Not the Triumph but the Struggle

CRITICAL AMERICAN STUDIES SERIES

GEORGE LIPSITZ, UNIVERSITY OF CALIFORNIA–SAN DIEGO

SERIES EDITOR

Not the Triumph but the Struggle

The 1968 Olympics and the Making of the Black Athlete

Amy Bass

Critical American Studies

University of Minnesota Press
Minneapolis • London

Copyright 2002 by the Regents of the University of Minnesota

Published by the University of Minnesota Press
111 Third Avenue South, Suite 290
Minneapolis, MN 55401-2520
http://www.upress.umn.edu

Printed in the United States of America on acid-free paper

Library of Congress Cataloging-in-Publication Data
Bass, Amy.
    Not the triumph but the struggle : the 1968 Olympics and the making of the Black athlete / Amy Bass.
        p. cm. — (Critical American studies series)
Includes bibliographical references and index.
    ISBN 0-8166-3944-2
    1. Olympic Games (19th : 1968 : Mexico City, Mexico) 2. African American athletes. 3. Olympic Project for Human Rights. I. Title: 1968 Olympics and the making of the Black athlete. II. Title. III. Series.
    GV722 1968 .B38 2002
    796.48 — dc21

                                2002005310

The University of Minnesota is an equal-opportunity educator and employer.

12 11 10 09 08 07 06 05 04 03 02   10 9 8 7 6 5 4 3 2 1

The most important thing in the Olympic Games is not to win but to take part, just as the most important thing in life is not the triumph but the struggle. The essential thing is not to have conquered, but to have fought well.

—The Olympic Creed, 1896

We believe in fulfillment—some might call it salvation—through struggle. We reject any philosophy that insists on measuring life's success on the achieving of specific goals—overlooking the process of living. More affirmatively and as a matter of faith, we believe that, despite the lack of linear progress, there is satisfaction in the struggle itself.

—Derrick Bell, *Faces at the Bottom of the Well*, 1993

Contents

Note on Usage   ix

Acknowledgments   xi

Introduction: A Tiger in the Woods   xv

1. **The Race between Politics and Sport**   1

2. **What Is This "Black" in Black Athlete?**   37

3. **An Olympic Challenge: Preparing for the
    "Problem Games"**   81

4. **The Power of Protest and Boycott:
    The New York Athletic Club and the
    Question of the South African Springboks**   131

5. **Tribulations and the Trials:
    Black Consciousness and the Collective Body**   185

6. **"That's My Flag"**   233

7. **Whose Broad Stripes and Bright Stars?**   291

Notes   349

Index   425

Note on Usage

On February 19, 2002, Vonetta Flowers became the first African American to win a gold medal at an Olympic Winter Games. In an Olympics that had already established speed skater Derek Parra as the first Mexican American medalist in winter history, Flowers's achievement created a flurry of panic throughout the ranks of U.S. media (of which I was a freelance member) regarding how she should be described. All agreed that she was not the first black medalist; Debi Thomas assumed that title when she won a bronze medal in figure skating in 1988. The more difficult question was whether a black athlete had won a medal since Thomas. Everyone seemed certain that a black face had not graced a skiing or skating victory podium, but who could be absolutely sure that the fourth member of the Swiss bobsleigh team in 1994 was not black by some definition? Who could claim to know the self-identity of every single Winter Games medalist? Deeming Flowers the first African American, then, seemed the most precise route to follow, and it was the one that I—in my capacity as a broadcast research supervisor—helped NBC settle on for its coverage of the event, thinking that the word *black* might be too ambiguous for the television audience. I did not foresee, with this decision, that a commentator at the bobsleigh venue would then erroneously describe Flowers as the first African American *from any country* to win winter gold.

As Matthew Frye Jacobson eloquently points out in his own note on usage in the ever-important *Whiteness of a Different Color: European Immigrants and the Alchemy of Race*, making decisions regarding racial terminology is a complex procedure for reasons of style and substance. Many scholars take the safe route of putting quotation marks around racial terms in an attempt to further emphasize how such terms are culturally and socially constructed. Additionally, such practice removes responsibility from the writer if any reader finds a term objectionable. Yet it is the rare individual, as Jacobson points out, who finds it necessary to encompass terms like *white* and *Caucasian* in these scare quotes, making clear that when we talk about race we tend to be talking about color rather than the lack thereof. Such practice grants whiteness a spurious authenticity, and therefore value, while further highlighting the constructed nature, and perhaps inferiority, of blackness.

The decision to remove the scare quotes from archaic—and often uncomfortable—terms like *American Negro*, *Negroid*, and *Negro* was difficult to make and required much prodding, for which I am grateful, from my editors. Terminology and semantic shifts are key arguments of the pages that follow, and I hope that I have historically situated them well enough to stand on their own, and that each reader will understand the meanings and consequences of each one.

Acknowledgments

The idea for this project began when I asked my brilliant brother about "Olympic" topics that might be appropriate to research for a graduate class titled "Race, Class, and Culture." During the course of our conversation, he mentioned Tommie Smith and John Carlos. After preliminary research, I realized their story encompassed everything I wanted to emphasize in my work. The seed was planted.

The professor of that class, Nikhil Singh, helped cultivate that seed, as well as many others. He has profoundly changed the way I see the world, and he helped me gain the capacity to articulate clearly the thoughts that wander in my head. His impact is everywhere throughout my work; I hope I have done his influence justice. Equally, Matt Jacobson has remained my most trusted adviser on any matters that I (constantly) put before him—intellectual, professional, and pedagogical—despite a variety of geographical distances between us. I thank him for remaining as "in touch" as I ever could want.

I owe much to the faculty at the State University of New York at Stony Brook. They cultivated a creative, progressive, financially supportive, and collegial environment under difficult gubernatorial circumstances. Nancy Tomes has been an exemplary teacher, advocate, friend, basketball fan, and scholar. Femi Vaughan offered kind words, good conversation, and a sensitive critical eye. Thanks also to Gene Lebovics, Barbara Weinstein, Ned Landsman, Richard Kuisel, Joel Rosenthal, and Gary Marker.

Many people have offered valuable encouragement and critiques. Beth Vihlen MacGregor has been involved from day one, providing uncountable hours of support and advice. I never imagined I'd find such a friend amid the chaos that is graduate school. Brian McKenzie, noted casino maven, has provided steady camaraderie and studied intellectual input—my respect for him is boundless. I am greatly indebted to the keen perspective of Rachel Buff; the book is much better for her numerous contributions. My editor, Richard Morrison, has occupied the knotty role of friend and critic, and I am forever grateful for his attention, abilities, and good humor. Members of audiences at Stony Brook, Yale, Plattsburgh State, Michigan State, the Newberry Library, the American Studies Association, the Organization of American Historians, the Berks, and the NEHA provided good insights. Thanks also to George Lipsitz, Alejandra Osorio, John Bloom, Michael Willard, Seth Spiro, Emily Kelly, Tom Bailey, Victoria Allison, David Wiggins, Eric Zolov, and Patrick Miller, and to my colleagues at Plattsburgh State University, especially Jennifer Scanlon, Vincent Carey, Anita Rapone, Donald Maier, Wendy Gordon, Peter Friesen, Erin Mitchell, Tracie Church Guzzio, and members of the Cultural Studies Faculty Seminar.

Practically, there were many who helped me get what I needed, whether that be experience, video tape, or answers. Special thanks to Peter Diamond (who got me "up close and personal" to several Olympic Games), Wayne Wilson, Joe Gesue, Glenn Morris, Brian Brown, Jimmy Roberts, Kirby Bradley, Dave Gabel, Maria Pagano, Aaron Cohen, Evan Silverman, Erin Davis, and the library staff at both Stony Brook and Plattsburgh. Thanks also to a teaching assistantship from Stony Brook; a fellowship from the Institute for Ethics in Public Life at Plattsburgh State; and a Dr. Nuala McGann Drescher Affirmative Action/Diversity Leave from United University Professions.

I have been lucky to have much friendship around me, both near and far: Christina Kahr, Sue Blood, Christine Tynan, Julia Gaviria, Pauline Cullen, Sally Vihlen, J.R., Tom MacGregor, Chip Blake, Micaela Corkery, Ian Southwood, Joe and Debbi Welch, Mark and Mary Greengold, Jennie Thompson, Julie Jones, Andy Gluck, Huck and Char Finn, Mary Holt, Karen Davis Simms, Steph Stamatos, Pam Jacobi, and Courtney Stewart. Sarah Tynan Murray has, since the ninth grade, been the consummate confidante, consultant, and personification of best friend. Why I deserve her—why she tolerates me—is quite often beyond my intellectual capacity. And while Evan Klupt was lucky enough to arrive at this party late in the Games, if he hadn't come at all I don't quite know what I would do.

My family has been interested and supportive throughout this entire enterprise. Loving gratitude to Michael, who patiently provided access and answers; Lissa, who is Felix to my Oscar; Joe and Donna, who were brave enough to join us; and Sam, Summer, Emily, Max, and Jake, who are absolute wonders in and of their small selves. Finally, to my parents, Miltie and Ruthie, who gave me use of their phone card and so much more, I dedicate the following pages, and the years they represent.

A Tiger in the Woods

In 1997, when Tiger Woods won the Masters and donned the green jacket that accompanies the preeminent title, golf became thrilling to watch for an entirely new audience. The hush of the announcers, the roar of the golfing fans (yes, *roar*, and yes, fans), the screaming headlines in the next morning's sports pages, the discussions that surrounded the water cooler, and the unprecedented millions of dollars bestowed upon the young athlete by various corporate entities all indicated that something important had happened. On the hallowed (putting) greens of Augusta, where Woods would not have been allowed membership relatively few years earlier, history had been made. And America did not have a language with which to deal with the phenom.

Not since Lee Elder squared off against Jack Nicklaus in a sudden-death playoff at the American Golf Classic in 1968 had a black golfer gained so much televised attention. The sports press cast the feat of Woods as a breaking of a modern color line, yet no one, including Woods himself, could fully describe exactly *which* color line had been broken. The press conveyed his parental heritage as decidedly "mixed"— African American, Asian, and Native American. Yet overwhelmingly, people portrayed Woods as a "black athlete," a golfer who had accomplished something in the wake of path breakers like Elder, John Shippen, Dewey Brown, and Charlie Sifford.[1] However, he repeatedly told the press he did not consider himself to be black but, rather, tried to embrace a more nuanced racial heritage, one more representative of the melting pot imagery so prominent in American history and such a determining demographic factor of so-called Generation X. Nevertheless, most observers seemed almost past caring how the young star saw himself. In a nation that generally deals only in a racial binary of black and white, regardless of the multiplicities of "color," Woods was not white, and what was not white was black.

The moment of Tiger Woods works to show why the black athlete in American society cannot be considered an uncomplicated truth. Rather, the black athlete is a malleable and complex site, a place to look for discussions of race and nation in the most popular forums and to discover what kind of consequences go with the meanings uncovered. This book aims to be an examination of some of the many ways the black athlete is constructed in American cultural life. In no way is it intended as a comprehensive or even chronological discussion of all the complexities that encompass the black athlete. Rather, it serves as a cultivated historical disclosure of some of the consequential facets—scientific, political, social, cultural—that surround that figure. It is not a complete "history of sport" in any way, nor does it claim to encompass every moment when the black athlete has figured prominently in racial and national identity formations. Rather, it explores some of the most critical and compelling moments in the creation of popular *representations* of the black athlete, primarily spotlighting the amazing confluence of concerns that surrounded the black power protest of Tommie Smith and John Carlos at the Mexico City Olympic Games in 1968: transnational and national protests, the growth of minority and postcolonial expressions of identity, and the ways in which the sports arena, and those attached to it, reacted to the outpouring of subaltern movements that permeated the period.

This book, then, serves to connect concepts of nationalisms and internationalisms, movements of civil rights and human rights, and modes of political consciousnesses and collectivities within the arena of ever-proliferating postwar media industries. It is about public perceptions and, quite often, delusions, arguing that it often is more important to uncover what people *thought* about the black athlete on the medal stand in Mexico City than to pretend to know what the black athlete really was, especially as no historian should believe that *the truth* could ever be unearthed. In doing so, this book strenuously makes a case for a general need to consider culture as a primary vehicle for understanding national identity as well as the complex roles and issues, principally race, that accompany it, illustrating what can be historically grasped via cultural venues.

The discussion begins with an introductory overview of the reasons, to rephrase Cornel West, that "sports matter," by examining the expansive historical context for the black power protest at the Mexico City Games and the protest's importance in manufacturing ideas of race and national belonging. It considers the complex relationship between race and sport, with particular focus on 1968, a key year in both U.S. national and international history, making the seemingly obvious argument that the political trends of the time lent additional power to this narrative of the black athlete. Indeed, 1968 proved to be a year when the International Olympic Committee (IOC) could hardly settle on a workable definition of "woman," never mind "black," and remained seemingly blind to how issues of media, decolonization, and black militancy might mingle to produce an Olympics unlike any before.

Chapter 2 takes a step back, revisiting what many consider to be the "golden age" of sport. The discussion probes the relationship between the Progressive Era's scientific ideas of citizenship and sport at the turn of the twentieth century, as well as the scientific experiments of the 1930s that attempted to connect race and physical prowess. While these scientists were not connected in any kind of structural way, they formed what Sandra Harding calls "a historically located social group."[2] Thus, this discussion does not reflect the work of any one individual; rather, it reflects the consequence of a general interest in African American physicality that permeated the scientific community in the earlier part of the twentieth century, demonstrating how scientific suppositions both mirrored and preserved prevailing ideologies of racial difference. Instead of either verifying or invalidating their conclusions, the discussion problematizes the very foundations of such laboratory works. Because race is a culturally constructed category, it should not and, more important, *cannot* be used as a method of classification in the laboratory. Yet these studies explained physical ability, and therefore athleticism, along racial lines, forging a separate identity for the "Negro" athlete that African Americans would later challenge and reshape on the playing field.

One such figure, Harry Edwards, launches his charge in chapter 3, which moves into the period after World War II and toward the Mexico City Olympic Games, when the transition from "Negro" athlete, which had been resoundingly defined according to decades of scientific experiment, to a politically infused "black" athlete began. Three "problematic" developments surrounded the Olympics in Mexico: the rise of the Olympic Project for Human Rights (OPHR) and its threatened black boycott of the Games; the building of an Olympic city in a "developing" country; and the political uprisings of youth that seemed inextricable from both. Critical to the evolution of the OPHR was Edwards, who became synonymous with ideas of black militancy in the sporting world. While certainly not the first or necessarily the most important figure with this agenda, in 1968 he undoubtedly was the most visible. While one scholar has warned against falling under the charm of Edwards and elevating him to unwarranted heights,[3] more to the point of cultural discovery are the *whys* of his standing: Why did Edwards initially take up so much space, and how did the action that took place in Mexico City eventually overshadow him? By using the media-savvy Edwards, who personifies a conflation of topics that range from the problems of an African American student athlete to those of a militant civil rights activist, we can raise a series of questions: Where did the primacy of the OPHR come from in the political and social transformations in sport in the postwar period? How did various audiences—sports fans, sports columnists, news reporters, "concerned" citizens—watch the Games, particularly in terms of the perceived, although rarely verified, relationships between demonstrating Mexican students and African

American Olympic athletes? Last, what role did the American Broadcasting Network (ABC), which produced the first large-scale televised Olympics, play in determining which aspects of the discussion were to be manufactured as important and which were to be left out?

In this vein, chapter 4 examines the different geopolitical levels at which this series of events took place. The OPHR followed its decree to boycott the Olympics with resolutions to boycott events sponsored by the New York Athletic Club (NYAC) and any athletic meets with South Africa or Southern Rhodesia as participants. The NYAC was targeted because the club, which excluded blacks and Jews from membership, invited *all* athletes to its annual indoor meet, thus profiting from the participation of those it excluded as members. The African countries, of course, were targeted because of their treatment of black "citizens." The chapter, then, explores how an international forum, the Olympics, lent serious input to a local situation, the New York Athletic Club annual meet, and how a boycott of the NYAC served as a true experimental jumping-off point for the protest. This convergence of the local and the global—embodied by the African American protests, the movements against South African Olympic participation, and the aforementioned student protests in Mexico City—is a crucial element of the story. These different kinds of action must be considered in terms of their national, transnational, pan-African, and international valences, as well as their meaning in the context of the other protests ongoing in the key moment of 1968, allowing for a nationalist narrative of race and sport to be internationalized by both subaltern and dominant cultural forces.

As chapter 5 maintains, after the OPHR organized the successful New York Athletic Club boycott and helped prevent the reentrance of South Africa into Olympic competition, it appeared that a boycott of the Olympics was, indeed, attainable. Yet many athletes remained undecided, searching for answers as to what their role was within the broader political collective. By the time of the Olympic Trials, the question of how best to present a unified political front—whether to boycott or not—was pivotal, yet seemingly unsolvable. Differences within as well as outside the OPHR made it difficult for the movement to maintain its unified front. One of the most conspicuous internal difficulties of the organization, the chapter argues, was the lack of any kind of input from prominent *female* black athletes, with little room allotted in the quest for human rights to African American women.

Yet, as seen in chapter 6, despite the division within the boycott attempt, the action taken by Smith and Carlos on the victory dais in Mexico City largely solidified a politicized notion of the "black athlete" regardless of the continual fragmentation and reinvention of the label. The chapter explores the gesture's various interpretations by the International Olympic Committee, the U.S. Olympic Committee, journalists, fans, and athletes. While the gesture could have been seen as a sort of compromise, one that merely substituted for the loftier goals of the boycott, its devastatingly potent visual legacy indicates otherwise. The history of the evolution of the boycott effort that preceded the black power action certainly provided a meaningful context, but the gesture also stood powerfully on its own. Indeed, its shock value can be largely attributed to the difficulty that the media caused in understanding the *process* that led to the moment on the victory stand, often by pointing fingers at the individual actors, like Edwards, rather than at the communal issues he represented. The end result was a terribly public and *collective* transformation from "Negro" to "black," one that enabled various internal identities of political consciousness to be enunciated alongside a newfound cohesiveness that was previously beyond reach.

In an almost "where-are-they-now" format, chapter 7 examines the influence of the black power action, appraising how it became a permanent reference point for the so-called introduction of politics into the Olympics, with an extraordinary legacy that emerges any time a political action is accompanied by "The Star-Spangled Banner." Such transformative moments of national expression, most of which simply question who is able to speak for America, can be considered as *performative nationalism*, moments that enable organic figures, such as Smith and Carlos, as well as others, to create an alternative mode of protest when more traditionally sanctioned channels are unavailable.[4]

Yet despite such attempts, the athletic figures that represent the post–civil rights, post–industrial age of global capitalism—Michael Jordan, Tiger Woods—often work to erase, perhaps unwittingly, the concept of any collective struggle that attempts to bring to an end contemporary structures of racism.

When Tiger Woods donned green, he assumed an amorphous representative role that dealt with some mixture of youth and racial dignity. While Nike presented an assembly of characters who walked through grainy black and white commercials stating, "I *am* Tiger Woods," it was not clear what kind of identity was staked with such declaration. But it was apparent that it might be important to find out.

CHAPTER 1

The Race between Politics and Sport

In 1995, Robert Lipsyte initiated a public exchange with his tirade about what he described as the "emasculation of sports" in the United States, which provides a nicely summarized critical perspective of the athletic arena in American culture.

> As a mirror of our culture, sports now show us spoiled fools as role models, cities and colleges held hostage and games that exist only to hawk products. The pathetic posturing of in-your-face macho has replaced a once self-confident masculinity. And the truth and beauty of sport itself—a pleasure of the flesh to the participant, an ennobling inspiration to the spectator—seem to have been wiped off the looking glass.[1]

A writer at *New York Magazine* responded with his hope that "the real world"—a basketball game—protected readers from Lipsyte's article:

> Luckily, events in the real world kept traditional and not-so-traditional sports fans safely on their couches and away from Lipsyte, whose damning article appeared on a day when Connecticut's (somewhat unfortunately named) Lady Huskies capped their undefeated season with a dramatic, come-from-behind victory over Tennessee, in what was perhaps the most-watched women's basketball game in history.[2]

But it was documentary filmmaker Ken Burns who evoked the most nuanced reply to Lipsyte's observation that sport had fallen from grace:

> Heroes, as the Greeks have forewarned us, are intensely interesting inter-sections of courage, ability, timeliness and glaring flaws—ingredients always found in our sports figures. Most importantly, the critical question of race that has been at the center of American self-definition has always played itself out, heroically and tragically, in our national pastime and in other sports.[3]

Burns necessarily questioned whether grace had ever actually been achieved, and he conveyed an astute understanding of the central issues within "our national pastime and ... other sports," laying particular emphasis on the complex relationship between racial politics and American identity.

Burns, as one of the principle meaning-makers in contemporary society, grasps the central relevance of race in American culture, evidenced by what is now seen as his "American trilogy"—the Civil War, Baseball, Jazz—and his use of race as its primary organizing theme. According to Burns, a conversation with scholar Gerald Early clarified this mission. "When they come to study our American civilization 2,000 years from now, we'll be known for three things: the Constitution, baseball and jazz music," Early said. "They're the three most beautiful things Americans have ever produced." Burns's interpretation of Early's claim was that the Civil War presented both the greatest challenge to and maintenance of the Constitution and that baseball's key moment was its desegregation, with Jackie Robinson, rather than Babe Ruth, at its center. As for jazz, "it's the pie-in-the-face irony of all time that these people, who've had the experience of being unfree in a free land, created the only art form Americans have made," Burns argues. "If you want to know about your country, you gotta know about this music."[4]

Yet is it really so ironic? Or does it make sense that those who have been denied freedom can express it best, regardless of the format, whether it be music or any other accessible vehicle, including sport.

Indeed, the brief debate between Burns and Lipsyte over sport clearly demonstrates not only how much sport matters but also why it matters; it envelops nearly every aspect of American life and the complex cultural themes that accompany it.

A Siren Song Sung in Bass

As a part of the expansive relationship between popular culture and nationalism, sport provides a contradictory terrain upon which a multitude of questions and claims of identity—race, gender, ethnicity, class, sexuality—are constructed and contested, challenged and yet sustained. In particular, while sport is not the only arena in which national self-definition, and the questions of racial identity that go with it, "plays" out, it is one of the most central. The black athlete serves as one of *the most visible integrated* racial subjects in modern society, seen in all facets of media, cheered by millions of fans, teamed with white counterparts, and, at least on the surface, accepted. Yet cultural encounters of identity surround the figure of the black athlete because of its undeniably crucial place within the American imagination, as the athletic playing field also subsists as a central realm where black masculinity and physicality are visually represented and reproduced, whether on the television screen, sports page, or cereal box. The black athlete, then, forms a decisive site to explore ideas of nationalism and internationalism, the operation of mass media in the postwar period, multiple methods of civil rights struggles, and the numerous manufactures of both race and racism in American culture.

As a historical production, the black athlete emanates from many provinces—scientific, political, cultural—with wide-ranging speculation regarding its essential "nature" connecting to a series of speciously legitimated social theories of racial difference. These ideas remain greatly influential within mass-mediated discussions of sport and have generated multiple interventions by African Americans within numerous social movements in the United States, charging the appellation "black athlete" with political significance. Indeed, by the late 1960s a collective politicized movement of black athletes produced the Olympic

Project for Human Rights, spearheaded by sociologist Harry Edwards. The OPHR understood the elemental stakes involved in sport, demanded racial equality within it, and threatened a boycott of the Olympic Games in Mexico City in 1968 if demands were not met. After the boycott attempt failed, the work of the OPHR culminated in the black power protest of American sprinters Tommie Smith and John Carlos in Mexico City, an act that epitomized French philosopher Pierre Bourdieu's concept of "symbolic violence."[5] The action dislocated the normative staging of the nation, as well as the sprinters' own place as national subjects, and had heavy consequences for all it chose to represent. It quickly became a powerful symbol that both inspired and intimidated many and simultaneously acknowledged the *lack* of power of many more.

Based on the campus of San Jose State College, the OPHR represented a relatively rapid political evolution. In 1968, the collective presence of African Americans on prominent collegiate teams (other than in historically black schools) was a somewhat recent phenomenon that had not fundamentally occurred until after the all-black starting five from Texas Western (now the University of Texas, El Paso) defeated an all-white Kentucky squad for the revered NCAA basketball title in 1966. After the Texas Western victory, colleges actively recruited black players, creating new challenges on campuses and forcing new prescriptions for the fiercely fixed racial inequities that existed there.[6]

Largely peaking in the hands—fists—of Smith and Carlos, the narrative that unfolded after this turning point is best described as one of cultural collision, because no singular account can wholly represent black political action, or any other subaltern political action for that matter. After a diverse group of activists completed James Meredith's "March Against Fear" in Mississippi in 1966, it became clear that the increasingly pronounced generational and ideological differences between the Southern Christian Leadership Conference (SCLC) and the Student Non-Violent Coordinating Committee (SNCC) would further splinter *the* civil rights movement. With Stokely Carmichael's strategic introduction of "Black Power" in the face of Martin Luther King Jr., it was obvious that the seemingly unified national spectacles of civil rights that had dominated the first half of the decade were over, to be replaced by localized actions such as the Black Panthers' community programs.

Crucially, the OPHR presented a perverse twist within the ever-changing struggle for racial equality: rather than propel themselves into an arena where they were not wanted, members attempted to vacate an arena many considered already integrated. The organization fashioned embryonic political actions within older, incomplete civil rights struggles, synthesizing antediluvian tactics, such as the boycott, with the newfound dominance of Black Power popularized both by SNCC and the Black Panthers, as well as by the litter of identity movements that followed. In doing so, the OPHR resisted and confronted dominant forms of racial identity as it negotiated with hegemonic concepts of American national subjectivity. In addition, it intimately connected itself to an expansive international forum of *transnational* racialized politics in the late 1960s,[7] particularly issues surrounding independent African nations, South African apartheid, and student social movements in the Olympic host city itself. While these transnational conditions were rarely, if ever, organized formally but, rather, indirectly nourished one another, the critical relationship between the black athlete in the United States and a global discourse of human rights embodied the way in which various international arms of the "New Left" held comparable *geopolitical* objectives, regardless of the *geographical* divisions among the "Free," Communist, and "Third" worlds.[8]

Thus, the cultivation of the black athlete as a site for exploring racial and national identity formation in the twentieth-century United States is an imperative project, centered on the relationship between media and political strategy and the manner in which identity is manufactured on the most popular pages of news and sports as well as on the small screen. While often hailed as an icon of racial progress, the black athlete creates a potentially injurious basis for more comprehensive designs of black identity. Such investigation demonstrates how the figure of the black athlete has emerged as a critical ideological locus within popular culture, one that effects important intersections with capacious themes of black collectivity and consciousness and, as previously stated, (trans)nationalism. In addition, beyond the significance of sport *within* the nation, which fundamentally revolves around its nearly incalculable economic and political worth, is the import of sport *to* the nation, with national desires and needs deeply embedded in the competitive quests of American teams and heroes on international fields. Given the centrality of sport to popular constructions of the nation, it follows that unreconstructed sentiments of racial difference surrounding the black athlete have remained tenaciously pivotal in contemporary culture.

This connection between politics and sport can be perceived, of course, on many levels. Scholar John Hoberman makes interesting correlations among sport and "the subjective world of values, attitudes, passions, and temperaments, and ... the objective world of historical conditions," emphasizing that it is the state itself that provides the link between sport and politics. Yet Hoberman largely disregards sport's role in the formation, reiteration, and/or propagation of political movements by mistakenly viewing historical conditions as "objective" and excluding the United States from the process because sport does not exist in any "official" capacity within American nation-state formation.[9] This exceptionalist positioning of American sport alludes, of course, to the perceived "amateur" or "individual" nature of American athletes as opposed to state-sponsored (read: Communist) teams. However, it fails to examine how sport does play a sanctioned role in the United States. While perhaps more codified, sport acts as a symbolic field for the racially characterized political constructs of democracy. If we set aside an obvious example like the Olympic "Dream Team" in Barcelona, designed to ensure a gold medal in basketball, a historical pattern emerges of configuring sport as the basis for Cold War America's "official" claim of being a racially sound and harmonious country, with athletes such as Jesse Owens and Jackie Robinson continually heralded as figures that prove American fidelity to democratic ideals. In the aftermath of World War II, an increased awareness regarding the potential capacity of sport as a sound diplomatic tool vividly materialized, particularly while the United States reshaped itself, as global political underpinnings exploded, as the so-called leader of the free world.

This position created one of the intrinsic contradictions of the postwar age—that between the exemplary universal mission embedded in President Franklin Delano Roosevelt's prewar "Four Freedoms" speech and the ongoing consequences of Jim Crow—creating an uncomfortable position for the United States in terms of preaching but not practicing.[10] As Jules Tygiel contends in his decisive work on Jackie Robinson, sport played a vital role within this dichotomy, as "America's most visible example of interracial harmony had quickly become a weapon of Cold War politics."[11] In 1949, for example, the House Un-American Activities Committee (HUAC) instructed Robinson to publicly condemn former athlete and singing sensation Paul Robeson for his statement to a French audience that African Americans would be unwilling to take up arms against the Soviets. Although Robinson's testimonial, allegedly written by Lester Grange, head of the Urban League, included a powerful attack on prejudice, stating that American racism was not "a creation of Communist imagination," he also denounced Robeson. "I've got too much invested for my wife and child and myself in the future of this country," he announced, "and I and other Americans of many races and faiths have too much invested in our country's welfare, for any of us to throw it away for a siren song sung in bass."[12]

While Robinson later appeared somewhat distraught over his own remarks, writing to Robeson that what he said was "badly distorted," many took him directly to task. One prominent arm of the black press pointed out that Robinson left Washington immediately after his appearance before the committee in order to avoid "being Jim Crowed by Washington's infamous lily-white hotels."[13] However, for the most part the HUAC appearance made the Dodger standout more popular than ever, because the mainstream press accented his censure of Robeson rather than his promise to continue fighting racism, indicated by a *New York Times* front-page feature accompanied by an anti-Soviet, anti-Robeson editorial.

The use of Robinson in America's persistent battle against Communism standardized the promise of sport in the Cold War. The United States Information Service, for example, delivered articles with headlines such as "Negro Hurdler Is Determined to Win Olympic Event" to various points in Africa, implying that such feats were the direct outcome of a staunchly democratic system.[14] The success of such measures startled members of the Student Non-Violent Coordinating Committee on their African tour in 1964, during which they became acutely conscious of the control the U.S. government had in creating (misguided) imagery of African Americans in the black African mind. "There were all these pictures of Negroes doing things, Negro judges, Negro policemen, and if you didn't know anything about America ... you would think these were really commonplace things," remembers Julian Bond. "That's the worst kind of deceit."[15]

For his part, President Eisenhower was anxious to display integrated athletic talent to so-called developing nations, particularly because the Soviet Union devoted so much of its own attention in this area. In the midst of a domestic emphasis on physical fitness, in 1954 Congress appropriated a large part of the five-million-dollar Emergency Fund for International Affairs to sponsor international tours of athletes. As a result, over 50 percent of U.S. diplomatic posts reported that the United States was recognized for its athletic achievement, with one congressman proudly declaring that athletes were "some of the best salesmen for the American way of life."[16] President John F. Kennedy continued this trend by publishing articles on physical fitness in *Sports Illustrated*, emphasizing the importance of stamina to the nation, whether by creating fit and ready soldiers to do battle or, more simply, by maintaining a citizenry that was not "too soft" to deal with the rest of the world. His brother Robert concurred, observing in *Sports Illustrated* that "part of a nation's prestige in the cold war is won in the Olympic Games."[17]

As the first professional sport to integrate in the twentieth century, however, it was baseball that remained the earliest and most prominent facet of such cultural diplomacy. Issues of the *Sporting News* with photographs of black players sent to Africa's Gold Coast facilitated Catholic missionary work. In 1952, the publication avidly supported sending the Brooklyn Dodgers and Cleveland Indians on a world tour. While the tour never actualized, the role intended for black players made clear what its intention was, with Larry Doby and Jackie Robinson illustrating "the opportunity to reach the top which America's No. 1 sport gives all participants regardless of race."[18] Off the baseball diamond, perhaps the most vulgar example of the diplomatic use of sport came in 1955, when the State Department sent Jesse Owens to India on a "goodwill tour." Featuring a photograph of Owens in a madras shirt and a Sikh turban, *Life* magazine deemed him "a practically perfect envoy in a country which has violently exaggerated ideas about the treatment of Negroes in the U.S."[19] The State Department also sent world-class high jumper Gilbert Cruter to West Africa to help athletes prepare for the Olympics. Perhaps most famously, the Harlem Globetrotters, dubbed the "white man's favorite black road show" by *Sports Illustrated* writer Jack Olsen, toured Berlin, Indonesia, Burma, and Italy, playing, in the words of owner-coach Abe Saperstein, an "unusual role in helping combat the spread of communism."[20]

Sport provided a battlefield for the strain between the United States and the Soviet Union to take place without gunfire. In 1956, Eisenhower officially ordained physical strength to be as nationally critical as economic strength and created the President's Council on Youth Fitness (PCYF) to ensure that American youth were "physically as well as mentally and spiritually prepared for American citizenship." The domestic concentration on fitness, of course, was discursively connected to success on international playing fields. As PCYF executive director Shane McCarthy metrically proposed, "Perhaps as we consider the next Olympics, the theme should be not so much 'Win in Rome' as 'Win at Home' for if we succeed in getting our country off its seat and on its feet, the victories in the field of international competition will inevitably follow."[21] Perhaps nowhere was this clearer than in July 1958, when the U.S. track and field team met the Soviets in an unprecedented meet in Moscow. Two months earlier, Vasily Kuznetsov had assumed the title "World's Greatest Athlete" by breaking Rafer Johnson's decathlon world record. As the Americans worked out in Lenin Stadium, the Soviets played Louis Armstrong and gospel records on the PA system, while the American press worked itself into a frenzy over the pressures placed on Johnson to redeem his title in the name of democracy. He did.[22]

Sport lends itself easily to this kind of rhetorical display, because the image of a level playing field can be smoothly extended as a metaphor for racial and national equality on other platforms. Yet by 1968, sport had become an archetype for social action, drawing the concept of a categorically unbalanced playing field into a more abstract and ideological field. While this extension, as indicated by Bourdieu, might merely be governed by an embodied feel for the game that one is in— a feel that is itself socially and historically structured according to the particular "field" one inhabits within a vast hierarchy—it becomes critically important to discover the way that one plays the game rather than the way one is *portrayed*, by nation or otherwise, to play the game.[23] Thus, sport serves as a stage with the potential for tremendous symbolic power, one literally—physically—focused on human possibility, transforming budding speed, power, and facility into a broader quest for human rights and equality or, perhaps more succinctly, the *opportunity* to compete for such victories.

A National Race: A Restructuring of "Sports History"

Americans, of course, are not alone in the political utilization of and preoccupation with sports, evidenced most dramatically by soccer's global popularity and the sublimation of national issues that accompany it. On June 22, 1998, for example, a story about the World Cup appeared on the front page, not the sports page, of the *New York Times* under the headline "Enmity Past, U.S. Meets Iran and Suffers Bitter 2–1 Defeat," accompanied by a photo of visibly dejected U.S. midfielder Ernie Stewart surrounded by a jubilant Iranian team. Across the bridge, *Newsday* greeted readers with a front-page close-up of two smiling soccer fans, one face painted like an American flag and the other adorned with Iran's green, white, and red, headlined by "Face to Face—Clinton Hails Match as 'Another Step' toward Thaw in 2 Nations' Relations." For its part, Iran had prepared its citizenry for several months preceding the match, using billboards to exploit its expected victory for political gain. Yet once Iran's dominance had been "performed" on the pitch, the eagerly awaited match between the two hostile countries became considered by most, statesmen and fans alike, as a significant rung on the ladder to peace, as well as an athletic thrashing that symbolically settled an old score.

The global enormity of the World Cup is almost absurd. But with the marked exception of ethnic enclaves in primarily urban areas, Americans as a whole have not unabashedly joined the frenzy of "GOOOAAALLLLL" (in the long word of Andres Cantor), undoubtedly because the rules of soccer make a lucrative television commercial broadcast difficult at best. Yet the rest of the world, from the superpowers to the recently independent, embraces little else for the better part of a month every four years. An executive at a New York–based international investment company judiciously described the impact of World Cup fever, which lowers his weekly business by 30 to 35 percent: "Think of the Super Bowl happening every day for three weeks and you begin—and I mean only *begin*—to see the impact."[24]

In 1998, the effect was, indeed, extensive. According to *Sports Illustrated*, the World Cup organizing committee offered the final 160,000 tickets for sale over the phone and in the first hour received four million calls from Great Britain alone. The Italian parliament altered its schedule so as not to conflict with games. Hong Kong prison officials allowed two hours of game highlights per day to prevent prison riots, although they avoided screening live coverage to their incarcerated audience to avert rival fans from fighting. Iranian schools delayed examinations for the duration of World Cup play. In São Paulo, Brazil, thousands of auto workers at a Volkswagen plant walked off without permission to watch the match against Scotland; they were not docked any pay. For their part, the Scottish celebrated "Braveheart Day" at an Edinburgh tavern during the Brazilian match, replete with blue painted faces and a nonstop screening of the eponymous feature, which starred and was directed by American-born Australian Mel Gibson. An Edinburgh *Evening News* headline perhaps most succinctly summed up the frenzy: "COUNTRY GRINDS TO A DEAD HALT AS GAME IN A BILLION KICKS OFF."

As the United States slowly climbs out of its position of soccer apathy, especially with the command of American women on the pitch, its own frenzy in terms of hemispheric sporting experience principally revolves around the Olympic Games, not a unique obsession. Few, if any, events achieve the global nature of the modern Games, where some two hundred national delegations are represented. The *Olympic Broadcast Analysis Report*, published in 1997, pronounced the Olympics "the premier world event in terms of viewer interest." The Atlanta Games in 1996 had 19.6 billion accumulative television viewers in 214 countries, averaging 1.2 billion daily. According to the Amateur Athletic Foundation of Los Angeles (AAFLA), the Atlanta Games maintained an *American* viewing audience of 208 million viewers—91.7 percent of all those with a television.[25] Despite a far different media landscape strewn with cable and Internet options, the Sydney Games in 2000 actually bettered the global numbers, with an unprecedented 220 countries televising the event. While many emphasized that NBC's numbers went down from previous Games (averaging the lowest prime-time rating, 13.8, since Mexico City and with 36 percent fewer Americans in front of their television sets than during the Atlanta Games), the 2000 Games were still the most watched programming in the United States. During the first week of competition in Sydney, for example, NBC's prime-time ratings were 93 percent higher than average, with a viewing audience that surpassed that of the other three major networks—ABC, CBS, and FOX—*combined*, averaging 59 million viewers *per night*.[26]

In addition to the media, and therefore the economic, worth of the Olympics is their importance as a national and international symbolic encirclement of a kind of liberal idealism. Olympic chronicler David Wallechinsky makes a persuasive argument for the unparalleled international significance of the Olympic Games, claiming the United

Nations, largely populated by dictators, royal families, and the generally wealthy, comes in a distant second. Also important, the barrage of athletes that converges on an Olympic Village every four years composes a far greater cross-section of individuals, men *and women*, from a range of economic backgrounds, educations, and athletic training.[27] Without overstating the egalitarian aspects of the Olympics, it is important to recognize the jumbled array of human existence the Olympics provide in a spectacularly ceremonial setting. Yet their cultural weight has been relatively unexamined. While the monetary scandals of the International Olympic Committee have raised international eyebrows, and the number of athletes caught "doping" has caused much dismay, the Olympics necessitate far more serious consideration in terms of their weighty consequence *outside* the world of sports. While many scholars have noted that the Olympics can have grave political consequences, it is rather essential to determine how they affect the larger social order.[28]

Yet throwing the Olympics into a more widely defined ambit of study brings with it a string of practical considerations. Historian Gilbert Joseph, for example, has urged caution with regard to internationally scoped studies that merely explore "the technologies and discourses that conveyed empire to audiences back home."[29] Any cultivation of the Olympics as an academic site should carefully consider his point and appreciate that the Olympic community has *multiple* "homes": some within national borders, some between national borders, and some in an ongoing process of constructing and maintaining numerous transnational borders, with various subaltern voices informing how the narrative might be read. Perhaps most important to consider is that while the Olympics take place in a host city, they are replicated in different ways around the globe.[30] Thus, the same machinery that conveys to an American audience how many medals have been won in the name of country might also work to display multiple levels of discontent. While many celebrated Tommie Smith's gold medal as yet another victory for America, Smith capitalized on the moment to make a political point on behalf of an oppressed minority. This moment emerged through what Joseph describes as "a dialectic of engagement that takes place in contexts of unequal power and entails reciprocal borrowings, expropriations, and transformations."[31] Critical to such understanding is an acknowledgment of television's role in the athletic spectacle, creating an almost Benjaminesque proposal of determining the function of the Olympics in the age of mechanical reproduction, especially, as Bourdieu notes, because "every television viewer can have the illusion of seeing *the* (real) Olympics."[32]

This fantasy of authenticity engenders the very importance of the Games and necessitates a transnational framework with what Mary Louise Pratt has usefully termed "contact zones," defined as "social spaces where disparate cultures meet, clash, and grapple with each other, often in highly asymmetrical relations of domination and subordination."[33] Accordingly, an international scope of history is not one that includes merely a narrative of diplomacy or foreign policy but rather one that reveals, as Robin D. G. Kelley tells us, "how tenuous boundaries, identities, and allegiances really are."[34] In terms of using sport to such ends, one of the most fruitful studies is C. L. R. James's didactic analysis of cricket, which while not an Olympic event does illustrate how sport subsists as a fundamental model for other forms of social existence. James found the cricket pitch to be the consummate locale for an examination of the contests among race, class, and nation in conjunction with the politics of colonization. Indeed, when his gaze shifted from the playing field to his role as public intellectual, he found he was more than prepared. "Cricket had plunged me into politics long before I was aware of it," he writes. "When I did turn to politics I did not have too much to learn."[35] James provides an important methodological foundation that removes sport from those who know it—and perhaps only it—by putting it into an arena with different questions and an alternative charge. In his eloquent style, he prefaces his work as "neither cricket reminiscences nor autobiography" and poses his famous question "What do they know of cricket who only cricket know?" which directly outlines why such work is important. His query provides a needed paradigmatic shift, one that imparts an interdisciplinary look at cardinal questions of race, nation, and gender; discerns the historical, ideological, and cultural imperatives of sport; and firmly situates sport as an important, if not commanding, element of popular culture.

While there has, indeed, been an abundance of work in the field of "sports history," it is a relatively isolated sphere that needs to be reconfigured in a larger, more diversely contextualized field. In his historiographical treatment of sport history, Allen Guttmann notes that the increasing currency of social and cultural history produced a range of works that probed more deeply into the relevance of sport in society. Yet he found that the scholarly tendency to regard sports as "autotelic physical contests ... ends in themselves and not means" segregates most undertakings and prevents any kind of thorough academic examination with broader social relevance, creating a need for a more constitutive methodology that situates sport as an extended lens into a range of ideological consequences, particularly race and nation.[36]

Arthur Ashe took a significant step with his multiple-volume work *A Hard Road to Glory*, an extensive narrative with copious bibliographic references on every aspect of African American participation in sport. More recently, Jeffrey Sammons offered an unparalleled historiographical treatment regarding a cultural approach to sport and race in American society, exhaustively surveying scholarship on African Americans and sport from the 1800s to the present. Sammons initiates a more nuanced meaning of race in "sport history," citing the valuable cultural studies of David Roediger, Barbara Fields, and Evelyn Brooks Higginbotham to position an appeal for "those who remain insulated in the history of sport to move out into the larger scholarly arena."[37] Of course, Sammons acknowledges that some work already existed in this vein, such as Elliot Gorn's study on boxing, but finds it to be an exception rather than a rule, and further worries about "the reluctance of most contemporary black scholars to seriously address the athletic experience of African Americans." Among the notable exceptions, such as James, Henry Louis Gates Jr., and Gerald Early, Sammons makes the case for the importance of Harry Edwards's contributions to a politically defined conception of "black athlete," despite reservations regarding some of Edwards's other political activities.[38]

Some disagree with Sammons's perspective. Grant Jarvie, for example, finds a focus on "black athletes" tricky, because it diminishes "the diversity of sport by equating race with black and consequently obscures other cultural identities." Further, he argues that it implies a masculine identity.[39] What Jarvie ignores is the existing presumption of what a black athlete *is*, making it far more useful to ask why the *black* athlete, rather than, say, the "athlete of color," remains the principal focus, and why it is—if it is—an inherently masculine personality. Again, such questions beg for the inclusion of sport in a broader scholarly scope, pulling it out of a sheltered realm of study and into larger and more diverse fields that include racial, national, and transnational milieus. Such contexts work to understand the magnitude of moments such as the 1938 bout between German Max Schmeling and American Joe Louis; the triumph of Jesse Owens at the 1936 Olympic Games in Berlin; the integration of major league baseball in 1947; and, of course, the black power movement of the Olympic Project for Human Rights in 1968.

Yet these are not the only spaces to usefully locate sport; rather, they must be synthesized with its existence as a cultural entity, positioned not merely in terms of its social and political expressions, but alongside the more academically oft-mentioned cultural realms of music, film, and television.[40] Accordingly, it is important to note how popular culture generally functions, as Cornel West skillfully outlines, in determining the characteristics of the historical moment of postwar society, creating a genealogy with three decisive elements: the displacement of European high culture as universal; the emergence of the United States as a world power and global cultural producer; and the decolonization of the Third World.[41] It is the junction of these stages that is of central import: How does the ascendance of the United States and budding Third World sensibilities implicit in the numerous national independence movements of the postwar period feed into a perceived universal, and yet distinctly American, culture?

Although sport directly lends insight into such a question, it remains largely neglected in the increasingly prolific works of cultural studies, which fail to find sport, and especially the social construction of the black athlete, as a vital component of a cultural arena that operates as a dynamic, active force in challenging what it means to be an American and yet creates a simultaneous engagement, intentionally or inadvertently, in legitimating the American nation. This process acutely illustrates how the relationship between popular culture, whose often ambiguous and at times ambivalent nature creates indeterminate consequences, and the production of American national identity is enigmatic, at best, in the postwar period. Many "popular" civil rights strategies, for example, encode the internal social divisions in the United States, making it difficult for them to be enlisted directly into any kind of hegemonic national framework. Others, however, result in numerous celebrities sporting Malcolm X baseball caps at movie premieres. Thus, popular culture, along with its multiple components—music, television, advertising, film, *sports*—exists as an arena that is a democratizing force as well as a validation of U.S. Democracy.

The academic field of cultural studies provides essential tools for understanding popular culture and sports within this important framework.[42] Indeed, it is within cultural studies that a definition of *popular* can be found among other cultural designations such as *high*, *low*, *elite*, *mass*, *consumer*, *commercial*, and *folk*. Most often, *popular* is juxtaposed with *mass*, although the act of "choosing one's term," according to Michael Denning, is not always fruitful, because culture always exists as a "contested terrain."[43] In the United States, he argues, the central issue focuses on the question "What is American?"[44] In finding the answer, we see that the intersection between popular culture and national identity emerges most directly, creating the needed space for considerations of other identities, such as race, and generating an additional question: If popular culture negotiates between dominant and subordinate ideologies, how are dominant and subordinate versions (including subaltern and transnational identities) of nationalism arbitrated within it?

As some of the principal works on nationalism indicate, national identity is nothing if not a representation, ensuring that anyone who assumes the responsibility either to maintain or to challenge it does so with heavy risks and consequences. Benedict Anderson has influentially tied such representation to the birth of "print capitalism."[45] His idea of the nation as an "imagined community" is valuable in considering how nations are constructed, yet it begs for further interrogation: If there is no nation outside representation, does the strategy of representation change in the postwar period with the explosion of mass media stimulated by television? If "print capitalism" was critical in the formation of nationalism, how does the imagined community change with faster and farther-reaching networks of communication, particularly because television allows its audiences to closely view what they largely already presume? Does the dynamic of nationalism and its inscribed identities also change in the postwar period? Are mass media, as posited by Stuart Hall, increasingly accountable for the "construction of *social knowledge* ... through which we perceive the ... 'lived realities' of others," and do they allow us to create some kind of "world-of-the-whole" that makes sense?[46]

Whom, then, does the national framework include? Whom does it exclude? From its inception, racism, as Matthew Frye Jacobson skillfully phrases, has been "a theory of who is who, of who belongs and who does not, of who deserves what and who is capable of what."[47] In this vein, a study of a radical, racialized political action, such as that of black athletes at the Mexico City Olympics, is a cultural study of nation, determining who has been denied access to full citizenship, what such citizenship might entail, and how such denial has been both rationalized and opposed. Further, it seeks to determine where identities that are both subnational and transnational (sometimes simultaneously) fit into the imagined community, arguing that it is often the newly prominent cultural actors excluded from the nation, and yet physically residing within the national border, who produce the forms of representation crucial to the staging of national identity, making subaltern identities constitutive of a more general sense of belonging.

The central question, then, seeks to discover how cultural actors, such as black athletes, who are constructing oppositional versions of national identity, fit into the American citizenry. What has loosely been defined as "black cultural studies" provides important foundations to such a question and yet has largely failed to incorporate the relevance of the black athletic figure. It is the multifaceted negotiations of citizenship that such a figure brings with it, allowing for the examination of how compound identities can be considered together rather than in binary opposition, that many black cultural critics have found to be important.[48] This struggle of what W. E. B. Du Bois famously dubbed "double consciousness" vividly emerged at the Mexico City Olympics when Smith and Carlos raised black-gloved fists over their heads during the playing of "The Star-Spangled Banner," an act that vividly demonstrated just how difficult the declaration of a racially identified people could be. In their moment, Smith and Carlos created a politically infused cultural strategy of "blackness," one designed to represent the needs and wants of a racial community, and simultaneously inhabited the same space as the dominant presentation of national identity—the American flag. While oppositional to that presentation, Smith and Carlos were confined by its terms, and they somewhat conceded to the dominant version by simply trying to address it. Further, with their red, white, and blue uniforms, the ever-present embryonic imperialism implicit in earlier occasions of American national construction haunted the historical moment of the two athletes, as their revolutionary image was broadcast throughout the world via modern modes of mass communication, dominantly positioned within a broad spectrum of political events lending to the social anxiety and political renovations inherent in the 1960s.

The Mythological Canon of 1968:
The Political Visual of the "New Left"

Indeed, what Nikhil Pal Singh has called "the national allegory of 1968" provided the key moment within which this occurred.[49] It emerged as a crucial year within the formation, maintenance, and solidification of the American imagination in terms of new styles of political consciousness and radical action, especially in terms of civil rights and its collective offspring, the New Left. The increased visibility of a militant "blackness" that vividly materialized indicated that civil rights had definitively altered its directions, illustrated by the short-lived merger of the Student Non-Violent Coordinating Committee and the Black Panthers. The ephemeral merger created a coalition that fully illustrated a revolutionary politics characterized by an anti-imperial, transnational sensibility, further augmented by the founding of the Republic of New Africa, with delegates from Mississippi to Louisiana declaring that African Americans were no longer under the authority of the United States.

Pivotal to this political transformation was the proliferation of popular modes of cultural communication, because most of what was played out was performed, often live, on television. Of course, 1968 was not the first historical moment in which the political ramifications of television played a critical role in movements of civil rights, which produced political spectacles such as the Montgomery Bus Boycotts in 1955, the student lunch counter sit-ins in 1960, the March on Washington in 1963, the March from Selma in 1965, and the aforementioned March Against Fear in 1966. All of these events solidified a national gaze on issues of the racial inequities deeply embedded in American society, and all played upon the visual power exemplified by the publication of the horrifying images of Emmett Till's mangled body in *Jet* magazine. One of the most vivid examples of television's direct impact occurred on May 2, 1963, during the Southern Christian Leadership Conference campaign in Birmingham. With SCLC leader Martin Luther King Jr. in jail composing his famous letter, organizer James Bevel gathered six thousand black children to demonstrate peacefully, only to be met by the violent force of Police Commissioner Eugene "Bull" Connor while national television cameras watched. Images of children crumbling under the force of water sprayed by fire hoses, one hundred pounds per square inch, became critical in awakening Americans to the fight taking place in the South, and the simultaneous presentation of American racism and American democracy finally forced President John F. Kennedy into action.

As Singh argues, the 1960s presented "a series of attempts to transform the normative staging of 'race' in American culture."[50] In so many ways, then, the revolution *was* televised, in no small part because of the expansion of television's role in society. As a news and entertainment organ, television rapidly developed from its origins in the 1950s to its present-day dominance via the introduction of cable, VCRs, big screens, stereo sound, satellite dishes, and so on. Throughout these modifications, it has remained a central source of national desires and fears, largely because of its broadcast of news, a somewhat conflicted synthesis, observes Daniel Hallin, of "journalism and show business, a key political institution as well as seller of detergent and breakfast cereal," reminiscent of the penny papers of the early 1800s.[51]

Television has yet to replace print journalism, but it has influenced which events newspaper readers want to pursue by visually establishing the moments that should be further realized in print. The history of television news is instructive in terms of how powerful and persuasive a national political medium it is. The modern version of the evening news began in 1963, when both CBS and NBC extended their news broadcasts to half-hour segments. This alteration occurred largely as a reaction to the "quiz show scandals" of 1959, which severely strained public trust and eventually led to Newton Minow's famous declaration that television is "a vast wasteland." The networks attempted to generate a more honorable image through a renewed interest in news, aspiring to the allegedly higher standards of print journalism and conceding news as a "loss leader" rather than an attempt at profit. Despite such ambitions, early news productions contained only rudimentary reports from Washington, remaining fairly unchanged until the spectacles of Watergate and Vietnam, while print journalism continued to work actively at presenting "the real story."[52] Yet it is important to recognize the expanding role of television in public emotion, even at its earliest stages, as illustrated by the eventual attention paid to civil rights movements and the unprecedented degree of "direct" participation in national mourning during both the assassination and the funeral of John F. Kennedy in 1963.

The very outset of 1968, when Communist forces attacked U.S. strongholds in South Vietnam on January 31 during the Tet offensive, made clear the intimate connection of television to politics, establishing a realm of what can be termed the *political visual*. Timed to make prime-time network news in the United States, Tet demonstrated how conscious the Vietnamese were that their war was televised.[53] The political potency of the imagery crystallized as Americans watched the brutality from their living rooms, horrified by sights such as the brutal point-blank execution of a prisoner by General Hguyen Ngoc Loan, head of the South Vietnamese National Police. The violent imagery definitively redirected American sentiment regarding the military effort, ensuring that within weeks of Tet public opposition to the war doubled and President Lyndon Johnson's popularity rating plummeted to unprecedented depths, persuading him not to run for a second term. Using the carnage that surrounded Tet as evidence, network news anchors doubted the veracity of "official" versions of events and produced editorial condemnations of the war. Even trusted newscaster Walter Cronkite deviated from his customarily steady and seemingly impartial on-screen analysis to instruct his audience that the U.S. was "mired in stalemate" with little end in sight. "To say that we are closer to victory today is to believe," he observed, "in the face of the evidence, the optimists who have been wrong in the past."[54] After the broadcast, Johnson reportedly responded that "Cronkite was it," indicating that the administration was powerless against the ever-increasing public sentiment that "Amerika" was no longer "beautiful," abroad or at home.

On April 4, the political command of the visual persisted with the assassination of Martin Luther King Jr. in Memphis, Tennessee. In the wake of events such as Tet and the escalating antiwar sentiment that accompanied it, King had begun to revise his strategies in the time before his death. With his newfound censure of "white colonialism" and his recognition that "the bombs from Vietnam are exploding in our own country," he abandoned his original desire for America to fulfill the potential of its own system and urged the creation of a new one altogether.[55] According to Clayborne Carson, King's death produced "a unique display of nationwide racial unity" as African Americans took rage and grief to urban streets, fashioning major riots in over sixty cities that culminated in over forty deaths and twenty thousand arrests, some of which took place on television.[56] The course continued two months later on June 6 with the assassination of presidential hopeful Robert Kennedy at the hands of Palestinian activist Sirhan Sirhan. The upshot appeared on television later that summer during the Democratic Convention in Chicago. Thousands of antiwar protesters descended on the city, clashed in the streets with barbaric tactics of law enforcement, and taunted the brutalizing police and their weapons with the nascent slogan of politics in the media age: "The whole world is watching."[57]

The exceptionalist assumption by radical American youth that the whole world was, indeed, interested in the turmoil-laden domestic politics of the United States somewhat ignored other extensive international student social movements. Yet it also illustrated how such revolutionary stances to some extent did focus on American youth, largely because of the hegemonic positioning of the United States in the postwar period, and furthermore illustrated how these youth engaged in a transnational culture. "The worldwide episodes of revolt in 1968 have generally been analyzed from within their own national context," George Katsiaficas acknowledges, "but it is in reference to the *global constellation* of forces and to each other that these movements can be understood in theory as they occurred in practice." Katsiaficas deems such events "synchronic" because of the role of the mass media, which conveyed events across the globe and produced an "eros" effect that tied together various disparate events, generating "a year of world-historical importance."[58]

The demands of staging an event such as the Olympics in this period, then, had far-reaching effects, generating expressions of dissent from African Americans, Africans, and Mexicans that generated protests with national, transnational, pan-African, and international valences. Furthermore, while these voices occupied the global stage most centrally, the Olympic administration had to deal with the Soviet occupation of Czechoslovakia, "Prague Spring," which created several complications: Czech Olympic champion Emil Zátopek called for any Warsaw Pact country occupying Czechoslovakia to be suspended from Olympic participation; several European countries threatened to withdraw from any competition against the Soviets; and separate dining facilities had to be planned for Czech and Soviet athletes in the Olympic Village. Eventually, Olympic spectators dealt with the situation their own way, wildly applauding the Czechoslovakian squad when it entered the stadium during the 1968 Opening Ceremony, creating an ovation more munificent than that received by the home team.[59]

With such a range of spectacles secured on the political front—Tet, Memphis, Chicago, Prague—on October 16, 1968, a critical image emerged in Mexico City, one with enough political power to generate a mythological legacy. With an enduring effect within the popular imagination of both sport and political radicalism, this image exemplified the multiple political connections of identity in a period when the mass media, accessible organs of information, played a central role in informing radical action. The image created a range of public perceptions regarding racial and national identity, and was understood in many ways: through the terms of the apparent course of events, the words of athletes, the analyses of sports columnists, and the narrations of television anchors.

Just as Jack Johnson, the first African American heavyweight boxing champion, won his title in 1908 in Sydney, Australia, because no U.S. city would host the fight, and Jackie Robinson made his professional debut with the Montreal-based farm team of the Brooklyn Dodgers, Smith and Carlos staked their complex symbolic claim of national citizenship and racial dignity outside their assigned national border. Their action vividly demonstrated how movements of civil rights had saturated multiple spaces in society, redefined for many what constituted civil rights, and illustrated how such rights were intimately connected to a supranational discourse that took the surrounding international influences and ramifications of American citizenship and African American identity into serious consideration. Indeed, in a period in which displays of race often were cultivated against the backdrop of sweeping youth movements, the Olympic Project for Human Rights had ensured that sport played an increasingly significant role in manufacturing meanings of racial and national identity and forcefully recast the role of the black athlete in society to make it integral to both local and global struggles surrounding race and human rights. Smith and Carlos then sealed the metamorphosis from "Negro" to "black," heavily supported by a series of events the OPHR largely initiated in the preceding months. When located within the ongoing Black Power movement, the duo's action stands as a prominent facet of the radical political transformations occurring in the United States, shaping a period when some Americans felt their world was coming apart at the seams while others welcomed whatever change might bring. Within these political transformations, then, sport played an increasingly significant role that constructed meanings of racial and national identity on a broad playing field.

Official reaction to Smith and Carlos's defiant raising of black-gloved fists during an Olympic medal ceremony was swift and severe. Forced to leave the Games, the duo headed home to the United States, where they were denied the housing, employment, and respect they had sought through their silent protest gesture. In their attempt to speak out against racial oppression, Smith and Carlos employed a cultural strategy that contested the dominant tradition of American nationalism. Further, their action took place in an international, *televised* realm, forcing a crucial role upon the media in amplifying the tension of their act of insubordination by bringing it directly to the living rooms of America and, on the next morning's sports page, to breakfast tables, where it was digested alongside coffee and eggs. It was a moment of central significance to both sport and politics, forever frozen in full-color during the unprecedented Olympic coverage by ABC, with strains of the national anthem providing the audio backdrop. The protest created what became the defining image of Mexico City, an image that has had residual effects on the sports world as well as a more generalized historical and cultural resonance that fuses the racialized anger of 1968 with the broader imagery of black masculinity in American society.[60]

Of course, the 1960s presented a key decade in terms of the prescribed identities of athletes, reflecting many other social changes of the moment. Black power and antiwar movements, of course, animated other voices that collected under the appellation "New Left," epitomized by the wave of feminism produced by groups as diverse as the National Organization for Women and the Society for Cutting Up Men, which combined civil rights strategies with a strong desire to move away from the masculine world systems underlined in Vietnam.[61] In sport, alongside well-publicized racial battles, women, whose stake in the athletic arena was already unquestionably overshadowed by male counterparts, found their "femininity" scrutinized in terms of their Olympic eligibility. Just as the International Olympic Committee, helmed by eighty-one-year-old Chicago business mogul Avery Brundage, would be unable to get its bureaucratic head around "black," it increasingly stymied its own definitions of "woman," one of the two primary categories of entrance into international athletic competition.

Absent from the inaugural modern Games in 1896, women made their Olympic debut in Paris in 1900 in tennis, golf, and equestrian events and in Amsterdam in 1928 in track and field, where American Elizabeth Robinson won the gold medal in the 100-meters.[62] Yet despite their swift success on international fields, American women had to contend with accusations of "mannishness" at home. After World War II, when athletic triumphs became vital Cold War victories for both the United States and the Soviet Union, the media began to transform images of athletic women, no longer disparaging the masculine female athlete most often associated with Eastern European nations. In 1963, for example, *Life* magazine recognized Soviet women for their "superb form" and contended that they had "the grace of ballet dancers." *Amateur Athlete* magazine divulged that while once "Amazons," Soviet women now wore lipstick. *Sports Illustrated*'s John Underwood understood the need to step back from deprecating remarks regarding Soviet sportswomen in order to garner more American support: "In deference to our own women," he declared, "we have quit calling the Russians 'muscle molls.'"[63] The former image, then, of the unfeminine, albeit physically skillful, woman battled with a new athletic image, which carried with it an interest in hair and makeup and, most essential, *hetero*sexual relationships with men.[64]

In this postwar period, the State Department put these women to work for the country by better preparing them for Olympic competition and by sending them on government-sponsored global tours designed to demonstrate why democracy should and would prevail. Yet while American men were able to keep up with the Soviets, Soviet women continually crushed their American foes. In 1963, *Sports Illustrated* inquired "Why Can't We Beat This Girl?" in an article about a "beautiful young [Russian] girl ... with auburn hair [who] not only looks better than the girl next door, she most certainly can run much faster."[65] Many of the excuses for the alleged athletic incapacity of American women derived from antiquated biological theories regarding female frailty. Throughout the nineteenth century, physicians emphasized the need for women to focus their attention, physical and intellectual, on human reproduction, with only moderate physical engagement encouraged to maintain good health. According to Carroll Smith-Rosenberg and Charles Rosenberg, the body was viewed as "a closed system possessing only a limited amount of vital force; energy expended in one area was necessarily removed from another."[66] The basis of such notions emanated largely from the work of Edward Clarke, whose *Sex in Education; or, A Fair Chance for the Girls*, published in 1873, disseminated the idea of "vital energy" to a vast audience, espousing a series of anecdotes on the perils faced by young women who overexerted their bodies, failing to lead a healthy, reproductive life.[67]

Yet the ever-changing vista of the postwar era altered the role prescribed for female athletes, illustrated "officially" in 1964 when the American Medical Association issued a statement *encouraging* women to get involved in sports. Yet despite the critical shift made by the influential organization, women in sport continued to be accounted for largely in terms of physical (in)capacities—biological determinism—rather than socially and historically discerned, with the remnants of nineteenth-century medicine most apparent in the correlations made between a woman's perceived frail physical state and her weak social position.[68] Such perception, of course, falsely identifies biological identity as a fixed construction rather than one that is both historically and culturally produced and that disallows any kind of preconceived rigidity in terms of gender.[69]

However, in international sport the category of woman has continually been contrived as cast iron, particularly with the requirement of "gender verification" testing, which in essence requires female athletes to prove that they are not really men (and presumes, of course, that men enjoy an unfair physical advantage). In 1966, "femininity control" debuted in international competition at the British Commonwealth Games, eradicating any notion that the male/female binary might be more complex. Furthermore, the test utilized—sex chromatin analysis—was both medically and scientifically controversial, because it often yielded false-negative or false-positive results, unfairly disqualifying some athletes.[70] While some cases are clear, such as Poland's Stella Walsh (Stanislawa Walasiewicz), who won gold in 1932 and silver in 1936 in the 100-meters but in a 1980 autopsy was found to have male sex organs, others are not. German high jumper Dora Ratjen was barred from further competition after a fourth-place finish in Berlin in 1936, for example, because she was a hermaphrodite, a sexual designation not recognized by any international athletic federation.

In 1968, the question of the female athlete came to a head when femininity control controversially made its Olympic debut under the auspices of a new IOC focus on equal playing fields. While gender verification tests were first given alongside systematic screenings for banned substances at the Winter Games in Grenoble, it was not until Mexico that the IOC required *every* female athlete to submit to a test administered by her sport's respective international federation. However, not all of the federations, most notably swimming (the Fédération Internationale de Natation Amateur, or FINA), agreed with the new requirement. Although many of its athletes volunteered to take the test and obtain certification for competition, FINA balked.[71] In the course of the dispute between the IOC and FINA, the discussion regarding gender verification widened, particularly as the majority of female Olympians underwent the test. Prince Alexandre de Merode, head of the IOC Medical Commission, held a conference to publicize the new program. "There are 962 women involved in these Olympics," he declared. "A total of 540 women have taken the test and they will be given cards to prove that there's no reason for them to take tests at any future Olympics."[72] Yet despite Merode's enthusiasm, the sports press focused on the ostensible absurdity of the test, relaying tales of women who had the inside of their cheeks scoured in the name of fair competition. The San Jose Mercury News, under the headline "OLYMPIC EDIT KEEPS 'EM GIGGLING," ran an Associated Press (AP) story about American fencer Maxine Mitchell, fifty-seven, to demonstrate why the test created more amusement than anxiety. "I must admit I was worried for a while," Mitchell told the press. "I have four children and eight grandchildren. I wondered what I was going back to tell them. Call me 'grandpa'?"[73]

From the perspective of mostly male sportswriters, much of the mirth emanated from the testing of women thought to personify femininity. The AP story highlighted American swimmers Linda Gustavson and Pam Kruse, both of whom took the test despite the refusal of FINA to administer it. "Looking at them, no person in his right mind could have any question of their sex," concluded the AP writer. Also interviewed was American platform diver Ann Peterson, "whose figure and flowing blonde hair have made her a photographer's delight around the Olympic pool"; Canadian swimmer Maureen Corson, who gave her statement while "tossing her long black hair"; and "statuesque fencer Yvonne Witteveen from the Netherlands Antilles."[74] Los Angeles Times columnist Jim Murray supplemented such visual "testing" with behavioral testing, producing a whimsical and revealing take on "separating the men from the girls":

For most of humanity, this poses no great difficulty. If it lisps, cries at weddings, stops speaking to you unaccountably for days at a time, can't get along with your mother, puts its hair up in curlers and stands in front of two closetsful of clothes and sobs "I haven't got a thing to wear!" it's a girl. Color it pink. If it sits around in front of the TV all weekend watching football, trailing cigar ashes on the rug, pudgy fingers wrapped around a can of beer, scratching its hairy chest and ogling pretty girls at the family reunion, and eats with its fingers and makes noise eating soup, and gets into political arguments with your best friend's husband, it's a boy. Color it ugh![75]

Murray's analysis, albeit crudely wrought, expressed the central criticism of those who felt the IOC—who, he said, "wouldn't be convinced by a topless waitress"—had badly complicated matters. While his criticism did not focus on the subjective nature of gender, he made strides in condemning the IOC's refusal to recognize gender's definitive *social* constitution, with its insistence that every female athlete be given "the barbarity known as the 'chromosome' test" rather than just the athletes he considered obviously questionable: "girls who speak baritone, have a mustache, or drive trucks for a living in the non-Olympic years" or men "in rouge and high heels." Murray acknowledged the gender stereotypes associated with various sports, but rather than use them to defame any individual, he wanted the IOC to take care to prevent "girl athletes" from becoming "one of the last persecuted minorities."

> As a general rule of thumb, I would not expect any creature who throws a javelin or a hunk of scrap iron or fights with a sword to be the kind of crinoline and old lace type Louisa May Alcott used to write about, or to be fresh off Sunnybrook Farm or Bryn Mawr. On the other hand, if a girl is born fat and ugly and has to shave twice a day, she's entitled to get her kicks sword fighting or spear throwing or shot putting. It's a cinch nobody's going to ask her to dance. It's the same way with a guy. If he grows up playing with dolls and crocheting and runs away to join the ballet, people figure his chromosomes are his own business.[76]

Thus, Murray understood femininity control to be a sham, because it measured gender exclusively in physical terms, while it was his opinion that "a great many more people are emotionally confused about their sex than they are organically."[77] He sought, in his unrefined yet waggish manner, to find an amalgamation of *sex*, meaning the anatomical and hormonal features that differentiate men and women, and *gender*, the perceived effects of such biological difference. The IOC, of course, disagreed and prevailed; after a few days of controversy and debate, FINA succumbed to the ruling and issued sex tests to all female swimmers.[78] With the question of feminine identity in the Olympics in 1968 seemingly settled, many felt the focus could return to attaining victory, although how exactly that would be defined, and by whom, was still up for grabs.

Thrill and Agony: The Actors and Actions of Sport in the 1960s

Even without the political debates that swept through the sport industry, 1968 would have been a remarkable year, as reflected in ABC's *Wide World of Sports*: "Highlights of the Sixties," which reviewed the nine years of sports coverage from the show's 1961 inception. During the show, commentator Jim McKay focused on the tremendous change, good and bad, that had taken place over the course of the decade. While some of the transformations revolved around the heightened commercialization of sport, such as the use of athletes in corporate advertisements and the increasing movement for unionization, McKay acknowledged another kind of shift: "We'll ... talk of the amazing decade of change. Do the sports and athletes mirror the time? Or in this era of massive television coverage, do they effect them? And for better or worse?... We relive the sixties—a ten-year *explosion of sport*."[79]

According to the program, the "explosion" began with figures like Olympic gold medalist Wilma Rudolph, jockey Eddie Arcaro, boxer Floyd Patterson, and baseball's notorious Casey Stengel. The unyielding Vince Lombardi commanded football, while players Paul Horning and Alex Karas were suspended for betting. Wilt Chamberlain and Lew Alcindor (Kareem Abdul-Jabbar)—the most sought-after high school player in history—dominated basketball, and baseball said good-bye to Sandy Koufax. Skiing saw the rise of bankable figures like Jean-Claude

Killy, while skating enjoyed the sublime performances of Peggy Fleming and mourned the tragic plane crash in Brussels in 1961 that killed eighteen members of the U.S. national team, as well as sixteen coaches, family members, and officials. There also was a series of underdogs to cheer throughout the decade, such as the Olympic hockey team in 1960; "part Indian American Marine" Billy Mills at the 1964 Olympics in the 10,000-meters; and Arthur Ashe, who in 1968 became the first amateur and first African American man to win a U.S. Open title. Also, there were figures of unparalleled "charisma," including Muhammad Ali, Arnold Palmer, Mickey Mantle, Willie Mays, and Joe Namath, and unmatched marks of both speed and endurance set by athletes like Ethiopian marathoner Abebe Bikila in both the 1960 and 1964 Olympics and four-legged track sensation Kelso. While McKay acknowledged that a *New York Times* writer had dubbed the 1960s a "slum of a decade," he countered that although "sport had its slum areas, all right ... it also had its Olympian heights," especially with the new elevations reached by Valery Brumel and Dick Fosbury and with Bob Beamon's renowned long—*very* long—jump, judged by ABC viewers to be the single greatest achievement of the decade.

Whereas McKay profiled the excellence demonstrated by a figure such as hoops phenom Alcindor, noting that "it's impossible to exaggerate his dominance of the college game," he said nothing about why the young star opted out of the Mexico City Olympics. The ABC overview designedly observed the decade in terms of the physical achievements of athletes, yet obviously many of these athletes were not isolated from the politics of the decade. "When the country changed, the athlete didn't stay crew cut," remembers hockey standout Derek Sanderson. "The athlete didn't stay where sports told him to stay."[80] The transformations that surrounded increasingly militant versions of civil rights in the United States via the proliferation of Black Power ideologies ensured a critical role for African Americans in how the industry that controlled their lives would unfold. While the media had often used the term *militant* in the past to brand and discount political figures such as Malcolm X, the social and national worth of the elite athlete made it nearly impossible to do so in regard to any black athlete who self-consciously took up any kind of confrontational role. As Jabbar summarized, "Black athletes were aware of exactly what time it was in America."[81]

Probing the questions behind the significant revisions made by black athletes in the late 1960s provides a way to answer the call of Robin D. G. Kelley for historians to "strip away the various masks African Americans wear in their daily struggles to negotiate relationships or contest power in public spaces, and search for ways to gain entry into the private world hidden beyond the public gaze."[82] One area for such study is, indeed, the Olympic Project for Human Rights. In his autobiography, Harry Edwards assessed the pragmatic, academic, and strategic use of the Olympics as a site for civil rights action:

> We knew that in 1963, activist-comedian Dick Gregory's proposal that the Black athletes boycott the 1964 Tokyo Games had been widely received as a joke. We had also witnessed the intermingling of politics, religious philosophy, and sports in the tumultuous sojourn of Muhammad Ali to the apex of athletic glory and into the doldrums of disfavor in the athletic world. But mostly it was the realities of the modern Olympics themselves that dominated our vision of what could be. More as sociologists than as political activists, we returned again and again to discussions of the games and how they were exploited for political purposes; how they had come to constitute little more than an international political propaganda forum; and how Black athletes had been exploited as both domestic and international propaganda tools.[83]

Edwards's incorporation of Ali was especially critical in his explication of how to utilize sport for radical action. Ali's importance cannot be underestimated in terms of awakening America to the germane role of the black athlete. In unprecedented fashion, he posed a dramatic contrast to challengers, exemplified by his sparring with Floyd Patterson, whose image revolved around an NAACP membership and a devout Christianity that diametrically opposed Ali's Muslim identity. Ali aptly (and continually) described and defined the relationship, declaring Patterson "the good American boy … the Technicolor white hope" and himself "the bad boy." Splitting few hairs about his beliefs, his rhetorical gifts brought issues into a crystal-clear focus. "The opposite of hot is cold, the opposite of right is wrong, the opposite of black is white, and if something is your opposite," Ali said, "it's automatically your opposition." While his refusal to fight in Vietnam was the last straw for many supporters, as well as the U.S. government, the antiwar stance enabled him to further transcend the sports arena, joining the ranks of figures like Julian Bond, who in 1966 was denied a position in the Georgia legislature because of his own draft opposition. Even after his title was revoked, Ali continued to battle, asking, "Can my title be taken without me being whupped?"[84] Without his title, he became a boxer who had to fight without gloves, and he remained strong by way of the wordplay that had brought the "Louisville Lip" both prominence and problems.

Ali's ability to maintain his fight outside the ring characterized a strategy of cultural resistance effective in a modern media age. His significance, indicated by his presence on the House List of Radical and Revolutionary Speakers (along with Harry Edwards), allowed him to serve as one who recentered political issues, popularized them, and laid necessary foundations for an eventual *collective* transformation from an athlete identified as "Negro" to one with the politically charged designation "black." This evolution greatly influenced other modes of resistance that could take place in a cultural arena, such as the black power action of Smith and Carlos. As Paul Gilroy explains in his discussion of "disasporic identity" and "Euro-American modernity," such action raises a series of important questions regarding culture and resistance for historians to consider: How is resistance understood? What is being resisted and how? How does one who is being oppressed think of it? And, perhaps most important, how does resistance picture and/or situate nation?[85]

From these questions, a framework can be established to determine where nationality lives within struggles against racial oppression and whether these struggles can be combined with other kinds of identity politics. Indeed, the gesture created by Smith and Carlos built on many 1960s strategies, ones that Ali politically illustrated and Gilroy has conceptually outlined, ensuring that the reaction of the Olympic administration was one based in fear of the possible consequences of Black Power rhetoric. Yet it is not sufficient merely to accept this reaction of fear on the part of the powerful; rather, we must probe where it came from and what rationale existed behind it. In his response to George Lipsitz's important treatment of "the possessive investment of whiteness," George Sanchez poses a key question: Why do whites ever feel threatened in *any* capacity? Why is white society not able to find security in its privilege?[86] The attention given to the OPHR, as well as to its leader, Harry Edwards, fully illustrates the degree of insecurity experienced by society in the face of images generated by black political groups. Indeed, Edwards's use of his own FBI file as a primary source for his autobiography shows the extent to which America felt threatened. According to his research, Edwards found that FBI agents attended the classes he taught at San Jose State University and went to his public speaking engagements, generating his reputation as a threatening figure rather than one *who was threatened.*

Matters of control and power figure importantly in determining why Edwards presented such a dangerous image. Since Jackie Robinson stepped up to bat in the major leagues in 1947, sport has been configured as an equal opportunity arena (for men), where success is possible—encouraged—for African Americans. Yet, although it emerged as this incipient sphere of possibility, in many ways it existed, still exists, as a more rigidly racist forum than any other because of the imposed limitations set within it and the rapidity with which the tide turned. In 1968, for example, Tommie Smith went from being a world-record-breaking Olympic gold medalist to a censured and banished political figure in a matter of days. By transgressing acceptable boundaries, he, along with Carlos, constructed and embodied a politicized notion of blackness that evoked hostile responses as it carved out a new role for the athlete and a fresh location for civil rights.

CHAPTER 2

What Is This "Black" in
Black Athlete?

Constantine is not a pure Negro, if that term has any meaning.
Any West Indian who took one glimpse at his father would know
that somewhere in his ancestry, and not too far back, there was
European blood. The Constantines, however, were black people.
Off the cricket field the family prestige would not be worth very
much. Constantine was of royal ancestry in cricket, but in
ordinary life, though not a pauper, he was no prince.

—C. L. R. James, *Beyond a Boundary*

The record shows that men with dark skin, wooly hair, broad
noses and thick lips, can run, jump, hit, throw and think as well as
those who have light skin, straight hair, narrow noses and thin
lips, and that many men in each group are better animals,
biologically, than many others in the contrasting group.

—Dr. W. Montague Cobb,
"Physical Anthropology of the American Negro"

Tommie Smith first had to combat and denounce the prevailing myths
of the black body, myths with roots that spanned almost a century. Early
African American boxing champions illustrate the historical precedent for Smith's predicament. In 1910, when Jack Johnson battled Jim
Jeffries—"the great white hope"—while the ringside band played "All
Coons Look Alike to Me," it was, as historian Gail Bederman notes,
"a national sensation."[1] While he had refused to fight any black con-
tenders during his own reign as champion, Jeffries yielded to national
pressure and came out of retirement to bring the coveted title back

to the white race. "I am going into this fight," he said, "for the sole purpose of proving that a white man is better than a negro."[2] Johnson, of course, successfully defended his title, leading many to make sweeping assertions about a fight that had been, remarks Bederman, "framed as a contest to see which race had produced the most powerful, virile man."[3]

The aftermath of Johnson's victory was chaotic, at best. Race riots violently emerged throughout the South and the Midwest. In an attempt to keep the fight out of the nation's nickelodeons, Congress signed a bill that censored boxing films. Johnson, dogged by the law for his relationships with white women, was ultimately forced out of the country. The photograph taken of his last bout, in which white boxer Jess Willard defeated him, enjoyed a lengthy tenure on tavern walls. Historically, as Bederman argues, Johnson became one of many figures through which middle-class America resolved to define "male supremacy in terms of white racial dominance and, conversely, to explain white supremacy in terms of male power."[4]

Similarly emblematic was the turmoil that eventually surrounded champion boxer Joe Louis. Throughout the pinnacle of his career in the 1930s, Louis transformed the role of the boxer from that of an individual fighter to one who embodied a variety of national desires. In 1935, for example, many viewed his battle against Primo Carnera as representative of the politics of Mussolini and Ethiopia, positioning the fight as a metaphorical clash between Italy and Africa. In 1936, Nazi adherents celebrated his loss to German boxer Max Schmeling as a victory over democracy, racial amalgamation, and non-Aryans. A year after winning the heavyweight title in 1937 in front of forty-five thousand fans, half of whom were black, Louis met Schmeling again in Yankee Stadium in a contest designed to settle the score between fascism and democracy once and for all. Indeed, Louis asserted that his single New Year's resolution for 1938 was to defeat Schmeling. His decisive victory a mere two minutes into the first round realized his goal. With it, he ceased to be solely a black champion, becoming a validated representative of the hegemonic American way of life.[5]

Yet in 1960, the man who once used his fists to personify democracy was condemned when his public relations firm negotiated a hefty deal with the government of Cuba. The Cubans intended to purchase an unprecedented $282,000 of advertising space in black newspapers in hopes of luring African American tourists with promises of beaches and equality. Louis, not realizing the Cold War implications of his agreement to such a proposal, encountered widespread criticism for taking part in the deal and lost much of his stature in the white press.[6] Such contradictions of Louis's representative societal role were further illustrated by a piece in the *Journal of the National Medical Association*, the journal of the "black" American Medical Association, in 1962. The article proposed to "treat certain features" of the boxer's "character" to establish him as a behavioral model for physicians, particularly "the Negro physician." It portrayed Louis as one who never did "anything to mar the public image of him as a gentleman." It praised him for wearing a tuxedo well and exhibiting exceptional conversational skills, commended his modesty, and emphasized that he should not be solely judged for his financial problems, as "many brilliant men have proved unable to handle sudden wealth wisely." The one exception to Louis's model behavior, however, was his fight against Schmeling. Despite his general refusal to "disparage an opponent," in this case Louis had demonstrated a loathing for his German foe. While understandable considering the situation, these actions were not to be celebrated. Thus, the moment that most Americans heralded as Louis's finest, the NMA denounced.[7]

The Science of National Belonging: Sport and Citizenship

The proper role of the athlete was firmly prescribed within American society, situating it as a cultivated site for explorations of race and nation. There is a misguided scholarly perception that before World War II, sport enjoyed a period of apolitical innocence, a so-called golden age that served as an escape from an amorphous "more real" world.[8] While World War II, indeed, served as a critical turning point, particularly with the introduction of televised sporting events, the prewar era cannot be discounted as an era of little consequence or significance outside athletic competition. Aside from the racial warfare waged over Jack Johnson and the national importance ascribed to Louis's victory over Schmeling, there have been continuous connections between sport and citizenship, as well as issues of masculinity, control, morals, and behavior, supplemental to national belonging. Indeed, the athlete, as Bederman points out with specific reference to Johnson, "was so equated with male identity and power that American whites rigidly prevented all men they deemed unable to wield political and social power from asserting any claim to the heavyweight championship."[9]

The extensive programs of the American "play movement" during the Progressive Era definitively illustrate the crucial connections made between physical and national fitness, laying an early but considerable precedent for the role of sport in postwar culture. As historian John Kasson explains, the movement attempted to refocus leisure time in the United States *away* from commercial mass attractions such as Coney Island's Luna and Steeplechase parks and inner-city nickelodeons and *toward* public parks and community-centered programs. The movement emphasized such leisure pursuits as a means to teach and reinforce national principles to children, putting sport on a national agenda as a way to raise good citizens. Although the play movement supposedly included all facets of society, it concentrated chiefly on children, especially males, because, as Kasson writes, Progressive reformers found that "the play-forms of childhood were the building blocks of a culture, upon which the future of American ideals depended."[10] Children, then, ideally engaged in "directed" play composed of activities that were coordinated as nation-building efforts. One of the movement's leading proponents, Luther H. Gulick, succinctly described its purpose:

> The sandpile for the small child, the playground for the middle-sized child, the athletic field of the boy, folk-dancing and social ceremonial life for the boy and girl in the teens, wholesome means of social relationships during these periods, are fundamental conditions without which democracy cannot continue, because upon them rests the development of that self-control which is related to an appreciation of the needs of the rest of

the group and of the corporate conscience, which is rendered necessary by the complex interdependence of modern life.[11]

Gulick's ideas clearly demonstrate the decidedly male focus of the "athletic" program, how it served as a critical component of a *national* program to raise "good" citizens, and how sport was positioned along-side dance as an important part of social engagement. Gulick's project had some durable results. Under his direction at Springfield College in Massachusetts, James Naismith invented the game of basketball to keep male youth constructively occupied during the winter, when they could not play football or baseball.[12] Arguably basing it on a game that native peoples played in South America, Naismith designed the new game as a civil, indoor alternative for boys, one that expressly forbade physical contact and encouraged passing the ball.

In a similarly "Progressive" manner, in 1897 W. E. B. Du Bois addressed the issue of athletics in his treatment of "the amusements of Negroes." In this discussion aimed at stimulating honorable leisure pursuits within the black community, Du Bois located sports firmly within a cultural tract and worried that "a proverbially joyous people like the American Negroes are forgetting to recognize for their children the God-given right to play." Although his reflections antedated the full-blown play movement, Du Bois urged people to "go into a great city today and see how thoroughly and wonderfully organized its avenues of amusements are; its parks and playgrounds."[13] He recognized these venues as indispensable to the health of the community and persuasively argued that legitimacy be granted to such endeavor.

We have an increasingly restless crowd of young people who are demand-ing ways and means of recreation; and every moment it is denied them is a moment that goes to increase that growth of a distinct class of Negro libertines, criminals, and prostitutes which is growing among us day by day, which fills our jails and hospitals, which tempts and taints our broth-ers, our sisters, and our children, and which does more in a day to tarnish our good name than Hampton can do in a year to restore it.[14]

Du Bois found play a pressing theme and felt those who were not of the same mind "simply open[ed] wide the door to dissipation and vice."[15] The clear objectives of organized recreation indicated by Du Bois, and ultimately launched by Gulick and others, were held widely. Secretary of War Newton D. Baker, for example, advocated movements of supervised play in urban areas, not for the physical benefits, but rather in hopes that time on the playground would protect children from the corruption most Progressives felt roamed in city streets.[16] In Chicago, settlement house activists Jane Addams, Graham Taylor, and Charles Zueblin of Hull House, Chicago Commons, and Northwestern University Settlement, respectively, pushed politicians to build playgrounds, especially in immigrant enclaves. They saw directed play as an effectual means of Americanization, a way, in Zueblin's words, to bind "people together as in a great melting pot on the playgrounds of Chicago."[17]

Along with those in Chicago, other proponents of the play movement included prominent reformers Lillian Wald, Mary McDowell, and Jacob Riis, all of whom became members, along with Addams and Taylor, of the Playground Association of America (PAA). President Theodore Roosevelt, an ardent champion of physical exercise, also heavily supported the organization. Closely inscribed within the PAA's mission to help remove children from allegedly dangerous city streets was an understanding that by doing so, staunch abilities of leadership and American identity would also be imparted. Joseph Lee, who followed Gulick as president of the PAA, further emphasized the sense of national belonging associated with directed play and aimed the movement toward activities that focused on democratic collaboration.[18] These efforts took a distinctly scientific mode of operation. The play movement was but one part of an expansive philosophical transformation regarding children that occurred between 1885 and 1910, stemming largely from influential theories of child psychology firmly rooted in Darwinism.[19] In this vein, the child was viewed as a wild animal, a savage, that had to be tamed through behavioral and moral instruction, intimately linking the physical realm, within which exists one's capacity for "play," to intellectual aptitude. Du Bois, for one, distinctly outlined the role of the athlete within his definition of amusements, recognizing schools as essential to organized recreation and, more directly, to sports:

> How are we to furnish proper amusement for these ... young people of all ages, tastes, and temperament? And yet, unless that school does amuse, as well as instruct those boys and girls, and teach them how to amuse themselves, it fails of half its duty and it sends into the world men and women who can never stand up successfully in the awful moral battle which Negro blood is today waging for humanity. Here again athletic sports must in the future play a larger part in the normal and mission schools of the South, and we must rapidly come to the place where the man all brain and no muscle is looked upon as almost as big a fool as the man all muscle and no brain; and when the young woman who cannot walk a couple of good country miles will have few proposals of marriage.[20]

Du Bois was not alone in staking such societal expectations in sport. There was a prevalent view in the early part of the century regarding what historian Patrick Miller has termed "muscular assimilationism," a belief in racial uplift via organized athletic participation that would enable the black community to participate directly in a most important segment of American life. The notion that sport could produce good citizens, accompanied by the idea that black athletic heroes held great potential for breaking down the barriers of Jim Crow, had widespread effects within the African American community. "For many 'New Negroes,'" argues Miller, "its potential role in forging racial solidarity as well as channeling the energy and aspirations of southern blacks seemed immense."[21] The most prominent muscular assimilationist was Edwin Bancroft Henderson. During his tenure as director of Physical Education, Safety, and Athletics of Public Schools in Washington, D.C., Henderson, who first learned his craft at the Harvard Summer School of Physical Education, promoted interscholastic athletic competition in African American schools in an unparalleled fashion. Dubbed the "Father of Black Sports History" by sports historian David Wiggins,

Henderson wrote prolifically on sport as a positive, vital element in the black community. He emphasized how, according to Wiggins, "African Americans were just as capable as whites on the playing field and, by extension, in other areas of American life."[22]

Largely based on the widespread convictions of figures like Henderson, a belief in sport as a principal path for economic success took hold. While the play movement was not directly aimed at African American youth at the outset, work by physical educators co-opted it for such purpose. In 1939, for example, William M. Bell, the director of physical education at Florida Agriculture and Mechanical College, wrote that "the American Negro problem" was rooted in the difficulties that surrounded emancipation, creating a population that was "illiterate and without either economic security or training for citizenship in the American society, one of the most complex in the world." To rectify such inequities, Bell called attention to the obvious benefits of education, accentuating the virtues of physical education within general education in order to "develop stronger bodies, keener minds, and shape fuller and richer lives." An even more specific purpose, according to Bell's research, was the ability of athletics to positively counteract forces of racism and poverty that directly correlated with high percentages of youth crime in the black community. "Under the proper supervision and in the proper environment," Bell posited, "physical education (and organized recreation) since it offers to many opportunities for socialization, may prove to be valuable in reducing this high crime and delinquency rate."[23]

In this vein, sport was widely understood as a means of upward mobility for African Americans, an inherently problematic position that largely eliminated other callings, namely, higher education and professional vocations.[24] In its earliest organized stages, sport, according to historian Allen Guttmann, operated "as a means of social mobility in that high school athletes are much more likely than nonathletes to graduate from high school and to attend college."[25] Yet such a path subsists in an intrinsically unequal domain. As Grant Jarvie has rightly observed, "We might all be equal on the starting line, but the resources (political, economic and cultural) that people have and the hurdles that people have to leap to get there are inherently unequal."[26] Many, of course, recognized such inequity, and thus even at the earliest stages not everyone embraced sport in this capacity. For some, the accent on sport that established athletic programs early on at many historically black colleges, such as Tuskegee Institute and Howard University, went too far. Controversially, Mordecai Johnson, the first African American president of Howard, stamped out athletic scholarships in 1927, toppling the athletic program in an attempt to shift attention back to the university's academic priorities. Du Bois was one of Johnson's chief supporters and applauded the president for his "attempt to purge ... Howard of those students who were not maintaining scholastic efficiency."[27] While obviously not an enemy of sport, Du Bois advocated a balance between endeavors of the mind and those of the body. He warned against the possible consequences of a college that took too seriously, and too exclusively, the priorities of sport. In 1930 at the Howard graduation, Du Bois counseled:

> The average Negro undergraduate has swallowed hook, line and sinker, the dead bait of the white undergraduate, who, born in an industrial machine, does not have to think, and does not think. Our college man today, is, on the average, a man untouched by real culture. He deliberately surrenders to selfish and even silly ideals, swarming into semi-professional athletics and Greek letter societies, and affecting to despise scholarship and the hard grind of study and research.[28]

Despite such admonition by a figure as influential as Du Bois, the belief that sport serves as a primary path of mobility has fundamentally triumphed in general society, largely on the basis of embedded convictions regarding black muscle.[29] Yet while the early stance of Du Bois, as well as the institutional influence of the PAA, submitted strength and endurance as features that could be closely connected to morality and citizenship, a central component of athleticism was its ability to determine one's role in society—however erroneous or legitimate the process might be. The level of science to which the PAA, in particular, took its program laid concrete foundations for later scientific inquiry. After the PAA connected the societal role of play to indicative evolutionary stages, scientists could then manipulate theories of evolution and authenticated versions of a scientific racism based on the athlete, manufacturing consequences far beyond anything Du Bois could have imagined in his call for black men to be of both brawn *and* brain.

Muscle Machines: Black Masculinity, Popular Discourse, and the Athletic Body

Despite Du Bois's intention that physical prowess and intellectual ability reside jointly, their historical legacy, particularly in the realm of science, has been one of cultural antagonism and mutual exclusion, with a continued reduction of sport as either a learned *or* an innate ability. In this vein, the implications for racialized understandings of physicality lend themselves to a recurring binary opposition of brain versus brawn, implying that the black body does not think as well as the white or possess the same level of self-control. Couched behind this tired yet familiar axiom are the influence and legacy of almost a century of laboratory work on questions of race and physical prowess. This work demonstrates how scientists, meaning those who measure data and quantify results in a controlled, Baconian, scholarly setting, have failed to grasp the unavoidable *social* construction of race when identifying and eventually compartmentalizing the black athlete. In short, this research epitomizes the impossibility of creating racially based groups for scientific laboratory research.

Any designation of an athlete as "black" has multiple and ambiguous meanings, particularly because of the multifacted role that athletes serve in the United States. In general, sport presents both a literal and a figurative field on which numerous facets of the media engage with corporate industry via sponsorship, advertising, and a money-generating fan base. Alongside this commodification of the black athlete, sport also emerges as a realm within which the black individual possesses what can be termed *corporeal capital*. Sometimes such capital materializes in the form of an attempt at social and financial mobility. Other times it is contained within the ability to make a political statement through performance, such as with Jesse Owens in 1936; through a direct engagement in civil rights, as illustrated by Jackie Robinson in 1947; or through overt political declarations embodied by Muhammad Ali in the 1960s. Regardless, it is a bodily commerce. Thus, any attempt to fully explicate the "black" in black athlete must identify and examine the so-called black body to prevent it from becoming a floating signifier.

As part of this larger sphere of popular culture, including television, music, advertising, and film, sport exists as a realm where black masculinity and physicality are visually represented. When applied to the athlete, the appellation "black" implies a variety of inherent or, more directly, *inherited* traits and abilities. Some popular constructions, such as those of hip-hop artists and gang members, create and contain so-called menacing images. Conversely, the athlete is designed as a more benign and "natural" figure, one intended ideally for consumption by a mass audience. For example, in the mainstream press, where the black male often is visible on the front page as a mugger or a rapist, on the sports page the black male body is transformed into heroic form. Cultural critic Kobena Mercer elaborates this process in his discussion of Robert Mapplethorpe's work, describing the body of an athlete as the "most commonplace of stereotypes" because of how the figure stands as "mythologically endowed with a 'naturally' muscular physique and an essential capacity for strength, grace and machine-like perfection."[30]

Yet regardless of the labels assigned, the assumption that there is *a* black body remains the same. Upon this body, multiple layers of black masculinity are challenged and maintained on a legion of levels.[31] Thus, whether rapper, criminal, athlete, actor, or, even more likely, simply none of the above, all modern manifestations of the black male become actualized in terms of, and must contest the various sociohistorical delineations of, racial identity, an identity overwhelmingly influenced by the various manufactures of the athlete. Such views, of course, have not been limited to American discussions of race and athleticism but have surfaced elsewhere as well. For example, in France, racialized notions of physical ability made dramatic appearances in postwar discussions of jazz. Many supporters of alternative cultural modes became increasingly obsessed with African American–generated forms of music in the postwar period. Numerous French jazz critics considered African Americans to have physical attributes that made them more athletically proficient, amplifying their capacity for playing a variety of musical instruments with greater power and dexterity.[32]

In the contemporary historical moment it seems almost too obvious to contend that race is, indeed, a social construction. Yet it continues to be constituted in biological terms. Despite its cultural and historical roots, race exists as an ideology with devastating and undeniable ramifications, a fiction with consequences fiercely rooted in reality. As Stuart Hall points out, because race is "not a transhistorical discourse grounded in biology ... it must function not through the truth of the 'biological referent.'" However, its constitution creates multiple, complex layers ripe for interpretation, largely because, despite the social circumstances of race, the biological vestiges continue to operate, making it critical to examine not what is true but, as Hall continues, "what is *made* to be true."[33] Thus, despite its eminent "social construction," race continues to be falsely discerned in biological terms, and unreconstructed sentiments of biologically derived racial differences have remained tenaciously pivotal in contemporary American culture. In her examination of this process, Sandra Harding astutely summarizes that while race is, indeed, a social creation, it is one that is "lived in," with both "manufactured" and "material" manifestations.[34]

In few areas is this more apparent than within the relationship that exists between the world of scientific research and the figure of the athlete, creating a forum in which biological definitions of race are, spuriously, *made to be true*. The question of the black athlete, a question that historically revolves around issues of success and dominance, has been a central scientific problem since the early twentieth century. While scientific taxonomies of race have continually shifted over time in response to a variety of factors, this period was notably volatile. As Matthew Frye Jacobson posits, in the early twentieth century the concept of race was "highly unstable.... It could connote a social difference whose basis was biological, historical, political, psychological, physiological, linguistic, or some combination of these.... What did remain stable ... was the degree of difference that the form was understood to describe."[35]

Beginning, primarily, in the 1930s during the large-scale breakthrough of African Americans in track and field, laboratory research resolutely attempted to quantify myriad racialized physical traits in an expert scientific dialogue. The projection of such traits upon the body of the black athlete added to existing racialized, stereotypical physical features derived largely from the representation of faces (fat lips, wide-open mouths, and large noses) as well as physical abilities (effortless, natural dancing and singing) portrayed on the nineteenth-century minstrel stage. These racialized differences were deeply ingrained as truisms in American culture, illustrated in part by the Mississippi planter who told Frederick Law Olmsted, "Niggers is allers good singers nat'rally. I reckon they got better lungs than white folks, they hev such powerful voices."[36] The credence of these traits and abilities, whether portrayed by a white performer in blackface or a black performer made to look like a white performer in blackface, led to what Paul Gilroy terms a "two-tone sensibility," emphasizing how the ability of the black body to be an object of pleasure or play and simultaneously an object of loathing was not contradictory.[37]

The black athlete occupies such a place in the American imagination. Accompanied by quantitative scientific analysis, the physical features scientifically attributed to the twentieth-century black athlete were more precise than those depicted on the minstrel stage. Yet in a similar fashion, they created the fetishization of a form of physical ability that lent widespread credence to some of the central mythologies of sport: blacks are naturally adept at sprinting, are more relaxed on the field, make better running backs than quarterbacks, and can jump farther. Within these fictions, the black athlete was reduced to a solely physical condition, with the removal of intellectual capacity from any scientific equation and the refusal to understand how, as phrased by

Michel Foucault, the body exists in a "political field."[38] In doing so, the scientific dialogue that surrounded the black athlete in the 1930s created erroneously legitimated social theories of racial difference regarding the "nature" of the black athlete and allowed the black athlete to sit scientifically beside other forms of racialized biology that emerged at the early part of the century. For example, the discipline of "criminal anthropology," which posed the criminal as biologically different—almost a savage subspecies—from the rest of society, began with the work of Cesare Lombroso in this period.[39] This biological emphasis on social behavior sought to exonerate society from responsibility for social problems, because it created a scientific basis for the actions of an individual.[40] In the case of the black athlete, however, such a pattern took a perverse twist, because the scientific understanding of the black athlete's success *removed* the individual's ability for achievement.

As with any scientific investigation, a pattern can be discerned in the scientific interest in the black athlete. Studies with a focus on the connection between race and athletic success emerged around periods of heightened interest in sport in general, such as Olympic years, periods when a specific athlete garnered particular interest, such as Jesse Owens in 1936, or periods when political and cultural interest, such as the black power movements of the 1960s, raised society's overall awareness of a particular group and thus stimulated a search for scientific explanation. Such trends are not unusual within the trajectory of science. As Harding points out, scientific discussions of race proliferate when "race as a structural system is changing or is perceived to be weakening," with emancipation and the civil rights movement serving as primary examples. Along these lines, scientific inquiry and, more specifically, projects of scientific racism also intensify in what Harding views as an attempt to "provide biological justifications for racist social structures and for meanings (symbols) of racial difference."[41]

In this manner, the work of scientists has contributed considerably to the popular discourse on the black athlete. Of course, these scientists by no means worked as a monolithic group, but rather produced studies from a range of fields, including physical anthropology, psychology, and physical education. To be sure, the background of one such scientist, W. Montague Cobb, the first African American physical anthropologist, certainly separated him from the core of his contemporaries. We can unearth many of the early fictions regarding African Americans' success in sports through an examination of a few varied (and sometimes tedious!) models of laboratory research that was done in an attempt, whether directly or indirectly, to quantify race and athletic ability. Perhaps more important, such research also demonstrates how laboratory science, initially published in academic and medical journals, becomes so-called popular science, helping to differentiate science's role in creating and maintaining authoritative social theories of racial difference. How the scientific construction of the black athlete has been propagated in a popular arena of perception illustrates that science is not merely a language of the laboratory but plays a significant role in popular discourse.

Because these scientific ideologies on race and physical ability eventually found themselves in more popular forums, they have great historical significance and provide critical evidence of where racialized untruths regarding physical ability originated and became reinforced.[42] Historian John Burnham situates the appearance of a popular science in the late nineteenth century and finds that its rise correlated closely with both the emergence of increasingly mass media and to the growing professionalism and specialization within scientific disciplines. In 1883, *Popular Science News* defined the field as "science put in a language which can be comprehended; it means science adapted to everyone's wants, to everyone's necessities."[43] Initially, scientists produced knowledge that was not accessible to a general public, and their conclusions needed explanation. This need was fulfilled by a series of different "popularizers," such as newspapers and magazines, and then radio, television, and advertising. Burnham describes this phenomenon as "a certain cognitive dissonance as the popularization of science and health developed a history that differed from the history of scientific ideas and institutions."[44] Once the popularization process has taken place, science takes on a life of its own, and the potential impact of scientists is greatly reduced when the power shifts to the popularizers or "gatekeepers," such as the media.

Of course, this process by no means takes a straight path, with scientific "fact" producing solidified racial ideologies, because science is not, as Andrew Ross observes, "value-free knowledge," but rather is attached to the institutions that both fund and utilize it.[45] Surrounding social beliefs, including ideologies of race, greatly impact scientific research. These beliefs contribute to the results, which are then co-opted into popular understanding with what Jacobson has aptly titled "supremacist baggage," producing conclusions that resemble few, if any, of the tenets of the laboratory work.[46] However, it is still crucial to begin our examination by exploring a sampling of the early experimental research on race and physical ability in order to determine where the popular science regarding the black athlete gained its authority.

A Record-Mad Country: Laboratory Athletes

One of the earliest illustrations of this development occurred in 1930, just before African Americans made a significant mark in international track and field competition. An article published by a group of physical anthropologists compared the calf muscles of "American whites and Negroes" to determine why differences existed along racial lines.[47] The study, which took place at the Department of Anatomy at the Washington University School of Medicine, was one of the first of many during this period that attempted to evidence a scientific, racially based hypothesis in the laboratory regarding physical difference and ability.

Of course, much of the scientific community had turned away from such eugenic-flavored projects in favor of the cultural emphasis established by scholars such as Franz Boas. But in a vein suggestive of nineteenth-century scientific racism, studies like this one circulated specious ideas of racialized athletic abilities, focusing on such things as heel length, body fat, and bone density and finding a parallel relationship between these attributes and athletic performance.[48] The stunning achievements of Jesse Owens at the 1936 Olympic Games in Berlin, where he won an unprecedented four gold medals in track and field, undoubtedly spurred the impetus for much of this kind of scientific research. Yet Owens was not alone in his accomplishments, nor was he the first. African Americans steadily climbed the international track and field ranks throughout this period, making questions of race and physical ability widespread matters before Owens even arrived in Berlin. Although the number of African American track champions would decline in subsequent decades, the number of black champions in the early decades of the century was considered phenomenal.[49] In 1924, while movements like the Harlem Renaissance and figures such as Marcus Garvey attempted to create alternative artistic and political realities for many African Americans, De Hart Hubbard became the first black athlete to win an individual gold medal with his leap of 24-5 in the broad jump at the Olympic Games in Paris.[50] In 1932, at the Los Angeles Olympics, Ed Gordon paralleled Hubbard's success with a gold in the same event. In addition, Thomas "Eddie" Tolan and Ralph Metcalfe finished first and second in the 100-meters and first and third in the 200-meters, respectively. Tolan, who set Olympic records in both events, had been considered by most to be the dominant American sprinter for the past several years. However, throughout the 1932 season, Metcalfe rose to success, beating Tolan at both distances at the Olympic Trials and making for an American rivalry that focused much attention on the emerging dominance of African Americans on the track.[51]

While African Americans won gold, the United States was under-going an economic nightmare. The social and economic climate of the 1930s created a difficult but critical interval for scientists. While the financial burden of the Great Depression considerably reduced the space that newspapers and magazines allotted to science, scientific authority was in great demand. As people lost their jobs and endured empty stomachs and bare feet, there was an exigency to promote and understand any possible social solutions that could be discovered in a lab-oratory setting, giving scientific research the prospect of greater social magnitude.[52] The number of scientific studies directly related to race and sport that emerged during this period was connected closely to both this increasing social responsibility of science and the international success of athletes such as Tolan, Metcalfe, and, of course, Owens. Further, the ongoing pattern of the "Great Migration," during which millions of African Americans moved from the rural South to the urban North, put an unprecedented number of African Americans in crowded city settings. Their attempt to escape from the violence of Jim Crow while seeking industrial opportunity magnified the seemingly ubiquitous fear of miscegenation and "race mixing," a fundamental undercurrent in all scientific (or social) inquiries into the black male at most any historical moment. As historian Glenda Gilmore affirms, by the late nineteenth century, interracial sexual relationships were definitively forbidden, because they "violated evolutionary principles.... Such liaisons resulted in mixed-race progeny who slipped back and forth across the color line and defied social control."[53] In the sporting world, Jack Johnson's enormously public relationships with white women created national uproar. When his liaison with eighteen-year-old Lucille Cameron became public knowledge, he was charged with the antiquated Mann Act: participating in a white slave trade. After an exhaustive federal investigation, Johnson eventually was jailed and levied a stiff fine.[54]

Of course, scientists never directly acknowledged the influences the surrounding social environment produced. In 1939, State University of Iowa physical educator Eleanor Metheny simply credited the rise of black sporting success as the spark for her own study. Her racialized science was an acknowledged quest to determine *why* Negro athletes were crossing the finish line first in such great numbers: "During the last few years, as a number of American Negro athletes have come into prominence, particularly in track and field competition, coaches and sports enthusiasts have raised the question: Is there some difference between Negroes and whites in proportions of the body which gives the Negro an advantage in certain types of athletic performance?"[55] Metheny maintained that despite the frequency of the question, an adequately quantitative answer had not yet been determined. Thus, she wanted to assemble "anthropometric data on American Negro and white male college students," as well as to establish the effects of differences in bodily proportions on athletic ability.[56]

The direct relationship between racialized anthropometric research and athletic success that Metheny sought to establish made her
study different from those of her contemporaries. For example, a study
drafted in 1941 in three laboratories—Indiana University's Department
of Physiology, Harvard's Fatigue Laboratory, and Duke's Department
of Zoology—aimed to assess quantitatively the difference between the
physical fitness of sharecroppers and that of "Northern Whites" and
yet never explicitly stated that *racial* difference was its primary focus.
Rather, its central point, according to its authors, was to find differences
in fitness between rural and urban men. However, with the sharecropper group broken into two categories—fifty-two "normal Negroes" in
one and eight whites in the other—and a comparative group composed
of white men, racial differences in physical abilities were implicit in the
conclusion.[57]

Conclusions from such studies were relevant because they claimed
to shed light not only on why athletes such as Tolan, Metcalfe, and
Owens were successful but also on why they won their races in such
record-breaking times. Indeed, with the superior marks of these athletes, their speed spurred rampant speculation as to why one athlete
was faster than another. Mere days before the opening of the Berlin
Games, for example, *Harper's Monthly* published an article on the "whys"
of speed. The author, Frederick Lewis Allen, observed, "We live in a
record-mad country and generation," and he outlined four reasons that
track and field athletes improved their marks with such rapidity: improved equipment, improved technique, larger physiques, and heightened motivation.[58] He argued the third hypothesis most cautiously,
phrasing it as a question rather than a conclusion. "Are the athletes of
to-day bigger, physically, than their predecessors," he asked, "and may
this increase in size be a factor in athletic improvement?"[59] Unlike
his other factors, which were environmentally and sociologically based,
his theory of physique was more pointedly scientific. While primarily
interested in the increased size of athletes, citing Gordon Townsend
Bowles's *New Types of Old Americans at Harvard*, a study of the physical
measurements of "Harvard fathers and sons of native American stock,"

he also discussed the racial and ethnic composition of athletes. He found it fascinating, for example, that although an American or British athlete had won every event at the inaugural modern Olympics in 1896, a wide variety of "civilized countries" produced gold-medal performances in later Olympics. However, "the most interesting athletic phenomena [sic] ... is the emergence of American Negroes as the best sprinters and jumpers in the world," specifically Tolan, Metcalfe, Owens, Eulace Peacock, and Ben Johnson.[60] Allen initially explained the emergence of such an abundance of African American talent as a "sociological phenomenon." Principally, he noted that new opportunities in higher education for African Americans likely allowed access to better training and more state-of-the-art athletic facilities. However, he quickly reverted to scientific assumptions about innate physical ability, emphasizing the physical features of the new black stars and alleging that "apparently they average somewhat longer-legged and longer-footed for their height than whites."[61]

This kind of correlation between speed and race was also a central tenet of a 1933 psychological study at Vanderbilt University. Psychologists Martha Lambeth and Lyle H. Lanier tried to determine if racial disparities on psychological intelligence tests were due to differences in reaction, presenting the question of whether reaction time is environmentally created.[62] Like the sharecropper study, this study was somewhat far removed from sport. However, it examined one of the central attributes—speed—connected to the success of African American athletes and also worked as a direct response to any sociological or cultural refutation of scientific studies of race.[63] With long-standing mythologies of "slow" plantation slaves, epitomized in popular culture by comic genius Stepin Fetchit, whose portrayal of characters like Highpockets in films such as *In Old Kentucky* (1927) solidified the stereotypical image of shuffling and dim-witted servitude, scientists undoubtedly wanted to discover the newfangled mystery of black men excelling in speed events. In doing so, Lambeth and Lanier directly juxtaposed an enduring concept related to African American participation and success in sport: intelligence versus physical prowess or, more colloquially phrased, brain versus brawn.

As the accomplishments of African American athletes continued throughout the twentieth century, claims that they were, by nature,
physically enhanced but mentally deficient evolved more fully, deriving
much sustenance from the supposed legacies of slavery as well as from
the conclusions of scientists who promoted false ideologies of black
strength. Thus, studies of speed and its relationship to intelligence
contributed to the broader understanding of human evolution. Such
considerations worked within a trend that had emerged largely in the
nineteenth century, when, according to Matthew Frye Jacobson, "scientific debate ... shifted away from static conceptions of various types,
toward more dynamic, evolutionary models."[64] In terms of the athlete,
Harper's Frederick Lewis Allen considered the continually improving
mark for the 100-yard dash as a general indicator of an evolutionary
societal progress. Comparing W. C. Wilmer's time of 10 seconds in
1878 to Frank Wykoff's time of 9:4.10 in 1930 (equaled by Jesse Owens
at the Big Ten championships in 1935), Allen found that the improvement "raises questions which concern not merely those who follow sports
but all of us who are interested in the riddle of human progress."[65]

Calf muscles had brought a similar conclusion in the aforementioned study at the Washington University School of Medicine in
1930. The study began with the premise that calf development was connected directly to a superior evolutionary state, positioning "man" as a
superior being partly because his calf muscles allowed for an upright
stance—one of the chief characteristics separating primates from the
rest of the animal world. The study also established that such upright-
ness was best and most often seen in white men, as "the colored races
in general, and the negroes in particular, show poorly developed calves,"
implying that nonwhites were more animal-like in their posture and
therefore, perhaps, in other areas as well.[66] While the scientists supported such an assertion by citing several international studies, they
acknowledged that previously there had been little agreement as to why
calves differed along racial lines. This study, however, declared a conclusion, creating a "scientific" analysis of which was the more "evolved"
being:

The tendinous part of either of the two bellies of the gastrocnemius muscle forms a greater proportion of the total length of the muscle in American negroes than in whites. Conversely, the muscle bellies of negroes are, in proportion to the total muscle length, shorter than in whites. These facts explain at least in part the slimmer appearance of the negro calf as compared to the bulkier appearance of the calf in whites.[67]

Other scientists had not been so extreme in trying unequivocally to establish indicators of superior evolution, but their findings, too, influenced perceptions of African American athletes in critical ways. For example, Lambeth and Lanier, in their study in 1933, moved beyond physical differences and speculated about how scientifically determined *behavioral* differences affected physical reaction, noting, "The possibility that two races might differ with respect to homogeneity of behavior traits ... is one which has scarcely been mentioned in race studies."[68]

Metheny's findings, however, more directly contributed to a connection between race and sport, generating relatively straightforward results. The "white" group was taller than the "Negro" group, for example, averaging slimmer hips and a shallower chest; but the Negro group weighed more, with less fat and more muscle. In addition, she found the Negro to have longer arms, hands, legs, and feet; wider elbows, feet, knees, and chest; and bigger shoulders, necks, and limbs.[69] She also tried to determine if such differences in bodily proportions affected athletic performance, seeking to establish what it actually meant to be *physically* "Negro," and, in doing so, what it meant *not* to be physically "Negro" (read: white). However, at no point did she attempt to "scientifically" determine exactly which physical features and abilities athletic excellence necessitated, negating any connections between her laboratory research and anecdotal assumptions regarding the actual athletic playing field. For example, she began with a finding that the Negro weighed more than the white, and then without discussion related her data of "sturdier construction" to prowess in football. She circumstantially reasoned that longer arms aided in throwing ability and increased momentum when jumping, while longer legs allowed for a superior running stride. Conversely, she wrote, a shallower chest affected breathing capacity and therefore possibly hindered stamina.[70]

Thus, Metheny, unlike Allen, linked a specific body type to athletic success. While Allen questioned whether a larger physique heightened athletic dexterity, Metheny conjectured that such a relationship was absolute and based her final conclusions on this assumption. While her goal had been to assess African American athletic ability "quantitatively," she admitted that her findings were based only on averages from her study groups and allowed for the possibility that huge variations *within* the groups existed. Last, the physical attributes she subjectively assigned for athletic success were not quantified in any way and failed to acknowledge the many factors that could not be precisely computed, such as motivation, technique, and training—all of which Frederick Lewis Allen considered in his nonscientific approach.

Like Metheny's study, the sharecropper study also tried to measure physical fitness but included additional factors such as age, occupational training, and financial status to provide some kind of finite conclusion regarding corporeal ability.[71] Yet despite the inclusion of these socially based factors, the study maintained a poorly argued scientifically racialized division and thus exemplified the problem of creating fixed racially based groups for precise laboratory research. The study on sharecroppers, for example, appraised metabolism and lung ventilation during moderate work, using additional data from sixteen northern Negro college students, but cautioned that the use of these students as a means for comparison presented a problem, because they were "commonly . . . of *mixed parentage*: many of them are predominately white." Undaunted, the scientists put forth a speculative conclusion: "We advance very tentatively the hypothesis that the trained Negro of relatively pure racial stock is more skillful in walking and climbing than the white man."[72]

The introduction of these "northern" students vividly demonstrates the impossibility of any kind of laboratory study that attempts to differentiate physical traits and abilities according to racial identification. Such an endeavor, as these studies demonstrate, is repeatedly based on an essentialist binary pseudoscientific racial classification of little complexity: white and Negro. Yet while entirely invalid, such essentialist classification provides one of the critical areas for examining the construction of race by science, making central the question, Who goes into which group? The answer to this inquiry clearly delineates how scientific conclusions concerning physical ability reflected and preserved dominant ideologies on racial difference. Rather than proving or disproving the validity of these scientific conclusions, then, it is imperative (and thankfully somewhat scientifically simpler) to question the very basis on which such investigations were approached, yielding a broad illustration of the strength of popularly held, albeit counterfeit, racial dogma.

Of course, several historians have, indeed, investigated the trajectory of scientific interest in race and athletic ability, generating important attention to the topic and producing comprehensive surveys of these kinds of social scientific and laboratory analyses, as well as some sharp critiques regarding the popularization of these scientific studies.[73] Yet while such scholarship regularly confronts and somewhat challenges the results of the laboratory, it can also engender troubling conclusions, often lending credence to scientifically derived notions of race.[74] Such works neglect their own historically fashioned tactics, intermittently falling under the spell of myths and stereotypes.[75] What is missing, and what remains elemental, is a renegotiation of the questions of such research in order to generate an interrogation of the very *premise* on which scientists stake their claims, rather than any kind of engagement over whether the scientists are correct in judging their results. In this renegotiation, two imperative questions emerge: How do the conclusions from these laboratories contribute to the overall understanding of the black athlete? And, perhaps even more edifying, how does science define race?

The pre–World War II studies typify this point. For example, the study on calf muscles used two groups of cadavers, one composed of seventy-three white males and the other of fifty-nine "negro" males. The scientists provided no categorical definition of race when describing the groups, merely stating, "The whites are of various national and racial derivations.... negroes were not differentiated as to purity of negro blood."[76] With a variety of national identifications within the white group, ethnicity clearly was not a factor, indicating that anyone who *looked* white was put into this group. This ignored, of course, the social construction of whiteness that so many historians have recently elucidated.[77]

For their part, Lambeth and Lanier attempted to create a more nuanced division of subjects, acknowledging, "Direct comparisons of the psychological test performances of races differing widely in general cultural background are of doubtful scientific value." They overtly worried that if differences were found as a result of the research categorization procedure, the data could not "be assumed to represent either the fact or the extent of hereditary disparity between the two races." Thus, they feared that the cultural disparities and economic conditions *within* a racial group might negatively affect the integrity of the study's scientific outcome, invalidating their suppositions. Yet regardless of such trepidation, which might lead to a conclusion that race could not be scientifically determined, they resolved that the absence of needed evidence merely prevented them from making any finite claims about behavioral racial differences. Their conclusion, then, did not indicate that science should avoid racially derived research because of the social and cultural aspects of race, but rather shifted the question of racial difference to one of scientific methodology. In doing so, they issued an urgent call for similar experiments to be more scientifically based on "fact" in order to create a forceful response to the various emerging social theories regarding racial equality. Such theories troubled Lambeth and Lanier, because they lacked a scientific basis. Therefore, in their view, there was "no immediately apparent *a priori* reason why the race equality principle should have found such favor in sociological circles."[78]

Accordingly from their perspective, the inability of science to find a basis for cultural differences along biologically conceived racial lines was not an indicator that such differences did not exist; this certainly presupposed that racial equality was not yet to be a factor in their work. For example, when examining the possible interpretations of their results, they were confident about their own sample: "30 12-year-old white and 30 12-year-old Negro boys in certain public schools of Nashville, Tennessee." Their white subjects were from the Warner School, while the Negro subjects were from the Meigs and Cameron schools. They stated that the socioeconomic status of the students was "average for the respective races," but they defined white and Negro according to which school each subject attended, failing to acknowledge the methodological problem inherent in the process. The doctrine of Jim Crow, which had legally permitted southern schools to segregate via the notion of "separate but equal" since 1896, ensured that this scientific study was based on the state's classification of race. It is doubtful that the schools had comparable environments, lending to an unequivocal social disparity within the scientific study. Yet Lambeth and Lanier confidentially asserted "one could scarcely secure a more homogeneous group than one of this sort, in which age, sex, and school grade are controlled."[79]

Their results belied their conviction and indicated, again, misgivings. While the two scientists acknowledged that their data indicated that the Negro did not perform as well as white subjects on "speed" tests, they allowed that such results might indeed have been environmentally rooted—lack of adequate schooling, for example—and encouraged prudence in future research. Further, they conceded:

> The general significance of the specific experimental results of this study is, of course, problematical. The question of the extent to which these samplings represent the American Negro, and of the effects of race mixture on test performance in the "Negro" group for which no allowances can be made in our figures, suggest the appropriateness of reservations concerning the *general* meaning of our figures.[80]

With this retreat from establishing any kind of firm *biological* racial deduction, the problematic of pitting black against white in the laboratory became singularly evident. Rather than focus on the results of this experiment, which was significant for its indirect attempt to juxtapose intellect and innate physical ability along biologically formulated racial lines, we must focus on the critical importance of scientists' inability to analyze a *scientific* and *homogeneous* racial classification for their subjects.

Interestingly, Eleanor Metheny, whose work was most directly a racialized scientific investigation of athletes, was one of few who admitted that the complexity of race created a problem in the laboratory. For example, when summarizing a 1937 anthropometric study of college students at the State University of Iowa (since renamed Iowa State University), in which the measurements of fifty-one male Negro students were taken and analyzed, she conceded that "it was not feasible to obtain histories of possible mixture of ancestry from the Negro students, and no attempt was made to determine degree of mixture by any objective method." With this disclosure, Metheny acknowledged the heterogeneity of any category designated merely as Negro. However, she did find the Iowa results to be of some value, relying on the 1928 study by Melville Herskovits, *The American Negro: A Study in Racial Crossing*. Citing Herskovits, she asserted that the American Negro was or was close to becoming "a stable type," and found her study to be balanced because of the racial complexity of the white study group, making the Negro classification "as homogeneous a group as the white students, whose ancestors, early or recent, have included many nationalities."[81] Thus, despite a variety of amalgamations of race, nation, and ethnicity, she discovered the complexity of whiteness as a classification to be no more stable or certain than that of American Negro and therefore rationalized the soundness of her data.

However, it was the physical potential, and therefore athletic ability, of the American Negro subject, not the white subject, that was an emerging central concern in the period. Like other studies representing several different scientific fields in this period, Metheny's work, while problematic in premise, probed into reasons behind the striking success of athletes such as Tolan and Metcalfe. The final analyses, whether from physical anthropologists, psychologists, or physical educators, created and sustained the foundations of mythologies that surrounded record-breaking performances—particularly in the case of Jesse Owens.

W. Montague Cobb: The Study of the "American Negro"

One of the most absorbing studies to emanate from the interest surrounding African American athletes in the pre–World War II period came from Dr. W. Montague Cobb, a physical anthropologist who applied the racial mythologies and scientific methodologies of his day to the most famous of possible subjects: Jesse Owens. Cobb's results, like others, are important in understanding how racialized science was practiced; however, his work is further significant because of his own social location—who he was and the kind of science he wanted to engage in. While much of the scientific examination of the success of African American athletes stemmed from fears about the decline and even exclusion of white athletes, Cobb's work represented alternative motives: he labored to produce a somewhat effective counternarrative on the subject.

As the first African American Ph.D. in physical anthropology and a prominent public intellectual, Cobb, unlike other scientists who worked on similar topics and remained relatively anonymous, has been the focus of many historical treatments, with a great deal written about his career as a physician, scholar, and activist.[82] During his medical studies at Howard University, Howard president Mordecai Johnson endeavored to increase the number of black faculty, which resulted in Cobb training in physical anthropology at Western Reserve University under T. Wingate Todd.[83] As reflected in his willingness to take on an African American student, Todd had progressive leanings, staunchly opposed racial determinism, and worried about the potential danger of the relatively new field of anthropology.[84] In 1932, upon the completion of his graduate work, Cobb returned to Howard to launch the Laboratory of Anatomy and Physical Anthropology, encouraging African American students to make their own "contribution not defense" of racial biology.[85] At Howard, he began working on a skeletal collection at the Smithsonian Institution under the direction of Ales Hrdlicka, curator of physical anthropology. Unlike Todd, Hrdlicka believed that the Negro mind was inferior to other races and supported eugenicist Charles Davenport. Indeed, he hoped to forge a connection between Davenport's work and physical anthropology to link two seemingly diametrical areas—biological study and societal advancement.[86] Hrdlicka's ideological dissimilarity to Todd unquestionably had tremendous impact on Cobb's own understanding and positioning of race, a topic that increasingly consumed him.[87]

In 1939, Cobb published his first full-blown treatment of race, in which he delineated seven "essential facts" of "common knowledge" in the biological construction of the Negro, finding this designation to represent a hybrid and intrabreeding group that was physically strong and mentally able. Without ever incorporating any direct historical reference to slavery, he linked each of the seven "facts" to its legacy, positing that environmental and physical trials and challenges served as the basis for explaining the ability of African Americans to succeed in the modern world rather than exist as a preindustrial, premodern people.[88] In 1942, he offered more detail, issuing a direct call to physical anthropologists to engage in further study of "the world's largest minority, the thirteen million American Negroes of the United States."[89] He began this seminal project, entitled the "Physical Anthropology of the American Negro," with an analytical critique of the existing work—numbering 412 studies—on the American Negro, work that he found to be largely unsatisfying because of its lack of scientific substance.[90] Yet notwithstanding such a lack, Cobb admitted that some of what existed was compelling, particularly Herskovits's claim of the "surprising 'homogeneity' of the American Negro" and Hrdlicka's pursuit to work on "data on the unmixed negro before he becomes non-existent."[91] Nevertheless, Cobb feared further decline in the field, especially with the reduction, by both attrition and death, of the ranks of those interested in such academic pursuits, charging that future studies by "well trained Negro scientists" were of critical importance, particularly as he saw a need for the creation of a "popular" volume on the subject for schools and "general lay use."[92]

Notably, the trajectory that Cobb laid out in this project displayed both a scientist's interest in the subject matter *and* a political agenda. He established a need for a more expansive scientific bibliography of anthropological studies, encouraged more African American scientists to engage in the work, and, perhaps most important, called for the dissemination of such studies to a more general public, indicating that despite his insistence on the pursuit of laboratory science, even in his earliest work he demonstrated a desire to produce significant *social* change. Further, as his work progressed, he began to make noteworthy concessions to social and cultural constructions of race along the lines of contemporaries such as Boas.[93] However, at no point in his project on the American Negro did Cobb identify his field, physical anthropology, as anything other than biological. He continually narrowed his own objectives along the lines of hard science, where the laboratory and the data it produced remained central, but he concurrently envisioned an ideal environment incorporating "living Negroes and their records, and human remains, soft parts as well as skeletal" with "more Negro workers" to combat the institutionalized racism he saw in the American educational system.[94]

This amalgamation of scientific objectives and social concerns produced a quest to determine the "scientific justification of the study of the physical anthropology of the American Negro," which forced Cobb to negotiate a space for himself between his two mentors, Todd and Hrdlicka.[95] This negotiation resulted in a definition of the American Negro that separated his discipline, which centered on scientific evidence and conclusion, from its subject, the American Negro, which, he concluded, was not a scientific creation. He wrote: "Social and not scientific dictum defines an American Negro." Nowhere did he reference factors such as blood and heredity; instead, he found that the American Negro was delineated not by science but rather by "various arms of the federal, state and municipal governments and ... the courts." Thus, he concluded, the American Negro was not a race, especially because as a group it was far too physically diverse.[96] Yet despite this conclusion, he maintained that the American Negro had "racial significance from a biological standpoint ... because the extant social system compels the people so designated to be essentially an intra-breeding group." Furthermore, he argued, if intrabreeding were to continue, the level of homogeneity eventually might constitute a race. So, rather than designate the American Negro as a racially based category, Cobb altered it to "a physical type intermediate between the African and the European in those traits in which the two differ most markedly, such as skin color, hair form, lip eversion, nasal dimensions and form and interpupillary distance."[97]

Thus, his explication of the American Negro, although somewhat based on physical traits, differed from those of other physical anthropologists, because he tried to create a more complex understanding of race that compounded social and scientific implications. His work was not based on a simple essentialist binary of black and white but, rather, understood that within the anthropological classification "American Negro" existed "almost every possible combination of features" instead of one precise racial type. Of importance, then, is his suggestion that race was not a fixed category. While a physical type such as the American Negro had the *potential* to become a race, he argued that with interbreeding, this evolution was not likely to occur, because "the American Negro is becoming a blend of three racial stocks, African Negro, European White and American Indian," with little "pure African ancestry."[98]

With his complex racial definitions set, Cobb began the most detailed part of his work on the American Negro, designated in the broadest of terms as "somatology." In this crucial discussion, Cobb argues that American sport provided one of the critical areas in which a popular understanding of these kinds of scientific discussions existed. "A fact which has occasioned much comment in the public press," he wrote, "is that Negroes have demonstrated superior ability in nearly all fields of athletics in numbers much greater than would be expected on a basis of opportunity or population proportion." Referring to his own study of Jesse Owens, written six years earlier and considered at length below, in which he determined Owens to be "Caucasoid rather than Negroid in type," Cobb refuted the increasingly popular theories that

"Negro excellence" was limited to sprinting and jumping, contending that such ability had no connection to "Negro blood."[99]

Cobb rephrased the question of Negro athletic prowess so that it did not ask why just one racially defined segment of the population excelled at sport but asked why *anyone* did. In this refocused pursuit, he never denied that racial traits were a possible factor; instead, he brought the query a step back before making any conclusion. "The important problem is the identification of the factors that make for excellence," he resolved. "Their racial incidence may readily be determined."[100] However, within Cobb's examination of athletic excellence, the inveterate possibility of "racial incidence" in no way unseated a possible connection between race and athletic ability. He continued, "Researches of this nature should be very enlightening if conducted upon Negro athletes and non-athletes, and might possibly be decisive in determining the relationship of race to athletic ability."[101] Cobb was convinced of the noteworthy strength and adaptability of the American Negro. Cobb was a former athlete himself, and his personal understanding of physical strength was prevalent throughout his academic work; indeed, one of his seven "essential facts" was physical strength. It was a concept he found to be racially understood throughout American society. "The ability to work hard and long is today so firmly fixed in the white man's mind as an attribute of the Negro," he wrote, "that when himself required to make strenuous exertion he commonly remarks that he has had to work like a Negro."[102]

Yet Cobb offered few scientific foundations for staking this claim. With no answers to be found in the laboratory, his initial assertion that the American Negro was not a race paralleled his contention that science was unable to prove or predict superior athletic ability. Rather, he admitted that neither anatomy nor physiology—scientific disciplines— could explain remarkable strength. He suggested that perhaps a different kind of scientific discipline, such as biochemistry, might be useful in the pursuit of this knowledge, persisting in his belief of a scientific explanation for what he still found to be the exceptional physical attributes of the American Negro, exemplified by athletic excellence.[103]

Cobb used his own study on Jesse Owens to close the door on any kind of anthropological answer to the question of the athletic supremacy of the American Negro. In the study, he brought into the laboratory the range of myths and explanations popularly offered to explain Owens's record-breaking success, using Owens as a diagnostic subject and producing perhaps his best-known contribution to both the field of physical anthropology and the understanding of the construction of the black athlete. The study appeared early in 1936, before the Olympic Games in Berlin began, in the *Journal of Health and Physical Education*, published by the American Physical Education Association. Cobb argued that track and field, specifically the Penn Relay Carnival (known during this period as the Negro Olympics), worked as an ideal anthropological laboratory, with a variety of bodies performing a multitude of tasks—running, jumping, and throwing. In this environment, he found, one could observe that while there were many ingredients to a successful athlete, such as training, desire, and technique, certain body types had apparent advantages in certain events. However, he found that Owens's specialty—sprinting—was not such an event, despite the claims of other scientific studies, with no single physique providing an advantage.[104]

Whereas he generated few conclusions about sprinting, he found the broad (long) jump, which Owens also excelled at, more appealing in this examination, because, as he posited, "only three times in the last sixteen years have white men been able to win the national broad jump title." He primarily sought to refocus interest in the dominance of African Americans in the event, wondering why such a question was asked at all. Why, he wondered, was there such a public discussion about the success of Negroes in sprinting and jumping? His answer was relatively simple: it was in these events that black champions emerged quickly and in significant number, generating attention that "stimulated the notion that these stars might owe their success to some physical attributes peculiar to their race." Yet, he continued, questions regarding race and physical excellence were not new to the sports world with the emergence of African American stars, because athletes such as Finnish distance sensation Paavo Nurmi had sparked such inquiry in the past. Furthermore, they were not limited to track and field, especially considering the continued European dominance in events like weight lifting, which, despite or perhaps because of a conscious and determined pursuit by Americans in the event, had created much speculation about "inherent European capacity in this line of endeavor."[105]

To confirm his point, Cobb began his study on Owens by singling out the "Negroid characteristics" most often cited as beneficial to running and jumping ability—long legs, long arms, and so on—to see if such characteristics could be found in a "Negro star" such as Owens. While he clearly engaged in a sort of racialized biology (despite his eventual refutations of the American Negro as a race), he did not, unlike some of his contemporaries, make any direct connections between racial characteristics and athletic ability, evidenced by the data he gathered on the physique of Owens and the way in which he compared those data to the so-called recognized standards. The exploration of Owens focused on three areas: skeletal proportion, calf muscles, and neuromuscular coordination. He concluded that Owens exhibited some Negroid characteristics, such as his lower limb, which formed 52.7 percent of his height. However, his foot, which was "relatively short and somewhat broad," possessed none of the qualities Cobb felt were "commonly but often erroneously designated as Negroid," nor did his heel bone. His description of Owens's calves was further emphatic: "Owens is of the Caucasoid type rather than the Negroid."[106]

The study's primary conclusion argued that, according to scientific data, Owens did not have the standard body of a "Negro star." Further, Cobb argued, there was little uniformity among such athletes to be found along racial lines, and it was unreasonable to emphasize just one characteristic, such as a foot or a heel bone, as *the* necessary feature—the sole enabler of superior athletic endowment:

> The physiques of champion Negro and white sprinters in general and of Jesse Owens in particular reveal *nothing* to indicate that Negroid

physical characters are anatomically concerned with the present dominance of Negro athletes in national competition in the short dashes and
the broad jump. There is not a single physical characteristic which all the
Negro stars in question have in common which would definitely identify
them as Negroes.[107]

Cobb summarized his conclusion with the example of Japanese
broad jumper Chuhei Nambu, in order to demonstrate further how
Negroid characteristics had no bearing on sprinting and jumping success. Nambu held the world record, 26-2¼, on the eve of the 1932 Los
Angeles Olympic Games, when a leg injury reduced his performance
to a bronze medal. Two days later, he won the hop, step, and jump
with a world record leap of 51-7, making him one of a few to hold the
world record in both horizontal jumping events. Nambu, Cobb found,
belonged to "a people with an anatomical build the opposite of the
Negroid in pertinent features."[108] Hence, Cobb determined that the
criteria for a champion jumper could not be limited to one physique
or, most important, to one kind of *people*.

With his work, Cobb pondered the concept of race in a more
layered and nuanced way than that of his contemporaries, all of whom,
of course, were white. Although he did not completely abandon what
he considered to be the necessity of scientific inquiry into race and its
connection to athletic success, his emphasis on the complexity of the
subject differentiated his writings from others, particularly those who
assumed and relied confidently on the ability of science to determine,
or even presume, who belonged in a group labeled American Negro and
why so many records were broken at the Penn Relays. Yet despite the
counterfeit nature of the essentialist designations "black" and "white"
(re)affirmed in the laboratory and in the counternarrative created by
Cobb, many, including those who guided and coached the athletes
themselves, felt they had the answer to the question of why athletes
such as Metcalfe, Tolan, and, of course, Owens emerged so quickly and
in such great number.

"Closer to the Primitive":
The Physical Anthropology of Coaching

While Cobb found the Penn Relays to be an ideal laboratory for the physical anthropologist, he maintained that his quest was not one solely reserved for science. Rather, he found it necessitated the inclusion of another source of knowledge on the matter—coaches—whose primary role was to find and further talented individuals. By including this additional source from outside the confines of the laboratory, Cobb delineated the project as seemingly uncomplicated, yet difficult to execute:

> Let the track coach set down the factors that make a great sprinter and the anthropologist the distinguishing features of the American Negro. If on comparison the two lists have much in common, race may be important; if little, race is of no significance. Almost at once, however, we are beset with vagaries. The track coach cannot categorically describe the physique and character of the sprint champion, nor can the anthropologist define with useful accuracy the physique and character of the American Negro.[109]

With this proposal, Cobb more fully developed his previous contentions that the American Negro was not a race, avowing that a track coach would be incapable of designating one specific body type as sprinter material (just as the physical anthropologist was unable to characterize the African American physically) regardless of the physical patterns that he found to exist. While he acknowledged that certain physical types created a "natural capacity" for the sprinter, and also maintained that training and technique, with a coach, created the transformation of physical potential into successful performance, he made no attempt to quantify scientifically the necessary proportions of training and technique to more inherent attributes, such as physique or personality. It was this inconclusiveness and ambiguity that decidedly made his central point: between sprinting and jumping champions, the variability found indicated that no single body composition ensured success.

The very nature of track and field, grounded in measurements of time and distance, illustrated his argument, which is why he felt a coach would be able to recognize it as easily as a physical anthropologist could. Humans continually improve their athletic achievements, running faster and jumping and throwing greater distances, ostensibly without any sort of visible limit. While reluctant to quantify training and technique, Cobb found it a useful measure to attempt in his investigation. In particular, he made the conclusion that the flourishing of Negro stars stemmed from an increasingly integrated system of higher education, a system of which he undoubtedly considered himself to be a product. If training was insignificant, and physique the only critical factor in sprinting and jumping success, Cobb reasoned, the majority of the champions would hail from southern Negro colleges. However, Cobb noted that none of the "elite" athletes attended a Negro college, where, for the most part, few adequate athletic facilities existed. Rather, the majority of these new track and field stars came from integrated schools in other regions with premium training facilities, finding, in his view, incentive in "the desire to emulate their predecessors and to excel in a white environment."[110]

Cobb recognized the importance of sufficient athletic facilities and good coaching in producing a successful athlete, but he also found that the matter of athletic excellence could not be limited solely to those factors. The complication lay in whether science had a role in determining the other ingredients necessary for athletic success.[111] Unlike other scientific practitioners, Cobb understood the difficulty of connecting physical capacity and athletic ability with spurious racial designations. Thus, in his view, it was important that the role of the anthropologist was different. "He has to deal with men categorically designated as American Negroes, but they do not look alike," he wrote. "Genetically we know they are not constituted alike. There is not one single physical feature, including skin color, which all of our Negro champions have in common which would identify them as Negroes."[112]

Cobb exemplified these difficulties with detailed physical descriptions of the Negro stars themselves, noting that Howard Drew was often perceived as a white man and observing that Ned Gourdin had "dark straight hair, no distinctly Negroid features, and a light brown complexion." Jesse Owens had a lighter complexion than Ralph Metcalfe, but Metcalfe had straighter hair. "Not one of them," Cobb concluded, "even could be considered a pure Negro."[113] In a similar vein, he found that white sprinters did not resemble each other either, making it clear that the binary of black and white was a distinctly American construction that produced the question of why the American Negro excelled at sprinting and jumping and complicated it at all levels, scientific or otherwise. "We find blond Nordic and swarthy Mediterranean types and various mixtures," Cobb observed. "In fact if all our Negro and white champions were lined up indiscriminately for inspection, no one except those conditioned to *American attitudes* would suspect that race had anything whatever to do with the athletes' ability."[114]

Yet Cobb's unusual invitation for the anthropologist and the track coach to work together was, of course, problematic, because it provided no space for acknowledging these incongruities, which certainly existed for anthropologists and, likewise, would emerge as track and field coaches had their own competitive ideas about which athlete would excel in a particular event. However, one coach in particular possessed a remarkable amount of influence in track and field between the two world wars. Dean B. Cromwell, head coach of the University of Southern California track team as well as head coach of the U.S. Olympic squad in 1936, exemplified how a (mis)conception of race—heavily influenced by a scientific perception of the athlete—manifested in how he taught athletic technique and to whom. Cromwell's oft-cited book, *Championship Techniques of Track and Field* (1941), revealed, as Cobb had suspected, that the objectives of the scientist and the coach were not markedly far apart, particularly because numerical results, as gauged by the stopwatch and the measuring tape, were the primary indicators of sustained athletic improvement. The role of the coach, then, was to keep unearthing techniques and training methods with which to continue numeric advancement, somewhat similar to a scientific quest to discover what made for a better athlete.

Cromwell emphasized that the variety within track and field enabled most anyone to find a suitable event, regardless of anatomy, but that the choice needed to be connected to potential physical ability, something he found to be "built in" and racially derived: "Naturally heredity and to some extent inherited racial characteristics may affect the young candidate's choice of an event."[115] For Cromwell, heredity was a simple matter. If, for example, one had short parents, the pole vault was a doubtful prospective event. He theorized that some people were naturally suited for some events because of the physical attributes of familial lineage. Yet the role of race in the equation, he admitted, was more complicated. "The international competition of the Olympic Games in recent years has shown how racial history and racial physical characteristics contribute to track and field ability," he wrote. "In the past few games we have seen supremacy demonstrated by the Negroes in the sprints and jumps, by the Japanese in the hop, step, and jump and broad jump, by the Finns in the long distances, by the British in the middle distances, and by the central Europeans in the weight events."[116]

In his analysis, Cromwell created an ambiguous amalgamation of race, ethnicity, and nation. "Negroes" became a national entity, as he exemplified the Negro phenomenon with the usual figures, De Hart Hubbard, Ed Gordon, Eddie Tolan, Ralph Metcalfe, and Jesse Owens—all of whom were American athletes. Designating these individuals as "another colored athlete," "another colored star," or "an American Negro," he separated them from the rest of the American competitors—the white athletes. While he allowed that Negro stars were not limited to sprints and dismissed the idea that sprinting ability was attributable only to a longer leg tendon (because "no one has yet been able to back up any theory in the matter with positive proof"), he submitted his own hypothesis rather than deal with the anthropological specifics of inherent physical attributes: the rising success of African Americans in sprint and jumping events was a matter of evolution.[117] "I'll offer the opinion that the Negro excels in the events he does because he is closer to the primitive than the white man," he argued. "It was not so long ago that his ability to sprint and jump was a life-and-death matter to him in the jungle. His muscles are pliable, and his easy-going disposition is a valuable aid to the mental and physical relaxation that a runner and jumper must have."[118]

His emphasis on relaxation was furthered with his example of the broad jump, relating "the superiority that Negro athletes have shown" to their inherent ability to relax, as well as to their "natural speed."[119] He found that relaxation was key to Negro technique. "The body-over-feet landing seems splendidly adapted to athletes who are perfectly relaxed," he wrote. "Jesse Owens and practically all great Negro jumpers have used this type of landing. Upon hitting the dirt they would roll over as relaxed as a kitten."[120] In Cromwell's eye, then, Negro jumpers had an ability to jump a particular way because they were intrinsically relaxed and must be coached accordingly, providing a vivid demonstration of how racial (mis)perceptions directly influenced athletic training.

Yet Cromwell's conclusion was somewhat complicated by the success of Japanese athletes in jumping, forcing him to shift from a racial designation ("Negro") *within* one national team to an entire Olympic team of a different nationality: that of Japan. Noting that "short stature and comparatively small size" should have prohibited Japanese success in most track and field events, Cromwell could find no explanation for their "sturdy legs" and therefore their success. However, he was able to make nationally derived inferences account for the Finnish success in distance running and javelin throwing:

> Seek the background of Finnish superiority in the long races and you will
> probably find it in the fact that Finland is a country of great stretches of
> forests and that the hardy people of this land for many hundreds of years
> had only their legs for locomotion in covering long distances. They kept
> up the development of their sturdy underpinnings in wintertime by trav-
> eling on skis and snowshoes. [Paavo] Nurmi is said to have been employed
> 5 miles from his home and to have made the trip each way daily by the
> old Finnish custom of running.... Finns used the spear in fishing and
> hunting, and it is only natural that they should become excellent javelin

throwers as well as long-distance runners. They were also wood choppers, as were the Swedes, and the shoulder and back strength developed in swinging axes contributed to the javelin-throwing ability of both races.[121]

In Cromwell's view, Finns and Swedes were a race much like Negro, although he delineated them along national lines—as a product of their physical environment—while he found the Negro, with no specific geographic origin, to derive success from natural ability. Yet Cromwell was able to create one critical correlation among the Finns and Swedes and the American Negro. None of these groups, he found, had any superior *intellectual* abilities or unusual levels of dedication that led to athletic achievement, unlike other national teams, namely the British, who performed exceptionally well at the middle-distance running events because they personified the smart and learned athlete. "We find that mental more than physical racial characteristics have played an important part in the British success.... those who excel do so ... because they are equipped with greater determination and doggedness than their opponents," he argued. "The Englishman has shown these qualities in ... political theory, and the same characteristics that have built the British Empire make John Bull's sons hard to beat in events that put a premium on strong-willed determination."[122] He admitted that his admiration for Great Britain stemmed largely from its similarity to the United States, a comparison inarguably racially determined, and in doing so implied that the American Negro was not part of this pan-national linkage but rather was set outside the parameters of the United States. "Racially, the American, although somewhat of a conglomeration, is admittedly closer to the British than to any other people ...," he argued, "excelling in the same events as the Englishman and closely paralleling the latter in athletic ability."[123] Accordingly, Cromwell posited that while the American (read: white) athlete worked hard, the American Negro had natural ability. With motivation and a desire to excel, in a nation more advanced and able to produce a better way to win, the American athlete represented the finest the United States had to offer—indeed, the finest in the world. Regardless of the uniform and the medals acquired in international competition, the American Negro was not included in this explication.

This racially founded hierarchy of ability established by Cromwell peaked with his assertion that an American athlete was a smart athlete. By delineating racial and national tendencies of non-American achievements, he was able to conclude his treatise on coaching with uplifting sentiments regarding the United States, critical on the eve of American participation in World War II. In Cromwell's view, success for the United States could be achieved through dedication and technique, as was historically proven. "We combine a love of these sports with a willingness to study them and develop scientific techniques," he wrote. "As a race it cannot be said that we are better fitted ... than other peoples."[124] Americans, then, were superior because they *learned* how to win, on fields of play and, along with the British as teammates, on any impending fields of war.

The legacy of Cromwell was considerable, and his ideas of an elaborate evolutionary ethnography on the Olympic track remained current for the next several decades. In 1964, for example, *Life* magazine emphasized how the Olympics offered "an 'anthropological' pattern of achievement" in what John Hoberman has called "the first of these popularizations" of racialized and scientific understandings of physical ability.[125] The piece focused on the success of "Mongoloids" (Japanese) and "Negroids" (African Americans) in some events, while not in others, to demonstrate how "the scientific fact that there are ... basic physical differences between races" could be played out on Olympic fields. Admitting that the subject was one with "hotly controversial implications," which kept many anthropologists from commenting, it argued for legitimacy because of the scholarly contributions of Carleton Coon and Edward Hunt regarding race and physical abilities.[126] The piece did acknowledge the work of W. Montague Cobb in the face of the racialized suppositions regarding athletes, as well as possibilities of individual ambition and social environment, but left the matter of scientific inquiry relatively open, concluding that there was much left to be done because of the apparent evidence that took place on Olympic medal stands. In the wake of such popular scientific wanderings derived from the multiple studies that emerged in the early half of the twentieth century, as well as the ever-increasing disparity regarding race and rights in American society that followed World War II, others in the 1960s would agree that there was much left to be done, but perceptibly in a far different manner.

CHAPTER 3

An Olympic Challenge: Preparing for the "Problem Games"

> Nigger Smith.... You don't know me and I don't know you,
> however I have heard that you are a fast nigger. You said off the
> track you are just another nigger.... Now call all your niggers
> together, plan your action (heroic type) and go out and snatch
> an elderly white lady's purse, or perhaps break a window out
> of an old man's shop. You know, do something real brave,
> something you and only you niggers are capable of doing.
>
> —Letter to Tommie Smith from "Just a YANKEE giving
> you the straight poop," reprinted in Harry Edwards,
> *Revolt of the Black Athlete*

> We like the Olympic Games, but we feel our cause is more
> important. These should not be related, because Mexico has spent
> a lot of money on the Games. But that is the way it is. The
> generation gap everyone speaks of has grown to world wide
> proportions now. It is everywhere. Your way of life, with
> your mechanism and your Olympics, does not suit us.
>
> —Mexican student leader, quoted in *Sports Illustrated*,
> October 14, 1968

Scientific studies between the two world wars authoritatively worked to establish Negro as a separate category of physique that habitually existed outside national and ethnic classifications. But the construction of the black athlete, obviously, was not left entirely to those in the laboratory. Rather, organic political discourse actively positioned the athlete in wide-ranging civil rights efforts that accompanied the close of World War II, creating the important social and cultural transformation of a "Negro" athlete into a decidedly "black" one. Individual victories over Jim Crow in the early postwar period—what historian Brenda Plummer has called "the age of 'Negro firsts'"—led to burgeoning yet counterfeit recognitions that American society was increasingly egalitarian.[1] By the late 1960s, it was clear to many that new strategies had to be implemented to fulfill the tenets of a more broadly conceived democratic citizenship. The Olympic Project for Human Rights emerged in this vein, arguing that U.S. society necessitated profound intervention because of its deeply rooted policies and attitudes of racism. Collectively, then, the OPHR attempted to convert the athletic arena into a source of empowerment rather than a forum within which racist interpretation and supposition could continue to run rampant.

Central to this metamorphosis was the rise to political prominence of Harry Edwards, whose autobiography provides a compelling interpretation of the various millstones, from the high school teacher to the college coach, endured by the amateur black athlete. The road Edwards forged clearly portrays how the societal belief in black athletic aptitude, held as normative by both the white institutions he worked within and the black patriarch with whom he lived, guided his way. Capitalizing on the talent he displayed both on the field and in the classroom, Edwards left his impoverished St. Louis home for San Jose State College, where he ultimately broke with the pattern of his "success" as an athlete. Combining his first-hand athletic experience with his academic aptitude, he established the foundations for an organization of politically revolutionary black athletes, the OPHR, and a strategy to boycott the Mexico City Olympic Games.

His father provided the initial necessary impetus. Between prison and marriage, the elder Edwards had trained to be a boxer, with Joe Louis as his model of how sport could be a vehicle of uplift, providing both escape and betterment. Yet unlike his father, Edwards questioned the spurious sense of equality the champion often was forced to symbolize. "He had knocked out the German boxer Max Schmeling," he remembers, "providing unequivocal 'proof' that … Jim Crow segregation was superior to Hitler's dream society based upon the ideology of

Aryan supremacy."[2] In 1956, through his father's engineering, Edwards attended the newly integrated East St. Louis Senior High School despite living in the wrong district. He found that the emphasis on sports was the fundamental similarity between his segregated junior high school and his integrated high school, with the focus on black athletic involvement perhaps even more pronounced at the so-called integrated school. Yet despite many reservations, Edwards became a standout student-athlete, motivated, in part, because "athletes could use the school's shower facilities *every day*," providing a luxury he could never be sure of at home.[3] However, he also remained well aware of the institutionalized lines of racial demarcation at the school and the inherent contradictions involved:

> Among my teachers, there prevailed an almost religious litany in praise of sports as the route to Black Salvation.... Sports were seen as an escalator up and out of poverty and nobodiness, as a way for Blacks to make it *now*. Blacks in sports were recognized by white teachers in the corridors. Black athletes were received differently in the classrooms than Black nonathletes. But to say that the Black athletes' reception was different is *not* to say that it was necessarily any better.[4]

However, within a few years of Edwards's high school experience, the widespread proliferation of civil rights movements complicated the belief in sport as a vehicle for social mobility, the concept of a level playing field, and the issues of (in)equality that accompanied both. As aggressive ideologies of racial equity began their foray into sports, it became clear that the Mexico City Olympics would likely transcend their "sports" identity because of their far greater potential as front-page news. The OPHR was but one aspect of the seeming chaos that encompassed the politics of race, rights, equality, modernity, globalism, development, and representation in Mexico City. Yet after the Opening Ceremony unfolded before eighty thousand spectators on October 12, 1968, *Newsweek* magazine comfortably reassured its readers that the Olympics would be a wonderful exhibition for all to enjoy. Portrayed in an unprecedented forty-four-hour television broadcast by the American Broadcasting Company (ABC), the Games would feature 7,225 athletes from 119 countries, a truly international spectacle. According to the magazine, the once "volatile setting of Mexico City" had been replaced by the grandeur and humanity inherent in an Olympic community. Everything that had threatened the very existence of the Games was all in the past: the OPHR, apartheid, Prague Spring, and so on. Most important, the demonstrations by Mexican students that had plagued the city had subsided. Quiet now were students who had loudly protested the Partido Revolucionario Institucional's $150 million Olympic investment, one made, they had shouted, while many lived in destitution.

Yet the assurances made by *Newsweek* were a far cry from the situation described in *Sports Illustrated*, which portrayed the approaching Olympics as an event in dire need of help. On its cover, *Sports Illustrated* represented "THE PROBLEM GAMES" by metaphorically transposing the Olympic rings to signify each category of turbulence, including "Boycotts and Riots" and an "Embattled" Brundage. The story that accompanied the anxiety-ridden cover questioned the ability of hallowed Olympic ideals to find a stable stage in Mexico, speculating that the Games might indeed be "the worst, as they are already the most troubled," with little hope for separating the politics from the sports.[5] Nonetheless, while the sports magazine emphasized such obstacles, the news magazine chose to put its faith in the Opening Ceremony. *Newsweek* remained confident that the "silvery blare of trumpet, clouds of pigeons swirling into the sky, [and] a throaty rumble of saluting cannon" would take care of the one possible remaining threat: protests by black members of the U.S. team, who after months of public debate about a boycott had decided to participate after all. Such concerns, *Newsweek* contended, could certainly be put to rest, as "the long-awaited black protests have produced far more rumor than trouble." Even New York sprinter John Carlos, considered one of the more militant members of the squad, seemed ready to run. "We've worked all year for our cause," he said upon his arrival. "Now we've got to concentrate on winning."[6]

The Way to San Jose: Creating the Olympic Project for Human Rights

Like Carlos, Harry Edwards was familiar with winning. As cocaptain of the San Jose track team and standout basketball player, his athletic scholarship enabled him to pursue his studies arduously and regain much of the educational opportunity he had lost in high school. As San Jose State record holder in the discus (180 feet), Edwards conceivably could have gone to the Olympics as a competitor. Instead, he quit the track team after extensive disagreements with coach Bud Winter and opted to redesign the rules of the game via his nuanced grasp of the prescribed roles for the athlete to procure a different kind of victory. He began by accepting a Woodrow Wilson scholarship for a doctorate in sociology at Cornell University, where his political awakening continued. He often traveled to New York City to hear Malcolm X speak and found the leader's assassination in 1965 to be the stimulus for a vital semantic move that later would provide one of the critical foundations of the OPHR. "I made a decision to discontinue use of the word *Negro*," he remembers, "... as Malcolm had said so often, that 'we' must take pride in our *blackness*, in ourselves, before we can do anything else."[7] In 1967, Edwards returned to San Jose State to teach a class entitled "Racial and Cultural Minorities." Ken Noel, a master's candidate in sociology and a nationally ranked middle-distance runner, took the course for graduate credit. Years earlier, while Edwards was quitting the San Jose State track team, Noel had been suspended from San Jose City College for trying to organize an action with out-of-state black student basketball players who had been denied some of the benefits of their recruiting packages. Noel also was held responsible for a protest at the State Junior College Basketball Championship Tournament, during which a player sat down in the middle of the court and had to be carried away. Edwards and Noel began to work together to spotlight incidents of campus racism.

While figures such as Noel provided important foundations for using sport as a form of social protest, Edwards must be considered, as both a social activist and a learned scholar, the central figure in the highly visible arena of race and sport in 1968. Jeffrey Sammons, among others, has criticized Edwards for trying to "speak for all black athletes."[8] Yet few can argue that Edwards remains synonymous with the critical issues, a constant presence, albeit at times a seemingly token one, in contemporary discussions. His unquestionable media savvy, crucial to his continued prominence, enabled him to take charge of the conversation but likely has prevented scholars such as Sammons from taking him seriously. Certainly, this talent could be problematic, because it often made him, rather than the issues, the story. In 1969, this predicament became clearly evident on the public television program *Black Journal*, hosted by Lew House. During a roundtable discussion with Bill Russell, Jackie Robinson, Arthur Ashe, and others, House asked Edwards if any kind of organization still existed after the events in Mexico City. "It's not a formal organization," Edwards boldly responded. "I think probably the only formality is that ... eventually it leads back to me in one way or another and I tend to hold the thing down."[9] Yet as the show continued, it became apparent that behind this somewhat egomaniacal reply was a man who understood the complexity of race as well as how sport functioned as an economic, industrial, and predominantly white-controlled institution. It was this very public voice conveyed by Edwards, whether as a professor, an author, a social critic, or an activist, that helped create and popularize the OPHR, an organization that almost produced a wide-scale boycott of the Olympic Games—an international spectacle—in order to make a political statement *within* the nation.

Of course, the connection between sport and civil rights did not originate with Edwards but enjoys its own eclectic history. On the eve of America's involvement in World War II, for example, students at New York University rallied against racial discrimination in college sports. As outlined by historian Donald Spivey, the movement began in October 1940, when school authorities told African American football player Leonard Bates that he, in accordance with a policy observed by most southern collegiate teams, could not travel with the team to play against the University of Missouri. In response, a throng of two thousand students marched in front of the NYU administration building-ing chanting "Bates must play," and in doing so brought the athletic "gentlemen's agreement" into question.[10] After the administration suspended seven members—the "student seven"—of the newly formed Council for Student Equality for circulating a petition regarding Bates, the radicalism spread, as is often the case. Paul Robeson, the NAACP, the Urban League, the Council on African Affairs, and the Communist Party all publicly condemned NYU, providing further sanction of the students' cause.[11] While the administration remained unmoved, the protestors had shed national light on the relationship between sport and civil rights. They made it clear that perhaps nowhere else was Jim Crow more in conflict with democratic ideologies than on the purportedly level playing fields of sport, particularly at the "amateur" level of collegiate competition.[12]

The following year the NYU Violets again played the Missouri Tigers at home, where Bates could have played had he not been injured. While little institutional change took place, the groundwork for using sport to this effect had achieved recognition and would soon be applied to a broader international field. In 1956, the first noteworthy boycott of the modern Olympics took place when Egypt, Lebanon, and Iraq refused to send teams to Melbourne in protest of the British-French-Israeli invasion of Egypt; Holland and Spain also withdrew in response to the Soviet invasion of Hungary.[13] The idea of a boycott by black athletes is generally credited to comedian Dick Gregory, who was a former track standout at Southern Illinois University. As early as 1960, Gregory suggested that African Americans boycott the Olympics and then encouraged them to boycott a U.S.–Soviet track meet. The idea gained further momentum when triple Olympic medalist Mal Whitfield passionately urged the necessity of a black boycott of the Tokyo Olympics in 1964:

> I advocate that every Negro athlete eligible to participate in the Olympic Games in Japan ... boycott ... if Negro Americans by that time have not been guaranteed full and equal rights as first-class citizens.... Even the

people of foreign lands know that we are still not free in this country. In Africa, South America, and all the nations of Europe, they know that day-to-day civil rights struggles of the American Negro are but expressions of his earnest desire to break loose from the shackles that keep him from making his place in the sun. They know this, and they watch with discerning eyes to see what the outcome will be.[14]

While the political climate simply was not ready for such an action to take place, the fact that a few people picketed the Olympic Trials in Los Angeles that year indicated that it might be close. On July 23, 1967, at the inaugural National Conference of Black Power in Newark, New Jersey, the idea of a black boycott of Mexico City again surfaced. But it did not generate much interest until adopted by Edwards a few months later. Edwards attributes the turning point to two pivotal developments. First, Tommie Smith told a reporter at the University Games in Tokyo that an Olympic boycott by black athletes was a possibility. His statement built upon earlier indications of his political leanings. In April 1965, for example, he gave a relatively controversial answer in a seemingly innocuous questionnaire for *Track and Field News* magazine's "Profiles of Champions" series. While most of his responses reflected his desires to excel on the track, maintain good grades, and "become an elementary school teacher," when asked what he disliked, he answered, "to be exploited."[15]

The second turning point was a rally Edwards and Noel engineered at San Jose State, protesting the treatment of black students at the school.[16] After the rally, which seven hundred people attended, including the college's president and dean of students, the United Black Students for Action formed and issued nine demands for equality. If ignored, the group threatened to block the upcoming football game between San Jose and the University of Texas at El Paso. Both occurred. The school met the demands but also canceled the game because of the intense atmosphere on campus. It proved to be a critical juncture because, in Edwards's adept words: "We had learned the use of power— the power to be gained from exploiting the white man's economic and almost religious involvement in athletics."[17] The successful blocking of the football game, the first major college athletic event to be canceled because of racial protest, motivated other campuses to follow suit. But perhaps most important, its impact went beyond political and social gain and attacked the economic underpinnings critical to American sport, making the protest a profitable, albeit risky, political endeavor. As Edwards explains:

> At San Jose State, the mold had been forged.... The college and the city had lost tens of thousands of dollars and substantial face, but Black people had made significant social and educational gains.... Shortly, we were to learn another lesson on both a personal and a political level: that any attack upon the sports institution of a society is intuitively and widely regarded as an attack upon the most central and preeminent values and beliefs of that society, as an attack upon the society itself. And only the naïve and the foolhardy could seriously expect such an attack to be inconsequential, regardless of how noble the motives or how grand the eventual accomplishment.[18]

According to Edwards, the next move came on October 7, 1967, when a group met at his house to discuss the problems of black athletes and their larger community. At the meeting, the group formed the Olympic *Committee* for Human Rights and designated the Olympic *Project* for Human Rights to focus on creating a black boycott of the Mexico City Olympics.[19] The difference in these designations presents two crucial points. First, to form a "committee" responsible for human rights indicated that the group felt it understood how such rights needed to be defined and that the struggle to achieve them was part of a larger, more universal, *human* quest. Second, undertaking the boycott as a separate task, or "project," indicated that it was a feasible devoir with a clear end in sight. To be sure, the language employed by the OPHR, and especially Edwards, would become increasingly important in terms of who was and was not responsible to the movement.

The meeting at Edwards's house produced the most significant foundation at that point for a black Olympic boycott. Rumors began to circulate in local newspapers, particularly the *San Jose Mercury News*, about whether such a boycott was possible, which athletes would support it, and what overarching effect it would have on the U.S. Olympic squad. Of particular concern was the poor American showing against the Russians in the so-called pre-Olympics that had taken place in Mexico that fall. Still, Payton Jordon, the probable head coach of the Olympic track team, dismissed the potential boycott. "I've heard about the meeting," Jordan told the press, "but I am confident these men are highly intelligent and will realize the overall importance of the games to our country."[20] Yet the idea that athletes had a responsibility to country prominently figured into such discussions because of the pre-Olympic results. To be sure, some, like Jordan, remained unconcerned about the apparent lack of international potential of the U.S. team. For example, U.S. swimming coach George Haines dismissed the pre-Olympic results: "If we were supposed to go down there and win the cold war, then we would have sent down droves of kids and done it." However, others, such as San Jose track coach Bud Winter, were more concerned. "The Russians started preparing for Mexico City one hour after the Olympics closed in Tokyo.... I, for one, am worried," said Winter. "The rest of the world is catching up."[21] Thus, while figures such as Winter steadfastly presumed that the United States, while lagging, remained on top, the proposed black boycott seriously jeopardized any certainty of superiority.

The decision regarding the boycott was scheduled to take place at the three-day Western Regional Black Youth Conference in Los Angeles, set to begin on November 23, 1967. Going into the conference, many sportswriters hinted at its implausibility. Many such reservations emanated from a *San Jose Mercury News* article that said Tommie Smith, arguably the most visible track athlete likely to make the U.S. team *and* a student of Edwards at San Jose State, did not support the boycott initiative. Without his advocacy, most felt it was dead in the water.[22] However, on the opening day of the conference, the paper reported that Smith was, indeed, going to be in attendance. Smith told the press that he understood how critical the Olympics were, but he emphasized that his beliefs also were important. "I am not willing to sacrifice my manhood and the basic dignity of my people to participate in the Games," he said. "And I am quite willing not only to give up participation in the Games but my life if necessary if it means that it will open a door or channel by which the oppression and injustice suffered by my people in America can be alleviated."[23]

The next day, the OPHR left the sports page for the first time when the *Mercury News* reported in a banner headline on its front page: "Negroes to Boycott Olympics." Flanked by photos of track stars Lee Evans and Tommie Smith, the boycott story took priority over news of gunfire between rival militant organizations at the conference. However, the decision to boycott, presented to the press by Edwards and Evans after the closed meeting ended for the day, was not yet confirmed by Smith. "Harry has taken it upon himself to say this," Smith later said in a tone described as angry. "No, I won't verify it.... I'm only one athlete out of a number at the meeting. The newspapers are not authorized to say anything."[24] Aside from Evans and Smith, the other well-known athletes at the meeting of approximately two hundred people included UCLA basketball standout Lew Alcindor, his teammate Mike Warren, and Otis Burrell, a former high jumper at the University of Nevada. Edwards claimed that other athletes also voiced support for the boycott, either by phone or in written statements. But in the midst of the athletic stars, it was Edwards who took center stage before the press. "Is it not time for black people to stand up as men and women," he dramatically asked, "and refuse to be utilized as performing animals for a little extra dog food?"[25]

The next day, Smith seemed just as adamantly supportive of the boycott as Edwards did, which was again front-page news. Pledging "I will not turn back" from a decision that would likely cost him at least one gold medal, he declared his cooperation with the boycott, as did an estimated fifty or sixty other athletes who participated in the vote.[26] Thus, with 197 conference participants in favor of the boycott and only three opposed, the symbolic Thanksgiving Day vote, now considered official and final, put the wheels of the boycott into motion. Concurrently, Edwards released a resolution that disseminated the specific mission of the OPHR. In skillful Cold War fashion, it pronounced that the United States had let its black population of twenty-two million suffer "more hell than anyone in any communist country ever dreamed of," despite its role as leader of the so-called free world. Therefore, the OPHR resolved to boycott the 1968 Olympics.[27]

Reaction to the proposed boycott varied both within and outside the athletic community. Bud Winter, Smith's coach (and Edwards's former coach) at San Jose State, said, "I have worked with the black man and I understand his problems, but boycotting just is not the way to solve them." While Winter appeared undaunted by the possible effects the boycott would have on American results in Mexico, he expressed concern over the individual athletes involved. "Smith and Evans are two of the greatest Negro athletes in history," he said. "I pray that the United States can clear up problems of racial equality ... so that they will never have to be confronted with such drastic action.... I am appalled Negro athletes have been driven so far as to consider boycotting a movement that epitomizes the very thing for which they are fighting."[28]

The Olympic administration, on both the national and international levels, agreed with Winter's assessment that it was Olympic *participation*, not abstention, that could aid the plight of the black athlete, arguing that the Olympics were the wrong event to target. In a television interview, IOC president Avery Brundage deemed the boycott "a very bad mistake" and faulted Edwards. "These misguided young men are being badly advised," he affirmed. While Arthur Lentz, executive director of the U.S. Olympic Committee, likely objected to the boycott because of its probable effects on the medal count (especially since the 50 African Americans on the 362-member squad in Tokyo had won 22 of the 125 U.S. medals), publicly he cited reasons in line with Brundage. "The officers and committee members have been aware of this situation for a long time," Lentz remarked. "They resent being used as an attention getter no matter how worthwhile the cause may be." Last, reports emerged from the host city that Mexican officials were worried about the negative ramifications a black boycott might have on their event.[29] Despite such indications, Pedro Ramírez Vázquez, chair of the Mexico City Organizing Committee, classified the boycott "an internal problem of the U.S.A." and insisted that it would not impair Mexico's ability to "greet the youth of the world."[30]

Many black athletes, or at least those pursued by the media, agreed with the men in charge. Jesse Owens, whom seemingly every reporter wanted to talk to, criticized the boycott from the start. "I deplore the use of the Olympic Games by certain people for political aggrandizement," said Owens. "There is no place in the athletic world for politics."[31] While the press underscored his view for numerous reasons, it was his performance in Berlin in 1936, obviously, that made him an authority on the proposed Mexico City boycott. Yet while most reporters knew and conveyed the legend of Owens's victories in the face of white supremacy, few gave any sense of the contradictions embedded in American participation in Berlin. When, for example, the Amateur Athletic Union (AAU) initially voted that the United States should not go to Berlin out of concern for its Jewish athletes competing in a Nazi state, the black press roared in protest that the AAU refused to alleviate parallel inequities suffered by African American athletes at home. Why, the black press asked, had the AAU excluded Owens from eligibility for the Sullivan Award, given to the nation's outstanding amateur athlete, in 1935?[32]

While a more shaded understanding of the politics that surrounded Berlin could have provided great insight into the situation emerging in 1968, few members of the press explored it. They focused instead on the story of how Owens won an unprecedented four gold medals before Hitler, an enemy so malevolent that he refused to shake Owens's hand on the victory dais. Indeed, the print space given to the tale of the missed handshake in stories regarding the Mexico City boycott demonstrated just how extensive its mythology had become. Yet historian David Wiggins explains that while Hitler refused contact with black athletes, it was not a direct reaction to Owens but rather an effort to prevent conflict with the IOC. On the opening day of track competition, Hitler personally congratulated all of the winners with the exception of the high jump medalists. The final event of the day, the high jump, lasted longer than originally scheduled. Two of the three medalists in the U.S. sweep of the event were black: winner Cornelius Johnson and silver medalist David Albritton. When IOC president Henri Baillet-Latour commented on the obvious oversight to German officials the next day, German IOC member Karl Ritter von Halt, a member of the Nazi Party, resolved that Hitler would "congratulate publicly either all or none of the winners." Hitler elected the latter option, and after the first day of track and field events shook no winner's hand, including Owens's.[33]

Regardless of the lack of validity of the story, Owens's Berlin performance remained a prominent part of journalistic analysis of the planned black boycott. For example, *New York Times* columnist Arthur Daley declared Owens "the best possible argument for Negro participation," a figure who proved "that the master race was not quite as masterful as Hitler would have liked everyone to believe." As proof positive, Daley called attention to Owens's friendship with broad jump rival Lutz Long. After failing to best Owens's record leap in Berlin, the German put his arm around his opponent's shoulders as they walked together, a move Daley described as "Olympic idealism in its ultimate form." The proposed boycott of 1968, he concluded, "would not put the slightest dent in the Olympics ... because [it] always has been the least discriminatory vehicle in the world of sports."[34]

While the most prevalent, Owens was not alone in voicing opposition to the boycott. World long jump record holder Ralph Boston, a likely candidate for the 1968 team, publicly objected to the boycott. Rafer Johnson, the 1960 Olympic decathlon champ, disputed the boycott because "the Olympic Committee and the Olympic organization always have been fair to the Negro." Yet others were not so sure and remained undecided, including basketball's most prominently rising star. "If you're in a racist society, it's up to you to do something.... We don't catch hell because we're Christian," said Alcindor. "We catch hell because we're black." Charlie Green, six-time National Collegiate Athletic Association sprint champion, disagreed and found little reason to hide his heavily patriotic position. "It comes down to a matter if you're an American or if you're not," said Green. "I'm an American and I'm going to run." Norvell Lee, who won a gold medal in boxing in 1952, concurred. "I personally don't see the need for this type of thing at all.... Athletics is the only field in which the Negro has been treated well," Lee said. "The athletes ... will be doing more to hurt themselves and their image than anything I can imagine."[35]

The press was so intent to find objections to the boycott that they moved far outside the Olympic circle to find them. One United Press International wire story quoted Emmett Ashford, who in 1966 had become the first African American major league umpire. Ashford declared that the boycott was "wrong, all wrong" and that only "impressionable kids" were involved. "The ones who came up the tough, tight way aren't complaining," he said. "Just look at gains the Negro has made in sports. It's been his major stepping stone."[36] Former Dodger pitching luminary Don Newcombe asserted that the boycott worsened the African American situation, and Dallas Cowboy Bob Hayes, a former Olympian, also voiced dissension. The press even found Joe Louis for a quote, albeit one from a hospital bed. While recovering from gallbladder surgery, Louis found the time to encourage everyone to participate in the Games. "Maybe they don't have equal opportunity in America, but they're gaining it every day and that's something you should realize," Louis opined. "Things are improving. If they were going backwards, it would be different."[37]

Edwards took such objections in stride. "I don't reconcile their stand," he said. "In this movement, we have not tried to destroy dissent."[38] Furthermore, not all prominent African American athletes objected outright to the boycott but rather found it a difficult issue to establish a firm position on. Most notably, Jackie Robinson, some twenty years after his momentous major league debut, announced that he had "mixed emotions" about the boycott. While he contended that initially he disagreed with the idea, he was "more sympathetic if the leadership is right and their motives are correct." Not surprisingly, Muhammad Ali, whose world heavyweight title had already been taken on grounds of draft evasion, supported the OPHR initiatives without reservation. "Giving up a chance at the Olympics and a gold medal is a big sacrifice," Ali said. "But anything they do that's designed to get freedom and equality for their people, I'm with 1,000 per cent."[39]

In addition to the athletes, sportswriters vocalized strong opinions about the boycott, puzzled by its motives but ably dealing with it as a potential political spectacle. Robert Lipsyte, *New York Times* columnist, offered perhaps one of the most nuanced perspectives of the situation. He maintained that the sports world could not simply relax, "patting itself on the back for its treatment of Negroes." It had "allowed" Owens to excel in Berlin and Robinson to integrate baseball for reasons of economics as much as humanity. But he also admitted that sport was often the antecedent for racial integration in America and had given "thousands of Negroes personal fulfillment, college educations and wealth." The boycott thus indicated a significant shift from a discussion of integration to one that recognized how young athletes had found the means for empowerment within sport and were even willing to jeopardize their own futures. The historical moment, Lipsyte argued, dictated newly extreme actions, because it was difficult to be a nonactivist college student. The politically defined athlete, then, had to decide whether to "sacrifice" the opportunity to compete while under "tremendous pressure ... by Black activists." Indeed, one of the most central goals "for this new generation of black athlete is the sense of obligation to the black community," Lipsyte contended. "Competing ... might seem hypocritical to those who believe that this country has offered black Americans only 'tricks and tokenism.'" As a consequence, the boycott could strengthen notions of identity for the young athletes involved and, "at best, embarrass the country."[40]

Other columnists were less sympathetic. Writers at the *San Jose Mercury News*, where interest in Smith was higher than perhaps anywhere else in the country, commiserated with him but often failed to see the driving force behind his decision. Sports editor Louis Duino, for example, dismissed the importance of the boycott and insisted that, even with the absence of some of its stars, "the United States will survive." Duino did not doubt the athletic abilities of those behind the boycott and contemptuously wrote, "To be sure the U.S. team can *use the services of boys* like Tommie Smith." But he stood solidly behind the Olympic movement and believed, in accordance with modern Olympics founder Pierre de Coubertin, that the Games promoted "a better understanding among men of all nations." This position, of course, indicated that the action at the Black Youth Conference directly impeded that noble mission, especially since athletes who had "been given equal treatment and equal opportunity to succeed in the field of sports" had taken it.[41] What he failed to realize, of course, was that it actually tried to drive more understanding among individuals *within* a nation.

Duino used long jumper Ralph Boston, who had already publicly stated his rejection of the boycott, as his example. Duino pointed out that sport "provided Ralph with the opportunity to travel the world and make many friends.... No one has enjoyed the life of an athlete more than Boston." In Duino's view, all Olympic athletes, "black and white," should appreciate their circumstances, because they are "pampered with special treatment and [their] path to the Olympics is strewn with roses." Duino recommended that if the athletes felt they had grounds for complaint, they should "read the history of the trials and tribulations of the first United States team." He recited the story of James B. Connolly. A Harvard freshman, Connolly became the first modern Olympic champion when he won gold in the hop, step, and jump after a grueling boat trip had left him with little time to prepare. Duino wondered if, in comparison, "today's athlete [could] match the courage and desire to win as did this group back in 1896?"[42]

Duino was unable, or at least unwilling, to recognize the specific plight that athletes such as Tommie Smith saw themselves in. He also failed, or refused, to see sport as anything other than an arena designed to envelop the purest demonstrations of grit and prowess. His stance stood in stark contrast with that of his colleague Dan Hruby, who solely focused on Smith to understand the boycott movement. Smith, of course, as a San Jose State student and world-record holder, was a familiar presence on *San Jose Mercury News* sports pages. With the boycott proposal, he appeared even more frequently in the paper, his athletic accomplishments increasingly attached to some sort of statement that identified him as an OPHR member.[43] Rather than chide Smith as Duino did, Hruby stressed the difficulty an athlete like Smith faced in deciding to boycott, knowing that in facing the world's best he could become the world's best. While Hruby praised the egalitarian nature of sport and wrote that one of the "biting ironies" of the issue was that "sports, which abhors prejudice—should be used as a vehicle for protest," he understood why Smith was a "cause celebre on a nationwide racial stage." He wrote, "Only a person of his stature can successfully make a case. . . . Similar action by a lesser person would only draw yawns."[44] The fear of such yawns was his primary point: without a figure like Smith on board, the boycott would not be unanimous. Without unanimity, it could not be an effective means for making a powerful political statement. It was Hruby's insightful contention, then, that the publicity surrounding the very declaration of the boycott could likely prove to have the greatest gain in the end, especially because the possibility of the boycott's working was, in his word, remote. Thus, Hruby respected Smith's position on the boycott, because it might do some needed good. In a nation that had experienced the riots of Watts as well as other places, "an Olympic boycott by Negroes wouldn't be telling the world anything," he wrote. "It would, however, be re-telling something in a big way."[45]

Hruby, unlike his counterparts, questioned the boycott's political impact on the broader community. While many sportswriters focused on the actions of Smith, Evans, and Alcindor and the reactions of prominent athletes like Ali, Owens, and Robinson, few dealt with the boycott as anything other than political posturing. It was seen as a disrespectful action and a strident display of disloyalty against the one thing that had presented so many opportunities to African Americans. But rather than believe that athletes such as Smith were acting on their own consciences, many felt they were badly advised. Those of this standpoint placed the blame squarely on the shoulders of Harry Edwards, portraying him as an autocratic character who dictated the game to the young ones who played it. Arthur Daley revealed such sentiment most directly when he sympathetically asserted that athletes like Smith and Alcindor were "victimized by those who would use them to promote a boycott that has no chance of serving its purpose."[46]

Eventually, as many predicted, the boycott effort would fail, and the majority of its supporters would go on to compete in Mexico. However, in a time when a plan for unparalleled media coverage of the Olympics placed a sweeping eye on its participants, any kind of demonstration by the OPHR would retell, as Dan Hruby noted, a familiar story in incomparable fashion. Thus, it was by design that the ultimate action taken by Smith, along with John Carlos, on the victory stand would coincide with the first large-scale Olympic broadcast, and it allowed an unimaginable degree of political worth. The television coverage of the Opening Ceremony that preceded it undoubtedly amplified its shock value. During the colorful Parade of Nations, black athletes marched proudly; one television critic described them as "smiling and waving and obviously eager," noting, "Harry Edwards, leader of the abortive boycott, should have been embarrassed."[47] On the first day of the Games, then, the carefully cultivated militant image of a black athlete had been replaced, momentarily, by a different figure on the small screen. The black athlete seemed just glad to be there, in living rooms throughout the United States and throughout much of the world.

Preparing for the Thrill of Victory and the Agony of Defeat: Developing a Modern Olympics

The moving image cameras that brought the athletes into viewers' homes first appeared in 1936 at the Berlin Olympics by the deft, albeit controversial, hands of documentary filmmaker Leni Riefenstahl and would be perfected, some three decades later, by television legend Roone Arledge. The historical trajectory between this unusual pairing illustrates the variety of consequences inherent in recording the Olympic Games in terms of both technology and content. Riefenstahl's renowned career began, of course, two years earlier with her propaganda master-piece *Triumph des Willens*, which chronicled Hitler's rallies at Nuremberg. In similar fashion, her treatment of the Berlin Games, *Olympia*, is a work of epic filmmaking but one that lionizes the Nazi state. Employing sixty cinematographers, Riefenstahl shot 1.3 million feet of film (approximately 248 miles) and pioneered a series of extraordinary athletic images that utilized slow motion, aerial, and underwater camera work. The film debuted in Germany on April 20, 1938, Hitler's birthday, to resounding applause. However, while many in Hollywood screened it privately, in awe of its cinematic achievement, the film never found a U.S. distributor because of its propagandistic nature, so it had little direct impact on the American public.

Twelve years later, the BBC took the next significant step in Olympic programming when it paid fifteen hundred pounds to the International Olympic Committee for the moving image rights to the London Games, the first time any television network had done so. By 1960, the money spent by the BBC paled in comparison to amounts that CBS shelled out to broadcast moments from Squaw Valley and Rome—$50,000 and $394,000, respectively. In 1964, NBC employed communication satellites to offer its viewers footage from Tokyo. However, the coverage, which appeared in late-night, fifteen-minute spots, was sparse at best, and print media remained the favored source for Olympic results.[48] Thus, when ABC procured the rights to the Olympics in 1968, both the Winter Games in Grenoble and the summer event in Mexico City, it marked the first time a major television network undertook the daunting task of an extensive broadcast. Estimates that four hundred million people throughout the world would watch events from Mexico ensured that it would be the largest media sports enterprise in history. From their own homes, spectators would learn about their favorite athletes and events from thirty-five hundred accredited media personnel stationed in the city—more personnel than were involved in any previous Games.[49]

While ABC undoubtedly appreciated its own role in manufacturing the grand scale of the event, it likely did not grasp its impending position within a longstanding racialized pattern of innovation in mass media. The minstrel stage, arguably the first form of mass entertainment in the United States, authenticated black stereotypes such as Zip Coon and Mammy to northern working-class audiences with a legacy that lingers in contemporary popular culture.[50] In film, D. W. Griffith's racist opus *Birth of a Nation* (1915) marked the debut of the full-length feature, while Warner Brothers' blackface classic *The Jazz Singer* (1927) unveiled synchronous sound. Riefenstahl perhaps exemplified how the means of representation often change at a crucial moment in the racial order. Her infamous contributions to her genre solidified the relationship between technical innovation and white supremacist ideology. In 1968, with a comprehensive broadcast of the Mexico City Olympics, we see once again this reinscription of racial hierarchy in mass media, this time at the hands of an American television network.

Responsible for the initiation of this full-scale Olympic broadcast was ABC sports president Roone Arledge, whose role in establishing the modern sport industry is nearly incalculable. After achieving some critical success at NBC early on, Arledge transferred to ABC in 1960, where he offered Tom Moore and Ed Sherick, respective directors of programming and sports, an unusual blueprint for televising football. His formula involved the use of several technological modifications, such as handheld cameras and remote microphones, as well as programming ideas that included a halftime show with game highlights and detailed commentary. Moore and Sherick made Arledge the producer of college football, and on the basis of his idea that "the marriage of sports and innovative entertainment techniques would produce higher ratings," in the words of Randy Roberts and James Olson,[51] Arledge subsequently changed the way Americans view sports. In doing so, Arledge revolutionized sport from a fan-based medium to a broader sector of the entertainment industry, a move that not all viewers appreciated. Traditional fans carped about how Arledge's most famous handiwork, *Wide World of Sports*, included events such as demolition derby, profiled individuals such as Robert Craig "Evel" Knievel, and accentuated "exotic" locations rather than activities themselves, such as

Acapulco's cliff diving. Furthermore, Arledge often broke what many considered to be well-established rules to cultivate a higher entertainment value. For example, upon the discovery that he had no footage of a crash at Le Mans, he restaged the event by setting several miniature cars on fire.[52] Techniques such as this expanded the number of viewers for *Wide World* and made sports programming a more lucrative venture. It developed its own personalities, such as Howard Cosell, and its own commercial worth to the network, particularly in terms of an increasingly targeted male market. When the image of Yugoslavian skier Vinko Bogataj crashing at the International Ski Flying Championships was inserted into the show's opening credits in 1970, personifying "the agony of defeat," the formula for commercial sports television was complete.

For the Olympics, Arledge followed the creed of realtors and emphasized location. He found the site of the Olympics to be a fundamental asset in generating mass appeal, like the *Wide World* cliff-diving segments. As the first Games to be held in Latin America, the Mexico City Games could be televised to people who perhaps were not interested in sports but wanted to know more about the place itself. Arledge understood how a sporting spectacle watched on the small screen differs from the one watched by the crowd in the stadium. It becomes, according to one scholar, a "technological translation of the event itself into another, two-dimensional language, and into a different cultural setting, the living room."[53] While the living room might offer a closer view of the game being played, it obscures the broader sweep of the exhibition. The producers of the coverage create what Pierre Bourdieu describes as "a very particular vision of the political field."[54] The television viewer watches the game through a lens that he or she does not control and has little command over the events shown and the individuals emphasized. Arledge, like Riefenstahl before him, understood the control he had and used it to full commercial advantage.

In 1968, the South American location of the Games was of further import because it necessitated a series of technical advances. Approximately six weeks before the Opening Ceremony, NASA prepared to launch *Intelsat 3*, described by the *New York Times* as "the newest and most advanced commercial communications spacecraft ever built," to relay footage of Olympic events.[55] While previous Intelsats had been stationed over the Atlantic and Pacific oceans, this marked the first time Mexico City would be included in satellite reach. In addition to the cameras in space, ABC's cameras in the air impressed many, with cameraman Neville Feldman and his three colleagues suspended 246 feet above the ground for aerial footage.[56] Also, the network employed a "Flash Unit," a helicopter outfitted with two cameras, and used both color "slo-mo" and stop-action instant replay in its broadcast.[57] Television critics largely rewarded these efforts and placed considerable emphasis on the sharpness of the televised images and the overall lack of mishaps. One writer, for example, marveled over the enormity of the production and asserted that Arledge "outdid himself" by assembling the necessary components "to cope with a multiplicity of athletic events occurring simultaneously."[58]

However, the ovations for ABC's technical accomplishments were accompanied by familiar criticism, such as the columnist who deemed the spectacle "saturation television coverage."[59] One disgruntled viewer found that ABC did "a rather poor job," particularly in terms of the number of commercials shown and the overemphasis on U.S. athletes.

> While I believe that an Olympic program aimed at American audiences should display properly the skills and talents of the outstanding U.S. participants, I also think that viewers should have been exposed more objectively to the wonderful achievements of many of the other fine athletes.... It should be in the spirit of the Olympics (and, one hopes, of the network as well) to reflect the true international atmosphere of the quadrennial celebration.[60]

One critic agreed wholeheartedly with the first point, noting, "Commercials were moving in faster than the sprint races and the network is sure to win a gold medal for selling cars and razor blades."[61]

However, extensive commercial sponsorship was not new to the Games, but began in 1960, when companies contributed their wares directly to the Olympic movement for the first time. In Rome, Gillette donated ten thousand shaving kits, Olivetti provided a thousand typewriters, Omega contributed stopwatches, Zanussi supplied refrigerators for the Olympic Village, Fiat furnished thirty-four cars, and Coke gave two hundred thousand bottles of its product. Banca Nacionale del Lavoro held the title of official bank, and Lambretta motorcycles exclusively transported journalists.[62] With over a hundred companies contributing various resources in Tokyo four years later, clearly corporate partnerships with the ostensibly amateur sporting extravaganza and the accompanying rampant commercialism were not limited to shoe manufacturers. Rather, they extended into other, often decidedly American, domains. While the *New York Times* claimed that the Olympics happened in "the universal language of sports" because no one needed an interpreter to decipher the timed result of a race, a walk through the streets of Mexico City indicated that such universality apparently never left the stadium. "Programs like Huckleberry Hound and Hogan's Heroes on television," the *Times* observed, "special English menus at the hotels and restaurants, Coca-Cola and Pepsi billboards, even a pitch for *Pollo Frito Kentucky* (Kentucky Fried Chicken) on a storefront near the stadium.... girls in orange uniforms peddled American camera film from plastic trays."[63]

Of course, the Olympic administration was not the only party guilty of forging corporate friendships. Throughout ABC's coverage, host Chris Schenkel continually invoked the names of the network's sponsors—Reynolds Wrap, Ford, Omega watches—as he introduced various segments of coverage.[64] One particularly vulgar commercial, arguably intended to undermine the countermeanings being instilled by the Olympic Project for Human Rights, featured Jesse Owens. Deemed in the voice-over as "America's greatest single Olympic hero," the spot showed Owens recounting his Olympic experience: "You're crouching in your starting blocks looking 100 meters down the runway. All the work and all your hopes are waiting there. It'll be over in 10 seconds.

Your palms get wet and your throat gets dry. [To the camera] Say, your throats look pretty dry, too.... I better pour you a Schlitz."[65]

While some critics blasted these kinds of advertisements as athletic heresy, others sympathetically argued that the financial demands on ABC made them necessary. Television critic Jack Gould, for example, placed blame for the number of commercials elsewhere, observing, "The moguls of the Olympic Games exact high fees for TV rights."[66] In addition to noting the $4.5 million ABC paid for the exclusive television rights, Gould noted that the travel and technical cost of the 450-person crew, which included positioning forty-five cameras in eighteen different sites, had to be "staggering." Rather than exhibit mercantile gluttony, the network represented "a model of enlightened reconciliation of economic needs with good sports journalism."[67] As for the other common complaint, the overemphasis on American athletes, Gould again held the International Olympic Committee responsible. He argued that the IOC stipulation regarding the playing of the national anthem during the medal ceremony invited "the political overtones that it professes to deplore." As for the network's culpability, he explained how the medium of television itself emphasized the nation and noted, "With the immediacy of live global television such emphasis on country participation, rather than the accomplishments of individual athletes, is bound to increase."[68]

As Gould seemed to understand, the commercial demands of television were bound to impact the very nature of the Olympics, whether in terms of an exaggerated presence of U.S. athletes or an increased weight put on the "exotic" setting. As the programming strategies of Arledge illustrated, sport had undergone a variety of alterations since the inception of the small screen. Football, for example, instituted manufactured time-outs to allow for commercial announcements. By 1950, before most Americans had sets in their houses, television was held responsible for the decreasing crowds at baseball parks.[69] Of course, even before the inception of sports television, games such as baseball had been continually modified to achieve the greatest number of spectators and remain profitable. As early as 1883, night baseball, which did not really flourish until the postwar period, was given a trial run in an attempt to procure a larger working-class audience.[70]

This desire to obtain the maximum audience produced the one facet of the Olympic broadcast vetoed by most television critics: professional commentating. Even Gould, who claimed that Arledge had "magnificently and consistently charted new territory in enriching the eye's appreciation of sports and already has next spring's Emmy ... staked out," dubbed commentators Chris Schenkel, Jim McKay, and Bill Flemming "connoisseurs of bland clichés and specialists in imparting the full details of the obvious."[71] Yet the commentator played a pivotal role in Arledge's programming design and continues to do so today. He, and now she, serves as the expert on the scene and, as one scholar points out, assists "the stupidest among us to begin to apprehend the superlative skill, courage, and abilities of star players."[72] However, in Mexico City, the "wonderful penetrating comments," as sarcastically described by one critic, seemed to give the audience too little credit and laid the groundwork for the battering of Olympic commentators that continues to be popular. In Mexico City, perhaps the most egregious incident was one cited by *Los Angeles Times* critic John Hall, who was horrified by ABC's explanation of how the word *gringo* originated during the first U.S. occupation of Mexico: "The U.S. soldier wore green uniforms. They weren't too popular. The citizens of Mexico, lining the streets as the troops marched by, would shout: 'Green, go home!' ... Hence, Greengo...." While Hall found the explanation "very colorful," he also discovered in the dictionary that *gringo* came from the Greek word for foreigner, *griego*.[73]

Such tales were not reserved to the network but also took their place among other notions of ethnic characteristics attributed to Mexico in stories the media generated about the "developing" nation's transformation into an Olympic city. Some such accounts praised the Mexicans for the spectacle at hand, exemplified by the unilateral applause for the Olympic torchbearer: twenty-year-old Mexican hurdler Norma Enriqueta Basilio, who was vigorously saluted by facets of the media. The first woman to light the Olympic flame, the farmer's daughter presented an image that emblematically spoke to an increasingly feminist political tenor in Mexico, simultaneously symbolic of both the preservation of a rural heritage and a quest for modernity. Arthur Daley commended how the Mexican hurdler "raced gracefully . . . around the track, pattered up the 90 steps to the ramparts—no mean feat at this altitude—and stood there with the torch triumphantly aloft."[74] *Sports Illustrated* found the presence of "a pretty Mexican girl instead of a muscular boy" to be decidedly novel.[75] And the *Baltimore Afro-American* found the choice of the "striking beautiful Mexican Girl" to light the flame "both fitting and remindful."[76] Alongside the newly built synthetic track and the hydraulic elevator at the platform diving venue, the farmer's daughter, it seemed, signified the newly modern trappings provided by the ancient city.

Many also praised the image of Basilio as one of the few non-commercial moments in an increasingly commercialized sport world. Yet this perspective failed to recognize how she was part of what could be considered a national advertising campaign for Mexico's "development." Avery Brundage had proudly hailed the decision to hold the Olympics in a Latin American country as progressive. He not only extolled Mexico as "the most stable and fastest growing country in Latin America" but also inflated the IOC's role in the process, remarking, "The Olympic Movement had no little part in making it so."[77] The ability and necessity of the Olympic host city to create its own image should not be underemphasized. The Mexican production of the Olympics becomes a key component in the discourse of development and dependency that has, according to Arturo Escobar, "been an integral part of the socioeconomic, cultural, and political life of the post–World War II period."[78] As Olympic host, Mexico tried to create several images, all of which tied in some way to the pioneering young woman who ran up the steps, torch in hand. As the first Latin American country to entertain the Olympic community, Mexico continually had to cope with media labels of "developing" and "Third World," both of which shed much doubt on whether the country would be able to manage its prescribed roles as host. As historian Eric Zolov points out, "The approaching Olympics were heralded by the PRI-dominated mass media as evidence of the nation's transformation from a bandit-ridden, agrarian economy into a modern industrialized nation."[79]

The transformation of physical space necessitated by the range of Olympic events and the people who want to watch them is one of the most significant changes a host city takes on, building athletic venues, hotels, roads, transportation systems, and housing. For Mexico, the pressure of the looming global spectacle expedited and intensified the construction of an urban infrastructure at a pace that the economy was not equipped to handle. Early on, for example, many considered transportation to be the primary Olympic problem for Mexico City, when its own population—estimated between six million and seven million, or 15 percent of the nation—ballooned because of an influx of migrants looking for work. Even without the added audience of the world's largest sporting event, getting through the city was "a trial," according to one "First World" observer, because "antiquated buses, streetcars and taxis cannot handle the demand." One could only imagine what the situation would be "when several thousand people simultaneously try to move from the Olympic Pool to the Olympic Stadium, from the Olympic Villadrome to the Olympic Auditorium."[80]

The building of these structures created some cause for concern. Unlike Japan, which had spent a reported $2.7 billion building roads, a monorail system, a high-speed railway, and sports arenas for the Tokyo Games, Mexico did not have limitless funds. Indeed, one member of the Mexican delegation that traveled to Tokyo to inspect its Olympic setup stated, "We are not sure we can guarantee the organization of these games. But the weather will be nice."[81] However, a member of the Mexican Olympic design team optimistically countered that whatever was accomplished would be a positive step for the city, with hopes to "set precedents throughout the city long after the athletes have gone home."[82]

The lack of capital was not the only thing to plague Mexico. Many in the media assessed the ability of the Mexico City Olympic Committee (MCOC) to complete its required tasks along decidedly ethnic lines, vividly demonstrating how writers, whether journalists or otherwise, are, according to Carlo Rotella, "in the business of imagining cities."[83] For example, *Fortune* magazine argued that the unqalified success of Tokyo in 1964 was largely due to the "industrious" nature of the Japanese, indicating that ethnic character had as much to do with designing an exultant Olympic city as hefty financial expenditures.[84] While never directly enunciated, the familiar ethnic stereotype of the "lazy Mexican" was evoked in the article. More directly, *Sports Illustrated* reported that the "stereotype of the Mexican peasant slumped against the wall, sombrero down to shield his eyes from the work left undone," was a widespread concern regarding the ability of Mexico to stage the Olympics. According to the magazine, the Japanese anticipated that its successors would produce an "Olympic doomsday," and a European member of the IOC admitted, "These people can't do it."[85]

In defense of the MCOC, Arthur Daley wrote that those who worried "that the supposed Mexican habit of doing everything *manana* would leave the games with incompleted facilities" were misinformed. "The Mexicans," he divulged, "approached their Olympic problems with the efficiency of Germans, turning tomorrow into today."[86] *Sports Illustrated* followed with an ethnic modification of its own. "It is not true that Mexicans are lazy," John Underwood noted. Rather, he wrote, they are a people of "great patience in getting things done." He fortified this revelation by informing readers of how "conservative Mexican thieves are known to risk capture by taking the time to remove the radio without stealing the car." Yet the observation of another *Sports Illustrated* staff writer further belied the magazine's alleged enlightenment with a reference to the Mexico City Games as "the hot-sauce Olympics."[87] By the end of the Games, a *New York Times* writer hoped, such rhetoric would be a thing of the past in terms of American ideas about Mexico. With 90 percent of all Olympic visitors to Mexico City hailing from the United States, the hosts "should have rid themselves of a lot of stereotype impressions created by too much reading about wetbacks and Mexican bandits. Nobody who has been here ... could look at another television commercial of a Mexican 'bandit' complete with big mustache, guns and cartridge belt without laughing."[88]

With this kind of uneven support behind it, the Mexican government reportedly allocated eighty-four million dollars for the Olympics, which did not include the budget for the six-lane highway between venues or the estimated seventy-five-million-dollar disbursement for the construction of four new hotels (two thousand rooms). Approximately half of the official budget was earmarked for the renovation of existing sports facilities as well as the building of new ones, and the remainder was set aside for operating costs and salaries. The nation regarded most of the expense as an investment, hoping to recover a good portion through the sale of concessions, tickets, television rights, and the general tourism from an anticipated two hundred thousand Olympic spectators.[89] Last, as with any Olympic hosts, Mexican organizers undoubtedly hoped that the creation of state-of-the-art athletic facilities would have positive long-term financial effects, attracting high-profile and large-scale events in the future.

Despite such hopefulness, the early media buzz regarding the building of the sports venues focused on reports of delays. Such rumors, of course, are commonplace in the months preceding most any Olympics. Most recently, the IOC reprimanded Athens for its delay in building an Olympic stadium for 2004. Even more dramatically, problems plagued the Winter Games in Nagano in 1998, with reports of a budget that ballooned from $644 million to $800 million, a downhill ski run that was too short, and a skating venue with too few seats. Yet Mexico City had to deal additionally with widespread notions that similar setbacks were indicative not of hosting an Olympics but rather of the Mexicans as a people. While Daniel Ruiz, director general of buildings in the Ministry of Public Works, confidently told the press that Mexico would be ready, reports of incomplete interiors, unfinished roofing, rough floors, and numerous imperfections, such as faulty lighting, continued throughout the summer.[90] However, photos of the eighty-thousand-seat Olympic Stadium featured in the *New York Times* in mid-July indicated that the so-called developing nation was doing just that, and eventually many, including U.S. Olympic Committee president Douglas Roby, declared the finished product "the finest ... ever."[91]

An important component of the "development" process was linking Mexico to global television connections to broadcast coverage of the Olympics. The presence of a major American television network undoubtedly added to the urgency of this objective. Seth Fein has argued persuasively that such endeavors occurred throughout the post-war period and "signified the deepening of state-to-state and transnational links between the United States and Mexico."[92] However, the role of the Olympics in expediting this process cannot be overlooked. According to the Mexican Ministry of Communications and Transportation, the Japanese financed the $6.4 million communication station constructed for the Mexico City Olympics, contracted to Mitsubishi and the Nippon Electric Company. After the Olympics concluded, Mexico was left with four television channels and twelve hundred telephone channels. Ironically, with such fast connections to European cities, the satellite enabled transcontinental communication to move more rapidly than domestic telephone service.[93]

The ideas of modernity and development that were deeply embedded in this focus on building, transportation, communication, and so on, were closely tied to a series of cultural and artistic modifications and contributions. The *Olympic Charter* mandates that the host city "organize a programme of cultural events," specifying that such an agenda "promote[s] harmonious relations, mutual understanding and friendship among the participants and others attending the Olympic Games."[94] This tradition dates back to the event's Greek origins, when poets such as Pindar sported their craft alongside the athletes. While some host cities situate the cultural agenda secondary to the athletic one, Mexico vehemently pursued its cultural mission and received a vast international response to its request to build a substantial cultural component. Some seventy-eight countries accepted invitations to participate in a portion of the cultural events, while only sixty-five indicated they would send athletes. Both Mexican president Gustavo Díaz Ordaz and MCOC chair Pedro Ramírez Vázquez publicly welcomed the positive response, indicating that the cultural program allowed for a greater number of Mexicans to be interested in the Olympics. Díaz Ordaz also indicated that he felt the cultural program provided a way for nations to enter the Olympics on more equal footing, particularly since it was cheaper to send an item or two for an exhibition than an entire athletic team and its entourage. "In loftiness of thought," the president said, "no nation, no one group of people can consider itself superior to the rest."[95]

Mexico City lashed its new infrastructure to the cultural curriculum with the permanent installation of sculptures along the twelve-mile "Friendship Route" leading to the Olympic Village. The city, represented by Oscar Urrutia as the general coordinator of the cultural program, commissioned eighteen sculptors from twenty nations—at least one from every continent—to create the pieces. The delegation from the United States included invited "guest of honor" Alexander Calder, who designed a seventy-ton piece of black steel entitled *Red Sun*, and Americans Herbert Bayer and Constantino Nivola represented their native countries, Austria and Italy, respectively. The cultural schedule reflected a mixture of artistic styles and expressions, from the very traditional to the increasingly modern, including performances by Soviet poet Yevtushenko, fourteen theater companies, five opera companies, seven symphony orchestras, jazz ensembles, the Bolshoi Ballet, the Martha Graham Dance Company, and American pianist Van Cliburn. Exhibitions ranging from a history of the Olympics to rare stamps from around the world to numerous paintings completed the program.[96] As one writer attested, "One of the most heavily insured athletes to go to the Olympic Games" was Salvador Dali's *The Cosmic Athlete*. Commissioned by the Spanish Olympic Committee, the work, which portrayed a discus thrower with the world in his hand, was insured for $28,570.[97]

"There was no change in programming": The "Generation Gap" Games and the Massacre at Tlatelolco

The cost of the insurance for the Dali painting was just one of innumerable expenses generated by the Olympics. Mexican students, however, opted for a less pricey form of art—graffiti—to make their mark within their increasingly modernized urban space. But while spray-painted messages such as "Everything Is Possible in Peace" and "Death to the Government" seemed a cost-effective mode to effect political statements, the social ramifications of such actions eventually created much higher expenditures. A series of student demonstrations, and their subsequent suppression by the government, ensured that the outlay for a peaceful Olympics was a violent death sentence for many.[98]

With a series of early foundations of social discontent, the younger generation of Mexicans did not fully embrace the Olympic vision promulgated by their government. As Eric Zolov argues, the late 1960s student counterculture, La Onda, got its roots in union strikes in the previous decade and was heavily influenced by the Cuban Revolution.[99] Just as the building of an Olympic city distributed a succession of modern facilities throughout the city, the rise of La Onda, or "the wave," symbolized the adoption of decidedly self-aware modern lifestyles and politics on the part of students. However, the Mexican government, undeniably in light of the approaching Games, zeroed in on squashing such youth, with *judiciales* scouring the streets of the stylish Zona Rosa for anyone with long hair.[100] While architects, engineers, and laborers hurried to finish building Olympic venues, strife escalated between such forces and the ranks of university students, creating civil disobedience on a par with the student struggles ongoing in the United States and around the globe during this period. The difference in Mexico, of course, was that an invitation had been presented by both the Mexican government and the IOC for the "youth of the world" to come and participate in the world's largest sporting spectacle. Recognizing the potential to provide far greater meaning to the chant "the whole world is watching," Mexican youth, like the stateside members of the OPHR, increasingly appreciated the global gaze provided by the Olympic Games.

Grasping the details of Mexican student struggles in 1968 is historically problematic, with relatively little, albeit growing, scholarship that directly deals with the course of events that eventually ended with the devastating loss of student life at the hands of Mexican troops at Tlatelolco. Of particular importance is the recent work of Mexican intellectuals Julio Scherer García and Carlos Monsiváis. On the basis of the testimony of Defense Minister General Marcelino García Barragán,

Scherer García and Monsiváis convincingly endorse the longstanding hypothesis that an elite army unit, the Presidential General Staff, effected the slaughter under the supervision of Luis Gutiérrez Oropeza. Their account, additionally backed by declassified U.S. intelligence documents, corresponds to an earlier assertion by Mexican politician Luis M. Farías. In his memoirs, published in 1992, Farías revealed that Gutiérrez Oropeza once admitted to organizing assault groups against the students along with Partido Revolucionario Institucional (PRI) leader Alfonso Martínez Domínguez.[101]

As described by Carlos Fuentes in his novel *Los años con Laura Díaz*, the massacre represents a defining historical moment for modern Mexico, because it vividly demonstrates how the Mexican administration "had no responses to the demands of the young men and women that were educated in the ideals of democracy and freedom and participation."[102] At the time, however, their European and American counterparts largely obscured Mexican student movements in the media. In the introduction of Barbara and John Ehrenreich's firsthand account of international student movements, for example, the authors admit to including "nothing … about the important movements in Japan or Mexico."[103] Today, as pressure mounts for the Mexican government to resolve liability, the American press, present in Mexico City in 1968 to provide Olympic coverage for the folks back home, offers one lens through which to situate the deadly battles that occurred that summer. Foreign correspondents and sportswriters alike witnessed much of the turbulence that took place on Mexico City's college campuses and streets and, because of the international importance of the Olympics, reported much of the turmoil in the American media.

Initially, the student protesters rarely invoked the Olympics directly in their discourse, but many observers, including the U.S. Central Intelligence Agency (CIA), saw the interruption of the Games as a distinct possibility, especially if the turmoil spread to city campuses. According to one CIA report, protests in early July at "provincial universities," likely advised by the Cuban consul, indicated that student unrest would probably grow, and "indications that agitators are planning disturbances during the Olympics have already led the government to tighten its controls on the students."[104] Yet despite such fears, in the weeks leading up to the Opening Ceremony student protests emphasized the siege that had taken place during the summer at various city universities and high schools rather than the approaching Games. One such campus was the Universidad Nacional Autónoma de México (UNAM), which boasted a population of ninety thousand students and had been moved outside the city center in 1952 by President Miguel Alemán because of what one scholar has called "the traditional propensity of Mexican students to demonstrate."[105]

According to historian John Womack, who provided his first analysis of the demonstrations before the Olympics even concluded, the conflict substantially escalated on July 23, 1968, when two hundred riot police, looking to halt altercations between students and gang members, invaded the campuses of trade schools, "cracking the heads of all in reach."[106] Three days later, the Federación Nacional de Estudiantes Técnicos, government permit in hand, demonstrated against the police brutality. The group's actions coincided with a fifteenth-anniversary celebration of the Cuban Revolution sponsored by the largely student-run Friends of Cuba, which also possessed the proper permit. When members of the two rallies eventually combined, riot police violently intervened. The students hid in university housing for three days supplied with Molotov cocktails, gas, knives, stones, and chains. They used burning city buses as barricades, only to be unearthed, according to one official U.S. report, by soldiers wielding fixed bayonets, "armored recon vehicles," and a bazooka.[107] While U.S. officials in Mexico acknowledged that there was no "accurate picture of the number killed, injured and arrested," they estimated that at least four students were dead and two hundred injured. The *New York Times*, but no Mexican newspaper, printed photos of the violence.[108] Within a few days, the students had assembled a list of central demands for surrender, including amnesty, restitution, indemnity, the expulsion of police chiefs, and the dissolution of riot squads, or *grenadiers*. The demands were, as Zolov points out, "carefully structured in terms of respect for the 1917 Constitution, which contained guarantees of free speech, democratic process, and economic redistribution."[109] Thus, like civil rights activists in the United States, the Mexican students, who often integrated both the national flag and the national anthem into their demonstrations, did not attempt, in theory, to reconstruct the nation radically. Rather, they wanted to hold it responsible to its own set of political values and beliefs, not to those of the patriarchal PRI administration. They worked, then, in a similar fashion to the OPHR, trying to make their specific demands about the university hold collective meaning for all Mexican people. Furthermore, they situated the demands as the foundation for sub-sequent student movements that permeated both the political and the physical landscape and concluded with both an unparalleled prison population and a still-unknown death toll.

Of particular concern to both the Mexican government and U.S. officials in Mexico, and substantially propagated by Mexican editorials, was the possible influence of "outsiders" on the students' actions, particularly in light of the impending Olympics. According to one U.S. intelligence report, Mexican police, in efforts to ensure Communist silence, arrested many members of the Mexican Communist Party, raided its headquarters, and searched the offices of its newspaper, *La Voz Mexico*, impounding various files and propaganda.[110] The U.S. State Department understood from the Mexican administration that there was "solid evidence corroborating public charges of Mexico City Police Chief that [the] Communist Party engineered [the] July 26 student fracas," particularly in light of the "Czech events." Further, just as the Mexican regime worried about "the image projected by the disturbances and the impact on the Olympics," the State Department felt it possible that the Soviets "may believe that Mexican anxiety to avoid any diplomatic contretemps with [the] Communist world as Olympics near gives [the] Soviet Embassy more room for subversive maneuver." Yet the CIA, despite locating the melee as "a classic example of the communists' ability to divert a peaceful demonstration into a major riot," ultimately doubted any direct participation on the part of the Soviets. It was unlikely, it theorized, they "would so undermine their carefully nurtured good relations with the Mexicans."[111]

The student siege continued throughout the summer, and both the American media, especially *New York Times* correspondents Henry Giniger and Paul Montgomery, and members of the OPHR paid close attention. On August 1, in a cursory attempt to bring peace to the city, Díaz Ordaz gave what is often referred to as the "extended" or "outstretched hand" speech. "Public peace and tranquility must be restored," he declared. "A hand is stretched out; Mexicans will say whether that hand will find a response."[112] The Mexican media jumped on the metaphorical possibilities of the president's words, generating celebratory cartoons of outstretched hands in newspaper space likely paid for by pro-government organizations. In protest of threatened academic freedom, UNAM rector Javier Barrows Sierra countered the "hand" of the president with what one U.S. agency described as an "orderly" demonstration of roughly eighty thousand students carrying signs that declared, "The outstretched hand has a pistol in it" and "The dead cannot shake hands."[113]

By one estimate, between July 23 and August 10 there were forty-seven student rallies, some topping 100,000 participants, with strike committees created by students and teachers alike.[114] On August 13, some 150,000 students, organized by the Teachers' Coalition for Democratic Liberties, marched through the downtown area. They chanted against the press, the police, and, in an unprecedented fashion, against Díaz Ordaz himself, as well as his notoriously poor occlusion: "¿Díaz Ordaz, dónde estás? Díaz Ordaz, saca los dientes." (Díaz Ordaz, where are you? Díaz Ordaz, get your teeth pulled.)[115] The CIA, for one, was impressed by the organization of the students, noting that the Mexican government underestimated their potential, because, despite what seemed to be a lack of any singular figurehead, "the students have made several spectacular, disciplined demonstrations of their willingness to confront the force of the government."[116] On August 27, that willingness materialized again with a march to the National Palace by over 200,000 students. Police and soldiers squashed the event in the early hours of the next day after the remaining few students defiantly raised the red and black "strike flag" up the national flagpole.[117]

Inarguably, the forthcoming Olympics added to the heightened anxiety following the August 27 march, in terms of both student intensity and government repression. The students realized that the Olympics gave them leverage to force the government to meet their demands, and the administration decided that what it considered a relatively lenient stance on the protests could not continue. According to one U.S. official, Mexican sources revealed that the August 27 march compelled Díaz Ordaz "to shift back to a get-tough, no-nonsense posture with the students," while another stated that he had "ordered army, riot police and police to use force if necessary to break up illegal activities and gatherings."[118] Undoubtedly, the Olympics provided the impetus for the stepping up of measures. Early on, their looming presence unequivocally affected the government's plan of action. Months before, city officials had confiscated firearms within city limits. Alfonso Corona del Rosal, regent of the Federal District, confirmed for the press that the Mexican Constitution allowed citizens to carry guns for personal protection, but such weapons had to be taken at that point in time to guarantee security during the Olympics.[119]

Closer to the Opening Ceremony, one of the more direct threats to the Games posed by students came from a controversial organization, the Comité Anti-Olímpico de Subversión (CAOS). CAOS claimed to represent a large student group determined to halt the ceremonies at Olympic Stadium, whether by a peaceful demonstration or a violent clash. But many, including U.S. officials and journalists, doubted that there was a sole group dominating the campaign, with the exception of the ever-present Consejo Nacional de Huelga (CNH), or National Strike Council, composed of representatives from the approximately 150 schools involved. Further, there was no set agenda for creating an Olympic-related rally, although one unnamed student source informed the press that there were "different projects to use the Olympics to embarrass the Mexican Government. Violence is definitely being considered—but right now it would be a last resort."[120]

However, on the basis of the series of marches that had taken place during the summer, most observers agreed that an ample number of students, a hundred thousand, would be willing to engage in some sort of Olympic action, and if Díaz Ordaz did not agree to a public meeting before the Opening Ceremony, such action would be inevitable.[121] Thus, on September 1, Díaz Ordaz finally addressed student concerns in his state of the union address by condemning those who tried to use the Olympics to pressure him politically. He pledged to use "all legal means within our reach," including force, to ensure the opening of the Games and denied knowledge of any political prisoners from the summer strikes.[122] Ten days later, surrounded by supporters and reporters, Díaz Ordaz confidently inaugurated seven Olympic sites, only to be greeted at his home, Los Pinos, by a silent student march.[123]

While the CIA optimistically felt the president had made some minor concessions to the students in his speech, it also realized that the Olympic time frame made negotiations difficult: "The students ... realize what is at stake in the Olympics, and while the majority would not try to disrupt the Games, the fact that the time for the Olympics is close at hand does not inhibit the students from airing their grievances."[124] The Mexican government's recognition of this became clear on September 18. After two and a half weeks of relative peace and with classes at UNAM commenced by Sierra, ten thousand troops and numerous armored vehicles entered the campus, an action sanctioned by a recent Senate act that officially allowed the president to use the military "in defense of the internal and external security of Mexico."[125] The government defended its action by stating that it wanted to prevent the realization of student threats to disrupt the Olympics, as well as, in the words of the minister of interior, any other "openly anti-social and possibly criminal activities." The press, as usual, was barred from the area. But one reporter, standing on top of Olympic Stadium, observed the tanks enter the campus and approximated that fifteen trucks exited with prisoners. Apparently the Díaz Ordaz administration, concluded the U.S. Embassy in Mexico, "could no longer temporize in view of the approaching Olympic Games and the location of a number of important Olympic installations on the campus."[126]

According to one U.S. report, it was with the army's presence that the picture changed from one of comparatively peaceful demonstrations to one of tension and potential violence, particularly when fierce clashes between students and police peppered the last days of September.[127] On September 24, yet another violent outbreak prominently positioned Mexican student unrest within the American media, with the front page of the *New York Times* announcing, "3 Dead, Many Hurt in Mexico City Battle." Considered "the bloodiest encounter since the wave of student agitation first [began]," the *Times* described an "all-night battle between the police and students" that resulted in anywhere from three to fifteen deaths. Two photographs accompanied the article: a front-page photo of soldiers searching a stopped car for weapons, a student standing with arms over head; and a runover picture of a grenadier driving a rifle butt into the stomach of a handcuffed student held by two others in uniform.[128]

While obviously not the first fatal battle since the student siege began, this clash became significant in the United States because of the play it received in the press, increasing doubts about whether the Olympic Games would be a safe venture for American athletes. The twelve-hour battle was further noteworthy, because, according to press reports, it marked the first time that the students responded to the police with firearms on a grand scale, killing, according to one report, at least three soldiers.[129] As the violence continued into the early hours of September 25, a Reuters news bulletin stated that a farmer and a nine-year-old boy were killed when police fired at students attempting to march to the National Palace in the face of some two thousand armed soldiers and "busloads" of riot police.[130] Among the observers of the violence were several foreign visitors who were in the process of arriving for the Olympics, now just two weeks away. Their presence prompted Avery Brundage to comment, finally, that Mexican Olympic officials guaranteed the situation was under control, and the Games would indeed go on.[131]

For the next several days, Brundage's reassurances seemed plausible, especially when reports surfaced that student leaders told a reporter that they would not prevent the Games from taking place. However, they also maintained that demonstrations would continue and that the imminent Olympics did not justify ending their militant stance. Indeed, with the vast price tag of the Games, from which few would actually reap profits, the Olympics likely reinforced their stance. "The Olympics are the Government's problems, not ours," said an unidentified student. "It is the Government that is going to sabotage the Olympics by creating a climate of repression in this city. The more the Government uses force the more it is going to have problems."[132] According to CIA observations, however, it was increasingly difficult for students to generate new tactics, because, while the Mexican government had been unable "to stem the crisis, its tough action against the demonstrators ... made it difficult for students to assemble and plan strategy."[133]

Despite the tenuous calm that pervaded the moment, many observers remained anxious about the possibilities the situation posed. The CIA, for example, worried about the scheduled visit from presidential candidate Richard Nixon. It cited "potential dangers inherent" in the trip "in view of the recurring troubles between Mexican students and the Díaz Ordaz administration," which it acknowledged had resulted in "scores of casualties and a number of fatalities on both sides." The conclusion of the CIA, then, was that "with or without the occasion of a prominent visitor from the US," the students would continue their efforts "to mount demonstrations during the Olympics in order to embarrass the Mexican government."[134] In a more popular forum, *Sports Illustrated* recognized how "Mexico's smoldering young activists" were similar to their counterparts throughout the world, especially "the young at Berkeley or Columbia." The magazine also appreciated how the Olympics granted the students their prominent platform, because they were "anxious to do their thing in front of plenty of witnesses" and, notably, acknowledged that "subverting the Olympics has never been just a local project" but rather "is an international undertaking."[135] In this understanding of the state of affairs, the sports magazine positioned the students alongside the OPHR and increased the political, if not the geographical, proximity of San Jose and Mexico City.

Yet despite these apprehensions, September ended and the moderate stance continued. Troops withdrew from the UNAM campus, and the students again reiterated their vow not to interfere with Olympic events. Unquestionably, with the Opening Ceremony almost at hand and an ever-increasing number of Olympic visitors and athletes arriving, both sides in the conflict were under heavy pressure to cooperate.[136] Indeed, according to one U.S. report, the impending sporting event had begun "to push student affairs off the front pages of Mexico City newspapers."[137] However, on October 2, two days after the students took back possession of the UNAM campus and one day after talks between the government and members of the CNH failed, the discord reached new heights. Details regarding the latest broil between police and students in the Olympic city appeared again in the forefront of U.S. print media. The death toll, as well as the responsibility for it, still remains under intense scrutiny today.

Initial press reports of what occurred during the evening of October 2 disclosed that approximately a thousand government troops, arriving in tanks, armored cars, and jeeps, fired on a demonstration of three thousand students. The CNH had organized the rally at La Plaza de las Tres Culturas (the Plaza of Three Cultures), a paved square named for its contiguity to Aztec ruins, a colonial church of Santiago, and the modern quarters of the Foreign Ministry. The site, located fifteen miles from the Olympic Village, was seen as a central meeting ground for students from the various city campuses. Located in the middle of Mexico City's largest public housing development, Tlatelolco, it is one of Mexico's most historic places, because it is where Cortés fought the battle to end Aztec opposition to Spanish subjugation. The rally began with the intent to march to the Santo Tomás campus of the National Polytechnic Institute, where government troops still remained. After the majority of the participants had assembled, somewhere around five o'clock in the evening, a speaker announced that the march had been canceled because of news that armed troops had gathered at the Santo Tomás campus. Further suspicions arose in the audience, ostensibly filled with both students and residents of the surrounding Tlatelolco apartments, who had become used to their neighborhood being used for such political gatherings, when news circulated that they had been infiltrated by a score of disguised *judiciales* and members of the elite Batallón Olimpia, trained to provide protection at the upcoming Games. By five-thirty, as student speakers began increasingly familiar speeches, soldiers began moving toward the gathering, arriving just after six o'clock, when shooting broke out.[138] Because of the cul-de-sac nature of the plaza, the crowd was trapped.

Reports as to what exactly took place differ, largely because of the extensive denial and secrecy maintained by the Mexican government. But an unusually high number of members of the foreign media, present because of the Olympics, generated fairly consistent eyewitness reports on the bloodbath that subsequently occurred. Carl J. Migdail, a member of the International Staff of *U.S. News and World Report*, surveyed the scene from behind a wall. His vivid description tells of full-blown war:

> Suddenly, while the meeting was still in progress, Army signal flares appeared in the sky above. More than 1,000 soldiers, with fixed bayonets, charged into the students. Shooting started. Machine guns on Army vehicles opened up against the sides of apartment buildings. Fires broke out. Nobody is certain whether the troops or armed students—of whom there were many—fired first. But within minutes a major fire fight raged. Its intensity reminded some of us of combat in World War II and Vietnam.[139]

Troops used both rifles and machine guns, killing anywhere from twenty to two hundred people, and wounding at least a hundred, including many women and children. Actual numbers remained difficult to determine (even to this day), because the army kept reporters away from the Red Cross hospital, reportedly full of civilian wounded. Defense Minister General Marcelino García Barragán determined that the conflict had begun when snipers fired upon riot police guarding the Foreign Ministry. Barragán told the press that the army had infiltrated the demonstration after a call from the police because of shooting among the students, yet both bystanders *and the police chief* denied this was true.

Whatever the case, as somberly concluded by the *New York Times*, "the night's events cast into serious question the prospects for the Olympic Games." The *Times* offered dramatic descriptions of the violence and bloodshed, emphasizing the number of students "led away, their hands behind their heads" and the number of Tlatelolco residents, including young children, maimed or killed. In the end, it produced likely the strongest and most consistent sentiments of sympathy by a member of the U.S. media toward the students.[140]

By the following day, the incident had been dubbed La Nueva Noche Triste (the New Night of Sorrow), a reference to the night in 1520 when Cortés's troops were massacred by Montezuma's army while retreating from the Aztec capital of Tenochtitlán. The death toll in 1968, again revealed on the front page of the *Times*, had escalated to forty-nine, with counts of five hundred wounded and fifteen hundred incarcerated. Among those hurt was Brigadier General José Hernandez Toledo, who had supervised the occupation of UNAM. Although so-called official counts put the numbers at twenty-eight dead and two hundred wounded, the *Times* claimed the higher numbers were "virtually certain" and that according to Barragán only one of the dead was a soldier.[141]

Many speculated over what effect the clash would have on the Olympics. The *New York Times* reported that news of the conflict between students and soldiers "cut the number of visitors expected ... hotels and travel agents reported cancellations."[142] The CIA, in light of the incident, cast strong doubts about "the Mexican Government's capability to keep the Olympic events and the many foreign visitors insulated from its domestic crisis."[143] However, Avery Brundage, upon emerging from a standard IOC meeting, adamantly declared that there was "absolutely no connection" between the discord and the Olympics and again resolutely reiterated and reaffirmed that the Games would proceed on schedule. The front page of the *San Jose Mercury News* assured readers, "Olympics Still On," while San Jose sports editor Louis Duino confirmed that "it would be a sad waste of physical endeavor ... for the whole world if the Olympic Games are cancelled."[144]

In addition to the international media that were on site to witness the violent spectacle, athletes from around the world were, of course, readying themselves a relatively short distance away in the Olympic Village. Yet for their part, athletes in the village seemed comparatively undisturbed, largely because their isolation prevented much news of the violence from penetrating. For American athletes, information about the massacre was firmly controlled by the FBI, who felt that the event had "definite bearing on safety and well being of internationally known U.S. athletes participating in the Olympic Games," but wanted only "responsible officials" of the U.S. squad to be given discreetly any "pertinent information."[145] When interviewed, the comments of many American athletes bore this procedure out. American canoeist John Pickett, for example, did not know that there had been any deaths as a result of the student rioting: "They don't tell us much out here," he said. "We don't get the papers, so we don't know." Comparatively, boxer John Coker of Sierra Leone had more to say about the situation, because he had spoken with a worker in the village who had lost a friend in the recent bloodshed. "Seeing what's going on leaves you appalled," he told a reporter. "I don't understand how the Mexican Government can present one face to the athletes in the outside world, and a different face to their own youths." However, he realized that there was little he or any of the other athletes could do. "It's the Olympics and we're proud to be here," he continued. "We just aren't in touch with what's going on between the students and the police. If I hadn't gone down to get my mail today, and talked to the girl at the mail desk, I wouldn't have known about how bad it was last night."[146]

The primary effect of La Nueva Noche Triste was a marked and almost immediate decline in radical student activity throughout the city. The day after the slaughter, the Mexican Senate praised the actions of the military, saying it was necessary to "protect not only the life and tranquillity of the citizens, but also ... the integrity of the nation's institutions."[147] With such applause, the massacre also signaled the reinforcement of armed soldiers throughout Olympic venues. Indeed, American water polo player Dean Willeford told *Sports Illustrated* that one of the ways he became aware that *something* had happened was the presence of "soldiers all around us" during a warm-up game.[148] While one sniper continued the cause inside a Social Security Institute building near La Plaza de las Tres Culturas, wounding at least two until reportedly killed by troops, the majority of students declared the October 2 affair "a massacre" and decided that any further agitation would be "suicide."[149] But despite their apparent retreat, the students vocally maintained their "six points." Some tension eased when two government representatives, Jorge de la Vega Dominguez (head of the Institute of Political, Economic, and Social Studies of the Partido Revolucionario Institutional) and Andres Caso (personnel manager of the Mexican Petroleum Corporation), and student leaders, including Marcelino Perello, a twenty-three-year-old physics student at UNAM and prominent member of the CNH, announced plans to organize some form of arbitration. However, in an interview, Perello indicated that present discussions were merely "exploratory," and formal negotiations would not begin until three demands were met: the removal of troops and police from the remaining campuses, the release of all students arrested since the government seizure of UNAM, and an end to the "persecution" of students trying to meet throughout the city to renew public support.[150]

However, reports regarding the involvement of government adversaries in the university movement jeopardized continued sympathy for the students. On October 6, authorities impelled Socrates Amado Campos Lemus, a senior economics major at the National Polytechnic Institute who had been held in a military camp, to state publicly the names of militant activists. The names Lemus disclosed included Carlos A. Madrazo, former president of the PRI, and Humberto Romero Perez, who in 1964 had publicly opposed the presidential nomination of Díaz Ordaz. Romero Perez denied any affiliation with the students, and Madrazo's family issued a statement that Carlos was ill, supporting reports that his nephew had been killed in one of the clashes.[151] With the testimony of Lemus, the Mexican government found itself in a contradictory state. While initial analysis of the student situation throughout the summer had consistently tried, according to the U.S.

State Department, to "divert attention from deeper local roots of [the] problem," Lemus directed the spotlight away from the notion of outside agitation and back into the local political arena.[152]

Ignoring the most obvious cause—the trying relationship between government and university—other theories of why violence had escalated to such a degree came to light. One such theory speculated that foreign youth were involved. Allegedly, French, American, Chilean, and Puerto Rican student leaders had coached Mexican youth in riot tactics; three such foreign students had been arrested and deported from Mexico in late July.[153] Also, rumors materialized that the CIA and FBI had attempted to force a situation that necessitated American intervention. The CIA countered that it was plausible, as the Mexican government had thought, that various Communist entities were involved. Yet despite its belief that such "outside agitators" existed, the CIA admitted that there was "no firm evidence that the Communists instigated the present crisis," but likely "capitalized on the disorders" after they commenced.[154] Still others proposed that Mexican politicians had instigated the discord, jockeying for political position before the presidential nomination in 1970. And still others pointed fingers at Detroit, Michigan—the alternate site for the XIX Olympiad—for trying to prevent the Olympics from taking place in Mexico.[155] Last, and perhaps most ominous, was the FBI theory of the Brigada Olympia, a "shock group" composed of members of the Liga Comunista Espartaco and groups of the Trotskyist Fourth International, including "extreme radical Trotskyists known only to each other" and in "contact with Guatemalan guerrillas and Cuban Trotskyists who are in Mexico on a 'secret mission.'" According to the FBI, the Brigada Olympia started shooting on the evening of October 2, with snipers located on top of the Tlatelolco apartments, intending to "commit acts of sabotage during the Olympic Games."[156]

Despite admitting that it found no evidence that the Brigada Olympia was even present at Tlatelolco on the night of October 2, the U.S. State Department deemed the possibility of foreign influence highly likely, because the friction originated not with the students "but rather [with an] organization already in existence and well developed . . .

[that] would disrupt [the] Games." Building on longstanding claims that a Communist undercurrent ran through the student movement, official State Department reports convey that the UNAM campus was originally occupied by troops in hopes that such "terrorist leadership ... would be rounded up," likely referring to the Brigada Olympia. The Mexican administration then allowed the gathering at Tlatelolco to take place, "because it had reason to expect that many of [the] extremist elements and leadership would be present." While the State Department further maintained that the Mexican government likely "would have preferred to accomplish this with minimum violence," it realized that with the number of foreign press present in the city, such an opportunity for political spectacle would probably not be lost, regardless of who controlled it. Indeed, the State Department admitted, "reports of usually reliable sources and on spot observers vary greatly and are often flatly contradictory as to who fired the first shots." It could have been either the students *or* "plainsclothes security agents"; would probably "never be known"; and was, "in any case, academic." A defense intelligence report, however, was surer, stating that "most accounts" indicated that it was the army who had fired first, at least into the air if nowhere else.[157]

Obviously the role of the Olympics in the deadly fray, while not the original impetus for the youth rebellion, was considerable. Despite the distance the students tried to create between their movement and the impending Games, the *New York Times* reported that a letter had been received by journalists, stating that a "constitutionalist army of liberation" would wage war against the administration and warning visitors from attending the Olympic Games because it intended to interfere with the Opening Ceremony.[158] Regardless of whether the writers of the letter were connected to the CNH, the Olympic Games inarguably shaped the situation. They enabled the students to operate on an international stage that otherwise would likely not have been there, which put intense pressure on the government to produce the largest of international gatherings, one that would be covered for the first time on (somewhat) live, national, American television.

While the Olympics had brought the enmity to the surface, many tried to put the violence of the preceding nine weeks behind. The *New York Times*, for example, after weeks of judicious reporting on the tenuous situation in Mexico City, inexplicably ran a piece that made light of the student demonstrations, labeling them "bloody (but isolated)." It placed the violence alongside sidesplitting tales of the Olympic city, such as rumors of Dutch women taking hormone injections and the laughable Olympic Village living conditions. The *Times* blamed these "yarns" on the "army of reporters seeking something more controversial to write about than the fact that nine more flags were raised in the Plaza de las Banderas," and it contradicted a previous piece that indicated that information regarding the violence had been withheld from athletes in the village.[159] For his part, Díaz Ordaz gave a speech affirming that "the immense majority of Mexicans—millions against only a few hundred—are enthusiastically desirous that the events be carried out with brilliance and success." On their front pages, Mexican newspapers carried similar assurances from Avery Brundage.[160] However, despite such attempts, the stark images remained. Visiting its serious side once again, the *New York Times* ran a photo of a cyclist practicing at the velodrome as an armed Mexican soldier stood by: "It's Not a Starting Gun."[161] On the day of the Opening Ceremony, the editorial page of the *Times* somberly noted that rather than be a "festive" event, "an atmosphere of youthful anger, political perplexity and family mourning" marred merriment.[162] And the front-page coverage of the ceremony by the *Los Angeles Times* emphasized that despite the grandeur of the gala, "sad reminders of the violence" continued. There were bleeding hearts painted on the banners of white doves that hung throughout the city. Rogue journalist Mario Menendez's independently run *¿Por Que?* sat on newsstands with a photograph of a corpse of a young boy at La Plaza de las Tres Culturas. At the time, Menendez was the only Mexican journalist who publicly contended that the massacre had been premeditated by the Mexican government. His paper created a stark contrast with government-controlled headlines that declared the end of the violence and the beginning of the Olympics.[163]

In *Sports Illustrated*, what had been termed "the problem games" for an array of reasons plummeted further into a harsh reality. Above all else, the magazine concluded, the event in Mexico City would be known as the Generation Gap Olympics, because the tragedy of October 2 pervaded the "grim countdown to the Games." Staff writer Bob Ottum mused, "Just when all seemed perfect, just when the only thing left was for that pretty young girl to run the torch into the stadium, the whole structure began to teeter back and forth and make ominous noises."[164] However, when Basilio lit the Olympic flame, many others felt confident that the final political statement had been made and the time had arrived to focus on the ostensibly noble endeavors of athletes. With a photo of the young hurdler on its cover, *Sports Illustrated* boldly declared "OLYMPICS ON THE WAY."[165] The magazine was finished, apparently, with the bleak reality of its own previous issues, and ignorant that La Onda, with unprecedented female political participation, likely influenced the choice of Basilio, making her symbolic of at least one battle the students had won.

Mexico, then, was armed and ready to put on a good face for the duration of the Games, and spectators patiently awaited the record-breaking performances that the high altitude was sure to produce in venues that Brundage declared "excellent."[166] Even *Sports Illustrated*, which had doubted the ability of Mexico to overcome its problems in time, predicted that the Olympic spirit would, indeed, prevail. "Never has an approaching Olympics been beset by more immediate and potential problems than Mexico City—altitude, racial and political boycotts, riots, red tape, delays—but the Olympic idea is still strong," John Underwood wrote. "The curtain is going up, perhaps shakily, but up."[167] With all that had occurred, likely few thought that the Olympic Project for Human Rights, so visible in the preceding months, had anything left to say. In the wake of the silenced Mexican students who had been slain mere city blocks from the expensive, and now rigidly guarded, stadium, what else could happen?

CHAPTER 4

The Power of Protest and Boycott: The New York Athletic Club and the Question of the South African Springboks

What is South Africa? A boiler into which thirteen million blacks are clubbed and penned in by two and half million whites. If the poor whites hate the Negroes, it is ... because the structure of South Africa is a racist structure.

—Frantz Fanon, *Black Skin, White Masks*

We hope to bring to the world arena the attention of the entire world that America is as guilty of racism as South Africa.

—Harry Edwards, *San Jose Mercury News*, 1967

American media focused a lot of attention on the spectacles of the Mexican student uprisings, particularly when the furor regarding the Olympic Project for Human Rights began to subside. Most observers felt confident that African American athletes would fall into line and the U.S. team would compete as a single, cohesive entity. Indeed, Stan Wright, the only African American member of the U.S. Olympic coaching staff, commented, "As far as we're concerned, the boycott issue is dead. We're here to win medals."[1]

What Wright did not count on, however, was the possible alliances that could be built, conjecturally if not officially, on the transnational possibilities of human rights struggles. Both the press and the FBI went into an uproar when Harry Edwards was alleged to have met (in San Jose) with Mexican students who claimed to be leaders of the Comité Anti-Olímpico de Subversión (CAOS). The students, according to Edwards, hoped to form some kind of coalition among groups publicly hostile to the Olympics and reportedly told him, "We are prepared to lose some lives in an initial charge on the stadium—but we will stop the Olympics by any means necessary." Edwards publicly responded with a statement that supported the students and expressed how the plight of African Americans was inherently connected to the battles Mexican students waged in the Olympic host city. "It seems ridiculous to us also to see a government spend ... million[s] on an imperialistic spectacle while millions of its citizens live at sub-human levels," stated Edwards. "... Your valiant efforts to dramatize the plight of oppressed peoples through use of the highly political Olympic Games will serve as a model to coming student generations."[2]

The FBI doubted the veracity of Edwards's associations with CAOS because it had misgivings about whether or not such a group even existed, finding no information in its official files. On the basis of its own reading of Edwards's public statement, however, the FBI did not deny the *possibility* of CAOS's existence, theorizing that it "could be a Mexico-based organization which may have sent three student-members to talk with Edwards relative to boycott and disruption of Olympic Games" and that it might even have U.S. chapters. Even more significantly, the FBI was not willing to underestimate the power of Edwards, who, it claimed, wanted to burn down the White House, kill Chicago's mayor Daley, and free the "Black Panther leader held in Oakland, California, for [the] murder of [a] police officer." A feasible scenario, according to the FBI, was that the meeting between Edwards and CAOS was a publicity stunt, "an attempt by Edwards to disrupt [the] Olympics and ... may not be factual."[3]

Yet the FBI, as well as others, worried that the mere prospect of a transnational alliance between Mexican students and the OPHR signified that some kind of radical conspiracy was working against them. Ironically, this belief implied that the FBI understood, perhaps better than any other outside observer, how complexly "troubled" the Games were because of the various modes of dual consciousness involved. According to the FBI, rioting students, a large number of Communist groups, and the "racial overtones of current boycotts ... give weight to fears by the Mexican Government of leftist attempts to disrupt the international proceedings." While no concrete evidence had emerged that any U.S. organization had openly supported Mexican demonstrations, the FBI claimed to know "that individual citizens of the United States, possessing histories of subversive activity, have been arrested for personal participation in the riots." The Black Panthers, the National Lawyers Guild, and "persons active in facets of peace and 'New Left' movements" were considered likely candidates, and the FBI recommended "that all offices be alerted to furnish information received indicating travel to Mexico of persons in United States with background and activity of nature described above."[4]

The FBI, then, understood that the Mexican students by no means stood alone in their militant antigovernment stance, but rather symbolically marched alongside students from other nations, particularly France and the United States, and furthered the global nature of the turmoil in 1968.[5] In the United States, the 1960s emerged as a period when the temperate, "golden" society that allegedly developed in the early part of the postwar era detonated, transforming the youth who had touched the dark—literally black—side of American culture through rock and roll, bohemianism, and nationally espoused trends of juvenile delinquency into a political body with tactics that played well on television. The bedrock of this burgeoning political activity remained rooted in the modern movements of civil rights that, as Nikhil Pal Singh elaborates, became "the 'trigger struggle,' or switch point for a host of other minority discourses and contestations and relay station for emancipatory impulses of decolonization from around the world."[6]

"It's all tied up in the visuals":
Looking "Black" in a Transnational Context

In San Jose, college students played their part in the generational rumpus by trying to effect change within their own institution of higher education. For example, in the fall of 1967, the same week the Olympic boycott was first proposed, the campus energetically reacted to the presence of a recruiter from the Dow Chemical Corporation, an increasingly multinational corporation with claims that an astounding 25 percent of its total sales occurred outside the United States. More important, Dow manufactured napalm for the Vietnam military effort, which is why students broke into a "riot" of approximately 2,000, of whom 150 were described in the press as "hard core" agitators. The police responded with tear gas and arrests, and Governor Ronald Reagan demanded all students involved be expelled, and any faculty who supported them fired.[7] Needless to say, such student behavior was not unusual for the time period, yet many commented on the vigor displayed by the San Jose student body. The focal point of the furor, Glenn Allen, western recruitment manager for Dow, told the press that while students at UCLA, the University of Oregon, Oregon State, Sacramento State, and Long Beach State also demonstrated upon his arrival, the San Jose protest was "the worst.... they were like animals, screaming 'murderers' at us and 'fascists' at the police. Their faces were contorted. I've never seen them like that."[8]

Campus administrators, as well as local politicians, saw the protests against Dow as working in concert with the militant foundations established by the OPHR in its demonstrations against the football game between San Jose and the University of Texas at El Paso, as discussed in chapter 3. Student activism had accomplished a lot in a short period of time and saddled San Jose State with a reputation as "problematic." For example, after the skirmish over Dow, Senator Clark L. Bradley (R-San Jose) blamed the "weak administration" of college president Robert Clark, who was in Puerto Rico when the demonstrations began, for the eruptions on campus, and he directly linked the anti-Dow activity to the cancellation of the UTEP game earlier that year. "When President Clark capitulated and called off the game," Bradley told the press, "I said the result would be more disturbances."[9] Assemblyman John Vasconcellos (D-San Jose) deemed Bradley's allegations "ludicrous," supporting Clark for a quick return to campus to speak with students and deal with the situation.[10] Before a crowd of five thousand, Clark announced his intention to work with students on an official procedure regarding campus recruiters, which curtailed student plans to storm the administration building but failed to prevent more students from being arrested. Clark's efforts were rewarded; Reagan himself chided Bradley for blaming Clark when he was out of town during the initial outbreak. Rather than call in the National Guard, which Bradley wanted to do, Reagan stated that he was inclined to keep Clark in the position of president, although he wanted the final word from legal affairs secretary Ed Meese, and the campus turmoil once again was put to rest.[11]

Thus, Bradley failed in his attempt to vilify both the students and Clark, but he inadvertently linked the anti-Dow, and therefore anti-Vietnam, rally to the Olympic Project for Human Rights. He placed its actions, especially the shutdown of the UTEP game, squarely within the broader context of the student movements on campus. The *San Jose Mercury News* furthered such connections in its "Inquiring Reporter" column by asking Harry Edwards what he thought of the protests against Dow, to which he answered that the police had "gone too far." As the only faculty member among those asked, his answer played dramatically on the page and lent additional legitimacy and authority to the OPHR as well as to the individual posed as its leader.[12] The OPHR, then, became located within the political context created and maintained by the San Jose State student body, feeding on the radical atmosphere to grow in terms of both sophistication and visibility.

In the period that followed, the demands of the OPHR expanded from the audacious boycott resolution into a well-crafted political strategy, with the athletes involved remaining visible in headlines that spotlighted both their political activity and their athletic accomplishments.[13] On December 13, 1967, before the Greater Los Angeles Press Club, Edwards announced that the OPHR had further extended its objectives to the following: a boycott of all New York Athletic Club (NYAC) events; a demand for the exclusion of South Africa and Southern Rhodesia from Olympic competition; the restoration of Muhammad Ali's heavyweight boxing championship title; and the desegregation of the U.S. Olympic Committee administration and coaching staffs.[14] The next day at a news conference at the Americana Hotel in New York City, another demand was added: the removal of Avery Brundage, whom Edwards described as "a devout anti-Semitic and anti-Negro personality," as head of the IOC. Edwards asserted that the aforementioned Olympic boycott would take place unless all demands were met.[15]

One of the most serious allegations Edwards made against Brundage was his connection to the Montecido Country Club, which, like the NYAC, refused blacks and Jews as members. According to *Ebony* magazine, a reporter once quoted Brundage as saying he would sell the club "before letting niggers and kikes" in as members, and while Brundage denied the statement, he declared that if the club members chose "to accept only red-haired barbers for members, I think it's their right." Brundage was also quick to respond to the demand to racially diversify the USOC, agreeing that "there should be a qualified Negro on the ... Board" and suggesting that (fifty-seven-year-old) Jesse Owens was "a fine boy" who might be considered.[16] Last, the IOC president waved off his own inclusion in the OPHR's agenda, retorting that the Olympics were "the one international affair for Negroes, Jews and Communists" rather than a place to rally for human rights.[17]

With this rejoinder, Brundage inadvertently validated the increasingly universal mien of the OPHR, expanding its civil rights mission as a critical component of internationalist politics and making the transnational location of the OPHR imperative and yet often overlooked. Brenda Gayle Plummer, in her important study on African Americans and U.S. foreign affairs, affirms that "an essentialist perspective on race, combined with the belief that the United States has little in common with other mixed societies," created a dearth of scholarly attention regarding black politics in an international arena. What has been done, according to Plummer, largely focuses on Africa rather than "Afro-American political behavior."[18] Of course, a significant exception is the work of black scholars in the late nineteenth and early twentieth centuries, undoubtedly influenced by trends of black anti-imperialism, working-class radicalism, and the diasporic legacies of a forced migration, producing histories within an international context that focused on the inability of the United States to realize its own promises of citizenship.[19]

It is a trend, then, with a long historical pattern. The meaningful manner in which a global discourse, centered primarily on issues of decolonization and human rights, informed African American political pursuits for civil rights began with intensity early in the twentieth century. Early examples emerged with Marcus Garvey and the United Negro Improvement Association and somewhat crystallized in 1941 with A. Philip Randolph's proposed March on Washington over the desegregation of wartime production. The tenets of the subsequent "Double V" campaign left little doubt as to the fashion by which World War II would recast American domestic politics, particularly as Randolph warned of a coalition of "the darker races" in its aftermath. Perhaps clearest of all was the NAACP's Walter White, who concluded his provocative book *A Rising Wind* (1945) with a solemn prediction of a global race war if racist and imperialist circumstances did not change:

> World War II has given to the Negro a sense of kinship with other colored—and also oppressed—peoples of the world. Where he has not thought through or informed himself on the racial angles of colonial policy and master-race theories, he senses that the struggle of the Negro in the United States is part and parcel of the struggle against imperialism and exploitation in India, China, Burma, Africa, the Philippines, Malaya, the West Indies, and South America. The Negro soldier is convinced that as time proceeds that identification of interest will spread even among some brown and yellow peoples who today refuse to see the connection between their exploitation by white nations and discrimination against the Negro in the United States.[20]

Self-secluded in France, Richard Wright echoed such sentiment from afar, clearly enunciating the global universality of American civil rights struggles: "Isn't it clear to you that the American Negro is the only group in our nation that consistently and passionately raises the questions of freedom?... The voice of the American Negro is rapidly becoming the most representative voice of America and of *oppressed people anywhere in the world*."[21] Throughout the 1960s, groups such as the Student Non-Violent Coordinating Committee and the Southern Christian Leadership Conference operated in agreement with Wright's understanding, connecting domestic and international politics in expressions of overt opposition to the Vietnam War, while more radical organizations made staunch anti-imperialist declarations.[22] Similarly, the OPHR, in its "human rights" stance, placed itself on a platform that not only proposed to understand what such universal claims entailed but also aligned itself with the plight of numerous groups whose social location dictated they were not on equal footing in the Olympic community, or anywhere else. Perhaps most important, the group encompassed an objective that incorporated international politics to better define and improve American citizenship. With the announcement of its final demand, the OPHR further highlighted this universal legitimacy, building on the earlier role of Muhammad Ali within its principal tenets, a figure who in 1967 had repudiated the Vietnam War because, in his own famous words, "I ain't got no quarrel with them Viet Cong."[23] Before Ali, Vietnam was a virtual nonissue for athletes, amateur and professional, because they discreetly served on their representative National Guards to avoid combat service. Yet once Ali declared his definitive opposition to the war, it became a central issue for athletes, building on his controversial conversion to the Islamic faith and his name change— "Cassius is not my name no more"—years earlier.

Significantly, Edwards made his announcement at the Americana Hotel, standing next to prominent civil rights leaders Martin Luther King Jr. and Floyd McKissick, both of whom lent an elevated credibility to the OPHR.[24] Despite its "militant" casting as a black power organization, whether by outside observers or OPHR members, this association firmly fixed the Olympic boycott movement as an integral component of a national civil rights agenda, making Edwards a major player within the movement, however briefly. From this position, the inclusion of South Africa in the OPHR's framework brought the organization to the same level as that of what it directly opposed, the Olympics;

established what Arthur Ashe has called "the first major partnership between the black athletes of Africa and America"; and extended the swelling "black internationalism" of the Cold War period—illustrated by the founding of the Organization of African Unity, the inaugural International Congress of Negro Writers and Artists, and the publication of *Présence africaine*—into the realm of sports.[25]

The influence of the mere *idea* of an extensive Olympic boycott quickly saturated the international field of sports. Weeks before the Winter Games began in Grenoble, France, in 1968, for example, the USOC encountered yet another boycott proposal, one that objected to American participation in a sporting event hosted by France. "We have gotten about 150 unsigned letters or cards," stated Arthur Lentz, USOC executive director, "of which the general theme is we will not support you financially if you insist on going to France for the games and so long as De Gaulle persists in his arrogant attitude to the U.S." Rather than appear antagonized over the latest demand for an Olympic boycott, Lentz stated that the USOC found the development "an amusing interval," particularly in light of the emergence of the OPHR in the preceding months. "We're more amused than annoyed at this," he said. "It's been a welcome relief from the boycott letters concerning Negroes we've been receiving.... of course we're not going to do anything about it."[26]

To be sure, while a proposed boycott of the Winter Games because of anti–de Gaulle sentiment was somewhat absurd, its direct concatenation of sport with a political situation most certainly was not, because it indicated that the language employed by the OPHR, particularly *boycott*, was increasingly popular. With few signs of anti-French Americans to be found, the Grenoble Games concluded as a grand sporting event, producing stars such as Jean-Claude Killy and Peggy Fleming. However, the Games did not end without controversy. Of far greater consequence to the OPHR, and others, was the secret IOC meeting that took place in Grenoble, producing the decision to readmit South Africa into the Olympic community. This IOC decision, intended to overturn the 1963 ban of the nation for apartheid policies, threatened political discord on the athletic playing field at a global level and forced a further restructuring of the perception of the black athlete. It complicated the OPHR's stance against the Cold War use of the black athlete as America's great success story, intensifying the situation with the issue of whether the Springboks, South Africa's national team, should be allowed into international competition. Thus, the readmittance of South Africa provided a larger, and yet more specific, field for the quest of human rights to take place, containing both symbolic presence and an intensely undeniable political situation that connected the varied pieces of the "Black Atlantic" around the political potential of international sports.

Indeed, intimately connected to the struggles and gains of independence that colonized peoples achieved in the 1960s were interest and participation in elite international athletic competition. For example, in 1963 the organization Games of the New Emerging Forces (GANEFO) was created, with Asian, African, and Latin American nations as members: Indonesia, the People's Republic of China, Cambodia, Guinea, Iraq, Mali, Pakistan, North Vietnam, and the United Arab Republic. Perhaps more important, in 1966 the Supreme Council for Sport in Africa (SCSA) was founded in Bamako, Mali, representing thirty-two African countries: Algeria, Burundi, Cameroon, Central African Republic, Chad, Congo (Brazzaville), Congo (Kinshasa), Dahomey (now Benin), Ethiopia, Gabon, Gambia, Ghana, Guinea, Ivory Coast, Kenya, Liberia, Madagascar, Mali, Mauritania, Morocco, Niger, Nigeria, Senegal, Sierra Leone, Sudan, Tanzania, Togo, Tunisia, United Arab Republic (Egypt), Uganda, Upper Volta (now Burkina Faso), and Zambia. Both organizations solidified a pan-African identity as well as provided organizational legitimacy. Like GANEFO, the SCSA was determined to establish and encourage sports within its member nations, such as the coordination of the African Games, but had the additional mission of engaging in political action against South Africa, with some arguing that its entire agenda was essentially focused in that direction.[27] Indeed, during the Bamako meeting, the newcomers drafted a resolution on South Africa that overtly targeted the Mexico City Olympics:

It is the firm decision of the Supreme Council to use every means to obtain the expulsion of South African sports organizations from the Olympic Movement and from International Federations should South Africa fail to comply fully with the IOC rules. Finally, the Supreme Council invites all its members to subject their decision to participate in the 1968 Olympic Games to the reservation that no racialist team from South Africa takes part, and to ask all national Olympic committees to support the attitude of the Supreme Council for Sport in Africa.[28]

Thus, as the Mexico City Olympics loomed, the relationship between international sport and politics, particularly racialized politics, underwent tremendous change. While the early postwar period presented sport as a critical tool within Cold War dialogue for many nations, in the 1960s the same international sporting arena became a vehicle for the identity politics that raged throughout the decade, creating a mode of empowerment for athletes within an arena that they largely had not built. In the United States, the rise in a militant black political visibility, with new forms and stances perfected by 1968, was critical to this shift, enabling the use of sport as a political mechanism. Harry Edwards, for one, was highly conscious of this evolution, finding that one of the primary reasons many observers were skeptical about the ability of black athletes to mobilize successfully was the failure to realize the significance of this new identity and how firmly grounded it was within the broader political moment, one with an ever-increasing "black" presence. "They were no longer dealing with the 'Negro' athlete of the past," asserted Edwards. "Confronting them now was the new black athlete and a new generation of Afro-Americans."[29]

The linguistic metamorphosis from "Negro" to "black" was a critical step in the creation of radical action in the 1960s. Sprinter Lee Evans, both an OPHR member and a student in Edwards's Racial Minorities class in 1967, acknowledged "black" as central to his radical stance. "We stopped referring to ourselves as colored or Negro," Evans explained. "You were black or you were not black."[30] However, the designation "black" was not necessarily a simple assumption of a racial binary, which Edwards's complex racialized political taxonomy of the sports press as white, Negro, or black exemplifies. In this classification system, "white sports reporters" ignored the problems of race in America but were not "dedicated racists." Rather, they refused to taint the American institution of sport with any accusations because of its political, social, and economic interests for the nation on both a domestic and an international level. More vilified by Edwards, the "Negro sports reporter," while similar to the white, had "misplaced completely all sense of responsibility and loyalty" and was therefore traitorous. Last, the "black sports reporter" was willing to risk his own career to fight those that violated the principles of sport, such as, according to Edwards, Sam Skinner (*San Francisco Sun Reporter*); Dick Edwards (*New York Amsterdam News*); Jerry Eisenberg (Newhouse Syndicate); Pete Axthelm (*Newsweek*); and Dave Wolfe (Time-Life Syndicate).[31] What made this seemingly simple system so complex, of course, was that not all of the writers Edwards deemed black were African American. He classified them, rather, by the nature of what they did and how they did it, locating black as something one could aspire to from the point of Negro or white. Thus, if white was to be insensitive, ignorant, and indifferent, as Edwards determined it was, to be black was to be the opposite.

He furthered this process with his choices of those he sought to aid the OPHR and those he excluded. While Martin Luther King Jr. and Floyd McKissick stood by Edwards as visible components of the OPHR at the Americana Hotel, lending on-the-spot authority to the veritable rookie, others were not invited. Edwards found both the Urban League and the NAACP to be "Negro oriented," but he welcomed the support of the Southern Christian Leadership Conference and the Congress of Racial Equality (CORE) and their leaders, King and McKissick. Despite King's and McKissick's elder statesmen status and the schism that had occurred between the SCLC and Student Non-Violent Coordinating Committee, Edwards undoubtedly realized the national media presence of such figures and, by deeming them both black, could stand in the spotlight beside them.[32] Even more critical to

Edwards was the support of Louis Lomax, whom he considered both friend and adviser. In particular, Lomax counseled Edwards on how to cultivate a black image, essential to the success of the OPHR because of the potential media harvest surrounding the 1968 Olympic arena. According to Edwards, the visual component of the OPHR, which would be critical to the eventual impact the group garnered through Smith and Carlos, was a strategic, self-conscious construction. It was Lomax who instructed Edwards, who held an Ivy League degree, to change his look and avoid becoming "another middle-class Negro with something to say about civil rights." He told Edwards to lose his suit and tie and deliberately replace it with something else: "There's a lot of noise out there. You're going to have to talk loud, to establish a separate image before anyone will stop long enough to hear what you have to say—especially about sports. That's just the way this damn medium is. It's all tied up in the visuals—in what they can project on that little screen to hold people's attention for thirty seconds."[33]

The image that the OPHR had to portray was one that needed to serve a multitude of communities, both within the world of sport—athletes, coaches, administrators—and in broader society. Crucial to the development of a political movement is an understanding of its various audiences, all of which are inherently complex, depending on the social location(s) of the community represented. Distinct communities, both marginal and dominant, are inextricably intertwined and dependent on one another to provide meaning. Thus, what is characterized as black, both by those giving self-meaning to the designation and by those assigning it to another, lends much to what actually constructs the black community. This community, which Harry Edwards wanted the OPHR to represent, did not merely exist. As Kobena Mercer argues, "Identities are not found but *made*; ... they have to be culturally and politically *constructed* through political antagonism and cultural struggle." It seems most obvious to contend that the black community emerged as an oppositional force in postwar America. But, asks Mercer, "if the 'black community' was not always there but something that had to be constructed, what did people use to construct it with?"[34] The OPHR relied on symbols of the black community that had already been assembled. The rise of the Black Panther Party in 1966 was instrumental to the OPHR's success. The Panthers nurtured what Mercer designates a "highly visible oppositional appearance."[35] At Lomax's suggestion, Edwards took up such an appearance quite handily:

> Thanks to Lomax, slowly and quite deliberately I broke down to pseudo-revolutionary rags and began to develop that separate identity Lomax thought to be necessary in gaining critical access to and the attention of the media. At times it was as much as I could do to keep a straight face, standing before crowded auditoriums, under blazing television lights, delivering a lecture developed for my race relations class from a rostrum festooned with reporters' microphones, or bombarding white America with rhetoric calculated to outrage. When I couldn't bedazzle them with brilliance, I bamboozled them with bull. But the Black cap, the beard, the work boots and jeans, the beads, the "shades" (dark glasses) and the black jacket with the occasional book of matches pinned to the front attracted more attention from more varied sources than I would have felt desirable. The mystique just may have worked too well.[36]

This strategic appropriation of Black Power occurred because of the increasing realization that traditional attempts to remedy the racial inequities in American society were in dire need of innovation.[37] It was important, then, for the OPHR to actively cultivate a confrontational, militant appearance, one that Edwards cynically described as "the going image … literally being bought and sold by a medium that thrived on packaging,"[38] to infuse the boycott effort as something fresh and therefore newsworthy. Of course, the fostering of this radical ethos had varied ramifications. For some, the very *appearance* of the Black Power movement provided the value of empowerment, if not power,[39] but for a broader audience it carried a different weight that held far less pressing meaning. As Black Power grew progressively more visible, it ran the risk of becoming politically diluted as it appeared in altered forms throughout a range of leftist politics. In the midst of the rise of the

Panthers, for example, the Young Citizens for Community Action, a Chicano nationalist group, changed its name to the Brown Berets, a reference not only to attire but also to the militant stance it had come to represent.[40] For the OPHR, the connection to radical iconography, whether a black beret, a goatee, or dark glasses, proved beneficial in its ability to situate the organization within the sweeping political landscape of racialized radicalism but also allowed many critics to dismiss the group, as well as its demands, as political posers engaged merely, in the words of one observer, in "a large symbolic confrontation."[41]

The OPHR countered such accusations at the annual New York Athletic Club indoor track meet, scheduled to commemorate the hundreth anniversary of the club and the inauguration of the newly constructed multimillion-dollar Madison Square Garden. The group's ability to forcefully halt an American event, which coincided and became more potent with the international outcry over the prospect of South African participation in Mexico City, created substantial fear that a boycott of the Olympics by African American athletes was, indeed, more than a threat and made the skeptics sit up and take further notice.

Taking a Bite Out of the Big Apple: Constructing the Blueprint for Boycott

From its prominent location on New York's Central Park South, the hallowed halls of the New York Athletic Club represent one of America's oldest and most distinguished sporting institutions. According to its own written history, the club has been committed to "encouraging and then enforcing the uncompromising law of the stopwatch, tape measure, and scales" since 1868.[42] With exclusionary membership policies, the NYAC was an obvious focal point for the OPHR. The refusal to compete under the auspices of a racist organization, one that would not accept many of the competitors as members, suggested that African American athletes objected to the role of performer, building on one observer's ironic suggestion that the NYAC mend its ways by asking Eartha Kitt to sing the national anthem at the beginning of its annual track meet.[43] By refusing to appear on the track on February 16, 1968,

African American athletes declared that if they were not allowed the designation "member," they would not play the game. This assertive move, which made it clear the athletes would decide where they would play and with whom, was one of power, indicating that the individual voice of the athlete was of critical importance to a sporting event. In addition to this figurative value, boycotting the NYAC meet also had pragmatic worth in demonstrating that the OPHR could infuse its political posture with a tangible action having the potential to effect substantial change. Thus, the symbolism of boycotting one of the most prestigious amateur athletic events in the nation was multifaceted, extant as an exercise that displayed the potentiality of the political athlete. The boycott could not be opposed, as many suggested, because of the gains made by African Americans in the sporting arena; it needed to be supported *because of* such gains. As one sports columnist posited, "In this arena where he excels, he is strong enough to assert himself, to tell the NYAC that he cannot support a policy that discriminates against him, and to make his absence felt."[44]

One of the significant benefits of using the NYAC boycott as a practice maneuver for the approaching Olympics was the outside support it garnered. The American Jewish Congress supported the boycott, for example, despite its members' inability to participate directly in any demonstration because the meet began at sundown on a Friday and conflicted with Shabbat.[45] Despite having been scorned by Harry Edwards as Negro groups, both the NAACP and the Urban League, in conjunction with the Anti-Defamation League, issued a joint statement in support of "the long overdue protest against the New York Athletic Club's discriminatory membership practices."[46] In addition to the organizations on it, the individuals on the list who helped the OPHR organize its efforts in New York were many and distinguished, including Jay Cooper, chair of the Columbia University Black American Law Students Association; Omar Abu Ahmed, cochair of the 1966 Black Power Conference; Roy Innis, Associate National Director of CORE; Marshall Brown of the Amateur Athletic Union; and, perhaps most significant, H. Rap Brown, chair of SNCC.[47] The involvement of such people, among others, greatly increased the impression that the OPHR was, indeed, a legitimate arm of the civil rights movement. Thus, the NYAC meet emerged as a formal coming out party for the politics of race within sport, indicating further that a large-scale boycott enterprise by African American athletes was feasible.

As the meet drew near, the prospect of its boycott put the central themes of the OPHR on the field for all to debate—race, nation, patriotism, equality, humanity—with one sports columnist deeming the impending event "the most significant racial breakthrough since Branch Rickey and Jackie Robinson broke the color line in baseball."[48] The central issues involved were to be tested by both the athletes *and* the fans, with the decision of whether to participate, as competitor or spectator, poised as a vote in support of or in opposition to all that the OPHR represented. Indeed, the emphasis placed on the spectator was crucial to the success of a boycott, because ticket sales from the event were a significant source of revenue for the NYAC, and empty seats in the newly constructed Madison Square Garden were critical to the symbolic success of the boycott action. A few days before the opening of the meet, one columnist, deeming the policies of the NYAC "intrinsically offensive," urged those who had already purchased tickets to "burn or swallow them," acknowledging that "each empty seat ... will be an affirmation of our better national instincts."[49] Another stressed that supporting the boycotting athletes was the patriotic move, an action necessary "if you care about what is happening in America."[50] By appearing on February 16, 1968, on the track or in the stands, an individual chose a side of the fence and, according to Edwards and company, would be held accountable.

Intimations of violence became a principal concern of NYAC organizers and were duly noted by sportswriters. Of particular interest was the presence of H. Rap Brown next to Edwards at the offices of the Tenants Rights Part for the final press conference before the meet. Already a controversial figure, Brown had publicly linked to the NYAC boycott the killing of three African Americans in Orangeburg, South Carolina, during a demonstration against a segregated bowling alley. Yet

Edwards emphasized that a nonviolent picket line would be the primary strategy of protest at the meet, predicting between three thousand and five thousand people in front of Madison Square Garden, and invited "anybody who is sincerely interested in doing something to help end racism in this society.... If George Wallace wants to get on the picket line he's more than welcome."[51] However, after Edwards finished outlining the essentially nonviolent strategy of the OPHR, Brown took his turn in front of the press on behalf of his own organization: "SNCC endorses and supports all liberation struggles.... Personally, however, Madison Square Garden should either be burned down or blown up."[52]

While Brown's statement was a figurative reference to extreme action, it was Edwards who repeatedly implied a graver manner of bringing the boycott to fruition, a strategy that proved fairly effective. Many institutions of higher education, including track and field powerhouses Georgetown and Villanova (ranked number one in the East), as well as Manhattan College, City College of New York, and all Ivy League schools, agreed with the tenets of the boycott and pulled their teams out of the event. All parochial and public high schools in New York City withdrew as well as the "predominantly Negro track clubs."[53] In addition, fifty alumni of the University of Notre Dame implored fellow alums to renounce membership in the club because of the university's belief in "human brotherhood."[54] O. J. Simpson, who initially said the meet did not fit into his training schedule, was even more direct: "I wouldn't run that weekend if my mother was holding the meet."[55]

However, despite these shows of support there were several key individuals who remained undecided regarding their participation. While one sports columnist noted that "a few Negroes on the floor may be a useful reminder of how many are not there," it was acknowledged that their presence might also impel a violent situation.[56] For example, the late entry of hurdler Larry Livers, a former standout of Villanova and member of Oakland's Athens Club, was met with rumors that it might be dangerous for him to cross the picket line. When Wayne Vandenberg, track coach at the University of Texas at El Paso (UTEP), stated that his team would include "six Negro boys," including indoor long jump world-record holder Bob Beamon, Edwards replied, "Bobby might come on up to New York, but when he sees that picket line, you can bet he won't cross it." In addition, Edwards confidently predicted that long jumper Ralph Boston, sprinter Jim Hines, and high jumper John Thomas—none of whom had publicly declared his stance—would also stay home, because it would be imprudent to do otherwise.

> Thomas would be very foolish to cross that picket line. There are some brothers in Boston who would be very upset with him. They might not show it that night, but within a week John would regret his decision. Hines says he wants to play pro football some day. If he runs in that meet, he'll never be able to play football for anybody. Some cats in Texas have personally said they'd fix it so he'd be on sticks if he's crazy enough to run in New York.[57]

After Edwards's incendiary remarks, Thomas became a focal point in the press. The *New York Post*, a newspaper overwhelmingly supportive of the NYAC boycott, declared, "The major question before tonight's New York AC meet is whether the boycott will force out the last big-name Negro athlete left, Olympic high jumper John Thomas."[58] A seasoned veteran, Thomas took the bronze medal in high jump at the Rome Games in 1960 (7-0¼) and the silver at Tokyo in 1964 (7-1¾). After Rome, he had been sorely disappointed by the reaction of the American fans and press when he failed to win the gold. Particularly bothersome were accusations that he had let the hype preceding the Games go to his head and proceeded to let two Soviet athletes best him for the gold and silver, marking his first defeat in two years. Months later, after dealing with nightmares in the aftermath of his loss, he complacently stated, "American spectators are frustrated athletes. In the champion, they see what they'd like to be. In the loser, they see what they actually are, and they treat him with scorn."[59]

Once again, Thomas was under vigilant scrutiny from fans and press, this time in regard to whether or not he would appear in Madison Square Garden. Within the athletic community, too, Thomas was defamed. Lee Evans declared, "Everybody knows he's the biggest Tom there is," to which Boston Celtic coach Bill Russell responded, "John is not a Tom, he's just naïve, terribly naïve."[60] After receiving three threatening long-distance phone calls, Thomas stated his doubts about competing, despite his participation in NYAC meets since 1959: "I've got a wife to think of—and a baby on the way."[61] Thomas's fears were not unfounded. When Bill Orwing, athletics director at the University of Indiana, entered African American Mike Goodrich in a sprinting event at the last minute, he, too, received a long-distance telephone call pledging that Goodrich would receive "acid in the face" if he crossed the line.[62]

Before the first competitor took his mark, the prospect of such violence, greatly emphasized in the press, had several considerable ramifications, including, as Pete Axthelm lamented, the transformation of the NYAC from a victim of its own policies to a victim of intimidation.[63] In an allegedly preventative move, the NYAC announced that tickets would not be available at the Garden for the meet; only spectators who had already purchased tickets in advance would be allowed admission.[64] In addition, in the midst of the widening turmoil, the Russian team, in a nicely conceived bit of Cold War maneuvering, withdrew from the meet altogether. News of their retreat came at the premeet dinner, when Colonel Donald Hull, executive director of the Amateur Athletic Union, announced that the seven-athlete Russian squad would not be on the roster.

> I talked to P. Stepanenko, the president of their track and field association.... He said that the athletes wanted to stay out in Los Angeles and train. I told him they could train here.... Then the real reason finally came out. He said they were guests in this country and they didn't want to do anything that would put their athletes in danger, and crossing a picket line might do that. They will still compete in our national championships later this month and we're not going to take any action against them. Why punish them without punishing our own athletes who have withdrawn from this meet?[65]

The withdrawal of this particular Russian contingent was considerable, because they had been the first to compete in the United States since a protest against American policy in Vietnam prevented a U.S.–Soviet match-up in 1966. The five-man, two-woman squad included high jumpers Valentin Gavrilov and Antonina Korokova, pole vaulter Gennadiy Bliznyetsov, long jumpers Tonu Lepik and Tatiana Talisheva, and runners Olveg Raiko and Vladislav Sapeya. The group, which had already participated in two indoor meets in the United States, had been training together in Los Angeles with the intention of competing in the AAU championships in Oakland.[66] Without their presence and that of the absent West German miler Bodo Tummler, the NYAC meet lost its international credentials, and the anticipation surrounding an East versus West meeting fell flat.

Also cautious because of the possibility of violence was ABC, who intended to televise the NYAC meet on *Wide World of Sports*. While viewers were not unaccustomed to violence on television—embedded in both fact and fiction—the situation posed a problem because it was violence in the context not of war or politics but rather of amateur athletics. Jim Spence, coordinating producer of *Wide World of Sports*, acknowledged the potential for problems. Spence told the press that ABC had considered dropping the meet but decided to go ahead with the broadcast with enormous precautions regarding technical equipment. Also, the network would allow for extra time in case the boycott prevented the meet from running according to schedule. While officials of Madison Square Garden augmented its own forces and communicated with the New York City Police Department in fear of violence, the prospect presented a much different scenario for Spence and the network.

> We've told the NYAC that if anything should happen during the telecast we're not going to shy away from it. We'll cover it like a news story. It's a messy situation and we're caught in the middle of it. If the NYAC had said to us there would be no Negroes in the meet we'd have said you're not going to see it on ABC either. We're disappointed the club has not

made any statement, but only if catastrophe hit us, like there being only 40 athletes and three events, would we not go ahead. That's not to say we condone the policies of the NYAC. The meet obviously is not going to be as good as it could have been, but our commitment was made in October and we're covering what always has been one of the major meets in the country.[67]

Critical to the perspective of the network was its contract to broadcast the impending Olympic Games, necessitating the creation of an enormous amount of visibility and viewer excitement to make Mexico City a televised success. Pre-Olympic events were crucial to the acquisition of a large audience, because they created a familiar relationship between the athletes who were likely to be chosen for the American squad and the viewing audience. The withdrawal of the Russians had already taken away a great deal of the meet's international appeal. To take the spotlight off the remaining American athletes would only worsen the situation of the network, which was concurrently broadcasting champion faces from Grenoble throughout the domestic athletic disorder in New York. While an anonymous network spokesman stated that initially ABC wished "the whole thing would go away," it was clear to one television columnist that it was not to be the case: "The land has become awake. The height a man can jump or the speed at which he can run no longer is as vital as how fast and how high he will be able to reach as a human being."[68]

While certainly not everyone agreed with such an assessment, the *New York Times* coverage of the first day of competition indicated that, if nothing else, the quest for equality attained the same weight of importance as the quest for the blue ribbon. A dual headline—"Young Sets 2-Mile New York A.C. Meet Mark; Police Repel Rights Pickets"—was accompanied by photos of both protestors and hurdlers as well as two stories: one focusing on the athletic accomplishments of the previous evening and another concentrating on the events outside the Garden on Seventh Avenue. Of equal importance, on the sports page at least, were both the meet itself and the political turbulence that surrounded it. Although the story regarding the athletic achievements began by revealing that the meet was inundated with politics—a picket line outside the door, a bomb threat inside the arena, and only "nine Negroes among the 400 or so athletes who competed"—its primary focus was that despite the less than elite field who participated, the 2-mile, the pole vault, and the long jump, all of which had African American competitors, did produce solid performances. Of the nine African Americans who did participate, three ended up victorious: Bob Beamon in the long jump (26-3½), Lennox Miller in the 60-yard dash (6.21), and Franzetta Parham in the women's high jump (5-5). The story also noted that the crowd who cheered on such achievements was significantly under capacity, with the likely inflated "official" count of 15,972 spectators—few of whom were African American—well below the Garden's 17,800 seats.[69] An unofficial count given by the *Los Angeles Times* estimated only 14,000 were in attendance, indicating that many who purchased tickets did not show up for the event, whether for political convictions or, perhaps as the *New York Times* contended, for fear of the rumored violence. In addition, twelve African American athletes remained on the meet's roster but did not surface, including, as Edwards had predicted, Jim Hines, Ralph Boston, and John Thomas.[70] Hines, who had intended to compete, stated he had received a threatening phone call the night before the meet, and with consideration to his family opted to stay home.[71]

Of those that did appear, Bob Beamon generated the most interest for press and fans alike. Unlike James Dennis, an African American sprinter who had his glasses broken as he attempted to enter the Garden, Beamon got inside the arena without any hassle.[72] Arguably the athlete with the highest profile participating in the meet, he walked through the door in his street clothes—a red leather jacket and black fedora—without his equipment, which was covertly brought into the dressing room by a UTEP teammate. While he waited for the long jump to be called, he remained in the dressing room with the rest of the UTEP squad, who opted to stretch there rather than out on the track. "I'm not going to warm up out there," said teammate Kelly Myrick.

"Might be a Lee Harvey Oswald up there." Jose L'Official, described by a *New York Times* reporter as dark-skinned, remained inside with his five African American teammates, despite the declaration by Leslie Miller that he had nothing to fear: "You're all right, Jose, you're from the Dominican Republic, you're Caucasian."[73] However, like L'Official, the rest of the UTEP contingent was uneasy about appearing on the track. Beamon, who won his event with his first leap, had decided ahead of time that that was all he was prepared to do—"one jump and out." Despite his victory and the steady applause that accompanied it, it was apparent that he was not pleased with the day he had inside the Garden, stating to one teammate, "It's not going to pay off, not never."[74]

Outside the Garden, the situation was comparably troubled. Chanting "Racism must go" and "Muhammad Ali is our champ!" and carrying signs with slogans such as "The NYAC needs a heart transplant" and "Run Jump or Shuffle are all the same, when you do it for the Man," between fifteen hundred and two thousand protestors attempted to storm the entrance to the Garden on Seventh Avenue as well as block the main entrance. During the chaos, police made three distinct charges into the crowd, at times using nightsticks, and arrested twelve people, at least two of whom had to be taken to St. Vincent's Hospital before going to the police station. Helping to keep the crowd somewhat orderly were Omar Abu Ahmed of the Black Power Conference, William H. Booth, chair of the City Commission on Human Rights, and Barry H. Gottherer and Sid Davidoff, two assistants to New York's mayor Lindsay. However, it was not until the police gave a bullhorn to Harry Edwards that some semblance of order occurred. When he shouted, "We aren't here to picket Penn Station or the Statler Hilton Hotel," many picketers followed him to the Eighth Avenue entrance of the Garden, at which point most of the athletes trying to get inside were able to do so. Marching around the three-block square, demonstrators, led by Ken Noel, deflected athletes from Holy Cross and Providence College to the wrong entrance, away from the Garden and into Penn Station. "Our coach," stated one Holy Cross athlete, "never told us it would be like this."[75] While some picketers favored rushing the building, such as the unidentified man who took the bullhorn from Edwards and shouted, "Let's break into twos and threes and go in and tear that goddamn building down," Edwards discouraged such behavior: "There are women and children around here and I'd just as soon let the damned thing rot."[76]

While not halted entirely, the meet did indeed fester, with few athletes producing any performances of note; one sportswriter lamented, "The program lagged.... the times were poor."[77] *Time* magazine, somewhat dubious regarding the political undertakings of Edwards, mused that the campaign against the NYAC likely "was enough of a success" to continue efforts against the Olympics.[78] In addition, the endeavor had tangible local results: the city of New York, led by Booth, pursued legal action against the NYAC for its discriminatory membership policies. While the NYAC invoked its status as a private club to refute the charges, Booth argued that the city had jurisdiction, because the NYAC leased several city-owned properties and held a state liquor license: "If they want to discriminate as a private club that's OK by me. But they can't then use the benefits of the city unless they want to abide by anti-discrimination laws."[79]

However, the militant symbolism of the boycott was perhaps its greatest offering. The "middle-ground," as posited by sports columnist Paul Zimmerman, "was swept under" in the boycott. While Zimmerman found the effort "successful" in putting the NYAC on notice for its racist policies, he was also somewhat disturbed by the loss of this so-called middle ground. Zimmerman invoked University of Tennessee track star Richmond Flowers Jr. to illustrate his point about how a militant stance could harm the larger movement. Flowers's father, of course, as Alabama attorney general, had battled George Wallace's segregationist policies throughout the 1960s before losing to Wallace's wife, Lurleen, in the 1966 gubernatorial race. Flowers Jr., who would go on to a respectable career with the Dallas Cowboys and the New York Giants, ideologically mirrored his father's politics. As a member of Tennessee's football squad, he often heard Alabama fans scream "Kill the nigger lover" in his direction. Yet despite his pro–civil rights stance, he ran in seven races, winning the hurdles, during the course of the NYAC meet and remained undisturbed by his participation. He said:

> When I found out that Rap Brown and Harry Edwards were running the boycott my conscience didn't bother me. I put them in a class with George Wallace, whose views I hate, but as long as you've got Wallace on one side and Brown and Edwards on the other, the views of the middle man won't be heard. And I consider myself a middle man, even though in Alabama they consider me as all the way over the other way. But you can't disagree with a Harry Edwards. If you do, then he says it's because he's a Negro.[80]

Zimmerman continued that other "white moderates" agreed with Flowers's position, such as a trio from Oregon University who had also competed in the meet. One member, Roscoe Divine, admitted that the team was "against the idea of a club with a restricted membership." However, he continued that at no point had they been compelled to engage in the boycott because of who was behind it:

> We're pretty interested in the civil rights movement, and if some black athletes would have come over to us in a rational way and said, "Look, you'd really be helping us out if you stayed out of the meet," we'd have stayed out, believe me. But the only people who talked to us were the black power guys. They threatened us with stuff like, "Don't run or else." Nobody's going to take that kind of stuff.[81]

What Zimmerman determined as "hard times for moderates" could be construed as the exact effect the OPHR intended. White athletes' perceptions of Black Power indicated how powerful the mere symbols of militancy were, marking a cultural phenomenon in which a fearful white America viewed the OPHR's stance without evaluating the politics and actions. Was a boycott, one of the most traditional forms of civil rights actions, really militant?

In the aftermath of the NYAC meet, African American athletes like Bob Beamon were not going to be able to sit on a well-lit fence between aspirations of Olympic gold and a growing movement of peers who were attempting to define victory in another fashion. Both Beamon and Lennox Miller, who later said that he, too, wished an athlete rather than an activist had explained the issues of the boycott to him, particularly because he was Jamaican and unfamiliar with American politics, asserted that a primary reason for competing was the trip to New York, where their families lived.[82] When stopped at the gate by Ken Noel, Larry Livers gave an answer along the same lines: "I wanted the plane trip to New York to see my family."[83] While their reason was similarly pragmatic to Harry Edwards's for participating in sports in junior and senior high school—a hot shower—it was clear that for many the time for individual interest in athletics was over. As one observer noted, "Anybody who viewed the passions and sensed the depth of feeling attendant upon the boycott of the NYAC ... must appreciate that life cannot go on normally in a social vacuum."[84] With the campaign against the NYAC that took place both inside and outside the newly constructed Madison Square Garden, new lines had been drawn in American sport. The next intended place of action to display the racial inequities of the United States was the Olympic Stadium in Mexico, although it was not going to be simple.

Playing with South Africa: The Diasporic Black Athlete

The aftermath of the NYAC boycott continued with the incensed reactions of several African nations as well as Eastern Europe to the announcement that South Africa had been readmitted to Olympic competition. The team had been suspended in 1963 at the Baden-Baden, Germany, session of the IOC on the grounds that its racist politics violated the Olympic code. The Baden-Baden decision encompassed substantial doubt about the verity of the South African team's promise to hold integrated trials to select its national team. The decision stated that it was the responsibility of South Africa to create substantial change regarding its racist policies in athletic competition, which began in 1954 when a Natal provincial council prohibited integrated sports in government-aided educational institutions. In 1956, when such segregation policy stretched to the whole nation, the IOC began overtly resisting it in regard to the Springboks' participation in the Olympic Games.[85] South African prime minister Hendrik Verwoerd reacted to the IOC resolution by persisting with his stance that "the principle of segregation must be maintained in sport."[86] Because of the refusal of the South African government to accede to the prescriptions of the IOC, its athletes were not allowed to participate in Tokyo in 1964. However, because of the pivotal role of sport in South Africa, the nation that produced the first African gold medalist in the form of R. E. Walker in 1908, the prospect of not competing in Mexico City in 1968 drove the Springboks to labor arduously in the interim to become reinstated.[87]

The prospect of the readmittance of South Africa gained enormous momentum early in 1968, particularly after a 113-page report was filed January 30, 1968, to the IOC by a fact-finding commission. The report included assurances from South African prime minister John Vorster and South African Olympic Committee president Frank Braun that a mixed-race team would be sent to compete in Mexico City. However, it also stated that the process for choosing the team would be segregated, because it was illegal in South Africa for athletes of different races to compete against one another on the same field. Such promises were glaringly ironic, considering the allowances the South African government had to make so that the committee, composed of Lord Michael Killanin of Ireland, Reginald Alexander of Kenya, and Ir Ade Ademola of Nigeria, could travel throughout the nation together. Before their arrival, Braun publicly declared that for the span of their stay, the rules of apartheid would be frozen, allowing Ademola, who was black, to stay with the rest of his cohort. Of the special circumstances provided, few were necessary, because the majority of the meetings the committee took part in were held privately. For example, when Ademola met the South African minister of sport Frank Warring for lunch, no photographers were permitted.[88] Thus, the trip avoided any uncomfortable incidents and proceeded smoothly enough to put together their substantial conclusions. Although they were not allowed to make an overt recommendation to the IOC, they submitted a report that many felt heightened South Africa's chances of participation.[89] If they were to participate, many felt that most other African nations as well as the Soviet Union would boycott Mexico City.

The day before NYAC competition was set to begin at Madison Square Garden in New York, Colonel John Westerhoff, secretary of the IOC, announced that South Africa was going to be allowed to partake in the Mexico City Olympics because of multiple assurances made by the South African government: "On the basis of these assurances the IOC had an absolute majority vote … in favor of letting South Africa send a team to the summer Games in Mexico." The judgment, attained through a mail vote and thought to be somewhere in the vicinity of thirty-seven to twenty-eight, was based on a five-part settlement between the IOC and South Africa: the team must be composed of both "white" and "non-white" athletes; the team must travel together as a unit; the team must be dressed in identical uniforms, live together, and march under the same flag in Mexico City; white and non-white athletes must compete against one another on the same field at the Olympics (and in other international meets outside South Africa); and a balanced number of white and non-white officials must select the athletes for the South African team. South Africa did not, however, have to hold integrated trials for the Olympic team; in events such as boxing, elimination rounds for team spots would occur once the team was outside the South African border.[90] Such a selection process differed greatly from that attempted in 1964, when the all-white South African Olympic Games Association (SAOGA) attempted merit selections, but without direct competition between whites and non-whites. When asked what procedure would be followed if the independent Olympic trials were to produce the same times, SAOGA responded that laboratory tests would be performed to certify which athlete was superior, prompting the IOC to suspend South Africa from the Tokyo Games, the nation's first dismissal since it first competed in 1908.[91]

In South Africa, the news of readmission was publicly heralded by Vorster, Braun, and Matt Mare, president of the South African Amateur

Athletic Union, who expressed gratitude at the "courage" of the IOC and reiterated that the country would send their "best team—white and non-white"; he also signaled an understanding that the exultation in South Africa at the announcement might not be mirrored elsewhere around the globe: "Now we hope that the I.O.C. will not allow the countries opposing South Africa's readmission to use their blocs to try to boycott the Olympic Games."[92] However, many expressed disbelief over the concessions the IOC granted to South Africa, particularly the separate Olympic trials, rather than over the concessions South Africa granted to the IOC. Historically, there was little reason to believe that South Africa would hold to its promise of selecting an Olympic squad solely on the basis of merit rather than race. From a pragmatic standpoint, merit selections were a near impossibility, because the elite training and facilities in South Africa were bestowed upon the official, national teams, all of which were exclusively white, preventing anyone else from competing internationally.[93] Although the South African National Olympic Committee promised the IOC that all athletes would be eligible to compete in Rome in 1960, black weight lifter Precious McKenzie, who defeated all white competitors in segregated trials, was disqualified on a technicality, ensuring that an all-white team was sent to Italy.[94] Further, when South Africa attempted merit selections for Tokyo in 1964, it furnished a track team composed entirely of white runners, despite two non-whites having run faster in their heats. When asked why Humphrey Khosi, whose time was 0.1 second faster than the white athlete eventually chosen, was not selected for the squad, Mare inanely responded "0.1 second does not really count."[95]

Furthermore, the decision to allow South Africa to compete was granted on acutely spurious grounds. It created a false sense of equality in the Olympic Stadium that did not exist in the nation itself. One columnist noted in apparent disbelief, "White and black may run and jump together outside South Africa, but they will not do it inside," and a *Sports Illustrated* writer emphasized that South Africa had not changed "socially, economically or politically. . . . Just with respect to its Olympic team," establishing a marked difference between a nation and a National Olympic Committee.[96] Ethiopia and Algeria, the two independent African nations that reacted immediately to the readmittance of South Africa with rumors of withdrawing their teams from the Mexico City Olympics, emphasized similar thinking. The Ethiopian Sports Confederation (ESC) made its announcement on February 16, 1968, from Addis Ababa. In the statement, Yidnekatchew Tessema, secretary-general of the ESC, asserted that all African and Asian nations would follow their lead, and many Latin American nations, particularly Brazil, were also likely to follow suit. "This was a victory for the policy of apartheid and not for the South African Olympic Committee …," Tessema stated. "What has the IOC achieved if the status quo is maintained in South Africa after the Mexico Games?" The withdrawal of Ethiopia, home of two-time Olympic marathon champion Abebe Bikila—both a national and continental treasure as the first black African to have won Olympic gold—was immediately followed by a statement from the Executive Bureau of the Algerian Olympic Committee, indicating that they, too, would be absent in Mexico. Word also emerged from Nairobi that the Supreme Council of Sport in Africa would meet to discuss a wide-scale boycott, with both Uganda and Zambia vocal about the decision of the IOC. In addition, official word came from Moscow that the Russian team might also keep away from Mexico because of the presence of South Africa, calling the IOC judgment a "flagrant violation of the [Olympic] charter … that forbids discrimination of athletes for political, racial or religious reasons."[97]

While the sentiments of nations like Ethiopia and Algeria became instantly clear, and the Soviet Union was posed as likely to follow, the position of the United States was rather vague. The American Committee on Africa (ACOA), with hopes that "all American athletes will boycott Olympics in solidarity with African nations against apartheid," contacted the IOC and Douglas Roby, both an IOC member and president of the USOC, via telegram to determine how he had voted in regard to the South African issue. Roby refused to answer: "It was a secret ballot. Nobody knows how I voted and I don't know how anybody else voted."[98] However, his vague response would not prove acceptable when the furor over South Africa increased and ACOA became increasingly focused on it. Eventually, the body gathered the names of sixty-five athletes, including Wilt Chamberlain, Arthur Ashe, Jackie Robinson, Oscar Robertson, Lee Evans, John Carlos, and Len Wilkens, as well as many members of the 1964 Olympic team, in support of the boycott movement. Robinson, a noted moderate regarding such issues, became particularly central, urging the USOC to "use its influence" to pursue a ban against South Africa.[99]

On February 17, 1968, five more African nations—Tanzania, Uganda, Mali, Ghana, and the United Arab Republic—announced their intended withdrawal from Mexico, and the UAR announced an intention of proposing to the Organization of African Unity (OAU) a collective African boycott strategy. In addition, Abraham Ordio, secretary of the Nigerian Olympic Games Committee, stated that the IOC decision was a "letdown of all African countries," indicating that Nigeria, too, would join the boycott effort.[100] The mounting strength behind the boycotting African nations, in addition to the simultaneous speculation and turmoil that surrounded the New York Athletic Club, greatly enhanced the perception that the approaching Olympics were in jeopardy. In the United States, perhaps the prospect of the default of the Soviet team was most consequential, because its absence would prevent the unofficial showdown between communism and democracy that took place every four years on Olympic playing fields. Within this head-to-head combat, athletes became emblems of their respective political systems, with a gold medal reifying governmental virtuosity. While American athletes were certainly portrayed as harbingers of freedom and liberty, emphasis lay on their existence as individuals within a team, whereas Soviet athletes were individuals within an entire national order. As articulated by *Sovetskiy Sport*, "In the socialist society the successes of the athletes belong not only to them, but first of all to the society of the country which has sent them. This is the duty of the sportsmen to their society."[101]

Moreover, the contemplation of a solid link of political solidarity between the Soviets and the independent African nations was a fearful one for many in the United States. While the relevance of Africa in American civil rights movements was increasingly evident in the post-war period, with the African continent no longer considered a refuge for African Americans but rather an ally intended to reinforce black identity *within* the respective national border, outside the arena of progressive politics a different perspective existed.[102] As conservative sports columnist Arthur Daley, who had continually lambasted Edwards for his work against the NYAC, remaining apparently ignorant of the national weight of sport on the American side of the Cold War coin, grumbled, "The Soviet Union and other Iron Curtain countries have assiduously been wooing the African countries for years and they could join such a boycott because they are pragmatists and always have used sports for political purposes."[103]

Although narrowly focused, Daley's perspective was correct in that the relationship between the Soviet Union and the emerging independent African states heightened in the postwar period, with a direct Soviet attempt to extend its influence both politically and economically on the "dark continent" as part of a broader strategy to abate Western authority. Sport played a critical part within this approach, in its alleged existence as a realm of solid values, morality, harmony, and peace, ideal for seemingly innocent financial aid and friendship. The Soviet program for African sport was based on six points: competing against African athletes; sending Soviet coaches to Africa; training African athletes in the USSR; donating money and equipment to African sports programs; exchanging sports delegations; and, perhaps most critical, remaining a constant and vocal critic of apartheid, monitoring South Africa's international athletic outings, and openly denouncing nations that competed against the Springboks.

In addition to this direct partnership, the Soviets also set precedents for placing African sports on a broader international level. For example, in 1961 the Soviet Union proposed to the fifty-ninth session of the IOC a resolution to aid in the development of amateur athletics in the so-called Third World—Latin America, Asia, and Africa. The proposal marked the beginning of the Soviet Union's creation of ties along athletic lines with over thirty African nations. This relationship had obvious political implications that could expand to other domains, implications that the United States found disconcerting in its worries that, as Penny Von Eschen points out, "resentment of American racism might cause Asian and African peoples to seek closer relations with the Soviet Union."[104]

Aside from the Cold War implications, the matter of South Africa was of critical importance in the United States when it became further incorporated into the revolt of the American black athlete. For example, before the readmission announcement was even made, a scathing editorial against the membership policies of the NYAC considered the perspective that, as a private club, no law required it to "admit any significant number of those once described by Dr. Goebbels as non-Aryan" but that, in 1968, if a group wanted to sponsor public events, it should consider promoting "a joint event with its equivalent athletic body in South Africa."[105] The correlation made between the NYAC and South Africa demonstrates how the land of apartheid served as a central reference point of odious racial policy even, or perhaps especially, in sport, extending the black collective—or black athlete collective—to a global black community with direct intimations regarding a binary relationship between black nationalism and white supremacy. As Rob Nixon submits, South Africa played a critical role in the American imagination of race and rights, a relationship of "transcultural echoes" that he defines as "the intense yet ambiguous ties between South Africa and the U.S.A., two frontier colonies notorious for racial injustice—the one with a black majority of some 35 million, the other with a black minority of almost identical proportions."[106]

However, the discussion of such critical issues in the global sporting arena was, at best, uncommon. Sport was historically positioned as a celebrated locale of parity and balance. For example, when defending the IOC decision, Avery Brundage asserted, "If there is one place an athlete, no matter what race, color, religion or political affiliation, can display his talents ... on an equal basis, it is the Olympic Games."[107] Many others based their opposition to the actions of the OPHR and the boycotting African nations on such a belief and positioned the Olympic Games beyond reproach by recurrently invoking imagery of the civilized Greeks and their sporting traditions.

However, the Olympic forum, founded by a European aristocrat and emphasizing Western athletic traditions, was not the wondrous site many projected it to be. As columnist Robert Lipsyte pointed out to his readers, such ancient icons "had long rotted away under creeping professionalism, bribery of officials and locker-room thievery," to be replaced by the modern Games, some twenty-eight years younger than any tradition of the NYAC. Thus, the African nations taking a stance against the IOC by boycotting Mexico City were not aligning themselves against what Lipsyte termed "the Hellenic heritage of the original Games or ... the European-oriented, genteel amateurism of the 19th century revival." Participation in the modern Olympics occurred for some other reason, whether it be what Lipsyte dubbed "an inexpensive way to communicate manhood" or an alliance with a gesture that, in Paul Gilroy's terms in his discussion of working-class British radicalism, "shrank the world to the size of their immediate communities and began, in concert to act politically on that basis ... [supplying] a preliminary but nonetheless concrete answer to the decisive political questions ... how do we act locally and yet think globally?"[108]

A partial answer to such a central query emerged on February 19, when the first non-African nations joined the dialogue regarding South Africa and the Olympics. An announcement came from Tayeb Safwat, president of the Higher Youth Welfare Council and vice president of the Syrian Olympic Committee, that Syria would join in solidarity with nations such as Ethiopia, Algeria, Uganda, Tanzania, Ghana, Gambia, and Guinea and withdraw from the Olympics. In addition, news emerged from New Delhi of India's displeasure with the decision of the IOC. President of the Indian Olympic Association, Raja Bahalindra Singh, avowed that the judgment of the IOC regarding South Africa was wrong and that, unless a reversal occurred, there would be a "mass boycott by most countries, including India."[109]

Further momentum occurred the following day when Kenya,

along with Sudan and Iraq, announced withdrawal.[110] The retreat by the Kenyan team, which was likely to have numbered fifty athletes, was significant largely because of the presence of runner Kipchoge "Kip" Keino, a Nandi tribesman who was considered a favorite in the 5,000-meters and the primary threat to dominant American champion Jim Ryun, as well as long-distance runner Naftali Temu, steeplechaser Benjamin Kogo, and the 1964 bronze medalist in the 800-meters, Wilson Kiprugut. In addition, a joint statement by Municipal Minister Helge Seip of Norway, Education Minister Helge Larsen of Denmark, and leader of the People's Party in Sweden Sven Weden, indicated that Scandinavia was also unlikely to participate if the IOC did not reinstate its ban on South Africa.[111]

Attention to the reactions by an increasingly diverse collection of teams moved off the American sports page with an editorial in the *New York Times*. While sportswriters such as Lipsyte were cautiously supportive and understanding of the proposed boycotts, the editorial page found such actions "a serious mistake." The editorial argued that while apartheid was most certainly a condemnable policy, it was essential to acknowledge that the concessions made by South Africa to the IOC were the first time the nation had "moved some distance away from its extreme application ... and agreed to send a racially integrated team to Mexico City," deeming the move a "revolutionary step" and hoping that such a foundation would persuade the South African government to "go further next time."[112] Columnist Arthur Daley adamantly agreed in his rejoinder to what he ruled a "thoughtful commentary on the editorial page." Elevating the IOC as an organization "unshakable ... in its purity of purpose," Daley argued that the group had "never surrendered even a little of its supranationality," and he exemplified his point with the numerous times the IOC was able to keep "the Olympic movement above politics and absolutely free from discrimination of any description."

> It slapped down Hitler when no one else dared so. It reunited East Germany and West Germany for the 1964 Olympics, a wedding that statesmen have been unable to achieve, not even on a shotgun temporary

basis. When Sukarno of Indonesia tried to bar Israel from the Asian Games a few years ago as a political ploy toward the Arab nations, the I.O.C. immediately exercised its jurisdictional powers and canceled the games. Wouldn't it be strange if the first breakthrough in South Africa's apartheid policy were to come through the high-minded idealists who form the International Olympic Committee?[113]

Daley was not alone in his support of the IOC. Writers of the British press, too, found that the Grenoble decision exemplified how sport could be put to favorable, diplomatic use. The *London Times*, noting the concessions made by South Africa, urged boycotting nations to reconsider and "occupy the ground gained in the Olympic decision, hold the Games successfully, and go on from there." The *Daily Telegraph* assented, arguing that any opportunity for the world to make contact with South Africa should be capitalized upon rather than shunned.[114] In addition to these ideological oppositions to the campaign against the participation of South Africa was Avery Brundage himself, who tried logistically to undermine the enterprise of the boycotting nations when he announced that the IOC had not been officially informed of any withdrawals: "I don't believe that any national Olympic committees have had time to meet and to take decisions on this matter so far."[115] In addition, Brundage made an appeal on behalf of the "underprivileged non-whites of South Africa," for whom Olympic participation was so important, admonishing the boycotting nations that it was "unfortunate that some who pretend to be their friends would deprive them."[116]

However, despite his remarks, the position of the boycott was further empowered when word came from Addis Ababa, Ethiopia, that the ministerial council of the Organization of African Unity, with thirty-eight member nations, unanimously recommended that African teams, as well as "other states and sports organizations that are inspired by the same racial equality," boycott Mexico City unless the ban on South Africa was reinstituted.[117] The pronouncement of the OAU was delivered the day before the Supreme Council of Sport in Africa was scheduled to meet in Brazzaville, Congo, to determine whether to pull out its member nations. Officials of the SCSA focused on pressuring Mexico to disregard the IOC decision and block the participation of the South African team. Both Dr. Eduardo Hay and Roberto Casellas, representatives of the Mexican organizing committee, were scheduled to appear before the executive bureau of the SCSA to discuss the possibility on the grounds that, when Mexico City was named as host, South Africa was still barred. However, Brundage made a direct appeal via telegram to Jean-Claude Ganga, secretary general of the SCSA, to avoid the "irrevocable decision" of a boycott until he received a committee letter clarifying the South African matter.[118]

In spite of Brundage's attempt to avert the mounting predicament, the campaign against South Africa continued to grow, particularly when the IOC representative for Tunisia, home of 1964 silver medalist Mohamed Gammoudi (10,000-meters), asserted that the readmittance was "regrettable," and Cuba made its first public criticism of the IOC in an editorial in *Granma*, the official Communist organ of the Cuban government. In addition, in the United States the spotlight on the activity of the OPHR expanded. The global boycott further ignited the campaign for equality by African American athletes to the chagrin of those who believed the Olympics were above racism. In addition, the situation undoubtedly spurred apprehension regarding the viability of a transnational, racialized political bloc. The prospect that an American racial minority, linked to an increasing global presence, could interrupt an event such as the Olympics was an emerging reality. "This new issue will force the black man to fight," allowed Harry Edwards. "They've virtually said the hell with us. Now we'll have to reply: Let whitey run his own Olympics."[119]

On February 26, Edwards's wish came closer to fruition when the executive committee of the SCSA, which embodied all but six of Africa's thirty-eight independent states, unanimously approved the boycott after two days of deliberation. Of the six nations not represented, three—Rwanda, Somalia, and Libya—requested affiliation. The executive committee represented ten membership nations—Congo, Nigeria, Mali, Togo, Gabon, Uganda, Malagasy Republic, Tunisia, Ghana, and

Guinea—although the last three countries sent telegrams of affirmation rather than attend the talks. The resolution meant that essentially the entire independent African continent would not compete in Mexico City, with the exception of Malawi, which did not field an Olympic team.

Other than, perhaps, Alan Paton's novel *Cry, the Beloved Country* (1948), the swelling boycott increased the visibility of South African politics in the American imagination with unprecedented ability. As George Katsiaficas argues, in the 1960s "only a few people in the industrialized countries supported the right of South African blacks to rule their country," and yet within a few decades, much of the globe supported an end to apartheid.[120] Heralded on the front page of the *New York Times*, accompanied by a map of Africa with SCSA members shaded and by a small article defining "what apartheid policy means," news of the boycott sparked a focused interest in Africa in geographical, political, and Olympic terms, impelling one journalist to remark, "Africa has become more important in track and field *and* in world affairs" and inspiring one reader of the *Times* to deplore an Olympics without athletes from the lands of Bikila, Keino, and Kiprigut.[121] Thus, the athletic arena began to fulfill its potential as "an indispensable mechanism for training the media spotlight on apartheid," in Rob Nixon's words.[122] In addition, the boycott created a spotlight on the relatively new independent African nations. Figures such as Keino, a veritable hero in Kenya, added a new layer to political national representation both within and outside their respective nations. As one scholar points out, when such athletes returned home from events such as the Olympics, "they received accolades previously reserved for the heads of new African states."[123] These athletes introduced much of the world to the new states, creating an increased level of popular understanding of Africa, as well as extending the notion of where in the world the "black" athlete existed. Last, the boycott introduced sport as an arena worthy of political discussion in the intellectual organs of the United States, as exemplified by an article in the *New Republic*, which emphatically demanded, "Keep South Africa Out!"[124]

Not only did the SCSA decision promise to more than double the number of boycotting African nations, it also furthered the prospect of the "Iron Curtain" joining the effort and crystallized the belief that the American OPHR boycott was, indeed, feasible. In short, the decision of the SCSA solidified realizations that the situation with the 1968 Olympics had reached crisis proportions, prompting one journalist to ask, "Where do we go from here?"[125] Although the spokesman for the Soviet team refused to answer questions regarding the boycott one way or another, he did reiterate disapproval of the settlement reached between South Africa and the IOC, stating, "We consider that the question of racial discrimination is not solved by including some colored sportsmen on the team."[126] Aside from the OPHR, whose force steadily expanded in light of the South African issue as well as the successful boycott of the NYAC, the position of the United States was more ambiguous than that of the Soviets. Although the IOC vote to readmit South Africa was concealed, most thought that all three American members—Brundage, Roby, and John Garland—had voted in favor of its readmission, particularly as they stood silent while others, such as Count Jean de Beaumont, chair of the French Olympic Committee, publicly announced his vote of opposition.[127] Harry Edwards outwardly accused the United States of supporting the move of reinstatement because of economic ties.[128]

While the silence of the Americans was increasingly difficult to justify, many felt that a boycott was not the proper approach. For example, despite his vote in the IOC, Beaumont publicly deplored the tactics of the boycotting African nations. A caustic editorial in the *New York Times* concurred, chiding Africa for refusing "to live by accepted rules of international conduct" and wondering if the behavior of African nations might someday "wreck the United Nations."[129] While Brundage remained firm that no one, individual or otherwise, would wreck the Olympics, proclaiming, "We are not involved in politics," Giulio Onesti, president of the Italian Olympic Committee, felt the situation dire enough to call for a special meeting of the IOC "to consider South Africa's participation, which is at the base of the present difficulties which threaten to grow even worse in the future." Despite Brundage's insistence that there was no chance such a meeting would take place, Pedro Ramírez Vázquez, head of the Mexico City Olympic Committee, made a statement that suggested his cohort was counting on such an assembly with hopes that South Africa would be barred once again.[130]

The prospect of the meeting taking place increased dramatically as tension regarding the issue of South Africa deepened, magnifying the degree to which politics existed within the realm of Olympic sport, despite Brundage's public protests to the contrary. There were overt and recent precedents of a political collision in the Olympics: Hitler in 1936; the East-West dispute of Germany, the Suez crisis, and the Soviet suppression of the Hungarian revolt in 1956; the withdrawal of North Korea from the Grenoble Games in 1968 because the IOC refused to recognize it as the Democratic People's Republic of Korea. Yet Brundage persisted with his more than familiar theme.[131] Indeed, beginning with his position on the Berlin Games in 1936, which many groups opposed for the well-founded fear that Hitler would use the global platform for his own propagandistic reasons, the IOC president had vigorously pursued separation of Olympic sport from politics, ensuring that an unswerving goal of the IOC was to represent the Olympics without dissent, with no regard for their political or historical context. Brundage held most dear his belief that sport transcends politics, apparently without regard to how deluded it made him seem to a broader audience. As enunciated in *Sports Illustrated*, Brundage held "that the Olympics have an almost supernal power for spreading goodwill and fellowship, that they are the only thing that has prevented one half of the world from giving the other half 24 hours to get out."[132] However, it was increasingly difficult for Brundage to maintain such a standing this time, particularly, as one journalist pointed out, in a world in which "Olympic medals matter almost as much to some countries as winning [a] vote in the United Nations."[133]

The reluctance of the Soviets to make a clear decision further exemplified this point. Although they had been ardently and publicly supportive of African independence, withdrawing from the Olympics was a severe step, again making clear just how closely connected a nation's global political stature was to Olympic medals. Thus, while one journalist acknowledged that "the Soviet Union may also feel compelled to follow Africa's lead, as it has on all other questions relating to South Africa," he understood why this would be a difficult step for the Soviet team to take, because "such displays of Soviet complicity previously involved no sacrifice. Leaving the Olympics would."[134]

However, before the month of February ended, it appeared that there was a chance that the Soviets, and others, would not have to make the difficult decision to boycott, as pressure to reconvene the IOC grew. While Brundage remained steadfastly against such a gathering, IOC rules mandated that one must be held if requested by one-third of the membership. In addition to Onesti's call, Major Raoul Mollet, head of the Belgian Olympic Committee, asked for a special meeting on the grounds that the readmission vote had been performed poorly, using only a mail ballot "on such an important question."[135] Most important, Mexican Olympic officials persisted in their appeal to Brundage, eventually sitting down in a closed meeting with him in the Versailles Suite at the LaSalle Hotel in Chicago to state their concerns regarding the proposed boycotts.[136] As their discussion took place, both sides of the debate continued, with South Africa setting up its first multiracial committee to choose the boxing squad for Mexico City and Saudi Arabia and India formally announcing an intention to boycott.[137]

The meeting with Mexico was the final push for the IOC to reconsider its decision. After two sessions totaling nine hours, Ramírez Vázquez, along with two Mexican members of the IOC, José de J. Clark Flores and Marte R. Gómez, successfully persuaded Brundage to call the nine-member Executive Committee, composed of representatives from France, Mexico, the Soviet Union, Pakistan, Great Britain, Lebanon, Italy, and Ireland, as well as Brundage, to put together a full emergency session of the IOC.[138] Rather than appease the situation, the announcement was greeted by its further intensification. For example, Harry Edwards, in a move seemingly designed to make any IOC decision almost irrelevant, announced a second competition to be staged in an African nation "in the true spirit of the Olympic movement."[139] Contemporaneously, Frank Braun reiterated South Africa's decision to send a team to Mexico, and Havana Radio announced that Cuba would not, resolutely adding its name to the list of boycotting nations.[140]

Despite Braun's confidence, it appeared that South Africans had lost some degree of faith of ever sending a national squad. One survey found that South African whites anticipated the IOC would reinstitute the ban, while Fred Thabede, administrator of non-white boxing, criticized the African boycott as a "slap ... in the face."[141] Such sentiment was not unfamiliar at this juncture, with many emphasizing that black South Africans wanted to go to Mexico City to compete. In addition to Brundage's appeal to the world to let such athletes fulfill their Olympic dreams, the *New York Times*, among others, also accentuated the point, stating that "South African black and 'colored' athletes told the I.O.C. they were eager to participate."[142] However, as Richard Lapchick submits, the "official" opinion of such athletes, or, apparently, their administrators, greatly differed from some critical personal perspectives. For example, at a press conference of the American Committee on Africa, former South African non-white soccer player Steve Mokone read parts of letters he had received from other non-white South African athletes, expressing what he contended were more genuine views than those deemed official. For example, one letter stated:

> The grapevine says everybody is against the idea [South African participation]. The trouble is that no one has the nerve—Robben Island is very near. Conditions are really bad here and they are getting worse.... We don't need the Olympics as much as they do because we have never been there. It hurts them more than being thrown out than it does us. None of us want to see them take South Africa back. But what can we do?... How do people outside feel about this?... We saw many of the countries are boycotting. We all hope Russia will join too. We have kind of lost hope the African states will stick together for the sake of their brothers here who can't do or say much.[143]

While the impending IOC meeting created a mixture of tenacity and discouragement in South Africa, it further galvanized the global boycott movement. Libya, Niger, and Tunisia announced their withdrawal from the Games, while Sweden and Lebanon publicly urged the IOC to reconsider its position on South Africa.[144] The Soviet Union made its most powerful statement against the IOC, accusing the administrative body of "sacrificing the unity" of the Olympics to "please certain imperialist quarters."[145] Two days later, it further erased any of the doubt remaining in terms of what action it would take if the IOC did not reconsider its stance, becoming what many saw as the first "major" global power to seriously threaten withdrawal. Calling for an emergency meeting of the IOC, a Soviet official stated that if such a meeting did not take place, the Soviets would "be compelled to come back to the question on participation of the Soviet athletes in the summer Olympic Games."[146]

The exigency of the situation was tagged by the *New York Times* as the "biggest crisis since the Games were staged in Hitler's Germany." An Associated Press poll revealed growing discord throughout the teams of the world, with few, such as Uruguay, Brazil, Turkey, Britain, Italy, West Germany, Greece, Denmark, Norway, Austria, and Israel, unequivocally stating that their squads would go to Mexico regardless of the South African issue. Other nations, such as Switzerland, had not yet met to discuss the problem, while still others, such as Bulgaria, France, Czechoslovakia, Hungary, Japan, and Belgium, urged the IOC to seriously reconsider South Africa's participation, waiting to make their own judgment. The statement by USOC executive director Lentz indicated that the United States remained firmly on the fence, far more ambiguous on the matter than the still somewhat hedging Soviets: "We are relying on the I.O.C. to come up with a logical solution. We are not going to make any move at this time because there is no need to do so. We support the Mexico City organizing committee."[147]

Notwithstanding the international turmoil, a survey of the numerous international sport federations by United Press International found that the actual Olympic program itself remained undiminished, curbing fears that the substantial boycott would hinder the competitions. While some, such as Donald Pain, secretary general of the International Amateur Athletic Federation (track and field), merely reiterated that the boycott did not affect their sport, others condemned the boycott, such as Rowing Federation president Thomas Keller: "The boycott is a most unqualified measure. It will not help anybody and ... is an affront to the Mexican organizers and all of Latin America." The president of soccer's organizing body found that his group had actually superseded the IOC, because it had already suspended South Africa from international play. Other organizing bodies were more concerned about which particular nations might follow the lead of the Africans. For example, Arthur Gander, head of the international gymnastics federation, was worried not that its three African members—Algeria, Morocco, and Tunisia— were pulling out but that the Eastern bloc nations would follow suit, greatly reducing the elite level of competition.[148]

However, the assurances that the international sporting federations would all be present and accounted for did little to encourage Mexican officials that the Games would go smoothly, prompting them to cable the IOC Executive Committee and ask that an emergency session take place by the first week of April in Dublin, Lausanne, Montreal, Chicago, or Mexico City. France's Beaumont staunchly supported Mexico's request, further stating that a meeting of just the Executive Committee was "not an acceptable solution"; only a meeting that allowed all members to debate the issue would suffice. In addition, Beaumont expressed anger that his initial design for South Africa, which had the athletes competing in Mexico City under the Olympic flag to give "to the world a coherent and united image of the Olympic movement," had not been seriously taken into account and perhaps would have alleviated this problem altogether for the IOC.[149]

However, it was doubtful that the mere removal of the national ornaments of South Africa would have sufficed. With forty-one nations publicly declaring intent to boycott, the situation had gone beyond mere symbolic solutions. While Brundage admitted that it was within his power, as president, to convene a full parley of the IOC, he still refused, despite the urging of five of the nine members of the Executive Committee—Constantin Andrianov of the Soviet Union, Gabriel Demayel of Lebanon, Giorgio De Stefani of Italy, France's Beaumont, and Mexico's Flores—to assemble the entire body, bypassing their own role.[150]

The Executive Committee, which was finally scheduled to meet on April 20 and 21, was actually powerless to make and enforce a decision regarding South Africa. Rather, its role was to decide whether to call a general meeting of the IOC. With a majority of executive members asking for the meeting anyway, it was clear what their decision would be. Brundage's insistence that formal procedure be followed gave the appearance that he hoped the issue would be dragged out beyond the deadline for entries, putting the debate into the dead letter office. As the Executive Committee waited to congregate officially, the situation continued to swell; Mongolia, Jamaica, Trinidad, North Korea, and Cambodia declared a boycott position, followed by the staunch assertion of New Zealand, with a historically tumultuous international reputation regarding competition against South Africa, that it would send a team.[151] In Italy, Onesti made a final attempt to influence the IOC, publishing a letter that described South African participation as "legally absurd," arguing that the *Olympic Charter* instructed National Olympic Committees to ensure that discrimination did not take place in their respective countries, thereby relinquishing South Africa's right as a competitor. In South Africa, preparations for the trip to Mexico increased when the Springboks received their official accreditation from the IOC, readied what Braun described as a "multiracial team," and made the announcement that a non-white athlete would carry the national flag and lead the team into the Opening Ceremony and a white athlete would carry the flag in the Closing Ceremony.[152] While the flag-bearer decision was obviously an attempt to exhibit the seriousness with which South Africa intended to abide by the IOC stipulations, it also provided further evidence that the country was unable to assemble an integrated team based solely on merit without definitive assignments of "non-white" and "white" team members.

Under the building pressure, Brundage seemed to bend his stead-fast position a bit when he emphasized in a statement to the press that the readmission of South Africa was not an IOC endorsement of its racist political structure, stressing that while the Grenoble vote allowed the team into the Mexico City Games, it was not a permanent invitation but rather one requiring further examination before the 1972 Games.[153] However, after Brundage's brief trip to Johannesburg, where he received South Africa's list of Olympic team athletes directly from Braun, who had earlier expressed fear that the IOC president would personally ask South Africa to withdraw, it became even clearer that Brundage was not preparing for any kind of temporary situation in terms of having the Springboks compete under the Olympic rings.[154]

The convening of the Executive Committee elevated the question of South Africa to its highest level, with most observers finding the entire future of the Olympic movement to be at stake pending the IOC's decision. For the first time, the IOC reconsidered a majority decision because of the power of the grassroots protest against it, revealing the wide disparity between the organization and its constituency. One of the clearest examples of the representative shift was the language invoked by the press to describe the Executive Committee. In its account of the first day of the meeting, after which no judgment was reached, the *New York Times* referred to the nine men as "elderly aristocrats," meeting under an "air of exclusivity" in a chateau while drinking mineral water and port out of a "crystal goblet" and eating "foie de veau" in the "lux-ury and comfort" of Lausanne, beside "old model Rolls Royces."[155]

The next day, who was involved mattered less than what they were saying. The committee ended its emergency session with the unanimous recommendation that another vote be taken regarding South Africa and the membership withdraw its invitation to the apartheid nation. It issued a cable to be sent to all members of the IOC, reading:

> In view of all the information on the international climate received by the Executive Board at this meeting, it is unanimously of the opinion that it would be most unwise for a South African team to participate

in the Games of the 19th Olympiad. Therefore, the Executive Board strongly recommends that you endorse this unanimous proposal to withdraw the invitation to these Games. This postal vote is submitted under rule No. 20. Please reply immediately by cable CIO Lausanne.[156]

Although the committee's statement was not a direct suspension of the Springboks, because it was not in their power to issue one, never had the IOC opposed an executive recommendation, and it was doubtful the body would in this instance. However, somewhat more important than the actual vote were the grounds on which it was made. Rather than cite, or even acknowledge, the odious policy of apartheid as a basis for South Africa's dismissal, a teary-eyed Brundage emphasized that the decision of the committee was a preventive one, rooted in the "international climate" and "present atmosphere of violence around the world," and indicated that the committee members were fearful for the safety of South African athletes in Mexico City.[157] Without question, the recent assassination of Martin Luther King Jr. had influenced the decision, particularly with the OPHR ever-present in the collective imagination of the IOC. For example, one member of the Executive Committee invoked Edwards directly: "We did not want that chap from California coming down to Mexico City and setting off riots. We had to think of the safety of the young people involved in the Games themselves, especially the white South Africans competing. Suppose one of them should be killed in a riot?"[158]

South Africa, not in the least grateful for this supposed compassion on the part of the IOC, issued a call for all members of the Executive Committee to resign.[159] Acquiescent that the executive vote likely meant the end of South Africa's Olympic dreams, a furious Frank Braun argued that the "shocking miscarriage of justice" marked the end of the IOC "as a reliable body" and maintained that the resolution set a dangerous precedent: "It will mean that every time characters like the Communists or black states start, the I.O.C. is going to do what they say."[160] An article in *Time* concurred, anticipating future trouble if, for example, Egypt were to try to force the expulsion of Israel with a little help from its friends.[161] The *New York Times* editorial page, too, agreed, chafing that a reinstatement of the suspension translated into "a victory that will encourage the use of similar tactics in other international bodies, including the United Nations" and might serve only to strengthen apartheid, sending a message that "there is no point in South African concessions since the black countries of Africa will be satisfied with nothing less than total abolition of apartheid."[162] Such fear that an example had been set quickly came to fruition; Republican congressman Jack McDonald impelled the IOC to avoid a double standard and suspend the Soviet Union because of its "brutal physical and spiritual persecution of the Jews."[163]

An editorial in the typically more conservative *Chicago Tribune* furthered a Cold War line of fire, concurring with Braun that "South Africa's conciliatory attitude failed to appease the Communists and the black African nations which are always seeking to make political capital out of racial separation in South Africa." Domestically, the *Tribune* found the IOC decision a great loss for the United States, yet another example in which Americans "have truckled to the prejudices of the anarchic countries of black Africa," further confirming that the United States did "not have the courage to stand up to the communist enemy in any arena." Thus, the *Tribune* lamented, the IOC vote did not salvage the Olympics but rather "probably wrecked them for good," irrevocably inserting politics into the formerly unscathed Olympic Games.[164]

It took little time for the necessary thirty-six votes to be obtained through the mail by the IOC to suspend South Africa from competition. Within two days of the conclusion of the Executive Committee session, forty of the seventy-one member nations elected to bar the Springboks.[165] For its part, South Africa announced it would accede to the vote in what Braun termed "a gentlemanly manner." He continued, "We feel, at this stage at least, no useful purpose would be served by standing on house tops and shouting our anger to the world and vilifying the I.O.C. as such. The Lausanne decision is illegal, immoral, and unconstitutional."[166] However, there can be little doubt that the ruling elevated South Africa's worst fears about mingling with the rest of the world, something it had been wary of for some time. For example, as Rob Nixon demonstrates, during this period, the National Party of South Africa outlawed television primarily "because it was thought to transmit all the 'contagions' of 60s counter-culture, the end point of which would be racial integration and national disintegration."[167]

Ironically, Braun and company had little to fear along such lines. In the midst of the furor, apartheid lost much of its presence and importance in the situation. As the emphasis on the potential for disruption and violence in Mexico took precedence over the crux of why most nations threatened to boycott, the discussion of racial inequality came to an abrupt halt. Perhaps most serendipitous of all was the effect it had on the OPHR. Elucidated by a distraught Arthur Daley, who wrote that the decision was one based on "pragmatism" to prevent "the great international show in the ancient Aztec capital" from collapsing, many found that the OPHR would now cease to exist because of the suspension vote just as quickly as it had gained leverage over the Grenoble resolution. As Daley explained,

> The temporary return of South Africa also lit a fire under the virtually dead and barely smoldering movement by Harry Edwards to have all American Negroes boycott the Olympics. They had been shooting at the wrong target because the Olympics has always been devoid of racism. But South Africa's readmission made too many blacks hesitate and wonder. Now they need wonder no longer.[168]

Daley's reaction, along with others, seemed almost improbable. With the executive decision, the IOC transformed from an ideologically sound organization to a body that had altered a policy for practical, logistical reasons that were in no way attached to any of the petitions of the protesting nations, whose objection was, namely, apartheid. Such a rejoinder made it difficult to map what the remaining options of the OPHR were. On the one hand, the suspension of South Africa indicated that the Olympics did, indeed, present a viable and feasible arena in which to base racial protest. On the other hand, the suspension fulfilled one of the six demands posed by the OPHR. Payton Jordan, head track coach of the U.S. Olympic squad, suggested the latter was true, arguing that the IOC resolution would compel OPHR members to compete. Tommie Smith seemed to concur, stating, "This is one of the things we were after. The chances of my going to Mexico City would have been much less had South Africa been allowed to participate." Lee Evans indicated similar feelings: "This certainly changes my mind some about participation."[169]

However, Harry Edwards saw the situation much differently: "The boycott is still on. One of our targets was South Africa, but the main target is still the racism right here.... If Rap Brown and I and the other brothers say don't go, the black athletes won't go."[170] The action at the New York Athletic Club annual indoor meet, in conjunction with the announcement reinstating South Africa, had solidified the growing belief that a black boycott of Mexico City was a possibility, provoking one columnist to write, "What seemed like a forlorn hope of such as Prof. Harry Edwards now seems more real fury and less froth." Yet the aftermath of the IOC vote once again to suspend the Springbok team left the situation notably unresolved.[171]

The standing of the OPHR was not the only one in question. While the global boycott produced the desired effect, apartheid lost its venom as the issue of the moment, although Edwards recognized the event as a crucial victory, not merely in terms of Olympic justice, but also in creating a multinational relationship focused on what was becoming an increasingly less ambiguous struggle for human rights: "For the first time Afro-Americans had united with other black nations to defeat forces in the world that were seeking to perpetuate racism and discrimination."[172] However, as could be expected, little, if any, change took place within the South African borders. As the various Springbok teams made plans to travel abroad to counterbalance the Olympic void, it was obvious that they would do so along segregated lines, with black African cyclists scheduled to compete in Ireland in July and a white track team scheduled to go to West Germany in June.[173]

Regardless of the internal operations of South Africa, the action necessary for the Supreme Council of Sport in Africa to take was clear. Within days of the final IOC vote, a statement from Jean-Claude Ganga sent notice to all member Olympic committees to repeal their threat of boycott: "Since the International Olympic Committee has annulled its decision authorizing the participation of South Africa in the games, we no longer have any reason to boycott the competition."[174] But as they did so, it became increasingly clear that their renewed participation was not so much a blow against South Africa as it was a triumph for independent Africa and its supporters. For example, *Newsweek* exalted the Lausanne decision as "a major diplomatic triumph for the black African states and the Soviet Union," indicating that they should be pleased about their power play working rather than about South Africa's global penalization for its political system.[175] Within a few weeks, with announcements from North Korea, Morocco, Sierra Leone, and Congo (Brazzaville) that they would send teams, the number of teams scheduled to appear in Mexico City totaled an unprecedented 110.[176]

The IOC unquestionably subjugated apartheid in deference to the "safety" of athletes in Mexico City Games. However, the matter concretely produced a new plane upon which battles of equality and human rights could take place. The essential role of 1968 was critical—politically, socially, culturally—in terms of what it produced for both the local team and the global athletic arena, making the eventual decision of the IOC almost compulsory. Recognizing this early on, Robert Lipsyte pointed out that "if 1968 pragmatism is to prevail, how can the I.O.C. afford to support racism, the world's greatest present problem?" And a *New York Times* reader deemed South Africa "one of the greatest offenders against human dignity in the world," scoffed at their promise to compete in the Olympics in "unequal togetherness," and subsequently chastised the IOC for its "profound insensitivity to the tenor of the times."[177] While the Grenoble decision, in the words of one scholar, "showed international sports administrators were still unable or unwilling to grasp the true criminality of apartheid,"[178] the amends made in Lausanne provided the first beacon that the focus was no longer to rest on sport *regardless* of politics as much as sport *in spite of* politics. It was

Brundage, himself, who ironically elucidated this most clearly, stating, "In an imperfect world, if participation in sport is to be stopped every time the laws of humanity are violated, there will never be any international contests."[179] Inside the U.S. State Department, there was much agreement. The chair of the Inter-Agency Committee on International Athletics, Captain Asbury "Red" Coward, in an expression of sympathy for the "colored athletes in South Africa who could have competed in the Olympic[s], and now can't," found that the decision to ban South Africa created grounds to revamp the IOC entirely, removing the national basis for entrance "so that innocent athletes are not penalized for political purposes."[180]

The extensive and eventually successful threats of boycott that greeted the Grenoble resolution made it impossible for apartheid to be rationalized in the international sporting arena, shedding more light on the odious political system than anything since the Sharpeville Massacre in 1960. With little room to turn back, in 1970 the IOC instituted a full-fledged ban on South Africa, joining virtually every other international federation in isolating the racially exclusive Springbok teams. On April 22, 1971, Vorster launched his inconsistent "Multi-national" sport plan, an elaborate program that entailed a new, supraracial identity for South Africa and emphasized that, while sport would remain racially segregated, the miscellaneous "nations" *within* South Africa would be allowed to compete against one another under the guise of international competition as long as non–South African athletes were involved. Despite Vorster's various explications, the new terminology surrounding "multinationalism" meant little, if any, real change toward national integration, prompting most of the world's sporting organizations to increasingly sever the Springbok colors from the teams allowed to play and crystallizing the degree to which sport in South Africa was, as specified by one scholar, "distinctively politicized."[181]

South Africa would not make another Olympic appearance until 1992. However, although absent from direct participation, it remained a factor in Olympic competition. For example, Tanzania led a boycott by African nations of the Montreal Olympics in 1976 because the IOC did not ban the participation of New Zealand, which had sponsored a South African rugby tour. While the IOC argued that rugby was not an Olympic sport and therefore not within its jurisdiction, the African nations stayed home, as did Guyana and Iraq. Thus, when the Springboks finally marched into the stadium at the Barcelona Olympics sixteen years later, it marked a symbolic new beginning for the world. As the broadcasters for NBC noted during the Opening Ceremony, "The world is in its most fluid state since the end of World War II. In some cases, it's as if pieces of a jigsaw puzzle have been tossed into the air, and some have yet to land." Broadcasters from around the world agreed: Canada's CTV noted that the athletes were "marching into a new era ... a dramatically altered new world"; an Ostankino 1 (Russia) sportscaster described the moment as the "first Olympics that hasn't been disturbed by political intrigues and disagreements"; and an SBC 12 (Singapore) commentator declared Barcelona "the first boycott-free Games" as well as the "first Cold-War-free Games."[182]

The media relished putting the vestiges of the Cold War to bed with the racist policies of apartheid once and for all. Like athletes from the former Soviet republics, the Springboks marched under the IOC flag. And it was decided beforehand that, should a South African win a gold medal, Beethoven's decidedly Western "Ode to Joy" would play rather than "Die Stem" or "Nkosi Sikelel' iAfrika." But while South Africa's admittance into the Barcelona Games seemed to occur with relative ease, in 1968, issues of political equality and citizenship were not finished. The (in)ability to separate politics from sport ensured that an enhanced interrogation was foreordained in the United States. It was time for the American "Negro" athlete to be forever shelved, never again taken out to "play."

CHAPTER 5

Tribulations and the Trials:
Black Consciousness and the
Collective Body

Boycott is a political word. I don't like the word boycott.

—Avery Brundage, *Sports Illustrated*, 1968

As Bob Beamon waited for the long jump to be called at the New York Athletic Club meet, his coach, Wayne Vandenburg, who had suspended team members for political activity in the past, reminded him that he did not have to participate, saying, "It's your decision, it's an *individual* decision."[1] Vandenburg failed to recognize how Beamon's decision to take part in the meet had consequences that extended beyond his own immediate future. Increasingly, the collective force generated by the OPHR ensured that such choices impacted everyone connected, voluntarily or not, to the designation "black athlete."

Both the NYAC and the South Africa controversies further secured the designation within the parameters of civil rights, making it recognizable to athletes and spectators alike. The barrage of responses the *New York Times* received to one of Arthur Daley's rampages against the NYAC boycott, for example, suggested that a widespread audience at least acknowledged the expanding circle of athletes who identified with an overtly racialized political cause. Some expressed outrage at Daley's "patronizing" and "disturbing" tone; took his "reactionary stand" to task; and praised the athletes for capitalizing on the "inherently democratic" nature of sport. Others supported Daley for his "cool, clear head"; found his to be "the only true appraisal of the ... situation"; concurred, "politics do not belong in sports"; and worried that the actions of the black athletes might "trigger violence resulting in death and injury to innocent persons."[2]

The *Times* brought both sides of the row together under the headline "Sports and Civil Rights," making clear that whichever side of the fence someone chose, the fence itself was established with unprecedented durability and visibility. Critical to this consolidation was the change in the identity itself, one that OPHR members clearly demonstrated at the final press conference before the NYAC meet, when they refused to respond to questions from any reporter who used the word *Negro* instead of *black*.[3] Unmistakably, the campaigns against both the NYAC and South Africa had contributed greatly to the creation of a black athlete collective that had emerged from an organic political interest in racial formation rather than from the scientific classification or conventional social stratification conventionally maintained in U.S. society. By the spring of 1968, an essential change had transpired as the focus moved from individuals often dismissed as militant (e.g., Muhammad Ali) to a collective political force. As columnist Robert Lipsyte pointed out to his readers in the aftermath of the NYAC protest, "Until last Friday night's boycott of the N.Y.A.C. meet ... the thinking had never been translated into effective group action."[4]

Yet despite this recognition that a sound connection between sport and civil rights had been collectively forged, for many athletes the question of Olympic participation remained largely unresolved, foundering upon a painstaking examination of the role of the individual within a political community. For some, the question was not so complicated. Basketball star Lew Alcindor, his teammates Mike Warren and Lucius Allen, and other cagers throughout the nation—Elvin Hayes, Neal Walk, Bob Lanier, Wesley Unseld, Larry Miller, and Don May—withdrew from the Olympic Trials early on, citing "academic concerns." While the *Pittsburgh Courier* had hoped that other players would not follow Alcindor's lead toward "the Edwardian philosophy," many did.[5] Alcindor's resolve to abstain from the Olympics gained negative attention after he attempted to explain his stance to Joe Garagiola on NBC's *Today* show. After telling Garagiola that a trip to Mexico might interfere with a timely graduation, he added that he also did not want to go because the United States was "not really my country." Garagiola suggested that he should move if he felt that way. Feeling misunderstood, Alcindor later clarified his stance: "What I was trying to get across was that until things are on an equitable basis this is not my country. We have been a racist nation with first-class citizens and my decision not to go to the Olympics is my way of getting the message across."[6]

While Alcindor demonstrated strong convictions, for others the question of Olympic participation remained unsettled. Central to the predicament, as *Los Angeles Sentinel* sportswriter Clint Wilson Jr. articulated, was the divisive identity endured by African Americans of being both athlete and citizen, meaning that "special problems arise when one happens to be Black in addition to being an athlete." While the sports public seemed willing to tolerate political movements for athlete unionization on the one hand, Wilson observed, "Black sportsmen have come under sharp criticism for making their desires and beliefs public." Thus, while Alcindor, for example, might be out of line as a basketball player, he was "perfectly within his rights as a conscientious young man." The issue of Olympic participation, then, remains particularly difficult. "Many Americans cry that the Olympics should not be a 'political' event and that Black athletes should choose another time and place for such activity," Wilson concluded. "But what are the alternatives of Lew Alcindor, Tommy [*sic*] Smith and others who share a deep personal obligation to less fortunate Black people?"[7]

In addition to the domestic inequities that motivated the possible boycott, the question of South Africa accentuated the various dilemmas individual athletes faced, and at the same time it ensured that the Olympics were, indeed, a viable domain for successful political action. This newfound reality already had a variety of implications for a diverse range of people. Some observers, for example, took the IOC to task for its verdict on South Africa, illustrated by one *New York Times* reader's lament that the organization had transformed itself into "a professional institution of international politics."[8] For the independent

African nations, the common adversary of South Africa enabled affirmative links that produced the likes of Games of the New Emerging
Forces and the Supreme Council of Sport in Africa. For the United
States, South Africa furthered its status as a powerful cultural reference
point on the basis of the potent parallels between its apartheid and the
American portents of racism, illustrated by the eventual media characterizations of the Bronx as "New York's Johannesburg" and Chicago
as "Joberg by the Lake."[9]

Of course, the covenant to oppose South Africa did not certify the
stability of a movement centered on political notions of blackness.
While Stuart Hall warns against using "black" as adequate in defining
"progressive politics,"[10] it remains tempting to do so, as demonstrated
by Harry Edwards's use of the label to determine who or what was a
positive force for the burgeoning OPHR. Clearly, political appellations
are everything but simple, because a unified collective is a near impossibility, in the black community and most anywhere else, as difference
lies within a movement as well as within that which it opposes. It is
useful, as such, to examine how the OPHR attempted to put together
what Robin D. G. Kelley has termed a "collectivist ethos" rather than,
as Kelley warns against, "begin with the presumption that a tight-knit,
harmonious black community has always existed ... across time and
space."[11] Such presuppositions have been a repeated tendency within
the writing of African American history as scholars continually have
looked to unearth the history of a cohesive black community battling
against inequality and repression.[12] In like fashion, many contemporary
voices often question why there is *no longer* a single black voice in America rather than ask the antecedent question: *Was there ever?*

Just as W. Montague Cobb contended from his laboratory in the
earlier half of the twentieth century that the American Negro could not
exist as a biological category, because too much *physical* variation existed
within the group, the *political* body of the black athlete has experienced
a comparable obstacle that has prevented the establishment of any kind
of singular, cohesive unit. While the racism that the black community
battles against makes political homogeneity appear inherently legitimate

and concrete, the OPHR could not exist outside its own historical moment, in which social prescriptions of nation—as well as the nationalist strategies that attempted to reconstruct them—operated in gendered terms, ones that most often privileged men.[13] The exclusion of women from the ranks of the OPHR most centrally demonstrates how the group was limited by its own political context, ensuring that the collective body was an overtly masculine one and therefore flawed in terms of both number and content. Just as Cobb, again, and his contemporaries focused entirely on African American men and defined *scientific* racial classifications wholly on masculine attributes when establishing the idea of the "Negro" athlete, the OPHR, in an age when Black Power often wore a male face, excluded women from its *political* collective voice in establishing the "black" athlete.

Despite their increasing athletic importance to the U.S. squad in 1968, African American women—Wyomia Tyus, Barbara Ferrell, Madeline Manning, Doris Brown, Margaret Bailes, Jarvis Scott, Mildrette Netter—were unilaterally counted out of the ranks of the OPHR. The perceived difficulty, of course, in dealing with the collision of race and gender in grassroots political struggle is the unofficial hierarchy of social priority that emerges. It can be, and has been, argued that the story of women in sport is one of cultural resistance, merely because their very existence in such a conventionally male sanctuary—a realm one scholar describes as "the last bastion of male domination"—denotes a crack in the foundation.[14] In terms of racial struggle, the presence of the female is further complicated. The assumed "right on" priority becomes that of placing the black male on equal footing with his white counterpart before dealing with the inequities faced by women—white and black.

Such a case arises within the OPHR, where the support of black women was presumed along racial lines, and yet the language of the radical black athlete was codified without gender (via "human rights") despite its almost entirely masculine construction. Such an imbalance stems largely from the way in which the broader black collective, as Paul Gilroy indicates, is often expressed via "the trope of the family," creating disproportionate gender relations within a movement, because family is traditionally a fundamentally patriarchal structure.[15] If the crisis of the collective is expressed as a crisis of the family, meaning community but operating as an actual nuclear kinship arrangement, the communal formation is transformed into one that revolves around the pursuit and maintenance of black masculinity. This consequence prioritizes the problem of creating collective action along gender lines, because it manufactures automatic consent for the black man to deal with his own house before finding out where his female counterpart is. This privileging of race over gender corresponds to what Derrick Bell has christened "the rules of racial standing."[16] In 1968, it was assumed that black female athletes did not mind their exclusion from the OPHR, because in the face of the USOC and the IOC, both elite and white institutions, it was understood that they would, quite literally, stand by their men.

Of course, sport did not become masculinized with the OPHR's exclusion of black women from its order, but rather an emphasis on masculinity was a dominant feature of the context in which the organization emerged. In 1968, as discussed earlier, female athletes were scrutinized at every level, exemplified by the IOC's mounting difficulty in defining the gendered categories it used as the very basis for entrance into competition. Within the OPHR, such confusions became magnified because of what was at stake and further complicated the attempt to bring a relatively disparate group of athletes together under a racialized tag. The organization, then, and those it tried to represent could not be compelled to act as one even by something as powerfully odious as racism. Even the dramatic rallying points, such as the assassination of Martin Luther King Jr., that permeated the landscape and further "closed ranks" could not manufacture a comprehensive harmony. While Tommie Smith and John Carlos, once in Mexico, would solidify the notion in the midst of intensifying political fragmentation through their individual actions, their actions were not the empowering symbol that Harry Edwards had originally envisioned and were not the challenge he wanted to pose to the existing power structures of the

Olympics and beyond. Rather than rally a concentrated identity around a symbolic move *at* the Olympics, Edwards maintained his objective to produce a solidified stance in absentia. However, as he and his cohort found, it can be all but impossible to make a diverse body into one and translate ideological political values into effective political action.

A unified political core, then, was critical—mandatory—to the way radical political change in the arena of sport was positioned. As a result, within the comparatively short period of time between the IOC decision on South Africa and the Opening Ceremony in Mexico, the OPHR faced its toughest and most direct question: to boycott or not. In order to find an answer, the organization had to determine whether some kind of internal hegemonic disposition could be mustered to subsist as a consequential social organization. In this process, it subsequently crystallized the political parameters of the black athlete. By securing this widely shared recognition of a political, racialized, and *unequivocally masculine* identity in the sports world, this identity became the fruit of the OPHR's labor, fully illustrating what Bell terms "racial realism," in which fulfillment is not achieved with tangible accomplishments but rather with the very struggle engaged in.[17] Accordingly, the struggle of the black athlete, which became newsworthy because of events such as the Olympic boycott announcement, the NYAC boycott, and the debate over South Africa's participation in the Olympics, became a story unto itself. As the media fostered the idea of an athlete that existed within ongoing struggles of civil and human rights, it became clear that the meanings found, perhaps, were the OPHR's most significant, if not only, success.

Featuring the OPHR: Media Attention and Retention

One telltale sign of this paradigmatic shift unfurled throughout the course of the NYAC boycott and the debate over South Africa. Throughout the century, observers of the sporting arena, whether physical anthropologists, IOC administrators, sports columnists, or fans, discussed the "American Negro" or the "Negro athlete." By the middle of 1968, such terminology had largely been put to rest, and when it was used, it generally indicated a certain refusal to acknowledge the political sweep of the times. Print media in particular played a growing role in creating the black athlete. A feature in *Life* magazine illuminated the paradigmatic shift. In a series of vignettes, the magazine made a valiant attempt to encompass the widespread movement of the black athlete throughout the United States. The center of the feature was the core of the OPHR—Tommie Smith, "the prototype superstar," and Harry Edwards, "the man with the microphone"—and the position of their organization within the blossoming political stands of athletes. But the magazine did not merely focus on the West Coast politics initiated by the likes of Smith and Edwards. *Life* further situated their cause, as well as the issue of South African participation in the Olympics, on a broader domestic plane by sending staff writers to seven college campuses throughout the nation. The magazine concluded that "at every one black athletes considered themselves in a second-class position compared to whites" and that "a majority of the black stars were prepared to forfeit the chance for Olympic fame to better conditions for their race."[18]

The report started at the origination of the movement, San Jose State, where the complaints of athletes such as Smith and Lee Evans focused on unfulfilled promises of housing, exclusion from fraternities, the grouping of black athletes together on road trips and in locker rooms, the emphasis on "gut" or "Mickey Mouse" classes in their academic schedule, and the overall discomfort at the hands of white classmates. As expressed by Smith to one reporter,

> You leave high school, you come to college and you're on your own, but you can't understand this new pressure. What is it? I'm here in college and I'm a great athlete. What's wrong with me? Just walk outside and you feel it.... Sit next to a girl with long blond hair and you feel her tense up and try to move over. Talk to a couple of white girls in the cafeteria and see what happens. People are reading papers, and first thing you see the papers drop and eyes peering over. For quite a while Lee and I were so naïve we thought, "Man, we're just great athletes, that's why they're staring at us."[19]

Despite the problems that college presented, it also provided the tools with which to fight such situations. The article portrayed Smith, in particular, as aware of why the collegiate athlete was primed to take up the fight. The combination of books and an environment conducive to intellectual stimulation and development, with the additional benefit of travel throughout the nation to competitions, was ideal in laying the foundation for political activity. In their travel, and the widespread exposure that went with it, both Smith and Evans slowly began to distinguish the different levels of existence that revolved around their athletic status. As stated by Evans, "I began to notice a lot of little discriminatory things that I had simply accepted. I finally began to realize what was being done to me, how I had been stereotyped as a black athlete."[20]

With this label came consequences of every extreme. Edwards, as leader of the group, often bore the brunt of the racist reaction, such as the day he returned to his home to find the remains of his two dogs splattered throughout his house and neighborhood.[21] But *Life* indicated that the ramifications of association made each individual athlete a target as well. "Tom and I receive tons of hate letters calling us black bastards," Evans continued. "One professor gave Tom a D in a course when he was doing real good work. I talked to one television cat, and two hours later I hear him saying that Tom and I are against each other and we're both against Professor Edwards.... And the average honky goes for that."[22]

Rather than emphasize that which attempted to pull the movement of the black athlete apart, the article focused on the pursuits that pulled it together—racial tolerance, decent living conditions, fair student evaluation, courageous identity—and endeavored to exhibit its broad roots throughout the nation, beyond just the San Jose epicenter. It unveiled, for example, the story of "loner" Calvin Murphy, the African American basketball star with the average of 38.5 points per game, at Niagara University in upstate New York; the thirteen black athletes at the University of Washington who created a list of provisions for its administration, including a call for football coach Jim

Owens to publicly endorse Muhammad Ali; the eight black football players at UCLA, "the Athens of Athletics," who charged, among other things, that summer school tuition "was given to whites but only loaned to Negroes," white athletes received more free tickets to games, and the team trainer rarely believed a black athlete to be severely injured; and the decision of three UCLA hoopsters (Alcindor, Warren, and Allen) to abstain from Mexico City for academic reasons, although each acknowledged that by refusing to enter the Olympic Trials they were virtually supporting the boycott.

Perhaps the most revealing piece of the story lay at Berkeley, where basketball player Bob Presley clashed with his coach on an issue *Life* deemed "minor": getting a haircut. In the midst of a campus where tension on the playing fields was high, particularly after thirty-eight black athletes organized to air their common grievances publicly, the question of Presley's "natural" hairstyle was seemingly insignificant but works well to demonstrate, as Kobena Mercer has argued, that "where race is a constitutive element of social structure and social division, hair remains powerfully charged with symbolic currency."[23] Working within what Mercer defines as "the cultural politics of 'race' and aesthetics," Presley's hair took on cultural and political designations and significations in the same manner as Edwards's own self-conscious cultivation of a black militant appearance under the tutelage of Louis Lomax. In the case of Presley, the political ramifications were pronounced, because, as Mercer resolves, "within racism's bipolar codification of human worth, black people's hair has been historically *devalued* as the most visible stigmata of blackness, second only to skin."[24]

Presley's "natural" worked within the framework of the proliferating notion that "Black is Beautiful." The idea of such a political aesthetic had been greatly enhanced by Muhammad Ali, whose continual reiteration of being "so pretty" helped foster the concept that a black man could, indeed, be beautiful. It was a stance allowed by coaches such as UCLA's John Wooden, who permitted athletes such as Lew Alcindor the opportunity to play with "pride" by wearing hair "natural," and one that historically, according to Mercer, "implied that hairstyles which avoid artifice and look natural ... are the more authentically black hairstyles and thus more ideologically right-on."[25] Such symbolic resonance worked in an ironic dialogue of identity embedded in a historical cross-cultural collision. In the previous decade, of course, another Presley, Elvis, fashioned his own rockabilly hair with Royal Crown Pomade to imitate the black "process" of straightening, which was designed to enable African American performers to *appear* more white. Elvis's use of this process created what Andrew Ross succinctly describes as "everyday, plagiaristic, commerce."[26] At UCLA, Bob Presley's hair became entrenched in the middle of the broader quest to attain a positive position on the marking of "black athlete."

By itself, the debate was minor, as deemed by *Life*, and with little overall relevance. But the evolving political and ideological revolution in sport ensured that its meaning was understood, especially when the media spotlight widened on the OPHR's efforts and their subsequent effects. Reporters always mentioned, for example, if a black athlete had facial hair—a goatee. In an age where most athletes were not allowed to sport either a beard or a mustache, the press made much of anyone who did, such as Harry Edwards and John Carlos. Thus, while on the one hand, athletes of "America's national pastime," baseball, kept their faces clean shaven, members of the OPHR were not held to the same standard, indicating that they existed outside the normative cultural status allotted to athletes. Further, this emphasis on particularized aspects of style amplified the false notion that the wave of black athletic militancy was limited to an unruly few, despite the intention of the OPHR to mobilize black athletes in great number.

In particular, much of the media's focus remained on Edwards, largely because his was the (bearded) face most commonly associated with the various facets of the OPHR. In a biographical profile, the *New York Times Magazine* presented him in perhaps the most complete light to get at the broader movement he had helped instigate. Like *Life*, the feature located Edwards in his collegiate setting at the Center for Interdisciplinary Studies, an office adorned with various components of the OPHR: a poster with the caption "Rather Than Run and Jump for Medals / We Are Standing Up for Humanity / Won't You Join Us?" and a banner that read "Traitor (Negro) of the Week" with a photo of Jesse Owens beneath. The *Times* writer understood the importance of the parenthetical *Negro*, which signified "the gut- and gutter-tough language of Black Power, a language in which 'Negro' is a word of contempt, no better than or different from 'nigger.'"[27]

The upshot of the *Times*'s placement of Edwards firmly within a militant context was twofold. While it allowed ample understanding of where the OPHR was coming from, naming as his heroes H. Rap Brown, Stokely Carmichael, and "St. Malcolm," it also displayed how, from a journalistic standpoint, Edwards made good copy. The story described him as a "colorful phrasemaker," dubbing the president "Lynchin' Baines Johnson" and depicting in great detail what needed to occur in the United States for human rights to be achieved.

> For openers, the Federal Government, the honkies, the pigs in blue must go down South and take those crackers out of bed, the crackers who blew up those four little girls in that Birmingham church, those crackers who murdered Medgar Evers and killed the three civil-rights workers—they must pull them out of bed and kill them with axes in the middle of the street. Chop them up with *dull* axes. Slowly. At high noon. With everybody watching on television. Just as a gesture of good faith.[28]

In the midst of the retelling of such rhetoric, the bottom line of Edwards's message was also captured. Above all, the article portrayed him as a good teacher, although it pointed out how he did not dress "like an instructor," quoting the head of the San Jose State sociology department, Dr. Harold Hodges: "From the start, Harry showed a unique ability to empathize with students, to identify readily with them, black and white."[29] Edwards's three classes boasted a combined enrollment of eight hundred students, many of whom were white despite his adamant and vocal declarations that he did not want to teach "crackers." But such apparent contradiction, according to the *Times*, provided the key. Edwards avowed that blacks "cannot and must not" work alongside whites, but his office was populated by both. He continuously described the police as "pigs in blue," yet the *Times* pointed out that at the NYAC boycott he worked with them to avert a potentially violent situation outside Madison Square Garden. The upshot, the *Times* concluded, was to understand that Edwards existed as "moderated *and* militant" and that he conscientiously occupied both of these roles, appreciating how the public perceived both characterizations.[30] While understanding that the OPHR existed within "the nation's racial struggle," the *Times* also saw his quest in global, postcolonial terms. According to Edwards, "The crackers are losing all over. In Vietnam, Thailand, Laos, Bolivia, all over. The blue-eyed devil is in trouble. The third-world power—black, red, yellow, brown—is taking the white man apart in chunks. We must get the cracker off our backs, by Olympic boycott, by out-and-out revolution, by whatever means."[31]

While some journalists reveled in Edwards's grandstanding oratory abilities, some members of the African American press countered his dramatic vocalizations by putting U.S. track coach Stan Wright on a pedestal. While the OPHR continually dismissed Wright as an "Uncle Tom," others, such as columnist Bill Nunn Jr. of the *Pittsburgh Courier*, championed him as a "black man who ... has fought and survived." Nunn found Wright's refusal to capitalize on the Olympic spotlight for political gain to be a thoughtful stance and his words about Edwards, in particular, to be diplomatic and free of "ill feelings."[32] Yet despite this emphasis on his peaceful perspective, such writers were careful not to make Wright out to be an apolitical entity, as illustrated when the black press highlighted his role in smoothing the relationship between members of his team and Avery Brundage. Wright led the charge, for example, for the team to voice its disapproval of comments Brundage made regarding the possibility of Olympic protests. "I heard him make the remark that if the black athletes demonstrated in Mexico City, we'd be rushed right back home," Wright confirmed. "A lot of the fellows here thought the remark was derogatory, intimidating and completely out of line." Yet Wright denied that he demanded Brundage's resignation. "All we did was send Brundage a letter protesting his remark," Wright corrected. "It wasn't a petition for his resignation.... Somebody sure took that out of context and made something out of nothing."[33]

The celebration of Wright often blurred the bigger picture that articles about Edwards seemed to encompass. The *New York Times Magazine* profile of Edwards, for example, featured a succinct assessment of the status of the black athlete, both collegiate and professional, in American society. Acknowledging that the numbers indicated black success and even dominance in many major sports, the article also recognized that discrimination ran rampant. The bottom line was most clearly explored in regard to the matter of housing. While on the road, for example, the Los Angeles Lakers were the only professional team to have integrated roommates. Perhaps more striking, the most "successful" of the star athletes were unable to find housing on a more permanent basis, with the same collegiate examples that had been cited by *Life* accompanied by shocking examples within the elite professional ranks. The *Times* outlined how Willie Mays was unable to purchase the house he wanted in San Francisco; St. Louis pitching standout Bob Gibson was unable to obtain a bank loan to build in Omaha, despite his salary of fifty thousand dollars a year; when moving into his California home, St. Louis outfielder Curt Flood was greeted by an armed white landlord; despite a signing bonus of three hundred thousand dollars, football star Mike Garrett was powerless to rent an apartment in a white Kansas City community; and Tommie Smith, accompanied by his pregnant wife and numerous world records, was turned down by thirteen landlords in San Jose.[34]

Despite the access to financial gain that such athletes achieved, they still endured what Henry Louis Taylor Jr. brands as "occupational exclusion," in which a job is not solely about monetary reward but also about the quality of life that such reward can purchase.[35] With such explicit depictions of racism generated toward the stars of America, it became clear within the pages of the *Times* that it was around such indignities the boycott was posed, impelling the belief of Edwards that the cause *was* justification enough for collective mobilization:

I don't think any black athlete will go the Olympics. If they do go, I don't think they'll come back. I am not threatening. I am not encouraging violence. I am assessing reality. I know the demeanor of the black people. They see a black man back from the Olympics, and they'll say, "Look at the devil, with his medal hanging around his neck." Some of them are going to have accidents. You can't live with the crackers and come back to Harlem. The athlete who goes will face ostracism and harassment. People are fed up with those shufflin' niggers. Them days are long gone. The black athlete who goes will be a traitor to his race, and will be treated as such.[36]

However, in terms of producing some kind of tangible effect, the movement mobilized by the OPHR did not create more equal housing for these athletes or make any facet of day-to-day existence easier on any level. What the move to boycott did create was an increased awareness of the politics of race within sport. For example, in the midst of the South African controversy, the *Los Angeles Times* ran a six-part series by Charles Maher entitled "The Negro Athlete in America." Despite its use of an increasingly obsolescent term, *Negro*, the series indicated a profound interest in probing more deeply into the topic. The questions posed in the sequence were fairly mundane, with little focus on the proliferating political movements surrounding the subject matter. Rather, its emphasis lay within a more traditional, guarded, and familiar line of questions that often implicitly juxtaposed the successes of the Negro athlete with those of the white.

The premise of the series was immediately apparent in the first installment, which offered little more than a quantitative breakdown of "the Negro" in professional sport and hinted that the presence was more often than not one of dominance, leaving the question of why for the remainder of the series to tackle. Of particular interest was Maher's reason behind excluding "Latin American" athletes from the analysis; he claimed that it was "impossible to tell whether a Latin is predominantly Negroid." With his incorporation of a simple binary of analysis, reminiscent of earlier laboratory studies dealing with similar subject matter, the manifesto to answer why "the Negro has excelled in many sports … in numbers greatly disproportionate to his share of the general population" became a relatively futile task that produced little innovation on previous writings.[37]

For example, the series continued with the relatively age-old question of whether "the Negro's success" could be attributed to physical superiority. The response to this query was presented in the words of others, with virtually the entire article composed of a succession of quotations from numerous scientists, academics, and sports figures, including Vince Lombardi. The trajectory proceeded from a familiar biological position, although it did, like the work of Eleanor Metheny, question whether the assumed physical gifts could even be connected to athletic prowess. While Maher devoted much space to the role of environment, or nurture, in creating this alleged physical superiority, the authoritative tone given the biological argument dominated, particularly when the reader was alerted that *further* "scientific comment" was right around the corner in the third installment, where the question of racialized physical superiority would be put entirely within a framework of scientific debate.

This third installment began somewhat ironically, with a quotation from W. Montague Cobb asserting that physicality was in no way related to "the present dominance of Negro athletes in national competition." Maher built on this assessment by emphatically stating that, indeed, there did not exist conclusive scientific evidence in terms of racialized athletic ability. But because of the amount of space granted to this "scientific debate" and the simple acknowledgment that there *was* an existing scientific discussion, a lack of evidence did not mean that racialized athletic ability was not a possibility, particularly because much of the article was devoted to those who believed in it. Like the preceding installments, this one displayed little original research—eight entire paragraphs were direct quotations from Cobb—but the assemblage of information demonstrated that, regardless of conclusions, race and physical ability were, indeed, questions for science. Such inference was furthered with the point upon which the article ended: If innate physicality cannot be accounted for, which Maher acknowledged, "why no Negro quarterbacks?"[38]

The fourth and fifth parts of the series attempted, indirectly, to supply the absent proof by outlining two of the classic examples used by those who believe in innate physical and intellectual differences in athletes along racial lines: the lack of African Americans who occupy the positions of quarterback in football and pitcher in baseball. While again Maher assembled extensive statements regarding the issue, and while environment, training, coaching biases, and so on were included, much credence was lent to scientific reasoning. Thus, their quickness, combined with their lack of stamina and, of course, their inherent ability to relax, explained why so few African Americans played at the so-called thinking positions. Again the point was made that "it has not been scientifically established that there are innate differences between whites and blacks," but, more important, it also was emphasized that "there is also no absolute proof that such differences do NOT exist."[39]

In the conclusion of the series, Maher's focus shifted dramatically to be more compatible with the ideas of Harry Edwards and the problems of Tommie Smith and Lee Evans: the social relationships among athletes. He observed, "On the field, Negro and white athletes learned long ago to function almost as parts of a single body," while "off the field ... the parts fit together less snugly." Further, he asked why there was little mixing among teammates along racial lines, noticing that the disparities in lucrative endorsements among athletes paralleled the relationships among roommates and dining companions.[40] Maher argued that players were *informally* segregated *by choice*, rather than examining a more institutional explanation for the separate spheres of white and black, and he concluded such social observations with his first discussion of the black athlete as a political entity rather than merely a physical anomaly. Incorporating the opinions of many sports figures, Maher used the last few paragraphs of the series to show that the central question for many of the athletes themselves was a decision of what to do with their so-called success. At one end of the spectrum was Willie Mays: "I don't picket in the streets of Birmingham. I'm not mad at the people who do. Maybe they shouldn't be mad at the people who don't." At the other end was Edwards, who *was* mad at the people who don't, and football great Jim Brown, who clearly delineated the complexities that made the situation of the black athlete so difficult to construct and so difficult to present as common experience:

> A Texan named Y. A. Tittle ... goes on the Ed Sullivan Show and calls you the best football player he has seen in his time.... And the first man to relay this great compliment to you is a TV viewer named Lyndon Johnson, who has invited you to the White House. Well, don't go popping the buttons off your vest, big shot, because a few miles away in Virginia, white folks are closing public schools lest their kids have to sit in the same room with your kind.[41]

Trials and Error: When Losers Can't Lose and Winners Can't Win

Like the *Los Angeles Times*, *Ebony* magazine did not unequivocally embrace the political transformations emerging around the shift from *Negro* to *black*, but the notoriously antiquated publication did pose the most direct query: "Should Negroes Boycott the Olympics?" On the basis of its own poll, the magazine determined that African American athletes were nowhere near consensus in terms of a boycott, with a mere 1 percent behind the idea, 28 percent undecided, and "a massive 71 percent" categorically against it. Significant was the basic reason the magazine offered for such outright rejection: "Some don't like what they think is an infringement of their right to *individual* rather than *group* thinking." Along a similar vein, *Ebony* further argued that in addition to economic concerns and the tantalizing prestige of Olympic participation, many athletes were disgruntled that "they were not even consulted before the boycott proposal was made," an indirect indictment of the role the OPHR had assumed as representative. At the center, despite a general objection to the mission of the OPHR, was disdain for the authoritative position taken by Edwards, who *Ebony*, despite acknowledging his collegiate career, described as "an Ivory Tower–type who knows nothing about the world of sports and the thrill of victory and public adulation."[42]

On the other side of the coin, the magazine found others who adamantly agreed with Edwards, despite the fact that the percentages indicated they did not exist in any great number. Along with the two hundred delegates at the Black Youth Conference, where the idea was first officially announced, the magazine acknowledged just how visible the movement had become, with speeches and pamphlets commanding "Where do you stand?" and the support of figures such as Martin Luther King Jr. and Floyd McKissick, as well as Ron Karenga, leader of the Los Angeles black nationalist group US. Outlining the six demands of the OPHR, the magazine posed yet another critical question: "Are these wild demands, mere buckshot aimed at targets in outer space?" Turning to Arthur Lentz, it found the answer was an unequivocal yes, particularly because he contended that few of the demands were within the power of the USOC to grant, such as the restoration of Ali's title or the expulsion of Brundage as president of the IOC.

Yet the magazine did not deny that, if successful, the boycott could have sweeping effects, particularly because, in the six Olympic Games since World War II, African Americans were responsible for 34 percent of American track and field gold medals and 18 percent of the nation's total gold in all sports. In terms of 1968, *Ebony* supported such numbers with the predictions of Dick Drake, managing editor of *Track and Field News*, who is quoted as saying, "The U.S. should garner 33 medals if this country sent its best team.... Negro athletes would account for 18 medals—or 55 percent.... The U.S. would lose a net of 15 should the Negroes boycott, for Caucasian athletes could make up for only three of the 18."[43]

In agreement with Drake's calculations was USOC public relations officer Bob Paul, who focused more of his own concern on the tactics of the OPHR than on the actual effect such a boycott might have. Along with Stan Wright, Paul purported to *Ebony* that threatening mail had been sent to at least four members of the renowned Tennessee

Tigerbelles, arguably the epicenter for American women on the track. While Tennessee coach Ed Temple, who trained the likes of Wilma Rudolph and Edith McGuire, as well as 1968 star Wyomia Tyus, denied that any such letters existed, and Edwards claimed that he did not "believe in castigating people who don't go along with us," Wright claimed to have seen the letters and maintained that he, too, had received threats calling him "a dirty s.o.b." and an "Uncle Tom."[44] Perhaps most disturbing about Paul's and Wright's allegations was that until needed to make a point about the dangerous side of the boycott, African American women had been treated as virtually a nonfactor in terms of the OPHR, by both boycott supporters and the media, reflecting both the masculinist tendencies of black radical actions and the subordinate position of women within athletics.

The magazine found that others disagreed with the premise of the boycott rather than with the actual tactics being taken. Temple worried that such an effort would not subdue racist attitudes but rather soothe them, striking from the Olympic arena a despised black presence. Others, such as sports columnist Red Smith, took up the familiar song that the Olympics were "the Negro's best friend," making the Games the wrong target for such protest. Yet *Ebony* also realized that as a "best friend," the Olympics tended on the side of fair weather, with few black stars able to capitalize on their gold medal success in the days following their athletic careers.

Nonetheless, *Ebony* posited, the pull of Olympic gold was greater than any kind of a symbolic statement regarding racial equality. The magazine claimed that the identity of "athlete" was one great enough to supersede that of "black athlete"; as enunciated by sprinter Willie White in preparation for her third Olympic appearance, "I can't see passing up the Olympics.... I am an athlete."[45] The magazine found that many others concurred. Hurdler Larry Edwards's objection to the boycott was based on his perception that "the basic element of the Olympics is individualism." John Thomas, who was the center of so much contention at the New York Athletic Club meet, agreed, claiming,

"In the Olympics you're representing yourself. If you happen to be a Negro, you're also representing your race." And hurdler Larry Livers accused the OPHR of "overlooking the individual rights of athletes to decide." Still others understood the broader consequence of the black athlete in the red, white, and blue uniform but had difficulty supporting Edwards; high jumper David O. Smith maintained that while he agreed with much of the mission of the OPHR, he was not able to "go along with [Edwards] dictating the movements of Negro athletes." In the minority as represented in the poll were those who understood the necessity of collective action, articulated most succinctly by Lee Evans: "We know what we're doing.... There is need for anything that brings about unity among Black people and points up the fact that successful Blacks maintain their ties with the Black community."[46]

Despite presenting quantitative evidence of the opposition to the boycott, the *Ebony* feature ended on a note of power and pride, giving Edwards a strong last stand with a declaration that "black masculinity is no longer for sale." Further, it indicated an understanding that for the boycott to work—and it presented numerous reasons to hope that it would—the numbers produced in the poll would have to shift dramatically, and athletes would have to accept their celebrity role as a means with which to speak for others who did not have the same leverage. Political scientist Dr. Charles Hamilton, the figure who, along with Stokely Carmichael, produced a published articulation of Black Power, reiterated such a rationale definitively:

> The boycott is very necessary. It gives us another way of confronting the system of racism in this country. I'm not concerned with nit-picking about its effectiveness, or whether it is the best tactic, or whether it should be done at 5 or 6 o'clock this afternoon. What Black Power people are saying is that those of us who have made it, star athletes or whatever, have a responsibility to bring all our people along with us. The boycott expresses our concern for the plight of most of our people in this country. And it gives the problem international visibility.[47]

Hamilton's position coincided with Edwards's to the letter. At Martin Luther King's suggestion, the OPHR sent the list of its demands, as well as an informational booklet, to athletes throughout the United States to garner support for the boycott effort. In the booklet, Edwards defined the new role of the black athlete as a spokesperson for the masses, writing, "Those of us who have managed to make some inroads into the system have the responsibility of searching for new alternatives to violence for the effective expression of the plight of the masses of black people."[48] Whether this message was ever received was doubtful. While Edwards contended that it was a mass mailing, he worried that many, or perhaps most, athletes never saw it, because coaches screened their mail. But the message remained firm: with the boycott the OPHR hoped to create a position for black athletes as powerful representatives for their social community. Unlike more political figures, such as King, the black athlete held an unusual role because of the importance of sport in American society. The achievements of athletes such as Alcindor or, to a lesser degree, Smith were known by a large community, one that at times seemed to transcend racial classification and, as explored previously, was often displayed as a model for an integrated society. Thus, the achievements of Alcindor and Smith did not exist merely within a realm of privilege or a realm of "blackness" but also as a legitimate element of national culture. With this, according to the OPHR, it became obligatory for the black athlete to fulfill the role of responsibility to the black community.

In the eyes of Edwards, as outlined in the informational booklet, there were dire consequences for not fulfilling such a role. These consequences surpassed the individual athlete's position in society and extended into the larger collective of American society because of the façade of racial harmony created through the black athlete. This façade made collective action imperative:

> We must no longer allow this country to *use* black individuals of whatever level to rationalize its treatment of the black masses ... to *use* a few "Negroes" to point out to the world how much progress she has made in

solving her racial problems when the oppression of Afro-Americans in this country is greater than it ever was.... We must no longer allow the Sports World to pat itself on the back as a citadel of racial justice when the racial injustices of the sports industry are infamously legendary.... any black person who allows himself to be used in the above manner is not only a chump—because he allows himself to be used against his own interest—but he is a traitor to his race. He is secondly, and most importantly, a traitor to his country because he allows racist whites the luxury of resting assured that those black people in the ghettos are there because that is where they belong or want to be.[49]

Thus, African American athletes had a choice of action or inaction. Vice President Hubert Humphrey publicly stated that there was not "any better way to forward the cause of equal opportunity in America than having the champions speak up," beseeching black athletes to do the patriotic and harmonious thing, but Edwards saw patriotism defined in a much different light.[50] By joining the boycott, black athletes would not defame the United States but rather engage in a patriotic gesture that would help the nation fulfill its own promise and obligation to its people, and they would become, in Edwards's words, "heroes of humanity," not merely of sports.[51] For such a move to be effective, it had to occur with a great number of individuals behind it, something that was not ensured.

As the Olympic Trials approached, the question of whether to support the boycott quickly came to a head. Once assigned a space on the U.S. team, an athlete was in a position to declare officially whether he or she was going to go. Building on the momentum generated by the South African question, the OPHR called for demonstrations at the West Coast Relays, the California Relays, and, of course, the Trials, which were scheduled to take place in Los Angeles. The turnout of demonstrators at the West Coast Relays was so great that the meet was dubbed Black Saturday. At this point, the OPHR realized that the boycott project had to be finalized and scheduled a vote to take place at the Trials; a two-thirds majority would be needed to declare the boycott official.

Unfortunately, determining the whereabouts of the Olympic Trials was no easy task in 1968. Initially scheduled to take place at the Los Angeles Coliseum, the USOC, in what some considered a preemptive political gesture, somewhat unexpectedly announced that the Los Angeles meet would serve only as rehearsal; the so-called official Trials would take place in early fall at South Lake Tahoe, California, where each of the top six finishers in the Los Angeles events would compete for spots on the national roster, creating what *Sports Illustrated* writer John Underwood sarcastically christened "the non-trial trials" and prompting him to describe the meet as one in which "losers did not necessarily lose and not even winners definitely won."[52] The USOC contended that the move to Tahoe was a necessary one to prepare the team for the altitude conditions it would face in Mexico City. Indeed, Tahoe levied great effort into the task at hand, spending a quarter million dollars to build a track that would rest at 7,377 feet, 28 feet higher than the track at the Olympic Stadium.[53]

Edwards saw the move in a different light, alleging that it was a selection process that gave the USOC broader options if the black boycott took place, creating a larger list of possible competitors at Los Angeles to replace any black athletes who made the squad in Tahoe and then opted to boycott Mexico. While the higher altitude seemed to provide adequate justification, the timing supported other reasons for the move; as Arthur Ashe pointed out, "Surely ... the USOC could plan better than that."[54] There were definite signs indicating that Edwards and Ashe had the right idea. Before the "non-trial trials" began, the USOC changed some rules in what appeared to be an effort to avert the political potential of the event. In addition to the decision that the results of Los Angeles would not be definitive for choosing the national team, on the second day of the meet the USOC removed all of the award daises from the infield and canceled the victory ceremonies and the march from the stadium, thwarting any windows for public, militant displays.

There are considerable historical analogies to the reaction of the USOC. As Robin D. G. Kelley points out in a discussion of the working-class political community, "When white ruling groups had reason to suspect dissident activities among African Americans, authorities tried to monitor and sometimes shut down black social spaces...."[55] Such action by the USOC was likely a direct response to Edwards's meeting with over forty athletes at the training facility in Pomona on the eve of the Los Angeles Trials, where the boycott was rumored to have been defeated in a vote. Despite waning interest in the boycott, many athletes remained committed to engaging in some form of protest, which kept the USOC on alert throughout the duration of the meet. The influence of black power remained highly visible at the Coliseum: spectators held placards reading "Why Run in Mexico and Crawl at Home?"; Edwards sat with Bill Russell in the stands; and Smith, his wife, Denise, and Carlos engaged in some sort of skirmish at the officials' table with Stan Wright and Hilmer Lodge, chairman of the United States Olympic track and field committee. The confrontation, which touched on lane assignments and the absence of Carlos from the 100-meters roster, created the first opportunity for OPHR supporters to become vocal, particularly, as Underwood noted, "when cameras and microphones were at hand" and occasioned Denise Smith to instruct Wright that he should attempt to be black first and American second.[56]

While such visible political pressure and tension intensified, many athletes remained on the fence about the movement at large. Long jumper Ralph Boston, despite being dubbed by one writer "the most prominent anti-boycott man among the Negro athletes," exemplified uncertainty when he told a reporter that although he did not want to boycott, he would support the majority, providing that he was not forced: "This is supposed to be a matter of human rights, isn't it? And as a human, I should have the right to do what I want and say what I think is right for me."[57] The indecision expressed by the 1960 Olympic long jump champion ran rampant throughout the ranks of athletes. The New York Times pointed out that athletes, regardless of how each personally felt about the prospect of boycotting, all dreaded "social and other reprisals from the Negro community should they defy a boycott."[58]

Such reprisal was rumored to have taken the overt coercion displayed before the New York Athletic Club meet to new heights. Wright was accompanied by two bodyguards throughout the course of the meet at the Coliseum; other athletes claimed to have been threatened. Underwood observed that the training facility in Pomona was not of the usual "carefree" atmosphere, and he placed much of the responsibility for this on the leader of the OPHR:

> … the atmosphere was always heavy. There was the abiding and exotic and massive presence of Harry Edwards, stalking around in a camouflage-colored jacket over a brown T-shirt, pants that were tight and short, a black beret, beads and sunglasses; Edwards' meetings with knots of black athletes were carried on under the eucalyptus trees out in plain view. The talk that came out of these meetings, however, was not so much that they would boycott but what they would do *after* they got to Mexico City—like sitting down during the national anthem and sewing their own emblems on team uniforms and generally raising hell to "embarrass The Man."[59]

Thus, despite the turning of the tide from a boycott movement to a protest movement, one that perhaps better understood the difference between revolution and reform, the OPHR remained the epicenter for a radicalized black militant identity in sport. While it became increasingly apparent, albeit still unofficial, that the necessary two-thirds majority to boycott did not exist, the grounds for creating the movement in the first place still existed; the identity endured as the image of the black athlete as a political entity continued to grow. This growth was illustrated by investigative pieces written by two of the most respected sports journalists in the United States: Pete Axthelm and Jack Olsen. Through these two writers and the expositions they produced, the black athlete continued to have resonance and relevance when the boycott movement significantly subsided. Further, these writers built substantially on the work that Edwards and the OPHR had instigated on college campuses and then moved beyond it. In doing so, they acknowledged the collective nature of the movement rather than the key individuals involved and how necessary it was for them—the sports press—to deal with "real-news" issues.

As sports editor for *Newsweek*, Axthelm produced a cover story exemplified by its photo of Tommie Smith, in full stride with black shades covering his eyes, next to the words "THE ANGRY BLACK ATHLETE." The story outlined both the athletic and political intensity that athletes such as Smith displayed at the Los Angeles Coliseum, where, when a radio broadcaster said to Smith, "Tommie, you ran with real power out there ...," Smith cut him off with "Call it *black* power" and ended the interview. In the article, Axthelm captured the breadth of Smith's position, noting that the movement encompassed thirty-five college campuses with demands for "black coaches, black trainers, black cheerleaders—and new black dignity," creating what he succinctly observed to be athletic prowess as "a means toward an ideological end."[60]

Axthelm's piece was perhaps the fullest articulation of how a range of athletes was connected in some way to the OPHR. Within his comprehension existed the belief that black success in sport was social rather than scientific and that the black athlete had not "more muscles" but "fewer opportunities." Axthelm found that, rather than fall into the comfort zone of "older Negro sports figures,... the black athlete is an angry *young* man suddenly aware of years of exploitation and discrimination ... not attuned to the cautious pronouncements of those who tell him that 'sports have done so much for you.'"[61] Axthelm also outlined the broader historical process that created the militant stance by black athletes in 1968. He recognized the double existence of the black star, illustrated by tales of Jesse Owens racing against horses and motorcycles to make money two years after his Berlin performance and Muhammad Ali's famous complaint that even with his gold medal hanging around his neck he was not able to get a cheeseburger in a Louisville eatery. The sports editor outlined the numerous problems that greeted the black athlete at the collegiate level—low graduation rates, racial slurs, biased coaching, poor housing, social isolation—and concluded overall that the situation was "a mess." His examples paralleled those discovered by *Life* magazine, including biographical accounts of key figures such as Smith, Carlos, and Evans, and provided closure to one prominent tale: UCLA hoopster Bob Presley, who never gave in to the demand that he cut his hair, was kicked off the team for missing a practice session a few days after his adamant refusal.[62]

In a similar vein to Axthelm's story was Jack Olsen's seminal series in *Sports Illustrated*: "The Black Athlete—A Shameful Story," which he eventually turned into a book. Of course, the series was not the magazine's first foray into the subject of race and sports. For example, it covered the group of black players who withdrew from the American Football League All-Star game in 1965 in New Orleans because they were not provided with the same hotel accommodations as their white counterparts. Even more significant was the magazine's devotion to coverage of Muhammad Ali, including the boxer's relationship with Malcolm X, who once told *Sports Illustrated* that Ali would "mean more to his people than Jackie Robinson." Also, there was an insightful reading by George Plimpton of the incident when the world heavyweight champion was denied a meal at a roadside restaurant in the South. While the magazine initially wavered over whether to employ Ali's chosen Muslim name, particularly because many sportswriters refused to acknowledge the boxer's religious conversion, in 1967 he appeared for the first time on the cover with his proper appellation.[63]

With this kind of foundation, by the time "The Cruel Deception" appeared—the first installment of Olsen's series—the magazine was able to outline its mission expertly:

> Sport has long been comfortable in its pride as being one of the few areas
> of American Society in which the Negro has found opportunity and
> equality. But has sport in America deceived itself? Is its liberality a myth,
> its tolerance a deceit? Increasingly, black athletes are saying that sport is
> doing a disservice to their race by setting up false goals, perpetuating
> prejudice and establishing an insidious bondage all its own. Now, when
> Negro athletes are shaking numerous college administrations with their
> demands and a boycott of the 1968 Olympics is no idle threat *Sports
> Illustrated* explores the roots and validity of the black athletes' unrest and
> finds them well-founded.[64]

The series continued with "Pride and Prejudice," an in-depth examination of the problems of campus life for black collegiate athletes, taking the initial explorations of *Life* to the next step. The third installment, "In an Alien World," was a case study of the racist athletic policies at the University of Texas at El Paso, the school whose football team provided the impetus for the founding of the OPHR. Part four, "In the Back of the Bus," took the analysis to the level of professional sports, outlining the similar inequities black athletes faced in the most elite ranks, and the concluding exposition, "The Anguish of a Team Divided," used the St. Louis Cardinals as a vehicle with which to explore such discrimination.

Olsen's series answered a heated debate at *Sports Illustrated*. While realizing the centrality of political issues in the sports arena, the magazine still feared estranging its readership by putting too many African Americans on the cover. Between 1954 and 1959, a mere 6 percent of the ninety-six covers that featured male athletes presented a black face.[65] As one of the most trusted writers on the staff, Olsen was given the assignment of the black athlete because the editorship realized that entering the political conversation regarding race and sport meant incorporating a range of figures, from "positive" role models like Floyd Patterson to "militant" individuals like Ali.[66] The magazine was so apprehensive about the repercussions from powers at Time, Incorporated, the series was kept secret, with no mention of it in the "Next Week" teaser in the issue that preceded it. Days before the first installment ran, all those connected with the series left for their summer vacations, rightly assuming that all hell would break loose at Time, Incorporated.

While corporate headquarters tried to deal with the impact of the relatively revolutionary series, members of the black press reacted to it in a mixed fashion. *Pittsburgh Courier* columnist Ric Roberts, for example, found "The Black Athlete" to be "no way to keep July and August on the 'cool' side." Rather than focus on "the dark side" of sports, Roberts pleaded with the magazine to concentrate on the positive aspects of the subject matter, such as the financial gross of black athletes in professional sports. "It is historically logical," Roberts suggested, "to abstain from irritating the American mystique—black or white—during any part of the three zodiacal 'fire' interims...." Besides, the writer concluded in reference to Olsen's piece on El Paso, "the racial paranoia of a mutating Anglo-Saxon people, in Dixieland, is no news."[67] Somewhat at odds with Roberts's view, the *New York Amsterdam News*, which quoted Olsen's words at length, found the series to make for "hard-socking reading which should be read by every so-called red-blooded sports fan—and especially the blacks who differ with the Afro-American athletes' negative attitudes to the forthcoming Mexican Olympics." One of its readers, signed "Black Male," agreed in a letter to the editor, writing that "every American desiring the real facts underlying the increasing racial hostility in this country should read the July 8, 1968 issue of *Sports Illustrated* magazine."[68]

In this vein, Michael MacCambridge rightly argues that the series was "the single most important piece in *SI*'s history."[69] The magazine received over a thousand letters, the largest number received for any sequence, and, along with Axthelm's investigation, disseminated the ideas of the OPHR to a more mainstream, national audience than had previously been reached. Joe Paterno, football coach at Pennsylvania State University, remembers reading the series and then talking to the African Americans on his squad about it: "That series had such an impact on coaching, on our whole social consciousness in this country that all of a sudden we were doing these kinds of things to people and exploiting them."[70] Looking at the rejoinder of figures such as Paterno, MacCambridge contends that the series "set the agenda for discussion about blacks and athletics."[71] In reality, the work of Olsen and Axthelm merely added to and popularized an ongoing dialogue, the terms of which had been set almost a year earlier by a group of young men in the house of a professor in San Jose, California.

Equal Yet Separate: The Gendering of Human Rights

Pieces such as those by Axthelm and Olsen indicated that the black athlete achieved a reality that was not necessarily connected to the possible eventuality of a boycott. Yet in this transformation, it became glaringly apparent that as a political entity, the black athlete was constructed, defined, and maintained as familiarly masculine, even when not directly connected to the male voices—Edwards, Smith, Evans, Alcindor—that propagated it. With these men as the leaders and central figures of sport and the overwhelmingly male readers and writers of *Sports Illustrated* as its spectators, its use as a vehicle for achieving "human" rights included little room for the involvement of African American women. While some, such as David Wiggins, have argued that the exclusion of women was a central downfall of the boycott effort, there has been little scholarly effort to fully flesh out the collisions that implicitly occurred between race and gender in the workings of the OPHR.[72] Neither the athletes nor the observers made any visible attempts to include women within the militant dialogue, and the gendered suppositions of the (un)spoken maleness of Black Power and the seemingly inherent whiteness of feminism left little space for any kind of political articulation of a female notion of black athlete.[73]

When women did enter into the conversation, it was generally as objects in the context of coaches and/or administrators posing OPHR members as a threat to "their" (white) women, an unquestionable legacy of the popular "black rapist" imagery that further illustrated the clash of identity surrounding the organization. Historians generally root the so-called fissure between civil rights and feminism in the mid-nineteenth century, when suffragists and abolitionists split over the issue of the franchise for freed*men* and established, according to Christine Stansell, that "if the 'negro' was male, then the 'woman' was white." Vron Ware further complicates this history in her exploration of how race and class bisect "woman," demonstrating the important point that various categories of identity exist in somewhat contradictory ways: women and gender are not knowable outside class and race. Ware's examination of the nineteenth-century synergetic relationship between women and slaves, for example, situates abolition and feminism as a transatlantic vinculum of concerns, with feminism the "midwife" to imperialism via the spurious colonial presumption that all women are the same.[74]

In 1968, the exclusion of the African American female voice from the increasingly transnational dialogue of civil rights was not a new phenomenon with the foray of Black Power into the world of sports. While the Student Non-Violent Coordinating Committee, for example, made some attempts to address the existence of sexual discrimination within its ranks, the budding waves of feminism induced female members to recognize and somewhat challenge the inequities they encountered within the generally progressive group. Women in SNCC found that their tasks centered on the secretarial; they were allowed little input on the broader issues of the movement, and few held leadership positions. According to Clayborne Carson, SNCC, like other such groups, "had not developed an egalitarian ethic regarding sexual relations similar to racial egalitarianism," as epitomized by Stokely Carmichael's infamous response of "prone" to a question regarding the suitable "position" of women in the organization.[75] Whether stated jokingly, as he claimed, or not, Carmichael's notorious rejoinder mirrored the dearth of regard paid to any kind of feminist preoccupations.

Indeed, a distinctive characteristic of Black Nationalism has been the elevation of race over any other element, including gender.[76] The subjugation of gender to race has long historical antecedents, ensuring that the issue of "woman" as a political entity, particularly that of "black woman," took a secondary, if any, role within the quest for racial equality. As Elaine Brown explains in her memoir about her days as leader of the Black Panther Party,

> A woman in the Black Power movement was considered, at best, irrelevant. A woman asserting herself was a pariah. A woman attempting the role of leadership was, to my proud black Brothers, making an alliance with the "counter-revolutionary, man-hating, lesbian, feminist white bitches." It was a violation of some Black Power principle that was left undefined. If a black woman assumed a role of leadership, she was said to be eroding black manhood, to be hindering the progress of the black race. She was an enemy of black people.[77]

The lack of the inclusion of the black female athlete in the movement by the OPHR and its observers, then, occurred despite the marked importance of African American women to the U.S. Olympic team. With the placement of sexism as secondary to racism in political movements in general, there were few means for any kind of political stance on the playing field, where women would not receive so-called official recognition until the passing and enforcement of Title IX in the 1970s.

Issues of inequality are pronounced in the relationship between African American women and athletics. It was twenty years after the Olympic debut of women tracksters that an African American woman won an Olympic medal. After the Olympics had been canceled because of World War II in both 1940 and 1944, Audrey "Mickey" Patterson (Tyler) took the bronze in the 100-meters at the London Games in 1948. For her achievement, the Tennessee State University alum was named Woman Athlete of the Year by the Amateur Athletic Union in 1949 and went on to a successful coaching career in San Diego.[78] The breakthrough accomplished by Patterson was reinforced by that of teammate Alice Coachman, who won the high jump in London to become the first African American woman to win Olympic gold and the *only* American to win an individual medal in track that year.

Of course, Olympians were not the only black women making an athletic splash in the postwar period. Tennis star Althea Gibson, who in 1950 became the first African American—man or woman—to compete in the United States Lawn Tennis Association National Outdoor Championship, broke down many of the color barriers in the ostensibly patrician sport. The *Chicago Defender* proudly declared that Gibson was "to the tennis world what Jackie Robinson was to major league baseball."[79] As the first black woman to grace the cover of *Sports Illustrated*, arguably Gibson was the first female sports figure to play a salient representative role in the African American community. While Arthur Ashe often is touted as the breaker of the color barrier in tennis, Gibson pioneered the role. For example, to help her pursue her dreams, African Americans in Detroit raised $770 to help defray the cost of her trip to

Wimbledon, and Joe Louis furnished both her plane ticket and hotel accommodations.

Despite the support, Gibson recognized the problems with representing the collective. Of accusations by the black press that she was shirking her duties as a "goodwill ambassador," she lamented, "It was a strain always trying to say and do the right thing, so that I wouldn't give people the wrong idea of what Negroes are like." Gibson's frustration as a role model mounted, sending her into a retreat from a public persona when she began to emphasize the *individual* aspect of her position: "I don't consciously beat the drums for any special cause, not even the cause of the Negro in the United States, because I feel that our best chance to advance is to prove ourselves as individuals."[80] This disengagement from direct representation of the black community fell into the common line of "liberal integrationism." The central argument, as explained by Manning Marable, dictates that "if *individual* African Americans are advanced to positions of political, cultural, or corporate prominence, the entire black community will benefit," resulting in "symbolic representation."[81] Yet Gibson's belief in this kind of racial trickle down did not prevent her from beating her drum in the name of nation; she agreed to travel throughout Asia on a "goodwill tour" sponsored by the U.S. State Department. In 1956, she traveled around the globe, playing exhibition matches and displaying the image of a prosperous African American citizen.[82] While the general diplomatic use of female athletes by the State Department was not unusual, African American women, in particular, highlighted such tours, representing racial integration as well as female fitness.

The State Department was not alone in its embrace of black women in the role of athlete. Others argued that their inclusion was critical to the advancement of the black community in the broader society. The African American press did not devote nearly the same amount of coverage to women as it did to men on the sports page, but most of the leading papers printed information on sportswomen, helping to promote the notion that the athlete—male *or* female—was critical to social mobility.[83] In 1951, Edwin B. Henderson, arguably the most influential African American voice on physical education, postulated that the participation in sport by black females would aid in the broader quest to use sports achievement as a means by which African Americans could improve their image in the white world:

> There are those who condemn strenuous athletic contests for women, who fear women will lose some of their charm and possibly what is more important, health. But so long as women of other races and nations engage in these sports with no proven evidence of detriment, our girls have reason and right to compete. Victory in physical contests, as with high rating in mental or spiritual measurements, helped kill off the Nazi-inspired doctrine of inferiority.[84]

Henderson's reference to the perception that women should not engage in sports for biological reasons indicates the ubiquity with which such thought still existed in the postwar period. Yet African American women often were not held to the same standard customarily stipulated for women, even as traditional gender roles became markedly reemphasized within the domestic execution of Cold War containment policy. The feminine ideal encompassed by the good suburban housewife was considered critical to America's global strength, as exemplified in no small part by the infamous "kitchen debate" between Richard Nixon and Nikita Khrushchev, in which Nixon asserted that the strength of the U.S. democratic system lay in its ability to relieve the burden of the American woman in, of course, her proper location—the home.[85] Yet the domestic ideal was by no means a universal reality, because the daily lives of women were not as prevailingly staid as the dominant imagery of middle-class white suburbia indicated.[86] Further, not many African American women had *access* to these suburban roles, nor were they *expected* to conform to them.

In sports, African American women did not compete in the more "feminine" events but rather displayed speed and strength on the track and in the field. Swimmers, such as the darling of the 1968 U.S. squad, sixteen-year-old Debbie Meyer, who would become the first woman to win three individual swimming golds in one Olympics, embodied a more traditional feminine aesthetic and thus did not encounter many of the "masculine" associations that plagued women in sport. While swimming thrived as a suitable venue for women, producing athletes more closely associated with Esther Williams than with the legendary Mildred "Babe" Didrikson (Zaharias), track and field, largely because it included "weight" events such as discus and shot put, did not. In 1929, one critic published objections to the display of strength and skill on the track that were "profoundly unnatural" for women, placing at risk their ability to mother as well as their "health, physical beauty, and social attractiveness," while another deemed the Olympics an "animalistic ordeal for women."[87] As Susan Cahn has argued, "By mid-century the sport had a reputation as a 'masculine' endeavor unsuited to feminine athletes," so much so that despite the success of athletes like Patterson, Coachman, and, of course, Didrikson, Olympic officials considered abolishing various events deemed "not truly feminine."[88]

African American women transcended many such associations, albeit for reasons different from those of swimmers. In general, black women inhabited the role of athlete more easily than their white counterparts, because they were not subjected to the same requirements of femininity, which has long been contrived along the lines of a distinctly white aesthetic. As Tricia Rose discloses in her discussion of hip-hop (another exemplary site to explore the everyday performances of black women), there exists a long historical trajectory of European dissection and exhibition of the black female body, as exemplified by the tour of "the Hottentot Venus" in the early nineteenth century and the fetishization of Josephine Baker in the 1920s and 1930s. Rose contends that in American culture, "the aesthetic hierarchy of the female body ... with particular reference to the behind and hips, positions many black women somewhere near the bottom."[89] In the 1950s, such a hierarchy of beauty proliferated, particularly among the ranks of young women, with white ideas of beauty and femininity being further enforced.[90] In terms of sports, the white-dominated discourse of femininity had far-reaching consequences. As one scholar has noted, because African American women faced a long history existing outside the white-dominated parameters of woman, "black women formed the vanguard of those individuals who broke new sports ground for women in general."[91]

Grant Jarvie and Joseph Maguire caution that, as with much of feminist criticism in general, "much of the feminist intervention into the sociology of sport and leisure has tended to be articulated in accordance with the structure of white middle-class oppression and thinking," with little work probing into "the historical specificity" of race, particularly with black and Asian female athletes and spectators.[92] African American women excelled in sports such as basketball and track and field, largely because they could participate in them either at school or on the playground, and both were relatively inexpensive.[93] When white women mostly abandoned the track because of its masculinist associations, black women began to dominate, running at unprecedented speed through the door left open, excelling in a new cultural arena, and fortifying conventions regarding their sexuality and their inherent "natural" gift to sprint, similar to much of the scientific language that surrounded their male counterparts. Thus, in addition to the established breach between supposedly masculine athleticism and femininity, the increased African American involvement and success on the track disclosed the dissonance between femininity and black women.

While black men, certainly, failed to live up to a white-defined aesthetic, their identity as men did not rely as deeply on physical appearance as female identity did.[94] Yet black females were able to cultivate their subversive athletic skills in relative isolation. Located at historically black colleges such as the Tuskegee Institute, black women avoided the rampant discrimination endured by their male counterparts, athletic scholarships in hand, at primarily white ones. Under the direction of Cleveland Abbot, the Tuskegee women won the first of their fourteen National Senior Outdoor Women's Track and Field Championships in 1937. Abbot began his tenure as physical education director in 1923 and instituted the Tuskegee Relays Carnival five years later to give men from black schools the opportunity for intercollegiate competition. At the third annual meet in 1929, Abbot added two women's events—the 100-yard dash and the quarter-mile relay. Other schools soon followed, and in 1936, Tidye Pickett became the first black woman on a U.S. Olympic team.[95]

After Wilma Rudolph's awe-inspiring performance in Rome in 1960, the position of African American women as a prominent feature of the United States Olympic team crystallized. With a poignant personal story that involved childhood illness and a dazzling gold medal hat trick in the 400-meter relay, the 100-meters, and the 200-meters, Rudolph became one of the unquestionable stars in Rome. The success of the woman who did not walk without aid until the age of eight shed much light on her home track at Tennessee State University (TSU) and on her coach, Ed Temple, who was an exception to the rule during this period, when women coached women's sports.[96] In 1955, Rudolph, still in high school, found her way to TSU as a participant in Temple's summer training program, which he had begun in 1953.[97] The following year, at the age of fifteen, she ventured to Melbourne, Australia, along with other members of the TSU team, taking the bronze in the 400-meter relay with Mae Faggs, Margaret Matthews, and Isabelle Daniels. The following summer, Rudolph began to blossom as an athlete, setting new AAU records in the 75-yard and 100-yard dashes and serving as a member of the record-breaking 300-yard relay team with women from TSU. In 1958, though, her remarkable success on the track abruptly halted when she dropped out to give birth to her first child, Yolanda. Despite Temple's rule that disallowed mothers in his program, he invited her back to the team, where she began to show the form that would dazzle the world in Rome.[98]

Following her astonishing Olympic performance in 1960, *Sports Illustrated* ran a feature on the indefatigable Tigerbelles, marveling that eight members of the U.S. women's track team in Rome wore the marker and emphatically declaring that "the star at the top of the whole Christmas tree" was Rudolph, dubbed by the international press La Gazèlla Nera and La Perle Noire.[99] In *Sports Illustrated* she was described, of course, as just a regular young woman in America, with a boyfriend in spiker Ray Norton and a hometown in Clarksville. But the magazine also emphasized the niche that Rudolph and her team-mates created with Temple at TSU, a place where black women were in training to dominate not only the American track but the world. Coach Temple understood the significance of Rudolph's feats as well as the importance of the inglenook he was chiefly responsible for creating:

> She's done more for her country than what the United States could pay her for. But she couldn't have done it alone. She's had tremendous com-petition, the three fastest girls in the country. Take Jones. She ran a world record 10.3 hundred yards at Randall's Island in 1958, although it wasn't official because she ran it against a girl with a handicap. *She* didn't have no handicap, but she ran with someone out in front. Jones would some-times beat Rudolph, Williams beat Rudolph, even Hudson was competi-tion right up to the last 25 yards when her little legs give out. Every time trial we had was like a track meet. Rudolph ran the hundred meters in 11.1 in a time trial because of that competition. Without it she wouldn't have won no three gold medals.[100]

According to *Sports Illustrated*, the unity and teamwork found at TSU was based on Temple's program, which began with training while the athlete was still in high school, indicating a conscious effort on his part to build a collective ethos among members of the squad. The article also marveled over how Temple and his team dealt with less than favorable conditions for producing champions. By no means was Temple able to focus exclusively on coaching; he was responsible for teaching six days a week in the sociology department. His coaching responsibilities were unpaid, as was his tenure working at the TSU post office. The facilities at TSU also left something to be desired; as described by *Sports Illustrated*, the track, located near the pigpen kept by the agriculture students, was "an oval ribbon of dirt, unmarked and unsurfaced."[101] Regardless, the end results from the group in Nashville were unparalleled: Faggs, Barbara Jones, Rudolph, Edith McGuire, and Wyomia Tyus all held a national championship in the 100-meters. By 1964, the Tigerbelles had set six new world records, twenty-one

American track records, and three Olympic records; in four Olympics (Melbourne, Rome, Tokyo, and Mexico City) the Tigerbelles won twenty-four medals—fifteen gold, five silver, four bronze.[102] Such feats did not go unnoticed; the U.S. State Department asked Temple to leave behind his teaching and coaching at TSU and travel to Ghana to teach his coaching methods.

Like Althea Gibson before her, Rudolph, too, proved to have great worth to the United States after she retired from the track. In 1963, she traveled to Senegal as the U.S. representative to the African Friendship Games. Of her trip, Wilbert C. Petty, cultural affairs officer at the American Embassy in Dakar, stated:

> I do not know of all the various parts of the world that Wilma must have traveled since 1960, but I rather suspect that this was her first time in an area where black rather than white is the color that counts. She seemed delighted to be among "the folks." She was struck by the handsome beauty of the Sengalese [sic] people—their flawless ebony skin, their excellent posture, the enviable grace with which the women wear their flowing *boubous*—a thin, chiffon-like overgarment which they drape rakishly off the shoulder. She was intrigued by the everyday life of the people, and one afternoon played "hooky" from a full round of sightseeing to spend it quietly with the family of her faithful student guide. A shy, but bright lad, he introduced Wilma to his large family, showed her all the rooms in the house and answered all kinds of questions she posed concerning the routine of their daily life. She retells this adventure with such nostalgia that I suspect it was among the fondest recollections of the Senegal visit.[103]

American diplomats found her resonance in French West Africa exemplary and continued to exhibit her throughout the region. The American Embassy in Dakar dispersed five thousand publicity shots of Rudolph, approximately a thousand of which she autographed. In addition, she made both television and radio appearances, gave press conferences, visited with Senegalese president Leopold Senghor, and handed out the gold medals to the Friendship Games victors. In the end, a French Embassy official reportedly said that the money the United States spent to send Rudolph to Africa brought a more positive and beneficial outcome than the some four million dollars France spent staging the Friendship Games. After the Games concluded, Rudolph— the "Ambassadress of American Sports"—went on to Ghana, Guinea, Mali, and Upper Volta, where thousands received her.[104]

Although without the international celebrity of Rudolph, Tiger-belle Wyomia Tyus became a prominent tool of the U.S. State Department after she led the U.S. sweep of the 100-meters as well as gained a silver as a member of the 400-meter relay in Tokyo in 1964. After being welcomed back from Tokyo to "Wyomia Tyus Day" in her hometown of Griffin, Georgia, Tyus was sent to Ethiopia with teammate Edith McGuire on a physically draining goodwill tour in 1966. Once in Addis Ababa, they met with several sports officials and athletes, including Abebe Bikila. A State Department representative wrote of the tour, "Perhaps the most impressed people at the reception were the girls invited from the Ethiopian YWCA. To them, Miss Tyus and Miss McGuire were a great inspiration who personified the freedom from reticence to which these young Ethiopian athletes aspire."[105]

In the four years after Tokyo, Tyus continued to excel, setting and defending world records. As Mexico City loomed near, an unprecedented feat lay before her: to defend the 100-meters Olympic championship, something no man or woman had ever done before. While the prospect of achieving such an unparalleled feat increased the celebrity of Tyus, both domestically and abroad, she understood that her achievements were still secondary to those of her male counterparts. As she remembered in an interview years later, "We could go and win 15 gold medals and . . . never get the attention we deserved. . . . the men are always going to get the glory and that was something we kind of accepted."[106] Even when the prospect of Tyus's achieving something special in Mexico was raised, it was never granted the scale it deserved, as illustrated by one journalist's excitement that she might "become the first *woman* in history to win the 100 meter dash in two consecutive Olympics."[107]

Consequently, Tyus's celebrity went largely unnoticed, or at least neglected, in another sphere of influence off the track: the OPHR. The course of action left for her then, as well as for her teammates, was limited to one of support rather than advocacy. Jarvis Scott, who finished sixth in the 400-meters in Mexico City, expressed disappointment over the lack of access presented to black women in terms of the political movement at hand. "We were most disappointed that our feelings were not brought out," she said. "While the men issued statements and held conferences, finding out what we felt was only a last minute thing."[108] The situation grew familiar, because, as Nellie McKay affirms, the historical pattern of the subjugation of black men by white society "entitles them to the unqualified support of black women."[109] Rather than find a part for herself in the quest for human rights, Tyus had to contend with the fact that no one figured out that she was competing for an unprecedented victory until she had actually achieved it. As she came to understand, there was little pressure even to win the second gold, because the media remained relatively unaware of the importance of such a feat. With such little media power, her political power—at least by OPHR standards—became greatly diminished, creating a terrible cycle that prevented her, in the terms set by the meaning-makers, from being a black athlete. Even though, as Gilroy has argued, gender is the means by which race is most familiarly inhabited,[110] the issue of gender was not going to get a chance to play itself out substantially in terms of the boycott, because by midsummer the boycott issue essentially was closed.

The Final Trial: The Black Athlete Stands Alone

The first word that the Mexico City boycott plan had been put to rest came with an announcement on July 31 by Lee Evans. During the Los Angeles meet, Evans said that an almost unanimous decision was reached to participate in Mexico City, although "the vote was also almost 100 per cent that we make some kind of protest.... What that will be I don't know."[111] Edwards responded that there was a possibility that Evans's statement had been constructed to create confusion for Olympics officials. "They can go ahead and depend on that if they want," Edwards told the press. "But if I was in Payton Jordan's or Hilmer Lodge's place I wouldn't put too much stock in what anybody says."[112] Within another month's time, Edwards conceded in a written statement to the third National Conference on Black Power that there would be no boycott and that "the majority of athletes will participate in the Olympics." Despite Evans's earlier contention that the vote taken in Los Angeles was close to unanimous, Edwards maintained that of the twenty-six athletes favored to make the team, thirteen had voted against the boycott, twelve supported it, and one remained undecided. The OPHR released those committed to the boycott to prevent any further divides within the movement. The fear, of course, was that the USOC might replace athletes who intended to boycott with those willing to participate. According to the *New York Times*, such speculation, which had been somewhat dismissed by John Underwood, was well-founded, because the USOC had "quietly made plans" to devise a special selection process if vacancies were left by boycotting athletes.[113] In terms of individual action, Edwards reiterated that many athletes might engage in some kind of "lesser protest," such as wearing black armbands and showing "their support of the black power movement in some manner during the course of the Olympic Games."[114]

Members of the black press took these words to heart. Columnist Howie Evans, for example, of the *New York Amsterdam News*, predicted that demonstrations not only by black athletes but by "student radicals from all over the world" would "surely cause havoc and possibly prevent some of the events from being staged."[115] However, many members of the black press also issued a collective sigh of relief that Edwards had, perhaps, been silenced and black athletes could get on with their pursuit of gold. The *Los Angeles Sentinel* proudly pronounced that "60 men of color" and "more than 10 of Uncle Sam's daughters of color" would now participate in the Olympics.[116] The *Pittsburgh Courier* issued a rather apolitical statement regarding the termination of boycott plans, claiming that the motivations behind the boycott "were circumstantial happenings" and that now "the talented blacks will do their best—as in the past." On its editorial page, a large cartoon entitled "End of the Season Good Deal" had three figures, Black America, HHH, and LBJ, dressed in baseball uniforms and engaged in an exchange. As LBJ (representing President Lyndon Baines Johnson) pushed HHH (representing presidential candidate Hubert Humphrey) toward Black America, he stated, "Better grab him.... He's the best man in the country for your team!"[117] Thus, while its written editorial musings on the boycott remained rather vague, its visual depiction of the situation located the black athlete—the ultimate team player—as important not only to the health of the nation but also, obviously, to the success of the Democratic Party.

Although the *Courier* subtly heralded the renewed possibilities of black Olympic participation, the *Chicago Daily Defender* took a much more caustic position against the disorder Edwards had created. Describing him as "an articulate and well-educated young sociology instructor whose speech is clouded by such endearing terms as 'Uncle Tom,' 'white man's nigger,' 'honky,' 'cracker administrators,'" the *Defender* held little back in its censure of the OPHR. It announced the defeat of the boycott in its news section, but on the cover of the sports section, it highlighted the defeat as a defeat of Edwards, with a large photo captioned with an explanation of what had happened.[118] *Defender* columnist A. S. "Doc" Young, one of the foremost, and few, black sports historians, gave his perspective on the decision not to boycott in an imaginary dialogue with a friend. When this friend asked him if he was "happy Harry Edwards called off the Olympic Boycott," Young replied, "It's too early to get happy. You never can tell what Harry Edwards will do." Particularly worrisome was Edwards's promise that demonstrations would take place in Mexico City, which would continue the path of "unsportsmanly conduct" that the OPHR had gone down from the beginning. Alleging that Edwards had hoodwinked both the athletes and the nation about the OPHR representing a cohesive revolutionary whole and taken focus away from the far more important presidential election, Young continued,

Harry Edwards and his disciples tried to sell the idea to Negro athletes. Most of them turned thumbs down on the plan, but Edwards browbeat them and vilified them and insulted all writers, Negro and Caucasian alike, who criticized the plan. The plan had no merit at all. But, these are tedious racial times and it's rather easy to make the unthinking people feel that they are "traitors to the race" if they don't fall in behind every publicized scheme proposed by people who make a profession of hollering at "Whitey." Fortunately, though, some of the athletes just wouldn't cave in. Jimmy Hines said he was going to Mexico City to run even if nobody else went. So. Edward's [*sic*] scheme failed.[119]

Despite these kinds of cutting remarks, Edwards and his cohort continued to affirm the OPHR as a successful organization. In his statement to the National Conference on Black Power, Edwards included a list of the tangible accomplishments of the OPHR and urged that future steps be taken, including the creation of an Olympic awards dinner for athletes "in recognition of their tremendous contribution to the black-liberation struggle" and a Federation of Black Amateur Athletes.[120] The OPHR had created, in his view, a "world-wide recognition of the plight of black people," illustrated by the banning of South Africa from the Olympics and the increased communication between black African nations and African Americans. Perhaps one of the most crucial achievements was the mobilization of what Edwards deemed "a sizable contingent of white athletes" to its cause.[121] Nowhere else was this more apparent than the relationship established between the OPHR and the Harvard crew team, which carved a space for itself within the political collectivity of the black athlete. The Harvard oarsmen composed the U.S. men's eight team for Mexico City in its entirety and supplied what many saw as an unusual source of support for the cause of the OPHR. Four members of the team, Scott N. Steketee, Curtis R. Canning, J. Cleve Livingston, and David D. Higgins, as well as coxswain Paul Hoffman, issued what Robert Lipsyte judged "an extraordinary statement": "We—as individuals—have been concerned with the place of the black man in American society and his struggle for equal rights. As members of the United States Olympic team, each of us has come to feel a moral commitment to support our black teammates in their efforts to dramatize the injustices and inequities which permeate our society."[122]

After qualifying for the Games at the Olympic Trials, Livingston and Hoffman set up a meeting with Edwards. Edwards said of their discussion: "It was beautiful to see some white cats willing to admit they've got a problem and looking to take some action to educate their own." The oarsmen decided that their best plan of action would be to talk to other white Olympians and try to create a body that would "stimulate an open-ended discussion of the issues" as well as "discuss means of voicing our support at the Olympic Games."[123] Coming from athletes who took part in inarguably one of the most elite of the country club sports, such spirit might be considered reason enough for the creation of the movement in the first place. But after the chaos of the Olympic Trials, which prevented many from believing that the move to Tahoe was merely about breathing at high elevations, it was obvious that the agenda remained unfinished.

Altitude would be responsible in many eyes for the mammoth athletic performances in some events at Mexico City, including twenty-seven medals and seventeen world records for the United States in track and field. Belief in the effect of altitude was so great that the USOC hired a breathing consultant, Carl Stough, to work with athletes on "breathing coordination."[124] Enlisting Stough seemed money well spent if Tahoe was any indication. Records were crushed with spectacular achievements, most notably Beamon's leap of 27-6½ in the long jump, an effort that foreshadowed even more miraculous things to come.[125] But for some, participation in the Olympic Games would not exclusively revolve around lane assignments and finish tapes, because it was apparent before the Games even began that a small but dedicated collection of black athletes had turned the attention of many to their struggle. While sportswriters such as John Underwood celebrated the excellence and unity displayed at Tahoe, all was not right with the world. In Underwood's assessment, the athletes, coming from all walks of life to be there, exemplified the Olympic spirit. In particular, he noted, and "in a very meaningful sense," that to appreciate the Olympic spirit one need only look at pole vaulter Bob Seagren, "the affluent, handsome-on-handsome Southern California college boy," and John Carlos, "a *goateed*, jive-talking slum kid from Harlem who remembers his neighborhood as a place where kids drank cheap Scotch and who believes that at least part of his mission in life is to point up the implications of that fact to the Establishment."[126] However, the calm before the storm that was Tahoe led many to rest assured that it was in the nation's best interest to send the speedy Carlos in a red, white, and blue uniform to greet the youth of the world. While Payton Jordan crowed that the team was "one of the finest we've taken to the Olympics,"[127] he failed to recognize that the starter's gun would not be the only thing to go off in Mexico.

CHAPTER 6

"That's My Flag"

You do not accrue prestige when you go the Olympics because when
you come back you're still a nigger.

—Harry Edwards, *San Jose Mercury News*, 1967

My whole life flashed in my face. I had two minutes to see everything.
Oh man, I never felt such a rush of pride. Even hearing the Star-
Spangled Banner was pride, even though it didn't totally represent me.
But it was the anthem which represented the country I represented, can
you see that? They say we demeaned the flag. Hey, no way man. That's
my flag ... that's the American flag and I'm an American. But I couldn't
salute it in the accepted manner, because it didn't represent me fully;
only to the extent of asking me to be great on the running track, then
obliging me to come home and be just another nigger.

—Tommie Smith, *Daily Telegraph*, 1993

When the U.S. Olympic track team, seventy-seven members strong, arrived in Mexico, it faced many questions from the international press regarding the political role of the self-proclaimed black athletes on the team. As reporters descended upon the athletes with questions about political militancy, the Americans sang the national anthem in the Plaza de las Banderas in the Olympic Village while Ambassador Fulton Freeman and USOC president Douglas Roby raised the American flag. Although U.S. track coach Payton Jordan assured reporters that there would be "no trouble whatever" and assistant coach Stan Wright insisted "there will be no demonstrations," the words John Carlos offered indicated otherwise: "We have no intention of disrupting the Games. But that does not mean we will not do something to accentuate the injustices that have been done to the black man in America.... If I win a gold medal, I will be up there to get it. I may throw it away afterwards, but nothing is going to keep me from getting it."[1] Yet Jordan and others shelved Carlos's statement in light of the harmonious participation in the traditional flag-raising ceremony. "We have a fine rapport on our team . . . ," stated Jordan; "I'm convinced John was speaking from his heart—but also only for himself."[2]

It became clear when the athletes began to settle into the Olympic Village that the pursuit of gold was but one focus at these Games. Despite Avery Brundage's quest for an apolitical arena, the turbulence of 1968 had saturated the arena of sport. While some wondered what kind of conflict might erupt between the Mexican government and Mexican students, the Soviet Union did not let the sleeping dog of South Africa lie. At a press conference in the Olympic Village, the Soviet contingent maintained its opposition to Springbok participation on any international playing field as well as assuring reporters that there would be no Soviet-Czech hostility for the duration of the Games.[3] The political circus even came close to bringing down Brundage himself, for he found his very presidency at risk upon his arrival in Mexico. French IOC member Conte Jean Beaumont, a critical player in the South African controversy, initiated the challenge at the apparent urging of IOC members from the United States, Iran, and Morocco. But despite an increasingly pervasive sentiment that the elite governing body was in need of change, Brundage held off the challenge and buttressed the more conservative facets of the organization, taking the reins of his fifth term.[4]

As host, Mexico made valiant attempts to steer attention toward the grandeur of the Games and away from its own domestic turmoil. Pedro Ramírez Vázquez welcomed the international press corps to the Olympic city at an extravagant dinner affair at the Hacundo de los Morales. The party, commented *Baltimore Afro-American* reporter Sam Lacy, "must have cost as much as it took to build the place."[5] Outside such festivities, however, officials struggled to avert the chaos stemming from the massive influx of people, while hopeful sports fans waited in lengthy lines for almost every service. Such lines seemingly solidified U.S. attitudes toward the Olympic setting, building on the observations made while the Mexicans had constructed their Olympic city. "It is not difficult to separate the natives from the foreigners," one Chicago sportswriter quipped. "The Mexicans, a patient people with a peon heritage, can stand passively in one line for hours."[6]

Yet regardless of native patience or the number of white doves instructed to fly through the air, the political turbulence of the moment persevered. By the time the smoke had settled at Tlatelolco in the wake of the massacred students and Smith and Carlos had thrust their fists into the air, any stability seemed crushed. One especially bizarre incident that graced the pages of the American press was the attempted murder of a Mexican resident, twenty-one-year-old Ramon Hernandez Vallejo. In a statement made to Mexican police, Vallejo alleged that four Cubans had thrown him from the bell tower of a local cathedral because he refused to kill a U.S. athlete, a plan designed, he explained, "so that Mexico would have problems with the United States."[7] Of course, anti-American sentiment would be the province not only of the unnamed Cubans. As Americans, Smith and Carlos would also challenge the United States by creating the definitive gesture of these Olympics as well as one of the most reverberant images in the collective memory of both American sport and American race politics.

Take the Stand: A Black-Fisted Salute to the Flag

Critical, of course, to the power of the statement made by Smith and Carlos was their use of a visual medium. They understood that their victory ceremony would be permanently fixed in the memory of anyone with access to print or televised media. While Mexico City's viewing audience achieved nowhere near the enormity of audiences of recent Olympics, the broadcast garnered a twenty-seven share and reached a prime-time peak of 14.3 rating points, gluing a huge number of eyes—approximately four hundred million worldwide—upon Smith and Carlos.[8] Harry Edwards had understood the visual component of the athlete's existence as crucial to the success of the OPHR, noting how sports stars' "access at a moment's notice to the mass media" made it imperative that they "take a stand."[9] Of course, some observers would misconstrue that stand, such as the *Los Angeles Times*'s description of the eventual action taken by Smith and Carlos as a "Nazi-like salute."[10] But even the misconceptions enabled a message—any message—to create space for the people it represented in the public eye, and they did so in an unparalleled capacity. As Edwards later pointed out, the action taken by Smith and Carlos

> was the only route both accessible to Blacks and promising an *international* protest platform, an escalation long advocated by many of the more militant spokesmen in the Black struggle who saw the oppression of black Americans, not as a domestic civil rights issue, but as a violation of *international human rights law and principles*. And increasingly in 1968, as the racial situation deteriorated and violent confrontation heightened, people began to see some advantage, however limited, in dramatizing Black America's plight before the international community.[11]

One of the earliest signs in Mexico that American black athletes refused to relinquish their moment in the international spotlight was an indirect demand that Brundage not present their medals should they win any. Rather than celebrate the possibility of an American IOC president presenting medals to an American athlete, those who made this request demonstrated how definitively Brundage represented all that the OPHR spurned. The matter was first raised in a query to Olympic officials by sprinters Jim Hines and Charlie Greene. "We asked them who was going to present the medals and they replied Brundage," Hines later told the press. "We didn't say anything. Neither did we smile. They apparently got the message." Although Brundage was scheduled to bestow the honors on the 100-meters champion, Hines, the first athlete to run 100 meters in under 10 seconds, received his gold medal, and Greene his bronze, from Lord David Burghley, British Olympic official and president of the International Amateur Athletic Federation, leading many sportswriters to believe that Brundage, who was in Acapulco watching sailing events, stayed away from the dais because of the black athletes' reluctance to receive accolades from him. While Stan Wright dismissed the incident as immaterial, saying, "I don't care who gives them the medals, I just want them to win them," Tommie Smith indicated that it was not immaterial, telling the press that if triumphant he did not want to receive his medal from Brundage.[12] In preparation, his and Lee Evans's wives purchased black gloves for their husbands to wear if either had to shake Brundage's hand. Smith, of course, would go on to share his gloves with Carlos.[13]

The medal ceremony was a natural focus of concern. The Olympics are organized around three rites of passage: the Opening Ceremony, the victory ceremonies, and the Closing Ceremony. As John J. MacAloon notes, the Opening Ceremony takes place to separate Olympic events from those of everyday life. In it, specific Olympic symbols—flag, torch, flame—transform the national identity expressed by each team into a universal one. In the victory ceremonies, another symbolic presence is added, the individual athlete, which represents the body itself. Through the body, the victory ceremony reinforces the results of athletic competition. Additionally, the nation and the Olympics also are reinforced through national flags, national anthems, Olympic medals, and the olive branch offered to each gold medalist. Thus, the athlete assumes a dual persona, because he or she stands on the dais as a member of both a nation and what MacAloon designates as "a wider human community." The Closing Ceremony reiterates this wider community by bringing both participants and spectators back to everyday life by having athletes march into the stadium together rather than as members of a national team.[14]

Smith and Carlos, under heavy media scrutiny because of their OPHR membership, did not wait for a victory ceremony to stake their symbolic claim. In their qualifying heats for the 200-meters, the duo wore tall black socks—what *Newsweek* described as ghetto "pimp socks"— unusual items for athletes gearing for speed.[15] In addition, Carlos wore a badge imprinted with "Olympic Project for Human Rights," which had been seen on other African American athletes, including Lee Evans, in the Olympic Village. While Stan Wright discounted the socks and the badge, stating, "If they can run 20.2 wearing badges it's perfectly all right with me," Smith, who claimed he did not wear a badge because he did not have one, stressed that their attire was symbolic, although he elaborated no further.[16] Jesse Owens, continuing his role as a talking head, dismissed the socks as impractical and, despite the resolute label of "Uncle Tom" by members of the OPHR, offered advice to the young men from San Jose: they should cut their black socks below their calves so as not to retard circulation while running. Watching Carlos strip down for the semifinal and reveal much shorter black socks than worn in the previous heats, Owens smiled to one sportswriter, "Maybe they're listening to their uncle." Yet he retained his stance on the OPHR. "I'm old enough to be their uncle," he acknowledged, "but I'm not their Tom. We don't need this kind of stuff. We should just let the boys go out and compete."[17]

In addition to wearing supposedly militant symbols, Smith also ensured a maximum audience for his final when he tied the Olympic record, 20.3, in his first qualifying heat. Australian Peter Norman, a relative unknown, upped the ante a few heats later by breaking the record with a career best of 20.2, which Smith matched in the third heat, despite a relatively slow start coming out of the blocks. His performance only added to the spotlight on American spikers that day. Al Oerter threw the discus for an unprecedented fourth consecutive gold, and Wyomia Tyus dominated a one-two U.S. finish in the 100-meters, with a world record of 11 seconds flat, making her the first athlete to defend a 100-meters Olympic title in successive Games, as previously discussed.[18] By the time Smith and Carlos took their marks in the 200-meters final, the United States had taken an early lead in the unofficial medal total. Many fans fully (and rightly) expected that the duo would add more gold to the American pile, with one of them likely to come out on top.

The gold medal that Smith won in the 200-meters on October 16, 1968, was a spectacular athletic achievement. Before the start there had been some fear that he would not be able to run because he had pulled an abductor muscle in his groin in the semifinal, clocking 20.1. Nevertheless, once in the starting blocks, Smith gave no sign of discomfort and shattered the world record with an awe-inspiring 19.83.[19] After effecting an exhilarating burst of speed that left the field behind with sixty meters to go, Smith raised both hands over his head in victory several yards before the finish line, a dramatic gesture not aerodynamically suited to a record pace. Carlos, who turned to look at his teammate, was caught by Norman's own burst of speed and lost the silver in the final charge, although both athletes were given the same time (20.0). It was the fastest 200-meters in the history of the timed track; no one would run it again in under 20 seconds until Carl Lewis in Los Angeles in 1984.

Despite the brilliant nature of the race itself, the symbolic medal ceremony that followed, of course, proved most historic, bearing out how, as Toni Morrison has argued, "spectacle is the best means by which an official story is formed and is a superior mechanism for guaranteeing its longevity."[20] The spectacle created by Smith and Carlos crowned the mission of the OPHR and, again, solidified a politicized notion of "black athlete" in spite of the continual fragmentation and reinvention the label had undergone. With their gesture, they created a moment of resistance and confrontation with dominant and existing forms of racial identity. They borrowed pervasive and normative conceptions of the nation and substituted new representations by replacing the dominant image of the American flag with a black-gloved fist. In front of a global audience of approximately four hundred million people, the duo used their moment to denounce racism in the United States, creating a cultural strategy effective in its attempt to change or shift the "dispositions of power," in the words of Stuart Hall.[21] Again, the arena of sport was already highly politicized when Smith and Carlos took their places. Their protest, then, exemplified a *collective* transformation from "Negro" athlete to "black" athlete, one that mediated various internal identities of political consciousness and enunciated a new cohesiveness to the protest's expansive audience.

When Smith and Carlos took their positions on the dais as gold and bronze medalists, they wore black stockings but no shoes, a black glove on one hand, and Smith had a black scarf around his neck. The silver medalist, Norman, wore an OPHR badge on his jacket. With their medals hanging around their necks, the athletes turned, as expected, to face the American and Australian flags. As "The Star-Spangled Banner" began, Smith and Carlos bowed their heads and simultaneously raised a black-gloved fist, and the stadium crowd slowly but steadily booed and jeered in reaction. Smith remained perfectly still, while Carlos raised his head slightly. The surrounding Olympic officials never turned to see what drew the catcalls from the stadium. As the two athletes left the stadium, the booing grew again in volume. Both athletes responded immediately by raising their fists again.

The following day, Smith's body language during an interview with Howard Cosell illustrated that he viewed his athletic performance and his performance during the awards ceremony in different terms. When questioned about the protest, for example, he held his arms tightly across his chest and gave somber answers, but when Cosell asked about the mechanics of his "extraordinary" victory, Smith relaxed, uncrossed his arms, and casually explained how happy he was with his impressive feat. Yet it was with arms crossed that he positioned the protest as a fusion of both the national and subaltern negotiations that had occurred in the period leading up to the Games. Cosell interjected little into Smith's explanations of the protest, saying simply before rolling the tape that "immediately after the victory the following awards ceremony took place," and let Smith do his own talking:

> The right glove that I wore on my right hand signified the power within black America. The left glove my teammate John Carlos wore on his left hand made an arc with my right hand and his left hand also to signify black unity. The scarf that was worn around my neck signified blackness. John Carlos and me wore socks, black socks, without shoes, to also signify our poverty.[22]

When Cosell asked Smith if he represented *all* black athletes, Smith continued: "I can say I represented black America. I'm very proud to be a black man.... I thought that I could represent my people by letting them know I'm proud to be a black man." When Cosell pushed him further, asking if he was "proud to be an American," Smith replied somewhat elusively, "I'm proud to be a black American," and said that through the action, he and Carlos had gained "black dignity."[23]

Thus, spectators and viewers alike listened to the national anthem while watching two American athletes powerfully display both their connection *to* and their criticism *of* the United States. Critical to the impact of the protest gesture was its silence. Smith and Carlos held no sign or banner, but rather made themselves visual beacons of discontent, figuratively illustrating Benedict Anderson's point that "nations can ... be imagined without linguistic communality."[24] Without words, the focus became the two athletes themselves, creating a symbolism that worked well within a realm where, as Stuart Hall notes in another context, the body has been used to such degree that individuals become "canvases of representation."[25] Smith and Carlos, as canvases, physically occupied their statement and therefore became the essence of the OPHR movement and the national community it signified in a multinational arena. Mike Marqusee has argued that the two invented "a complex new symbolism" that involved an action in which "the rhetoric of individual victory and national glory was replaced by a language of solidarity that amounted to repudiation of the United States and all its works."[26] Yet the protest took place *within* the dominant ritual, acknowledged its accompanying symbols, and then proceeded to revolutionize it, subverting the normative presentation of the nation-state with its own tools. Smith and Carlos, then, did not throw the iconography of America out, but rather pushed for a more inclusive politics of citizenship.

Following Cosell's interview with Smith, ABC Olympic host Chris Schenkel took a break from the stadium to tell his audience that the IOC held the USOC responsible for the protest, "which violated the basic principle of the Olympic Games that politics play no part whatsoever." After reading the entire USOC apology, Schenkel then promised to send his audience back to "the action now in competition," making certain that viewers would distinguish athletic from political action.[27] The print media further accentuated this distinction, putting the photograph of Smith's climactic victory—jubilant grin, thrown-back head, outstretched arms—in a separate context from his black-gloved fist. His triumphant image was but one exhibition of American excellence in the news that day. Pole vaulter Bob Seagren, for example, also had won gold and set an Olympic record of 17-8½, which missed his own world mark by half an inch. Sportswriters marveled, analyzed, and extolled such feats. While Schenkel diplomatically described the medal totals as "very close" on the air, newspapers resoundingly affirmed the U.S. lead (seventeen) in the medal count over the Soviet Union (fifteen), with the Hungarians (ten) trailing far behind.[28] Furthermore, sportswriters pointed out, it had not been easy for the Americans, particularly Smith's definitive win despite a groin injury and Seagren's draining seven-and-a-half-hour competition.

Yet along with the declarations of athletic ascendancy, most sports pages did juxtapose a photo of the black power protest with that of Smith's victorious stride. Detailed in smaller, separate stories far beneath the gleeful headlines were descriptions of how Smith and Carlos accepted their medals. The differentiation made between the day of *sports* and the day of *sport politics* transformed Smith-the-winner into Smith-the-revolutionary but ensured that until further repercussions of the black power action emerged, if any did, the principal story was not about an athlete's outlook on human rights but rather about his world record and gold medal. The *Los Angeles Times*, for example, acknowledged that there were two sides to Smith's day, but it decidedly preferred the sports to the politics. "Gambling Seagren" and his "heartstopper" victory dominated the coverage, followed by the coupled images—"The Winner!" and "Olympians Protest"—of Smith. While the fine points of his victory, such as the pulled muscle and the fast time, were relegated to page four, a full description of the "'Black Power' on Victory Stand" remained on the front page, culled from a *Washington Post* story off the newswire and reassembled as something that had little bearing on the day's results.

The article explained the protest, detailing how Australian Peter Norman "stood in respectful attention" during the American anthem while Smith and Carlos "raised a black-gloved hand in a closed-fist gesture." It noted that Lord Burghley presented the medals rather than Brundage, who in a threat to send home any protesting athletes had made it clear that possible repercussions were already on the table. The story also revealed that the two "Negro militants" had informed both Payton Jordan and Stan Wright of their militant intentions, but that the U.S. coaching staff had decided that it was an *individual* decision for the pair to make. Additionally, the article included a variety of explanatory remarks made by the duo, described as "mustachioed and bearded," including a description by Carlos of the gesture's durability. "If you think we are bad," he told the press, "the 1972 Olympic Games are going to be mighty rough because Africans are winning all the medals."[29] This caveat appeared to have merit at once. The article divulged that after the 200-meters victory ceremony, long jumper Ralph Boston, "never classed among the militants previously," began a turnaround from his initial position against the OPHR and its boycott threat. "I don't want Brundage giving me a medal, either, if I win one," said the world-record holder. "You gotta be black to understand it." In light of Boston's apparent transformation, the paper cautioned, such militancy was not perhaps finished with Smith and Carlos, particularly because the upcoming relays fielded "teams composed only of Negroes."[30]

The *New York Times* created an even more conscientious differentiation between the victories and the politics of the day but reversed the selected emphases of the *Los Angeles Times*. While Smith was the focus of the headline and the story on the sports page, the accompanying photo was of Seagren descending seemingly from the heavens. There was no mention of the black power protest in the headline story but rather an affirmation that the nation had "collected more gold and glory" with Smith's and Seagren's performances along with Willie Davenport's definitive win in one of the last qualifying heats for the 110-meter high hurdles.[31] The contrasting photos of Smith and a story regarding the victory ceremony were reserved for the next page of coverage. Describing the sprinters as the "most militant black members of the United States track and field squad," the article argued that the determination it took for the injured Smith to win came out of his desire to make his political statement rather than an aspiration to bring home the gold with pride. Without a victory by one of the Americans, "The Star-Spangled Banner" would have been absent from the protest, greatly reducing the protest's meaning. Carlos indirectly confirmed this, explaining why he turned his head and (arguably) lost the silver medal at the finish line. "I wanted to see where Tommie was, and if he could win it," he said. "If I thought he couldn't have won it, I would have tried harder to take it."[32]

Unlike its coastal counterparts, the *Chicago Tribune*, with a banner sports headline declaring "SMITH AND SEAGREN WIN GOLD MEDALS," provided little depth regarding the protest. The paper described it as "a somewhat discordant note," emphasized the world-record mark, and placed the photo of the protest as secondary to the one of Smith's "climaxing stirring performance."[33] On a more local level, Smith received a mention on the front page of the *San Jose Mercury News*, where his world-record mark dominated the sports page and paid relatively little attention to Seagren's accomplishment. The headline "TOMMIE IN RECORD 200 WIN" was accompanied by the drop headline "Then 'Salutes' Black Power," and the victory photo, as in more "national" papers, was accompanied by the protest image. However, sports editor Louis Duino did not remark on the protest in his extensive article, focusing instead on Smith's injury and, like the *Los Angeles Times*, ran the *Washington Post* wire story describing what occurred on the victory dais.[34]

Far more nuanced in terms of the black power action was the *New York Post*, which declared that the 200-meters was "the only Olympic race that was ever upstaged by a victory celebration." Yet while the more tabloid-oriented paper placed greater emphasis on the sensational political aspects of the day's events, the *Post* also gave an informative and detailed account of why the world-record mark was *not* the most important facet of Smith's victory and included a history of the gesture eventually rendered. That gesture, the *Post* contended, answered the question of what the paper designated the "'what-will-they-do-now' expectation that [had] hung in the air" since the athletes had refused to take their medals from Brundage and donned "pimp socks" in their heats. The *Post* further detailed the mechanics of the protest, explaining that the pair had bought the socks in the United States but purchased the gloves in Mexico City. It enumerated the symbolism contained within the gesture and noted that, although Peter Norman "smiled and waved" on the dais, he, too, was connected to the statement because of the OPHR badge on his chest. "I asked them for it," Norman stated. "They seemed delighted that I wanted one. Smith asked someone in the stands for his button. Carlos demanded it. He said 'Hand that thing over,' and that's how I got my button." The aggressiveness of Carlos was furthered with his statements at the postrace press conference. While Smith was described as quiet during the gathering, Carlos, described as loquacious, left little unsaid.

> Tommie Smith and John Carlos would like to put in the papers—print what I say or don't print it at all—that white people feel that black people are nothing but animals, something to do a job. We received many boos out there today. White people turned thumbs down on us. We're not lower animals—roaches or ants or rats. If we do the job well, we get a pat on the back or some peanuts. And someone says, "Good boy." I've heard boy, boy, boy all through the Olympics. I'd like to tell white people in America and all over the world that if they don't care for the things black people do, then they shouldn't sit in the stands and watch them perform.[35]

The *Post* also differed from other papers in that it included an Associated Press account of the possible upshot of the black power action, noting that the IOC called a special session with the USOC to discuss the events of the 200-meters victory ceremony. Deeming the session extraordinary, the small story stated that the IOC was "concerned by the action" and emphasized the uncertainty and ambiguity of the situation with a quote from the secretary of the acting executive director of the USOC, Everett Barnes: "The committee broke up for a few minutes and went back into session. It expects to have a statement shortly."[36] Yet the statement did not appear until the following day, and even then no one had any idea about the fate of the two American athletes. Rather, the attitude was more in line with that of Tommie Smith's wife, Denise, who laughed at the dour reaction of the stadium crowd as she watched the solemn statement made by her husband. "Wait until Avery sees this," she said. "He'll die."[37]

Heroes of Humanity, Enemies of the Village: Reaction to Action

While intentionally vague immediately after the protest, the USOC became decidedly clear the following day. Emerging from the five-hour emergency session, the USOC issued a formal apology to the IOC for the action taken by Smith and Carlos on the victory stand. In addition to words of atonement, the USOC also delivered what the Associated Press determined to be a "veiled threat" to other athletes, indicating that the committee would not permit any other steps of political agitation.[38] With the words of amenity and intimidation dispatched, the national sports press, which had only casually dealt with the black power action at that point, began to devote more inches on the front pages of sports sections to it, particularly when the various American Olympic authorities became directly involved in the responsibility for the situation. Within one day's time, then, the consequence of the black power action overtook the significance of the world-record race itself.

The apology and subsequent warning came from Barnes, who gave the statement, according to the Associated Press, "with his eyes damp from emotion." On behalf of the USOC, Barnes apologized for

> the discourtesy displayed by two men who departed from tradition during a victory ceremony.... The untypical exhibition of these athletes also violates the basic standards of sportsmanship and good manners highly regarded in the United States. The committee does not believe that this immature behavior by the two members of the U.S. team warrants any formal action at this time. If further investigation over subsequent events does not bear this out, the entire matter will be reevaluated....

a repetition of such an incident will be viewed as a willful disregard of Olympic principles.[39]

While Barnes asserted that no formal action would be taken against Smith or Carlos, he made it clear that no other athlete would be granted such reprieve. "We worded the statement in such a way that we hope that we will be able to solve the situation peacefully," Barnes later said. "This is a definite warning to athletes who disregard our rules. If there is a further violation, the committee will deal with it with a severe penalty. The practice in the past," he added, "has been to send such athletes home."[40]

Like the USOC, Avery Brundage demonstrated no conflict of interest regarding his own U.S. citizenship when dealing with Smith and Carlos. He further bolstered the USOC sentiment with the brazen accusation that Smith and Carlos had single-handedly altered the apolitical Olympic atmosphere he valued. In doing so, of course, he further yanked their action out of the historical context that had produced it, without any mention of the political turmoil of the months preceding the Games: "One of the basic principles of the Olympic Games is that politics play no part whatsoever in them. This principle has always been accepted with enthusiasm by all, of course, including the competitors. Yesterday, the U.S. athletes in a victory ceremony deliberately violated the universally accepted principle by using the occasion to advertise domestic political views."[41]

Brundage's statement put the USOC in a difficult position. He, like Barnes, referred to the *individual* action of Smith and Carlos, but he identified them by their red, white, and blue uniforms, not their OPHR badges, and located their politics as distinctly American in nature. Although the USOC also focused on the black power action as a result of the individual behavior of Smith and Carlos rather than as a larger political movement, it tried to separate their conduct from the rest of the American squad. The USOC, obviously, wanted put the situation to rest and end the emerging dialogue that surrounded the duo, likely in hopes of getting the incident out of the news as quickly as possible.

"I am embarrassed," Barnes confessed. "All of us are embarrassed. It makes our country look like the devil."[42]

The U.S. team more likely wanted to focus on the continued gathering of gold, particularly Davenport in his victory in the 110-meter hurdles in Olympic record time and Boston's Olympic-record leap of 27-1½ in the qualifier for the long jump. At the press conference following his victory, which occurred, many emphasized, without political incident, Davenport, described by the *New York Times* as "among the more militant Negro members of the American team," made it clear that the only race he wanted to address was the one he had just won. "I didn't come here to talk about black power or anything like that," he emphatically stated. Other athletes who also competed that day were not as certain. Some athletes wore the increasingly familiar black socks, others seemed to ignore or even resent the attention politics received, and still others seemed decidedly intent on keeping the press corps guessing. Triple jumper Art Walker even went so far as to wear distinctly white socks. Following his career-best leap of 56-2, good enough for fourth place, one of his opponents cracked about his socks, "How is everybody going to interpret that?"[43]

While such signs were complicated, they indicated that the USOC's attempt to portray Smith and Carlos as single entities was not going to be simple. As the press scoured the Olympic Village for opinions regarding both the protest and the ensuing apology, it became increasingly apparent that Americans were divided on the matter. One of the more moderate opinions came from the oft-sought Jesse Owens, who promised that no one else would step out of line in the manner of Smith and Carlos. "I want to talk to them," stated Owens. "I believe a man has a right to express his opinion and I don't think anybody should get mad. When the spectators booed Carlos and Smith as they left the stadium, they were expressing their opinion."[44] Owens's role, of course, went far beyond his personal testimonials regarding the protest. According to *Life* magazine, the USOC sent Owens to the Olympic Village to meet with a band of approximately twenty-five black athletes and to notify Smith and Carlos that the IOC wanted to send the duo home for breaking with Olympic canon in their action against the United States. Owens also warned the other athletes to avoid a similar fate by making only "humanitarian" protests rather than ones pointedly aimed against their country. His advice was greeted with marked objection. While not all of the athletes supported the mode within which Smith and Carlos made their statement, most felt that Owens, and therefore the USOC, had gotten it wrong: Smith and Carlos created a "pro-black," not an "anti-American," stance. According to Lee Evans, the situation intensified when hammer thrower Hal Connolly, who had won the gold medal in Melbourne in 1956, supported his black teammates against Owens. In response, Owens said to Connolly, "As far as I'm concerned, *you* don't even need to be here. I'm talking to my black brothers." Vince Matthews then pounced on Owens in defense of Connolly, who had been explicitly invited to the meeting by the black contingent of the squad.[45]

Such discord epitomized the atmosphere of the Olympic Village, where one poll found that of twenty U.S. athletes, "white and black," only five outright opposed the action, while thirteen claimed support for Smith and Carlos. Decathlete Tom Waddell, for example, said that he was "disappointed more Negro athletes backed down," and the irreproachable Al Oerter contended, "It's a free country. Perhaps if I felt as strongly about it as they do, I'd do the same thing." Connolly, who failed to qualify for the finals in Mexico, took a position similar to Oerter's, albeit in a more forceful manner. Deeming the black power gesture "great for our country," Connolly indicated that he found the black power action to be a *patriotic* gesture rather than one of embarrassment to the United States. "Let a Russian try that and see what happens," continued the 1956 gold medalist. "I know a lot of Russians who don't like what happened in Czechoslovakia, but they can't say a word." An opinion from the other side of the Atlantic concurred. "We all thought it was a bloody good show," remarked British distance runner John Wetton, with teammates Andrew Todd and John Davis nodding in unanimity. "It's bully that these blokes had nerve enough to express their feelings."[46]

Among those who voiced their opinions, Waddell and his support make for an important sidebar. While his sixth-place finish in Mexico did not make headlines (although he did beat eventual gold medalist Bill Toomey in five field events), his life eventually did.[47] Born Tom Flubacher, Waddell, a physician, came under terrific scrutiny for the various political battles he fought throughout his life. Drafted in 1966, he registered as a conscientious objector to escape serving in Vietnam and was assigned a domestic medical post. Undoubtedly, his political awareness enabled him to demonstrate a nuanced understanding of the Smith-Carlos action. For example, when asked by the international press if the pair had disgraced the American flag, Waddell responded similarly to Connolly: "I think they have been discredited *by* the flag more often than they have discredited it. Our image is so bad it can't get any worse.... Maybe this will help." Obviously, the army was not thrilled with his words. A few days after his remarks, an unfamiliar figure approached and notified him that Colonel Don Miller, the military liaison to all Olympians in the army, had ordered a court-martial; Waddell professedly shook the stranger off, because he was in the middle of the decathlon, and never heard anything about it again. Waddell, who died in 1987 of AIDS, became best known for the "Gay Games," which he founded in 1982 in a heavily criticized attempt to use sport as a vehicle for the acceptance of gay and lesbian culture in mainstream society, an idea with many parallels to the ideologies of the OPHR. According to Dick Schaap, Waddell's biographer, "Tom understood ... the feelings of the black American Olympians.... In Mexico City, Tom wrote press releases for black athletes, encouraged them, cheered for them."[48]

Like that of Waddell, the ardent support of the all-white U.S. men's crew team also was noteworthy. Plagued by illness and equipment pitfalls in Mexico City, the heavily favored rowers from Harvard finished their Olympic stint in sixth place overall, far from the gold medal many thought they certainly would capture. Alongside their discouraging difficulties on the water were those endured after the majority of the team announced support for the OPHR. Well into their stay in Mexico, for example, and after two of their riggers broke during their first qualifying heat, the disappointed team members were told by Olympic officials to cut their hair. While the IOC apparently found their look to be politically unacceptable, *Newsweek* argued that their hair was "no longer than current college styles," making it seemingly unfair, the magazine noted, that throughout their stay in Mexico the oarsmen were branded as "shaggies," "hippies," and "the grubby crew." The situation intensified when coxswain Paul Hoffman was "slammed against a wall and threatened by a boxing manager because he gave a protest button to a black boxer who requested it." Hoffman was then threatened with dismissal from the U.S. squad because he stood in sympathy with the wives of Smith and Carlos during the black power protest and allegedly was the one who supplied Smith with an OPHR button for Peter Norman. Hoffman understood the limits of his own participation, stating, "Let's face it, I'm not black," but he still had to endure the hazards of supporting the OPHR. The night before his final, the USOC called Hoffman into a meeting in the penthouse suite of the Reforma Hotel and charged him with transgressing the spirit of the Olympics. While Hoffman claimed he put on his "best prep school manner" and the committee finally determined he had not violated any Olympic code, its members did caution him that they could send him home. According to Hoffman,

> They asked me to pledge that even if I don't win a medal, I not demonstrate and the whole crew not demonstrate. I gave them my word. I had to get the boat to row. What the Olympic Committee has done here is to enforce its own opinions as to what is and is not proper behavior. And by law and by their own congressional charter they cannot do this. Our lawyers tell us what they did to Smith and Carlos violates the First Amendment.[49]

While controversial figures such as Waddell and the rogues from Harvard displayed passionate support for Smith and Carlos, many others disagreed with the notion that they had committed a patriotic gesture. Toomey, for example, diverged from teammate Waddell and argued that the Olympics were "strictly for competition," while New Jersey swimmer David Perkowski deemed the Olympics not "the time or the place for them to act as they did. They're members of a team and they should act that way." Bob Seagren, who shared headlines of victory alongside Smith the day after the protest, described the action as cheap. "If it wasn't for the United States they wouldn't have been there," Seagren told the press. "... If they don't like the United States, they can always leave." Some from outside the U.S. border agreed. Edward Belsoi, the head of the Kenyan team, which had threatened to boycott the Games because of South Africa, came out strongly against the perceived militancy. Although the Kenyans, in a move designed to demonstrate symbolically against apartheid, had recently fired track coach John Velzian because he was white, Belsoi claimed that politics had no place in the Olympic arena. In a vivid demonstration of what George Lipsitz has described as the "unexpected alliances as well as unexpected antagonisms" that often emanate within racialized struggles, Belsoi seemingly ignored previous allegiances to the cause and emphasized that his team was in no way associated with the American activists. "I think this is the wrong place to demonstrate," he said. "Politics should be kept out of the Games altogether. Let the politics of Americans be left in America."[50]

Many sports columnists agreed. For example, unflagging *Los Angeles Times* writer Jim Murray began his column on the "backward" technique of U.S. high jumper Dick Fosbury with an apology to his readers. "If this comes to you garbled, don't blame the transmission," he quipped. "I'm wearing my black glove." While seven years later Murray, an ardent supporter of the intersection between civil rights and sport, played an important role in forcing the Masters to permit Lee Elder to play, in 1968 his response to the black power protest was one of apathy. His focus on Fosbury's backward technique was inarguably a metaphor for what he found to be a mixed-up state of affairs in the Olympic Village. While he indirectly acknowledged that any notion that the Olympics could cultivate global amity and friendship was patently ridiculous, particularly because they had done so only to the point where they had not "started any wars," he remained critical of the manner in which Smith and Carlos made their point. "I don't care much for the Star-Spangled Banner, either," he agreed. "But I keep my shoes on." Most centrally, he criticized the black power gesture because it did not tell anyone anything not already known. "Our secret is out," he bantered. "We got race problems in our country." He continued that such a revelation would "come as a great astonishment to the reading public of the world." He also mocked how journalists looked for "the latest word in world politics" from the mouths of "19-year-old sprinters and long jumpers." In direct opposition to OPHR ideology, his point, obviously, was that Olympic Stadium was not where the important issues of the world should be discussed, and athletes should not be placed in positions of political authority. He proved his point with his own experiment: he asked a member of the Bulgarian track team—"I believe his name was Haravanko"—if he understood the protest that had taken place. "Oh yes," Murray claims the athlete answered, "Tommie Smith's mother is a political prisoner in America."[51]

Murray's colleague, columnist John Hall, took a different approach: outright hostility toward Smith and Carlos. He felt justified in his stance, because, as he pointed out throughout his column, some of his best friends were not only black, they were rich to boot. "Well, it takes all kinds," Hall began. "But I've got to tell you this morning I'm sick of Tommie Smith and John Carlos. I'm sick of their whining, mealy-mouth, shallow view of the world. I'm sick of apologizing and saying they are trying to improve things and that they have a right to take their best shot. Their best shot is a blank." Hall wrote this egregious column from Palm Springs at the annual baseball–celebrity golf tournament at the Canyon Country Club, surrounded by the likes of Gene Mauch, Don Drysdale, Bob Rodgers, and Bobby Knoop, as well as Willie Mays, Tommy Davis, and Willie Davis. He speculated that "somebody will probably make something" of the fact that Mays, Davis, and Davis were the only black players in the tournament and overlook the fact that Emmett Ashford, John Roseboro, Bubba Morton, "and a dozen other human beings" were unable to accept their invitations because of previous engagements. He emphasized that the white players conversed "with respect and admiration" about O. J. Simpson, and he regretfully pondered John Wooden, the sacred basketball coach, who "now pauses and carefully chooses every word lest he unwittingly offend Lew Alcindor." He continued with his reflection:

> ... the beautiful moments I've spent with Mike Garrett, a beautiful man ... [and] one of my first idols—Jackie Robinson ... of Bob Gibson, who will ask and get $135,000 to pitch a baseball next season ... of all the nation's top sportswriters standing around Lou Brock's locker during the World Series.... I thought of Nat Cole and Lena Horne and Louis Armstrong, whom I've loved all my life. I thought of the Southern California baseball writers, who were a little heartbroken last February when Bill Cosby was tied up in another part of the country and couldn't emcee their annual banquet at the Palladium.... I thought of driving up to the Truesdale Estates above Beverly Hills to interview a house—the $250,000 home Wilt Chamberlain was going to buy. I thought of Floyd Patterson, an uneducated, retarded and lonely child fighting and working to become a marvelous, articulate man as well as a millionaire. I thought of Joe Louis, Archie Moore and Dick Tiger—my good friends, kind and genuine gentlemen worthy of respect and contributing to civilization just by being what they are. Men.

Within relatively few words, Hall embodied all that Harry Edwards created the OPHR to oppose. He focused on a few elite, celebrity figures and their alleged riches and failed to look beyond those who made the headlines to see where everybody else lived. And because of that perspective, one designed to make the individual feel justified in his or her stance, Hall found latitude to criticize Smith and Carlos without any kind of acknowledgment of the broader movement they represented. His only sense of the world was one in which, in his view, "Tommie Smith and John Carlos do a disservice to their race—the human race," underscoring a global collectivity that simply did not exist and was not a viable category for critique.[52]

Columnist Clint Wilson Jr. of the *Los Angeles Sentinel* found that Hall, "with all the usual aplomb of a white person who can neither comprehend nor empathize with a sincere black gesture," epitomized why black journalists were "quite distressed over the reaction of some of our local White Press." Hall's piece, from Wilson's perspective, was merely "a pathetic and irrelevant sob story," one that simply reproduced the familiar "'some of my best friends are Negro super-athletes'" position. He continued:

> Well, it's too bad that John Hall didn't get the message Smith and Carlos had for him the other day. You see, it's the people like Hall who have a "shallow view of the world"; who won't face up to reality; who can't bring themselves to believe that black men have the dignity to show the world that they possess more than world-class athletic ability but also a love for their people that transcends politics and fear for their future careers in a white-dominated society. It has been said that when moral courage feels that it is in the right, there's no personal daring of which it is incapable. Black athletes are demonstrating that type of courage.[53]

Apparently out of Wilson's watchful gaze, in San Jose Louis Duino fell into a line of thinking comparable to Hall's, although via a different approach. Rather than focus on the reaction of other athletes or Olympic officials or take advantage of his local angle and unearth the sentiment of his San Jose audience to gauge the proper reaction, Duino looked to the response of those actually sitting in Olympic Stadium when the protest took place. While maintaining that the citizens of Mexico, "where demonstrations are common," were relatively indifferent, he found there to be "a great deal of comment among the 20,000 American visitors in the stands." He interpreted the whistles, boos, and turned-down thumbs to mean that the black power gesture was not successful in its consciousness-raising venture. Where it was successful, in his view, was in the international pressroom after the race, where Carlos, during interviews, "was right in the groove." Duino feared that the "press of the nations working against the United States" would exploit the incident as "good propaganda," and he further worried that other nations were "bound to get the wrong impression." Moreover, he was troubled that poor translation might allow for additional negative light to be shed on the United States. Sources informed him that the French, German, and Spanish press construed Carlos's oft-quoted words regarding the treatment of blacks in the United States, in which he made analogies to ants and cockroaches, much differently from how Carlos intended them.

What Duino failed to recognize, of course, was that Smith and Carlos—indeed, the entire OPHR—fully intended for this to occur in the interview room. While Duino charged that the pair displayed poor organization and strategy by not preparing written statements ahead of time, he ignored the possibility that Smith and Carlos, using the press to their own advantage, counted on misquotation and conjecture to confuse and broaden their central issues. Duino faulted Smith, especially, for his relative silence after the race in front of the international press and his failure to thank San Jose coach Bud Winter. When Smith was asked directly about who had contributed to his running career, he answered, "I would have to think about that question for an hour before I could answer." From this, Duino concluded that the young athlete "could have used some instruction in human relations ... [and] learn to give credit where credit is due."[54]

Perhaps most disconcerting to Duino was whether the ordeal was really over. He speculated, along with several others, that the appearance of Lee Evans in the 400-meters was sure to be the next phase of black power at the Games. When Howard Cosell, for example, asked Smith about any "more such incidents at these Games," Smith ambiguously replied: "I don't know because my events are finished. The other black athletes have a mind of their own and what they will do, I don't know."[55] While the USOC officially had indicated that any further protests would not be tolerated, the resonance of the Smith-Carlos action two days after it came to pass suggested that the press was willing to take notice of anything OPHR members had to offer. Thus, as the significance of the militant statement continued to overtake the significance of athletic performance itself, the perceived likelihood of more protests grew.

By the following day, a considerable change of heart in the USOC overshadowed any kind of gesture that Evans, or anyone else, might offer. As reporters increased the spotlight on the black-gloved fists, whatever tolerance and magnanimity that remained within the Olympic administration vanished, creating enough pressure for the USOC to revoke Smith's and Carlos's credentials, expel them from the Olympic Village, and force them to return home. According to the observations of the U.S. State Department, the IOC had not found the USOC's public condemnation of Smith and Carlos to be a sufficiently severe measure and insisted "suspension was minimum acceptable punishment." While the USOC argued that the black power demonstration was a "social act rather than political," the IOC countered that the USOC was "not controlling its athletes and that racial dissension might spread to other delegations."[56]

Unquestionably instrumental to the severe official sentence was the increasingly omnipresent image of two nationally uniformed black men engaged in an expression of defiance. The Olympic administration progressively became worried about the possibilities of an uprising of black athletes that came together over national lines. Henry Louis Gates Jr. has argued that the image of the black male is in itself a threatening one—an "already-read text" that evokes fear as a force that must be contained and controlled.[57] As the OPHR understood from the beginning, the bodies of athletes, particularly black ones, are not supposed to stage political movements. Deeply embedded in racism is what Kobena Mercer and Isaac Julien describe as "a logical dehumanization in which African people were defined as having bodies but not minds: in this way the super-exploitation of the black body as a muscle machine could be justified."[58] While the sporting arena is unusual, because it is an area where African Americans are urged to be superior in the name of nation, it closes when "misused" politically, as was the case with Smith and Carlos. Furthermore, the treachery embedded in their action was heightened because of their use of the black-gloved fist, a visual image that held weighty significance for audiences both within and outside the world of sports because of its connections to Black Power. Crucial to the development of any political movement, of course, is an understanding of its various audiences, all of which are inherently complex, depending on their social locations. Distinct communities, both marginal and dominant, are inextricably intertwined and dependent on one another to provide meaning. Thus, what was characterized as black in 1968, both by those who attached self-meaning to the designation (the OPHR) and by those who assigned it to another (the USOC), lent much of the import of the gloved gesture, momentarily knitting together an expansive black political community.

Many African American journalists felt that an emergent international definition of "black," bolstered by the success of not just U.S. black athletes but Africans and Latinos as well, intensified the heated reaction of officials. When the *Pittsburgh Courier*, for example, crowed about "the fast development ... [of] pigmented athletes" at any distance on the track, it contextualized the black power gesture in the broadest of terms. "In other words," contended the paper, "the threat here, last week, was the suggestion that 'Black Power,' an ugly specter to some whites, might be incarnated by a succession of insuperable blacks, ranging from a dazzling Jim Hines to the great [Abebe] Bikila." Olympic officials instead remained unaffected by any possibility of "a black takeover," continued the article. "'When we move back to normalcy, at the lower altitudes,' they conclude, 'the old relationship will again be in focus.'"[59] The *Los Angeles Sentinel* begged to differ with the USOC's viewpoint; the paper had predicted early on that the color lines of Olympic dominance would change in Mexico as "men of color from all sections of the world" competed in a variety of events.[60] The *Sentinel* continued to draw attention to what it saw as "a black man's show," noting that early on, regardless of the track event, "nothing but black men from black countries demonstrated winning talents."[61] Sports editor Brad Pye Jr. argued that such victories issued the loudest demonstration of racial pride of all, even when compared with the demonstration of

Smith and Carlos, who had, he admitted, ensured that "the Olympics will never be the same."

> Black athletes from America and from other black delegations around the world staged quiet and not too noticeable demonstrations in various ways. Tommie Smith's and John Carlos' black glove and black power gestures were seen over the world ... as they paraded around Mexico City's majestic Olympic Games stadium during ceremonies before a mass of humanity, which overflowed the stadium. The first real true black demonstrators were the three black men, who swept the 10,000, an event black people aren't supposed to win or even be considered as medal winners. But ... this myth was destroyed on the opening day of track and field.[62]

While many in the black press basked in the successes of a wide variety of athletes of color, the majority of Americans remained focused on the actions of Smith and Carlos. In Los Angeles, word of the expulsion came on the radio as the lead news story on the morning show of legendary Robert W. Morgan at KHJ. Newsreader J. Paul Addleston began the coverage:

> An almost unprecedented action by the U.S. Olympic Committee: they have suspended Negro athletes Tommie Smith and John Carlos and ordered them to leave the Olympic Village in Mexico City immediately. The committee cited what it called the untypical exhibitionism and unsportsmanlike conduct of the two runners when they accepted their medals after finishing 1-2 [sic] in the 200-meter dash. The men had raised their black-gloved arms and bowed their heads in a symbol of the black power movement. The Olympic Committee said the act was political, which is forbidden in the Games.[63]

The news continued with accounts of student activity at the University of Southern California, *Apollo* 7, the possibility of Russian intervention in Vietnam, George Wallace, and Jacqueline Kennedy's wedding to

Aristotle Onassis. However, when sports reporter Danny Baxter took the microphone, the story of Smith and Carlos returned:

> For a few moments it appeared the Olympic Games would run second to a black power demonstration by Tommie Smith and John Carlos of the U.S. Olympic team, and a follow-up statement such as this one by bronze medallist Mr. Carlos about IOC, the International Olympic Committee, president Avery Brundage: "I know Avery Brundage is a racist—definitely. I know this for myself. I'm from New York City and I went to track meets where they were supposed to have banquets and so forth ... and Avery Brundage told them he would not have any black people on his grounds. I know this; don't anyone have to tell me this because I have experienced this myself."[64]

While Baxter concluded that the discord in Mexico City had greatly subsided since the announcement of the suspension, sports pages throughout the nation indicated that in actuality the furor had only grown, because the USOC had granted "instant martyrdom," in the words of one sportswriter, to Smith and Carlos.[65] Along with lavish details of the wedding of "Jackie O," the front page now presented the Olympic saga, transferred from the sports section. The cover of the *New York Times* declared "2 Black Power Advocates Ousted from Olympics" and outlined the details of the suspension, which left the medals of Smith and Carlos intact, confiscated their Olympic credentials, and subsequently gave them forty-eight hours to vacate both the Olympic Village and Mexico.[66] In its official statement, the USOC stressed that the suspension occurred because of pressure from the IOC, which hinted that the entire U.S. squad was in jeopardy if Smith and Carlos were not punished accordingly.

> The United States Olympic Committee expresses its profound regrets to the International Olympic Committee, to the Mexican Organizing Committee and to the people of Mexico for the discourtesy displayed by two members of its team in departing from tradition during a victory

ceremony at the Olympic Stadium on Oct. 16. The untypical exhibition-ism of these athletes also violates the basic standards of good manners and sportsmanship, which are so highly valued in the United States, and therefore the two men involved are suspended forthwith from the team and ordered to remove themselves from the Olympic Village. This action is taken in the belief that such immature behavior is an isolated incident. However, if further investigation or subsequent events do not bear out this view, the entire matter will be re-evaluated. A repetition of such inci-dents by other members of the United States team can only be consid-ered a willful disregard of Olympic principles that would warrant the imposition of the severest penalties at the disposal of the United States Olympic Committee.[67]

Like the *Times*, the *Chicago Tribune* detailed "Black Power Show Causes Banishment" alongside the particulars of Kennedy's wedding, including speculation that she would be ostracized by the Catholic Church for marrying a divorced man. The *Tribune* also emphasized the pressure put on the USOC by the IOC. "I asked them what they would do if we did not take action," said USOC president Douglas Roby. "They said they might be forced to pull the entire United States team out of the Olympics."[68] Conversely, in the *Los Angeles Times*, Roby indicated that the situation was not so dire. While he admitted that the IOC was "incensed" and had "accused me and our committee of not having con-trol of our teams," he countered the report that the entire U.S. squad was in jeopardy. "I really don't think they would have disqualified the entire team," he confessed. "But there was concern that this might lead to a takeover, that there might be a broad demonstration."[69]

While the *Los Angeles Times* offered this other perspective from Roby, the *Tribune* seemed bent on demonizing Smith and Carlos and published an acrimonious editorial entitled "The Natural Right of Being a Slob." The vitriolic essay described the black power action as "an act contemptuous of the United States, which placed them on the team and paid the freight to Mexico City so that they could then insult their countrymen." It denied the pair any meaning behind their symbolic

gesture, stating that their black stockings were "emblematic of something" but never probing more deeply into what that something might
be. The editorial portrayed Carlos as an apathetic Olympian, one who
flung his medal to his wife "saying he didn't want it," and held the two
Americans responsible for creating "an unwarranted intrusion of domestic politics into international competition."[70] Of course, the *Tribune* was
not alone in such rancor, not even within the city limits. Its African
American counterpart, the *Chicago Daily Defender*, included a seething
editorial from editor and publisher John H. Sengstacke, who described
the black power protest as "inappropriate and perversive." While he did
find that the expulsion of Smith and Carlos proved to be "emotional
over-reaction" on the part of the USOC, he argued that there was
little to be achieved through such demonstration and asked, "Precisely,
what does black power mean at an international Olympiad?"[71] Outside
Chicago, *Time* magazine represented the national front with similar
contentions, finding that the events at Mexico City transformed the
exalted Olympic motto—Faster, Higher, Stronger—into "angrier, nas-
tier, uglier" and, in doing so, created "one of the most unpleasant controversies in Olympic history." The magazine held Smith and Carlos
directly responsible for ruining the atmosphere of the Games and
cracked, "East German, Russians, *even Cubans*, all stand at attention
when the 'Star Spangled Banner' ... is played."[72]

The degree to which such unsympathetic musings began to permeate the press coverage, along with the drama generated by the suspension and the debate over the possibility of other athletes protesting,
greatly skewed how the remainder of the Games was dealt with. In the
process, two magnificent occurrences on the track—Evans's world-
record 43.8 seconds in the American sweep of the 400-meters and
Beamon's world-record 29-2½ in the long jump—were eclipsed. Long
heralded among the greatest Olympic achievements, both records stood
for decades (American Butch Reynolds broke Evans's record in 1988
with a time of 43.29, and American Mike Powell broke Beamon's record
in 1991 with a leap of 29-4½). While both records astounded the sports
world, and some have since contended that Evans's mark was technically

a greater achievement, Beamon's leap had an enormous ocular impact that led to its greater worth in the media at the time. The jump broke the record by almost two feet; stadium officials did not have the necessary equipment to measure it. It would be eighteen years before anyone else (USSR jumper Robert Emmiyan) even hit the 29 mark. One sports physiologist went so far as to describe the jump as "a mutation performance," odd words at best, and judged it "an 84-year advance" in the event.[73]

Yet rather than exalt such athletic accomplishments, the media portrayed the two athletes as fulfilling a void created by Smith and Carlos. The *New York Post*, for example, rued that the feats took "second fiddle" to the political tones of Black Power. Neil Amdur of the *New York Times* resolved that the efforts of Evans, who had considered not running in deference to Smith and Carlos and wore black socks to the starting line, and Beamon "dramatically reaffirmed the tenacity and competitive spirit of United States athletics." Such a statement indicated that these values had been greatly disrupted by Smith and Carlos, despite the medals hanging around their necks and the world record achieved by Smith. Evans, continued Amdur, regardless of his close friendship with the suspended duo and his own OPHR involvement, displayed "the same fierce individual pride that earned him a berth on this strongest and most individualistic of American track teams."[74] But he did so, Amdur implied, without committing an act of treason. *Sports Illustrated* further confirmed this belief that Smith and Carlos acted by themselves, rather than as representatives of a collective body, and outside the prescribed norms of an eminent citizenship. The magazine decided that while "the Carlos-Smith affair took much of the play away from the Games themselves, and away from some marvelous performances," athletes such as Beamon "help[ed] brighten the Problem Games."[75]

Neither Evans's race nor Beamon's jump was featured prominently, if at all, on the front pages of the nation's newspapers. The focus continued to rest on whether they had created some sort of supplement to the protest of Smith and Carlos. The *New York Times*, for its part, determined that the Smith-Carlos suspension had "tempered the behavior of Negro American athletes" and speculated that little action would follow. It attributed this newfound calm to Roby, who had personally read the official USOC statement to the American sprinters, including Evans, before they took their mark in the 400-meters and allegedly told them that, while he was sorry he had to discuss such matters before their race, he wanted them "to be apprised of the serious consequences that may befall you if there is any outward demonstration today." The result, according to the *Times*, was that the victorious troika of Evans, Larry James, and Ron Freeman "in no way conducted themselves in a manner to incur official wrath" and were "apparently not defiant."[76]

Yet these athletes did create a sort of addendum to the Smith-Carlos action and invoked their own "Pantheresque" style. They took the victory stand "jauntily," according to the *Los Angeles Times*, with black berets on their heads and clenched, albeit naked, fists raised over them. After the long jump, Beamon accepted his gold medal in black socks and rolled up sweat pants, and teammate Ralph Boston accepted his bronze medal without shoes or socks. About his attire, Boston challenged the USOC—"Send me home, too, because I protested on the victory stand"—but like his compatriots in the 400-meters, he evidently did not cross the same line as Smith and Carlos and thus avoided a similar fate.[77] This perceived difference between the Smith-Carlos action, again pictured on the nation's sports pages, and those of subsequent American victors was succinctly illustrated beneath a *New York Times* photo of Evans, James, and Freeman on the dais. Entitled "Not Quite the Same Thing," the caption noted how the three smiling athletes lowered their fists and took their berets off during the playing of "The Star-Spangled Banner."[78] Their behavior, concurred Louis Duino, was "exemplary." Making an indirect reference to his previous portrayal of Smith, Duino pointed out that Evans "was most gracious in giving credit where credit was due," because he acknowledged his coaches, Bud Winter and Art Simburg. Such behavior, according to Duino, "put to an end the apprehension that has gripped the United States Olympic committee and millions of Americans all over the world." While he acknowledged that "some comment was made that the berets were a symbol of the Black Panthers," he insisted that these athletes were not members of the militant organization, and their berets should not be interpreted in any such way.[79] His point seemed validated by Evans himself, who later ascribed his black beret to the rain and said of his clenched fist, "It is just a salute. Some do it like this, some do it like that. This is our way of saluting."[80] Perhaps most important, the USOC agreed. "Everything has worked out fine," said Everett Barnes. "Evans accepted his medal in fine style." The ceremony was "perfectly all right," agreed Roby, who said he "found nothing objectionable in it."[81]

The restraint shown by Evans in his comments undoubtedly surprised many, particularly since a black beret on a black man in 1968—accompanied by a clenched fist, no less—may not have been a Black Panther membership card but certainly evoked a radical subtext. With gold medal in hand, Evans tried to infuse his victory with meaning but did so with a far less polemical tone. "I won it for all the black people in America," he told the press. Nonetheless, when asked by one reporter if he had also won it for some white people, he affably replied, "I have a lot of white friends at San Jose State and a lot all over the world. This was for them too."[82] As a member of the San Jose squad and an original member of the OPHR, Evans was considered by many to be closest to Smith and Carlos, a bond affirmed when he admitted the intense pressure he felt before his race and how he dealt with it. "I got things off my mind ... by thinking about winning," he said, "just like a friend of mine did."[83] According to the *New York Post*, Evans learned of Smith's and Carlos's expulsion on his way to breakfast, just hours after it had been handed down, and reacted with, "Damn it, damn it, I can't believe it." Later described as "teary-eyed and distraught and ... almost on the verge of collapse," many doubted that Evans would run. While rumors circulated that Smith tried to get Evans to forfeit, his decision to take his place on the starting line, he claims, was influenced by Carlos, who told him, "Get all the gold you can, and then do your thing."[84] Yet even after he decided to compete, his path to the starting line was not without conflict but rather was filled with confrontations with those he held responsible for the censure of Smith and Carlos:

I saw an Olympic Committee cat who said "Hi" to me real friendly and I grabbed him and shoved him so he almost fell down. "Mother, don't even speak to me after what you done to my partners!" ... The cat cut out and run into his room and slammed the door. I was cryin'. I went to the elevator and started beatin' on it with my fist. And another committee member says "hi" and I went for him too.[85]

However, this anger did not translate into any negative repercussions for Evans from the Olympic administration. Other athletes followed his diplomatic example and vocalized displeasure with the suspension of Smith and Carlos but, like Evans, did not take their dissent far enough to incur the wrath of the USOC. Ron Freeman, for example, found the suspension to be "terrible" and speculated that there would be "a lot of guys going home." "Some white ones, too," added Harold Connolly, who condemned a process that suspended two athletes without giving them "the opportunity to speak to the people who censured them and without any recourse to appeal." High jumper Ed Caruthers deemed the suspension "terrible, awful," while sprinter Vince Matthews declared the USOC response "unfair" and declared himself in "open opposition." Triple jumper Art Walker, who had worn the white socks during his event, pointed out that the U.S. squad never dipped its flag during the Opening Ceremony when passing the host country's head of state, as dictated by Olympic tradition. Wyomia Tyus described the situation as "awful" and contended that Smith and Carlos "did not hurt anybody. As long as they don't touch somebody and hurt them I don't see how they can be punished." Scott Steketee, one of the Harvard rowers so supportive of the OPHR, judged the suspension "unfair and very tragic" but said he would participate in the rowing finals because "rowing is a team sport and those of us who disagree with this decision have an obligation to the boat and to the crew." Yet some of his teammates, such as brothers Cleve and Mike Livingston, also expressed regret over the suspension. "I was with Hal Connolly, the hammer thrower, last night," said Cleve. "He was talking about how good it was to be from a country where there is freedom of speech and freedom of expression without fear of punishment. He said it was something to be proud of. Now there is nothing to be proud of." Hurdler Leon Coleman indicated a willingness to go further, however, stating, "If they make one of us go, I am pretty sure we'll all go. We're winning all the medals and the Olympic Committee is getting the credit."[86]

In the face of such ardent support for Smith and Carlos, other Americans defended the USOC decision. "I do not think it is so tragic," said water polo player Barry Weisenberg. "In my opinion an act like that in the medal ceremony defiles the American flag." Teammate Bruce Bradley agreed: "I think the U.S. Committee was well within its rights. It must maintain some sort of order." The American boxing contingent, including a flag-waving and victorious George Foreman, concurred and prepared to go on with its events. "Everybody has a personal opinion," stated boxer Harland Marbley. "I have got mine and I keep it for myself. I am for me." Boxing coach Robert "Pappy" Gault, the first black head coach of a U.S. Olympic squad, stated his feeling on the matter even more explicitly: "We came here to fight. We're proud to be fighting for the United States. This is our country. We're all brothers, aren't we?"[87]

As the international press struggled to make sense of Black Power politics, it became clear that international opinion varied. The *New York Post* apparently took great sarcastic pleasure in quoting a French reporter who called after Carlos, "We're weez you, Carlos."[88] Like Australian Peter Norman, Martin Jellinghaus, who anchored the bronze medal 4 × 400-meter relay team for West Germany, wore an OPHR button on the victory dais.[89] Noel Caroll, a member of the Irish track team, found "the demonstration by Smith and Carlos ... foolish and childish" but emphasized that "the punishment was even more ridiculous. It was too much for too little. It made heroes of them."[90] Tetsuo Ohba, head of the Japanese delegation, said that he would "not hesitate to suspend any of the Japanese athletes if they did the same kind of thing the two Americans did." Harry Jerome, described by the *New York Times* as "one of the three Negroes on Canada's track team," acknowledged the power contained within the Smith-Carlos action and why it raised so much debate:

Their action represented violence, a play for power. Fear is involved and I think the people in the United States are tired of violence. Have they been martyred? God, yes. I think they are sincerely trying to make an awareness that will lead to a better United States. The black man wants to be looked on not only as an entertainer, but also as someone with a place in the social structure.[91]

Others outside the United States did not have as clear a picture of the situation as Jerome. For example, Felicio Torregrosa, head of the Puerto Rican squad, speculated, "It is hard for Latin Americans to understand the attitude of the Negro athletes because in our country we do not have the racial conditions that may exist in the United States." He continued, "But, regardless of the Negroes' reasons, politics should not be brought into the Olympic Games." Perhaps even more significant than the nationalist secession of the Puerto Rican official was the unclouded position of Soviet track coach Gabriel Korobkov. "It's too bad," he told the press. "They are supposed to [be] free people. It wouldn't happen to us. We don't mix sports and politics."[92] Yet despite Korobkov's observation regarding his own purportedly apolitical state-funded program, it was overwhelmingly clear that there was little truth left to the incessant overture that the Olympics remained separate from the political underpinnings of the world.

Homeward Bound: The Problems of Legacy and Power

While the USOC revoked the credentials of Smith and Carlos and demanded they leave the Olympic Village within forty-eight hours, a spokesman from the Mexican government told them they could remain in the city if they went to the Mexican immigration department and solicited routine tourist cards.[93] The offer fit well with *Los Angeles Sentinel* reporter Booker Griffin's contention that Mexicans had welcomed African Americans with unusually open arms throughout the Games. "The most scorned spectator ... is the Joe (or Jane) Doe white American.... The brothers are received just the opposite," observed Griffin. "The brown brothers on the other side of the border roll out the red carpet for American blacks.... Black is truly beautiful to the Mexico City natives."[94]

Despite such hospitality, the intensity that surrounded Smith and Carlos became all but unbearable, making it was obvious to them that remaining in Mexico would do little good. According to the *New York Post*, for example, after the USOC announced the suspension, Carlos and his tearful wife had to combat roughly one hundred reporters between the U.S. headquarters in the Olympic Village and the main building. As Carlos, along with "two New York Negro friends dressed in black power costumes with beads," made his way through the crowd he lashed out at the media ring: "I want to be left alone—I told you I want to be left alone. If anybody puts another one of those things [microphones] in my face I will knock him down and stomp on him."[95] Of course, Carlos played a role in making his exit anything but subtle. In addition to his outburst against the press, Carlos stood in an eighth-floor window adorned with a sign declaring "Brundage Must Go" and taunted an outdoor press conference given by Douglas Roby.[96]

Largely because of the overwhelmingly jarring environment, the suspended athletes agreed to get on a plane and return to U.S. soil. According to U.S. State Department reports, Roby had phoned both Smith and Carlos at their hotels, the Diplomatico and the Reforma, to read them the official suspension pronouncement and offered to meet with them in his office at the Reforma to discuss it further. While both refused the meeting, they did see Roby in the Olympic Village in a meeting mediated by Jesse Owens and Billy Mills. The two suspended athletes agreed to leave Mexico via transportation arranged by USOC-contracted travel services.[97] Thus, on October 21, 1968, Smith and Carlos handed in their Olympic credentials to immigration and boarded Western Airlines flight 910 heading for San Francisco.[98] Once they exited the transnational Olympic context and returned to the physical space of the nation, attention shifted from the multiple messages they had sent around the world to control over the historical legacy of those messages. The early stages of this process made their homecoming contentious, at best. For example, when Carlos was leaving the Olympic

Village, a bystander asked where he was going. To his response of "home," someone sneered, "Do you mean the United States?"[99]

Stateside, the situation showed no improvement when a flock of reporters haplessly chased the world-class sprinters through the airport, badgering them with questions.[100] These sportswriters were concerned, too, about where the black power protest fit into history, and they worked vigorously at finding it a place. Initially, they tried to fit the gesture within a broader Olympic trajectory by finding historical precedents for the action. The "celebrated case of Eleanor Holm," as described by the Los Angeles Times, began to surface on American sports pages, making an odd juxtaposition between the battle against racism exhibited by Smith and Carlos and, of all things, social drinking. Swimmer Holm, of course, had been expelled from the team by Avery Brundage for drinking champagne on the ship to Berlin in 1936.[101] For her part, Holm lashed out against the actions of the Olympic administration in implicit defense of Smith and Carlos. "It's impossible to tell the right and wrong of a suspension from here," Holm stated. "But I will say that according to the committee, we should be like little sheep and allow ourselves to be herded."[102] American rower John Sayre, who had won a gold medal in Rome in 1960, raised similar issues when he spoke out against the Olympic administration's decision to limit the number of athletes, six per nation, in the Closing Ceremony in Mexico. "The athletes do all the running and jumping and swimming and participating," argued Sayre, who worked as a liaison between the USOC and the athletes, "but athletes never get a voice in the way the Olympics are run." Sayre contended that the conflict regarding Smith and Carlos was instrumental to the administration's decision to restrict the number of athlete participants in the ceremony, and he maintained that the lack of athletes in power prevented any discussion over the matter. "There ought to be guys like Jesse Owens, Billy Mills, Emil Zatopek and Abebe Bikila helping run the Olympics," he continued, "instead of just rich men that have a lot of time."[103]

Such attacks on the Olympic administration in the aftermath of Mexico City were joined by even more specific declarations of support for Smith and Carlos, some from surprising sources. While Democratic vice presidential nominee Edmund Muskie told the press that the black power action "probably should not have been made," he admitted that it was difficult to form any opinion, because, unfairly, Smith and Carlos "were given no hearing."[104] Jackie Robinson, considered to be politically conservative despite his pathbreaking role in baseball, said he "admired the pride in their blackness" and reproached the USOC for its actions. "The Olympic Committee made a grave mistake in suspending them," Robinson told the press. "I take pride in their proudness in being black. What they did had nothing to do with shaming this country."[105] Perhaps even more surprising than Robinson's endorsement was that of San Jose State College president Robert Clark, who publicly applauded the banished duo in the midst of his increasingly fragile position on campus. After the San Jose members of the OPHR left the campus for Mexico City, Clark became embroiled in a heated battle between the United Black Students for Action (UBSA) and athletic director Robert Bronzan. At a rally, the UBSA, represented by its president, Mal Whitfield, called for the removal of Bronzan on the grounds that he had withdrawn scholarship money from African American members of the freshman football team. The organization demanded that a black athletic director replace him. While Clark agreed to an inquiry into the matter, realizing that the charges put the entire athletic program in question, he defended Bronzan. His stance came only days after he unilaterally celebrated Smith and Carlos upon their homecoming, sent them a telegram, and described them as "honorable young men." He adamantly denounced the actions of the USOC and asked America the critical question of whether the action of the two athletes was actually that heinous, considering all that had been done to them:

> I hope their gesture will be interpreted properly. They do not return home in disgrace, but as the honorable young men they are, dedicated to the cause of justice for the black people in our society. . . . We at San Jose State College are proud of the achievements of Smith and Carlos in the Olympic Games. All Americans should be proud of their achievements. . . .

Millions of Americans must have seen Tommie Smith on television, as I did, explaining the symbolism of his and John Carlos' gestures, which have caused their expulsion from the Olympics.... [Smith's explanation] was calm and rational ... his sincerity unquestioned. The message he conveyed should be of real concern to all Americans.... I regret that our treatment of our black athletes has been such as to prompt them to feel they must use the Olympic Games to communicate their real concern for the condition of blacks in America.[106]

Of course, not everyone in San Jose accepted the protest as Clark did. Louis Duino, yet again, used his column to attack the two local students for their failure to understand the global Olympic audience, which he claimed remained puzzled as to what their protest meant. According to Duino, the world did not appreciate their position, as was illustrated by one member of the Barbados Olympic team. The Bajan athlete, according to Duino, stated that he did not "understand ... the protest" because "the black man in America is much better off than those in other parts of the world." Duino claimed that the Mexican audience also was baffled by the protest, and he cited an editorial in an unnamed Mexican newspaper that criticized Smith and Carlos. While the editorial contended that the two athletes had a legitimate cause, it argued that the Olympics were not the proper forum for it. What particularly disturbed Duino was another publication in the same newspaper: an apology from Smith and Carlos to the Mexican people, who they claimed had given them lots of support, and to the Mexican organizing committee. Why had they not apologized to the USOC, Duino wondered. Where was their apology to the American people?[107]

The letters to the editor in the *New York Times* both contradicted and reinforced Duino's position. Many realized the primary contradiction inherent in the censure of Smith and Carlos: as they attempted to secure human rights, they were denied American liberty. The majority of the letters the *Times* selected for publication unabashedly supported the action of Smith and Carlos and attempted to continue the dialogue begun by the two athletes. One such letter posed a critical question to the nation: "When are we going to treat these people with the dignity and individuality that they deserve as human beings?" Another declared the protest "poignant" and determined that the "racist attitude of the American Olympic officials will not be forgotten, four years hence, when black athletes are once again asked to put aside their just grievances to bring Olympic glory to the United States." Another letter pushed the blame beyond the USOC and postulated that "if the omnipotent [USOC] must play Simon Legree with someone and crack the whip, then let them crack it over the heads of A.B.C.-TV [and] the Republican National Committee ... [who] have used the nonpolitical Olympic games for baser reasons than that of black pride." Yet in the midst of the sympathy, compassion, and interrogation, others obviously felt much differently, as illustrated by a letter that described the protest as

> the most heartsickening thing of my life.... I have no objections to the black protest, but I am ashamed of any American who cannot look at the flag as it is being raised.... I feel that any person who cannot be proud of his flag and country should not be allowed to represent it. If it were not for the fact that they had the opportunity of being an American they might very well not be at the Olympics to win their medals.[108]

The verdicts rendered in the black press were as mixed as the sentiments conveyed by *Times* readers. The African American press, with a weekly rather than a daily publishing schedule, generally was not able to remain as topical on the course of events in Mexico City as the national press. But it did present its readership with a wide variety of perspectives on black protest, the banishment of Smith and Carlos, and the overall state of the black athlete—and the wider black community—in the United States. Many black journalists, for example, unilaterally hailed Smith and Carlos as heroes. *Los Angeles Sentinel* reporter Booker Griffin declared the episode "the most profound single act of this Olympics ... one of the greatest moments for the Afro-American in the 400 years of colonization in this country." The two were condemned for their actions, observed Griffin, not because they politicized the Games but rather because "they didn't have the power and protection ... the sanction of the polite inner circle of the power elite who respect the code of honor among thieves."[109] Colleague Clint Wilson Jr. agreed. Why were Smith and Carlos sent home? "All because the 'spirit of the Games' was violated?" he asked. "Phooey! You tell me if the 'spirit' of the competition calls for tallying of medals and team standings.... You tell me if the competition between the U.S. and the Soviet Union isn't political and in violation of the 'spirit' of the Games."[110] Columnist Maggie Hathaway was even more direct in her praise of the black Olympians. "There is no law against 'doing your thing.' How dare the officials ask them why they wore tams!" she wrote in reference to the men's relay team. "They don't ask Russians why they click their heels or wear monacles [sic].... The boys were BLACK and it took POWER to win so that's BLACK POWER."[111] Last, Jack Tenner, in his usual summation of the week's most interesting quotes, used the words of the British team as his own: "I don't know Tommie Smith and John Carlos, but one more quote from me to them: 'It was truly a bloody damned good show.'"[112]

Yet while such columnists praised Smith and Carlos, the front of the *Los Angeles Sentinel* sports section did not. Declaring in a headline "Olympics No Platform for Problems," sportswriter Brad Pye Jr. described the black power protest as "out of place" and, echoing the *Los Angeles Times*, as "a Hitler-type salute." "All countries and all people have a multitude of problems," observed Pye. "The Olympic Games is not a problem-solving platform."[113] Less blinkered, the editorial page took a more traditionally accommodationist stance. It noted that within ten days' time, two noteworthy events had taken place: the black power action in Mexico City and the flight of *Apollo* 7. The protest action, the editorial judged, "though widely applauded in our communities, was hardly as epochal" but instead revealed "just how diverse are the planes on which two groups of Americans operate today." Rather than make the focal point issues of education, housing, and family life, the protest was another relatively useless gesture with little impact.

On sober reflection, we suggest that American Negroes must begin to re-evaluate the actions of all who would be our leaders. For many years, we have paid tribute to people who have done little more than "holler at Whitey," or try to embarrass him, giving them credit for great courage and brilliance. But, time has proven that mere acts such as Smith and Carlos pulled off in Mexico City do not necessarily prove courage or brilliance, nor do they necessarily further our cause.... It has been said that Smith and Carlos represented all "black Americans" when they ran at Mexico City. The fact is, however, that [they] decided to compete ... after Harry Edwards' proposed boycott had failed.... Although we disagreed with the proposed boycott, we feel that Smith and Carlos would have revealed greater courage if they had stuck to their original plan not to compete in Mexico City.[114]

While the *Los Angeles Sentinel*'s writers could not agree as a whole, other African American papers were more decisive in their response to the protest. The *Baltimore Afro-American* obtained its own "up close and personal" view via sports editor Sam Lacy, who went to Mexico City to "bring AFRO readers on-the-spot, authoritative, and colorful stories of who's who and what's what among the world's greatest athletes."[115] In terms of Smith and Carlos, the newspaper rigidly separated the world-record race from the black power gesture that followed. In the sports section, the race was prominently displayed in both headlines and photographs, with news of the protest buried in the middle of details regarding Smith's run.[116] The protest, although on the front page, was presented as a small news item by Lacy. Although he had been an early OPHR supporter, Lacy editorialized that the protest "was childish and in extremely poor taste," dismissed it as "showboating," and found it to be "reminiscent of the 'heil' salute of the Nazis." While he understood the gesture was calculated to "embarrass the United States," his reaction was far different: "It embarrassed me more."[117]

Unlike its Baltimore counterpart, the *Pittsburgh Courier* hailed the image of Smith and Carlos in both photographs and political cartoons. With the caption "BLACK AND PROUD" beneath a photo of the black power gesture on the front page, the newspaper that had helped pave the way for Jackie Robinson some twenty years earlier boldly condemned the USOC and IOC for their "sudden eruption of Administrative Olympic racism." By banishing Smith and Carlos, *Courier* writer Ric Roberts argued, Olympic officials "promised to dramatize the American 'dilemma' for all the world to behold: and with an intensity nothing of the past ever produced." Rather than acknowledge the statement against U.S. racism, the "'red neck' response," Roberts concluded, transformed the two athletes into "global trouble makers."[118] The editorial page reiterated Roberts's point with a bold cartoon entitled "Pride Prevails"; it showed a large black fist punching a hole through the heavens, which was surrounded by doves and emitted rays of light over Olympic Stadium.[119] The following week, another cartoon adorned the editorial page: three black runners, "USA" emblazoned on their chests, running with heads held high and clenched fists held even higher.[120] On the sports page, the paper announced that the USOC had finally stopped "'making ado' about balled fists" with the realization that "'making a mountain of a molehill,' on an international stage, made less than good sense." However, while officials might be able to put the incident behind them, the paper concluded that the black community likely would not. "When the years have grown dim ... the spectacle of Smith and Carlos ... will be a folk tale, for black grandmothers yet unborn."[121]

The variety of these responses in the African American press mirrored those found in the Olympic Village and in other newspapers across the country, with some finding strength in the black protest gesture, and others finding it akin to the Nazi salute expressed on the Olympic victory dais so many years before. The nature of the gesture, of course, engendered such response, which Howard Cosell astutely sensed on the day following the protest. Realizing that the silent act opened the door for numerous misinterpretations, Cosell asked Smith if he expected any backlash. "To do something good, someone will always find fault, so I was prepared for this, Howard," Smith replied.[122] Thus, despite the circle of support for Smith and Carlos, the vitriolic judgments made by various sectors of the American public, including the press, necessitated that, upon their return stateside, they work to ensure that they take control of their message and situate it as they wanted. Carlos, in one of his first actions upon his return, announced a plan to sue the USOC. "I am going to nail them to the wall," Carlos told the press. "I have a lawyer in Los Angeles and a lawyer in New York. They have told me that the United States Olympic Committee acted in violation of the Constitution. I am going to see to it that they have to pay."[123]

Although it never came to fruition, one of the critical consequences of the planned lawsuit was that it brought some attention back to Harry Edwards, who had steered clear of Mexico City at the advice of Louis Lomax and, as he describes in his autobiography, for fear for his own life.[124] Whether his fears were founded, some journalists interpreted his absence in Mexico to be further indication that few, if any, still found any validity in the OPHR. "Where's Harry?" the *Los Angeles Sentinel* sniped under a photo of Jim Hines on the victory podium, informing readers that Edwards was "nowhere in sight" to witness the glory achieved by the black athletes who had finally opted to participate.[125] Despite such disparagement, when Smith and Carlos returned to California, Edwards immediately tried to become involved in the aftermath of the suspension. "These brothers were persecuted because of their political beliefs," he announced. "We are now organizing students on major college campuses throughout the country to carry out acts in support of these brothers." While Edwards remained vague about what these acts of support would include, he did specify that followers would "do exactly the same thing that John Carlos and Tommie Smith did—turn their heads down and give the black power salute whenever the anthem is played."[126] Within the next year, a smattering of such actions occurred. The University of Wyoming, for example, suspended fourteen black football players who wanted to wear black armbands in a game against the notoriously racist Brigham Young University team.

Perhaps most significant, Smith and Carlos announced the commencement of a national speaking tour, set to begin on college campuses in Washington, D.C. Stokely Carmichael, not Harry Edwards, announced the tour and issued a call for the banished duo to receive a "hero's welcome."[127] Howard University sent three busloads of students as well as the school's drum corps to the airport to ensure that a proper greeting took place, and Federal City College suspended classes for the day to allow students to attend the events. Once at Howard, an estimated two thousand people transformed the event into a formal coronation of the banished Olympians as part of the broader aggregate of Black Power in America. While Smith remained at home in California with his mother, who, according to Edwards, "nearly had a nervous breakdown because of harassment by the press," Carlos stood on stage beside H. Rap Brown and Carmichael. "From this day forward," Carmichael declared, "Black people will pick their own Black heroes." Carlos was presented with a relief medal of Malcolm X, which he designated "the real gold medal." The other medals that he and Smith had won, he argued, proved the hypocrisy of the USOC. "Since they disowned Tommie Smith and me," he charged, "let them disown our medals, too."[128]

Carlos articulated a key question enveloped in the battle between the individual athlete and the national collective. Should the United States count the gold and bronze medals from the men's 200-meters in its medal race with the Soviets if it does not "count" the athletes that won them? Should athletes continue to participate and win on behalf of their nation if they are denied full access to that nation's citizenship? While the *Pittsburgh Courier* proudly hailed the role of African Americans in the successful U.S. claim to the "unofficial but much-coveted" Olympic "team title," others hesitated.[129] According to "White-on-White" columnist Gertrude Wilson of the *New York Amsterdam News*, the United States is only the "home of the free and the brave when you are fighting for your country in Vietnam, or winning Olympic medals in international competition, but ... is a myth when you are black...." By banishing the duo but counting their accomplishments, observed Wilson, the nation obviously "values the metal called gold which they have won for us, far more than their personhood, their superiority, their manliness."[130] Of course, the case of Smith and Carlos was not unique in this way but, rather, typical within the history of black struggle in the

United States. During World War II, for example, many questioned whether African Americans should travel abroad and fight for a democracy denied to them at home. Eminent scholar John Hope Franklin, for example, anxiously wanted to do his part but found that overt transactions of racism prevented any meaningful execution of his willing support. "The United States," Franklin surmised, "did not need me and did not deserve me."[131]

Such issues came further to the forefront when Smith and Carlos, at the hands of Carmichael and others, became more fundamentally recognized as black power figures. The Cuban 4×100-meter relay team (Hermes Ramirez, Juan Morales, Pablo Montes, and Enrique Figuerola Camue) declared, for example, that they wanted to send their silver medal to Carmichael, "because we believe," explained Camue, "the American Negro's cause is a just and fair one."[132] Their action likely built on a mutual admiration that had developed in Mexico. "Many Negro Americans got a different picture of Cuba via Mexico City than they could have ever imagined," wrote Booker Griffin. "It was very illuminating for some of these brothers to have the opportunity to learn that there are more world views than the shallow, petty and self-centered ones passed to American citizens by our media."[133] The U.S. women's 4 × 100-meter relay team—Barbara Ferrell, Margaret Bailes, Mildrette Netter, and Wyomia Tyus—followed the Cuban example. Although *Sports Illustrated* claimed that "not even all the black girls on the track team were quick to back [Smith and] Carlos," the American women looked to add to their world record and gold medal by carving out a small and yet substantial space for themselves within the movement from which they had been excluded. "I would like to say," Tyus said to the press, "that we dedicate our relay win to John Carlos and Tommie Smith."[134]

Others were less sure than the Cubans or the American women about where Smith and Carlos fit after the Olympics. Mexico City's English-language newspaper, the *News*, editorialized that Smith and Carlos made "one hell of a mistake" but also arraigned the USOC: "Wouldn't it have been better to ignore the incident?"[135] Arthur Daley at the *New York Times* unequivocally agreed, arguing that the IOC-forced suspension of the two athletes by the USOC "so dignified the protest that they blew it onto the front pages of almost every newspaper in the world."[136] Most curiously, *Sports Illustrated*, notwithstanding its "Black Athlete" series by Jack Olsen and its insightful coverage of "the Problem Games," dropped the baton and buried any news of Smith and Carlos. Undoubtedly puzzled about how to cover an event that was, for the first time, being so well-documented on television, the weekly magazine failed to utilize its usually sharp journalism skills and color photography to promote any sense of the day-to-day particulars of the Games and chose to elevate a story on the Green Bay Packers to its cover rather than the increasingly famous photo of the protest.[137]

Despite the apparent journalistic confusion experienced by *Sports Illustrated*, the prevalence of the protest—and the suspension—in mass-mediated discussions that followed the Olympics secured it a substantial place in discussions of Black Power for years to come. Prophetically, among one of his many explanations regarding the gesture, Smith stated that the scarf around his neck had symbolized "blackness with a capital B."[138] Alongside all of the structural ramifications that the protest had in American society, many of which Harry Edwards submitted in a detailed sociological treatment, the notion of blackness is perhaps its strongest legacy, sustaining interest in it for the decades that followed. As John Carlos remembered years later, "The juice, the fire of '68, ... scared a lot of people. All of us were such strong personalities, and that scared people. It scared government and business, everybody. It still scares them."[139]

In 1969, the resonance suggested by Carlos emerged in ABC's *Wide World of Sports* wrap-up program, entitled "Highlights of the Sixties." As explained by host Jim McKay, "The political turmoil that swept the world in the 1960s did not spare the field of sport." McKay gave a brief historical overview of how this tumult affected the Olympics in 1968 in particular, remarking that the Mexican student protests jeopardized "the very existence" of the Games, as the possible readmission of South Africa did and, naturally, the "threatened American Negro boycott." McKay assured viewers that "eventually the American blacks came," but, he continued, "two of them, Tommie Smith and John Carlos, caused worldwide controversy by this symbolic gesture of protest, fists in black gloves, on the victory stand during the playing of the American anthem." To be sure, he noted, the protests were not limited to U.S. racial politics. Celebrated Czech gymnast Vera Cáslavská, for example, who shared the gold medal dais with Soviet gymnast Larissa Petrik after the floor exercise, bowed her head during the playing of her co-medalist's anthem to protest the invasion of her country, a move that reportedly put her into political trouble at home. "Now it seems that sport has become a stage for protest . . . ," McKay worried. "It's been a time of trouble all right."[140]

Another program in 1969, albeit one with far less exposure than *Wide World of Sports*, also focused on the ramifications of such political actions. Public television's *Black Journal*, hosted by Lou House, sponsored a roundtable discussion on the black athlete. Promising to "report and review the events, the dreams, the dilemmas of black America and black Americans," the show had carved a niche for itself in terms of black radicalism. Its premiere episode just a year earlier, for example, featured interviews with Bobby Seale and a jailed Huey Newton, days before his trial for murder.[141] Composed of "five of the country's greatest athletes"—Jackie Robinson, Bill Russell, Arthur Ashe, Johnny Sample, and Harry Edwards—the roundtable discussion began with a montage of children playing basketball on a playground, accompanied by soft music. As the beat grew more intense with heavier percussion, the images shifted to Ali in the ring, Robinson sliding into home, and a range of black athletes on the track and football field. "One area in this country where we have demonstrated our excellence is the athletic arena," a voice-over explained. "However, if we check it out, we find that racism in America knows no boundary lines—that the black athlete has also been a victim of foul play."

William Greeves, executive producer of the program, introduced and explained the athletic and political relevance of each of the roundtable participants. Robinson, he said, broke the color line in professional sports in the United States, was a former Rookie of the Year, and in 1962 had been inducted into the Baseball Hall of Fame. Russell, of course, led the Boston Celtics to eleven championships in thirteen years, was the first black coach in the NBA, but retired "because he could no longer derive satisfaction from the game and he refused to play for money alone." Greeves presented Ashe as the top tennis player in the United States, a member of the victorious Davis Cup team in 1968, the only African American in "the lily-white world of big league tennis ... [who] had to win most of his honors at country clubs and athletic clubs where he wouldn't even be considered for membership because of his race," and an architect in the movement to bar South Africa from the 1971 Davis Cup tournament. Sample, the left corner-back and defensive captain for the victorious 1968 New York Jets, had been sidelined with a back injury in 1969 but remained "one of the more outspoken black men in the world of sports." Last, Edwards, a former basketball and track star, was (somewhat erroneously) described as the "organizer of the dramatic and now historic black protest at the 1968 Olympics ... instrumental in moving our struggle into the world of athletics" while he completed his own doctoral work and attempted to organize amateur athletes nationally.

Greeves set the tone for the conversation with his first question: "I think the black athlete has had a very large role to play in the sort of spirit of the black community. How do you gentlemen feel about that?" In response, Ashe argued that the media, especially television, had played a problematic role in the equation. "You see black, white, Puerto Rican players playing together and superficially if you don't delve into [it] any further you say, well, they're living pretty nice but you never visit the locker rooms," he said. "You don't see what goes on beyond the cameras—how the off-field life [of] a black athlete is." Edwards concurred but held the sports industry accountable. Of importance, he refuted sport as an arena by which to gauge racial equality, an idea encompassed by the OPHR in the previous year, and argued that the achievements of the athlete in U.S. society, as well as the representations of that figure in the media, could not be used as sound measurements of civil rights success.

There's a lot of criticism of the mass media, the news reporting, et cetera, but I think that the sports industry in and of itself has a great deal of responsibility for the degree to which sports in fact has not brought people together in this society, because they haven't told the truth that would tend to undermine some of the established, institutionalized racism, discrimination, prejudice that exists between people in this society. They've tended to build up this myth that in fact what you see on the field is a microscopic portrait of reality in a mass society, and this is ... simply not the case.

Furthermore, interjected Russell, the athlete cannot be considered a typical citizen in *any* capacity. "It's like you gradually become a product, and not a person.... So you can't say that this is an example or this is the average guy because he's not.... The people that have this drive are your extraordinary, successful men in any field," he reasoned. "I think that I work this hard and had to have as much knowledge in my field to reach what I did as, say, the president of General Motors had to get to the top of his field." But this division between the athletic elite—black and/or white—and the rest of society, he continued, did have particular consequences for African Americans because of the dangerous perception that sport served as a vehicle of social mobility for black men.

For me, for example, if I were to say that I'm going to go to Harlem and go to one of the playgrounds and tell the kids: listen, if you work hard you can do the same thing I do—I did—that would be a lie and that would be unfair to myself and unfair to the kids. Now, I can say to the kids: do your best and fight it every day. But to say that I'm an example of the greatness of the country—that's not true. Because I feel, to be honest with myself and with the people I deal with, that I'm an exception and have been treated as an exception for years and years and years. The problem that we have is that they only want to treat me as an exception in certain areas.

Yet the issue of progress remained a fundamental concern, agreed the roundtable, because the role of the African American athlete had, indeed, changed in the sixties. Edwards acknowledged the accomplishments of individuals such as Russell but found the ongoing issue of collectivity problematic. The paucity of black coaches at the professional level, for example, revealed how "tokenism" remained the rule. Unlike for a white counterpart, noted Edwards, nothing existed "where a black kid can go into professional athletics and do a good job and say, well, I can look forward to being a manager or a coach with equal validity with some of the whites.... I don't think that tokenism necessarily means progress." Still, progress of a different kind—empowerment—had unfolded, Edwards maintained.

> In the last two years, since 1967, we've had more movement in athletics away from the status quo than in any other time ... because athletes are beginning to stand up. You find people in amateur athletics in particular—the whole movement around the Olympic Games, the black athletes who stood up and said we're not going to go to the Olympic Games because we do not feel that this country is giving us a just break as human beings. Therefore, we have to utilize whatever skills we have in order to demonstrate this. Maybe I'm not the kind of guy who can go out on a picket line or who can go to the South and try to register people to vote, but I am an athlete. This is what I know; this is my work and I'll use this as a tool. If I can use it as a tool to make a living, then I can certainly use it as a tool in order to live. In order to justify my humanity. In order to demonstrate my humanity.

With Russell and Ashe in staunch agreement, both of them emphasizing that the time for such demonstration was immediate and without delay, the roundtable clearly established that a new generation of black political consciousness had begun to articulate such sentiments beyond the individual figureheads of the past—Owens, Ali, Robinson. Indeed, Robinson seemed almost out of place sitting at the table. Even though he was inarguably one of the most prominent black athletic heroes of the twentieth century, his role had been continually questioned, along with that of Owens, by the OPHR. Yet in the presence of figures such as Edwards and Russell, Robinson spoke with unflagging respect for the revolutionary athletes in Mexico City and recovered a space for himself between the unwavering stance of Smith and Carlos and the alleged "Tom-ism" of George Foreman, who, like most of the other boxers on the U.S. squad, was audibly opposed to the encroachment of politics on the Olympic arena:

> I've never been so proud of individuals as I was of Tommie Smith and John Carlos's Olympic Games. I think this, to me, was the greatest demonstration of personal conviction and pride that I've really seen. To see these guys standing up there saying to the world, as I saw it, I'm proud, I conquered, my blackness and this sort of thing, and then all of a sudden you see a guy running around the ring waving a flag and you get sick inside. You know, that's just what happened to me—I go sick when I saw Foreman run out waving a flag.

While the members of the *Black Journal* roundtable, including Robinson, clearly enunciated the feelings of pride and self-respect that Smith and Carlos had marked as important in the protest, others were not as confident about granting it such a positive legacy. In addition to the aspects of a racialized pride and a renegotiated national identity that they performed *within* the national border were the consequences and ramifications of such a gesture *outside* the national border. Because of the ever-proliferating phenomenon of "Americanization," aided by the ever-burgeoning industries of mass media and information, popular forms and figures from the United States were in no way reserved for a domestic audience. As evidenced by the obvious ideological connections between the demonstrating Mexican students and the OPHR as well as the pan-African alliances surrounding the South African controversy, they operated on a much more global stage. These relationships enabled chords of similarities to be forged between something like the black power protest and struggles of people who existed outside the physical boundaries of the United States, serving as constructions and contestations of identities more universal than those of nation.

Moreover, this relationship between popular culture and this broader audience becomes further complicated because of the hegemonic position assumed by the United States in this postwar, Cold War, era. As the *New York Amsterdam News* explained in a headline over a trio of front-page photos of the medal ceremonies of Smith and Carlos, the men's relay team, and Bob Beamon, the "gestures in black" of the Mexico City Olympics were part of "spreading the U.S. gospel elsewhere."[142] This dominance enjoyed by the United States in the Olympic movement made the position of the USOC, which had claimed its hands were tied in regard to the Smith-Carlos suspension, somewhat suspicious. Following the suspension of Smith and Carlos, Robert Lipsyte rightly shed doubt upon the IOC's threat to disbar all Americans from the Olympics if the two were not adequately punished because of the significantly dominant status of the United States in the world. "The I.O.C. would no sooner suspend its main meal ticket for 'exhibitionism' than it would suspend its No. 2 meal ticket, the Soviet Union, for subsidizing its athletes on a national basis," Lipsyte argued, "or would risk losing delegations by standing by its guns with South Africa."[143]

Because of this swelling notion of national and international power, both political and cultural, a strategy such as the one employed by Smith and Carlos erased, at least within the American mass-mediated recollection, the very associations on which it was built. The action became somewhat of a perverse cultural imperialism, inadvertently complicit with a kind of exalted "Americanness" that would otherwise be expressly condemned in efforts to protest racial oppression, something seemingly without national boundaries. Paul Gilroy finds a similar circumstance in a different context, rap music, "a form which flaunts … its own malleability as well as its transnational character." Yet despite the fluid properties of what could be termed diasporic diversity, rap is perceived as an authentic voice of African *Americans*. "What is it about Afro-America's writing elite," asks Gilroy, "which means that they need to claim this diasporic cultural form in such an assertively nationalist way?"[144] Such tendencies further complicate identity politics in the international arena, making imperative Amy Kaplan's call to investigate how "diverse identities cohere, fragment, and change in relation to one another and to ideologies of nationhood through the crucible of international power relations, and how, conversely, imperialism ... abroad is inseparable from the social relations and cultural discourses of race, gender, ethnicity, and class at home."[145]

In terms of Mexico City, for example, *Sports Illustrated* determined early on that the tragedy at Tlatelolco would be "the scene that was to leave its mark on the 1968 Olympics."[146] However, by the Closing Ceremony, as the strains of "Las Golondrinas" conveyed farewell, few mentioned the slaughter and chose instead to scour the Olympic community for reaction to the two banished Americans, producing an almost despotic extirpation of the slain students. Harry Edwards, for one, reveled in the political preeminence of the protest action, particularly as the image of Smith and Carlos became firmly established as "the best remembered photo of the 1968 Games," according to sports scholar Richard Lapchick.[147] Smith and Carlos, according to Edwards, were "banished for having committed the ultimate Black transgression in a white supremacist society ... to become visible, to stand up for the dignity of Black people, to protest from an international platform the racist inhumanity of American society."[148] Reflecting decades later, Tommie Smith understood the moment in a similar vein, a moment that he described as a "prayer of solidarity":

> What hurt—an agonizing hurt—for the old heart of America was every-body saw it—the entire world saw it, and that it was done by black athletes. It was nothing but a raised fist in the air and a bowed head acknowledging the American flag—*not* symbolizing a hatred for it. The hatred for the flag was those people in the stands booing and not looking at the flag while it was playing. It was too interested in seeing those black devils on the victory stand.[149]

Days after the Closing Ceremony in 1968, *Newsweek* rued in its summary of the Games that the debate surrounding Smith and Carlos had "almost overshadowed all the brilliant performances and personal dramas of the XIX Olympiad—and turned it into what the militants had wanted all along, a showcase for black protest against racial injustice."[150] In a more nuanced vein, sports columnist Paul Zimmerman situated the black power protest in a broader, global political context with a tale of how an Olympic spectator in a "turban" felt about Smith and Carlos. "My friends, I was with Gandhi when we lay down and put our necks on the railroad tracks," he said. "We referred to that as a protest."[151] Zimmerman obviously wanted to reduce the magnitude of the black power gesture, particularly in light of the carnage that had taken place just days before the Games. "The protest that got the most publicity," according to Zimmerman, was greatly exaggerated in its importance because it was perpetrated by two Americans. It was the USOC, under pressure from Brundage and perhaps the U.S. State Department, that "awarded the two boys martyrdom and made them instant heroes to mass media audiences all over the world by sending them home." The administration justified such severity because the *Olympic Charter* had been violated, but the columnist asked, "Where was Mr. Brundage and Doug Roby ... when South Africa was brought up on charges of violating the Olympic charter—for more than half a century."[152]

Of course, while Zimmerman blamed Olympic authorities for creating the political imbalance, others censured the athletes themselves. In his own column, for example, Arthur Daley concluded, "Some thought it was legitimate to drag a protest movement onto a global stage, but a majority condemned it as disgraceful, insulting and embarrassing."[153] Yet despite the majority that Daley found, the aftermath of the black power protest suggested that its legacy was not going to be neatly compartmentalized but rather would have significant repercussions in terms of both the African American community and the nation at large. A letter from Leroy S. Rouner, missionary to India, to the editor of the *New York Times* perhaps best summarized the complexities embedded in the path ahead. In a lengthy treatment that dissected the reaction of mainstream America to the face of Black Power, Rouner articulated why the prominent role of the United States on the international stage not only enabled such an action to take place but also made it effective and ensured its tremendous legacy.

> The middle class white liberal establishment ... has asked black Americans to do something constructive, to make their protest quietly and peacefully. It has said, in effect, "Do this and we will be with you." But, as so often before, it turns out that these pleas and assurances are only a subtle means of keeping black men in their place. A black athlete who wins an Olympic victory knows that it is probably the only occasion on which he will ever have the attention of his nation and the world. Tommie Smith ... did not curse or scream hatred against anyone. He did not riot, or loot or burn.... His gesture was restrained, even dignified. What more can America conceivably ask from people who have been second-class citizens for so long?[154]

What more indeed?

CHAPTER 7

Whose Broad Stripes
and Bright Stars?

> They [the games] lost the spirit of the older days.... Winners
> were no longer contented with a simple olive wreath as a prize.
> They sought gifts and money.... The games were finally halted
> by decree of Emperor Theodosius I of Rome in 393 A.D.
>
> —Arthur Daley, *The Story of the Olympic Games*

The many classifications of the black power protest suggested that its legacy would not end in Mexico City. One *Ebony* reader's lament for the failed boycott, for example, saw the action of Smith and Carlos as a call to arms and pledged that "black people of these United States shouldn't participate in the Olympics, shouldn't be forced to pay income taxes, and shouldn't be drafted to fight these racist wars until they are accepted as first class citizens."[1] In Los Angeles, such propositions had an immediate effect. The city had drafted a substantial and welcomed bid to the IOC to host the Olympics in 1976, but the USOC suspension of Smith and Carlos threatened the proposal. Immediately following the return of Smith and Carlos stateside, Los Angeles city councilman Billy G. Mills, who had been in Mexico City to gather support for the LA bid, publicly backed the banished duo. Of particular importance, Mills pointed out, was "the restraint they exercised," which likely prevented the Games from becoming "completely uncorked" in the wake of the press, who "swarmed all over the (Olympic) village like ... coyotes and vultures."[2] The upshot, worried African American California state senator Mervyn Dymally (D-Los Angeles), was how the city now felt about hosting the Games. The actions taken by the Olympic administration, according to Dymally, greatly jeopardized the bid by weakening needed support from LA's black communities, where protests could be anticipated if the Olympics were to take place.[3]

While the IOC decided Montreal would be the best place for the Olympics in 1976, the degree to which Mexico City served as a political reference point vividly continued at the Munich Games in 1972. Munich was not without its own so-called political scandals regarding African American track athletes. In what many considered to be an extension of the purported "introduction" of politics into the Olympics by Smith and Carlos, the IOC banned American sprinters Wayne Collett and Vince Matthews from further competition for failing to pay adequate and deferential attention to the national anthem during the medal ceremony for the 400-meters.

Leading up to this controversial moment, a series of events had indicated what the spirit of these next Olympics might be. As Munich loomed closer, for example, the politics of solidarity between black athletes in America and those in Africa again emerged when the IOC announced its decision to allow Rhodesia to compete under the British flag. In response, Matthews and Collett, along with teammates Chuck Smith, John Smith, and Lee Evans, issued a declaration of allegiance with Kenya and Ethiopia, both of whom had threatened to boycott over the Rhodesia decision: "In the light of the Rhodesian acceptance in the Games, the United States black athletes ... believe it imperative to take a stand concerning the issue," they proclaimed. "We denounce Rhodesia's participation and if they are allowed to compete, we will take a united stand with our African brothers."[4] Perhaps having learned its lesson from the South African situation just four years earlier, the IOC rescinded the invitation and again banned Rhodesia. With Rhodesia out and the Americans in, another U.S. sweep of the 400-meters, which had occurred in Mexico, became a strong possibility.

Yet the tentative participation of Rhodesia was not the only factor that threatened the sweep. Although Evans intended to defend his gold medal in the event, he failed to qualify because of injury, so he traveled to Munich only as a member of the relay team. Matthews, to the dismay of his coaches, replaced Evans in the 400-meters, and John

Smith and Collett became favored to win. In the final, Smith pulled up injured after only eighty meters, and Matthews surged ahead of Collett to win. Later on the victory dais, the two Americans talked, twitched, and chafed throughout the medal ceremony. Upon leaving the podium, Matthews took off his medal and spun it around his finger, leading many to speculate that it held little significance for him. The stadium crowd booed them, and the IOC, not waiting this time for any kind of reaction from the USOC, banished them, quashing any hopes for the United States, with two injured athletes and two ejected athletes, to enter a team into the 4×400-meter relay. Furious over the matter, Avery Brundage fired off a letter to USOC president Stan Bock.

> The whole world saw the disgusting display of your two athletes, when they received the gold and silver medals for the 400m event yesterday. This is the second time the USOC has permitted such occurrences on the athletic field. It is the Executive Board's opinion that these two athletes have broken rule 26, paragraph 1 in respect of the traditional Olympic spirit and ethic and are, therefore, eliminated from taking part in any future Olympic competition.[5]

Both Matthews and Collett disputed the accusations that their actions signaled any kind of systematic political demonstration. Matthews claimed he stripped off his medal to demonstrate that it was his and on that day he was the best in the world, despite the viewpoint of many that he was a substandard replacement for Evans. "If we did have any ideas about a demonstration," he added, "we could have done a better job than that." Collett, however, belied Matthews's conviction of innocence. "I couldn't stand there and sing the words because I don't believe they're true," he said. "I wish they were. I think we have the potential to have a beautiful country, but I don't think we do."[6]

Of course, by no means was the alleged disrespect of Matthews and Collett the defining image of Munich. The horror of the massacre of eleven members of the Israeli team by members of the Black September movement, a Palestinian terrorist group, was far more momentous. The group raided the Olympic Village on September 5, 1972, for hostages in an attempt to procure publicity for its nationalist cause, demanding the release of two hundred Arabs and Palestinians held in Israeli prisons in exchange for the hostages. The terrorists killed two Israelis in the initial raid, and after a full day of futile negotiations and a bungled rescue mission by the German police, a shoot-out at the Munich airport left one policeman, three terrorists, and the remaining nine Israeli hostages dead. In one of the starkest moments of any Olympic broadcast, the shocking incident came to a close when ABC host Jim McKay, after bringing much of America through the siege, grimly delivered his now famous words: "Our worst fears have been realized. They're all gone." In the wake of the horror, the IOC suspended competition for a thirty-four-hour period, during which a memorial service was held at the Olympic Stadium. Despite the attempts at catharsis, the appalling exhibition of violence and terror scarred in perpetuity the Munich Games, which West Germans had staged in hopes of erasing the memory of Hitler's Olympics and celebrating their recovery since World War II.

The causal connections made between the black power protest in Mexico City and the Black September massacre in Munich reinforced the belief that many had not viewed the Olympics as a political forum until Smith and Carlos took their positions on the victory dais that day in October 1968. However, in the time that has passed since they voiced their dissent, it has been difficult to locate their exact legacy, because their complex enunciation of black power and dignity in no way guaranteed positive political or cultural results. Their image certainly has retained some kind of potency, continually reshaped and resituated as a political image that vividly remains within our imagination regarding race and sports and, indeed, within the images of the broader movements of civil rights. The interventions made by the OPHR ensured that the black athlete played an increasingly significant role in manufacturing meanings and memories of racial and national identity. Yet other factors complicate this historical trajectory. While both on and off the field the word *Negro* largely has been put to rest, many of the notions that surrounded the construction of the "Negro athlete" have not, generating little faith in any ideas of racial progress. Rather, the oldest of both scientific questions and social implications of race continue to weigh prominently in contemporary discussions, denying the collective transformation from "Negro" to "black" advocated by the OPHR, particularly in terms of the athlete's role in the postindustrial marketplace. The years between Mexico City and Michael Jordan, then, have taken a tremendous toll on the image of two black men with their fists raised, a toll that began in the wake of Black September.

Triumph and What? The Legacy of Blackness

With Munich, the Olympics, in its second major television broadcast, became transformed yet again. Instead of presenting an escapist immersion in the pageantry and spectacle of athletic competition, ABC had to fuse its news and sports divisions to bring its audience of millions reports regarding something of much greater consequence than the unofficial medal count. "At some point I learned that one of the athletes was [originally] from Shaker Heights, Ohio," remembers McKay. "And I realized that it was very likely that the young man's parents would be hearing from me whether he was dead or alive."[7]

Before the Montreal Games in 1976, ABC broadcast a documentary on the Olympics entitled "Triumph and Tragedy: The Olympic Experience."[8] An obvious attempt to reinvigorate viewer interest in the wake of Munich, the program ostracized and denigrated those who did not fully represent the true Olympic spirit, as defined by ABC, by revisiting those who made the Olympics "special." One of the first athletes featured in the early part of the program, "Triumph," was boxer George Foreman. Foreman, to the chagrin of OPHR members, had carried an American flag around the ring in Mexico City after he defeated Soviet opponent Ionas Chepulis for the gold. While OPHR members had been shunned, Foreman was embraced by the presidential campaigns of both Richard Nixon and Hubert Humphrey.[9] Of his victory, Foreman told Howard Cosell,

I think that in 1968, a lot of people paid more attention to my waving the flag ... than my boxing triumph. Although I was proud to be in the Olympics, I was also proud to be representing my country as an Olympian, and after I won the gold medal I wanted everybody to be sure where George Foreman was from. So I waved the flag and I was proud at that moment to be George Foreman, proud to be from the United States, and proud of the colors I had on.

While proud of the colors he was wearing, Foreman never mentioned his own "color." Jesse Owens, another "triumph," also fell short of fulfilling the distinction. The piece projected his gold medals in Berlin as triumphs over the racism and Aryan supremacy of Nazi Germany, but Owens's recollection, when asked if he had directly confronted Hitler, skirted issues of race and nation in terms of both Germany *and* the United States.[10]

Well, ... really I didn't. In other words, at that time I felt that I didn't because ... you didn't go over there to shake hands or fraternize with Hitler. You went there to run against fifty-five other nations of the world—and this is what we did. He was there, it's very true, his presence was felt there, but I don't think it was felt as far as the athletes were concerned. I, as an American and as a black American, wasn't too concerned with Hitler and his motives, because the social structure of our country at that time certain is [*sic*] not the atmosphere that it is today, where the blacks of our country at that time were not afforded all the social graces that are being afforded to athletes today.

While Owens staunchly believed that racial progress had occurred, he also made a critical comparison between the social state of the United States and that of Nazi Germany some forty years earlier. For Owens, at least in retrospect, domestic strife and the difficulty of being an African American Olympian somewhat paralleled anything that Hitler offered in terms of hate and discrimination. Yet because the OPHR had branded him an "Uncle Tom" and he continued to enjoy the support from figures like Avery Brundage as a "good boy," Owens was considered a positive athletic figure, regardless of his own stated cognizance of facets of racism in American society.

From Owens, Jim McKay's voice—increasingly synonymous with Olympic broadcasts—guided the viewer out of the war era, during which the Olympics were canceled, through their celebrated revitalization in a war-ravaged London in 1948 and into the turbulent 1960s. Images of the space launch, Kennedy, Johnson, and Vietnam; the creation of the Super Bowl; and figures as diverse as Vince Lombardi, "Mrs. Robinson," and the Beatles periodized the 1960s for ABC. Excluded from the network's historical trajectory, however, was any kind of identity politics that pervaded the age: civil rights, women's rights, and antiwar movements. Rather, McKay marked such political turning points by emphasizing that, as the Olympics persevered in the postwar period, "Americans of many ethnic groups were among the heroes," a statement that echoes the idiom of the "model minority." While generally used to describe Asian immigrants in the United States, the term plays a critical role in the broader politics of civil rights in the 1960s, used to demonstrate fallaciously that social change occurred because of governmental generosity, not collective struggle. "That some people of color achieve appreciable levels of success, for whatever reason," scholar Vijay Prashad argues, "is used as evidence that racism poses no barrier to success."[11] McKay highlighted, for example, the feats of Wilma Rudolph in 1960 and Billy Mills in 1964, accentuating their personal achievements rather than their representative role in any kind of collective political identity. Mills, the only American runner to win gold in the 10,000-meters, grew up as an orphan on the Pine Ridge Reservation, enjoyed a thriving running career at the University of Kansas, and became a commissioned officer in the Marines. While certainly inspiring, the story of the Oglala Lakota distance runner (canonized in the 1983 Robby Benson film, *Running Brave*) serves as a political reference point that parallels Owens: an account of an athlete who quietly, and *triumphantly*, defied the odds.

Mexico City's triumphs in the documentary ironically included

Jim Ryun's *loss* in the 1500-meters. A media favorite, the world-record holder managed "only" a silver medal in Mexico after a dramatic duel to the finish with Kenyan Kip Keino. (To add to the drama, in Munich Ryun fell in the first heat and failed to advance to the finals, where Keino again prevailed.) Other exultant Mexico moments included Bill Toomey's decathlon victory and Bob Beamon's magnificent leap. Left out, of course, was how Beamon accepted his medal: without shoes. Furthermore, no reference was made to the record-breaking achievements of Beamon's teammates, such as Tommie Smith and Lee Evans. By barring the details of their accomplishments and focusing solely on the visually stunning mark set by Beamon, the superiority of the U.S. squad in 1968 woefully went missing, making its legacy "tragic" by default. Indeed, the latter segment of the program dispensed a discussion of Smith and Carlos alongside a revisitation of the purported turpitude of Matthews and Collett in Munich. Howard Cosell took the narration reins from McKay and situated the two cases of banished black athletes within a somewhat longer historical scope, maintaining that the "prevailing notion that protests in the Olympic Games really began in Mexico in 1968 ... is untrue." As an example, Cosell reviewed the case of U.S. flag bearer Martin Sheridan, who refused to dip the flag before the king of England in 1908, stating, "I will not dip the American flag before any earthly king."

Many members of the OPHR had used the case of Sheridan as an example after the expulsion of Smith and Carlos. However, Cosell did not stand by it, instead continuing, "But it is true that the Olympic Games became a forum for international protest in the XIXth Olympiad in Mexico City in 1968." His use of *forum* spoke to an intentional politics of protest and also located the black power action as a tragedy. The source of empowerment that the black-gloved fists symbolized was lost in the ruination of sport that Cosell implied occurred on a wide scale in 1968. While Owens had been categorized as "triumphant" for his ability to prevail over Nazi white supremacy despite his allusions to American racism, Smith and Carlos were confirmed as a "tragedy." The segment offered no recognition of the possible social locations of the viewing audience. Black viewers, for example, could very well—and did—consider the black fists to be triumphant symbols of pride, dignity, and empowerment.

While the documentary attempted to situate the black power gesture within the broader political sphere that surrounded the Games, Cosell's timeline had a deliberate slant to it. He tendered that the political turmoil began with the Mexican student riots that occurred before the Opening Ceremony and that Smith and Carlos created "the first overt protest" during the Games themselves. By introducing the duo in this way, Cosell created a line of political demarcation between the two athletes and the collective movement of the OPHR, of which they were a part. The suggestion that the political turmoil began with the student slaughter erased the OPHR and its political campaigns from the larger perception of the Games and portrayed Smith and Carlos as solitary in their stance rather than as a smaller part of a greater historical whole. Furthermore, because the footage of the record-breaking 200-meter race itself was shown only in juxtaposition to the gloved-fist protest, the image of raised fists became the dominant memory established by the program. Cosell's narration only served to magnify its placement. "So, Tommie Smith won a great victory, a world record set," he stated. "But they didn't remember the world record, because something occurred after that was to shock the nation and create an international fury: the black power salute on the victory stand." By emphasizing that *they* did not remember the record, speaking to some unnamed spectatorship, Cosell attempted to convey his own objectivity on the matter. In doing so, he failed to acknowledge how *he too* had historically located Smith and Carlos outside the realm of Olympic triumph and as a signifier of Olympic tragedy instead.

Cosell situated Evans in a similar, albeit not identical, manner. Because Evans and his teammates took off their black berets during their victory ceremony in the 400-meter relay in 1968, Cosell said it was not a "reoccurrence of the Smith-Carlos affair." Conversely, the footage of Matthews and Collett on the victory dais four years later in Munich, in which Matthews appeared bored, stroking his goatee, and Collett stood barefoot, sighing visibly, served to represent some kind of augmentation of Mexico City's "tragic" politics. The two looked sloppy standing next to bronze medalist Julius Sang, who stood at attention in his formal Kenyan sweats. Collett wore shorts and an unzipped jacket, and Matthews wore full sweats and shoes but had left his jacket unzipped and his shirt untucked and hanging loosely. In the studio after the ceremony, with eyes averted from the camera and in a low voice, Matthews, wearing a USA hat, told Cosell: "Myself and Wayne, we didn't stand at attention on the victory stand, and a lot of people have read some sort of protest into this, but there was no protest intended." Cosell then asked if they would stand at attention if the situation were to present itself again. "Probably not.... As I said before, I couldn't stand with a clear conscience," Collett replied, arms crossed over his chest. "I feel that, you know, looking back on it now, that my actions on the victory stand probably mirror the ... attitude of white America toward blacks—total casual, ignoring them. As long as we're not embarrassing you, we're okay. And that's how I feel."

After reviewing the footage of Matthews and Collett, Cosell linked their banishment to the event that marked the Munich Games forever: the massacre of the Israeli athletes. With this segue, the black power protest of Smith and Carlos became designedly linked to the most horrific intrusion of politics into the Olympic Games. Cosell summarized:

> And so the use of the Olympic Games as a forum for protest, which really gained international attention in 1968, grew even further in 1972 and to some may be regarded as the genesis for the most horrible thing that's ever happened in any Olympiad: the grotesque massacre of eleven Israelis by members of the Black September gang, an offshoot of the Palestinian Liberation Organization.

Cosell's statement created a direct correlation between the Munich massacre and the Mexico City black power protest. Furthermore, because ABC defined Olympic "tragedy" solely through the events in

Mexico City and Munich, while Olympic "triumph" carefully included highlights from each and every Games, Smith and Carlos were linked to, and therefore implicitly held responsible for, the deaths of the Israelis. Cosell's use of the word *genesis* confirmed this historical sequencing and further buried the massacre that had taken place in Mexico City, albeit by government, rather than terrorist, hands.

This historical correlation and the amnesia that accompanied it persevered, and the black power protest continued to be heralded as *the* political turning point of the Olympic Games, with Smith and Carlos held liable for all that followed, despite oft-mentioned evidence pointing otherwise. Olympic chronicler David Wallechinsky, for one, maintains that the Olympics have been politicized since their modern inception, with the Greek royal family assuming a prominent position at the inaugural Games in Athens in 1896. The British royals undertook a similar role in London in 1908, and King Gustav as well as Czar Nicholas handed out the medals in Stockholm in 1912. Even more overtly, German athletes, as well as others, accepted medals in Berlin in 1936 with the Nazi salute, and numerous U.S. athletes put their right hand over their heart during the playing of "The Star-Spangled Banner," all without castigation of any kind. The question remains, according to Wallechinsky, a direct one: "If it was acceptable in 1936 to raise your right arm in the air with the open palm face down, and today it is acceptable to put your right hand over your heart, why was it *not* acceptable in 1968 to bow your head and raise your arm into the air with your gloved fist closed?" The answer, according to Wallechinsky, is one of perspective. Smith and Carlos had not merely made a political statement but had "made the *wrong* political statement.... Rather than showing support for a recognized nation-state, [they] showed support for an unrecognized political entity—black Americans."[12]

The continued focus on the black power protest indicates, however, that its resonance vibrantly remains because of its political potency and its service as this historical reference point. Its inclusion in various inquests of critical Olympic moments, as well as other treatments of the nature of sport in the United States and the turbulent politics of the 1960s in general, indicates that it remains a vital and multifaceted window. For example, the Home Box Office (HBO) presentation "Fields of Fire: Sports in the 60's" featured the black power protest at Mexico City as the decisive moment among numerous transfigurations that occurred throughout the decade. As José Feliciano's "Star-Spangled Banner" played in the background, the documentary began with a montage of familiar images of Vietnam, Martin Luther King Jr., civil rights demonstrations, a slain Robert Kennedy, Muhammad Ali, antiwar protestors, Smith's victory in Mexico, and, finally, the black power protest—presented as the last defining image of the decade.

While HBO prominently featured the gesture in this manner, it offered a confused and inconsistent trajectory of how it occurred. The sequence of the film used Vietnam and antiwar protest rather than civil rights struggles to provide the transition from the allegedly serene early postwar period to the tumultuous era personified by figures like Ali and Curt Flood. It then, toward its conclusion, used Julian Bond to summarize that it was the image of Smith and Carlos that undeniably unified black America, while narrator Ritchie Havens declared it "the most enduring image of the times." However, rather than allow the civil rights activist and historian or the Woodstock folk singer to have the last words, Bill Toomey, who had played such a considerable and vocal role of support for the OPHR in Mexico City, was given the honor of determining why the moment mattered so much and why the Olympics were, categorically, a political arena. "If a message has to be delivered," Toomey said, "this is perhaps the *most* appropriate place ... for somebody to finally say ... We're tired of being paraded as your Olympic pawns: King Us."[13] Thus, despite its odd historical arc, one that voiced the mission of the OPHR with an athlete who was not a member, the HBO documentary again confirmed the legacy of the black power action. While in 1968 Robert Lipsyte had lamented that the action of Smith and Carlos "seemed a little weak when compared to the clarity, the force and the brilliance of their organization," it is evident that their visual and physical embodiment of their statement had a lasting effect on the negotiations between the athlete and the nation that were still to come. The OPHR created what *Life* magazine had eloquently predicted to be "a lasting racial consciousness."[14]

Please Rise and Join US:
Declaring a National Order on the Court

The lasting racial consciousness, even before Smith and Carlos took their places, ensured that if nothing else, much of the viewing public regularly dissected images of black men in the athletic arena for whatever meanings they might hold. In 1968, while Smith and Carlos overtly made their own objections known, the intensely politicized atmosphere engendered by the OPHR made relatively small gestures recognizable. At the "unofficial" Olympic Trials in Los Angeles, for example, a vivid contrast appeared between two of the most visible advocates of the movement of black athletes, Bill Russell and, of course, Harry Edwards. Although the two sat together in the stands at the track meet, and Russell had publicly stated that he saw himself as a boycott sympathizer, a marked difference emerged between them when the national anthem was played: Russell stood while Edwards remained seated.

Edwards's immobility proved indicative of what was to come in subsequent months. Perhaps the most important aspect of the moment is that anyone noticed that Edwards did not stand. Indeed, his *inaction* appeared in the pages of *Sports Illustrated*, demonstrating the weight that the anthem holds in the sports stadium and in American culture in general.[15] In 1972, the magnitude of the national anthem also surprised Wayne Collett in Munich, although perhaps considering the consequences of Mexico City, it should not have. Looking back at his actions, Collett said,

> I did realize that what I did would not be looked on with a great deal of favor. But I had no idea that it would cause the furor that it did.... Probably every time there's a sports event in the United States a large number of people don't stand up—stand at attention for the national anthem—and nothing is, nothing is done, but in a forum like that, everything that happens is completely blown out of proportion.[16]

"The Star-Spangled Banner" has a long (and fabled) history within American sports culture. The ritual use of the national anthem during sporting events began early in the twentieth century and can be quite directly connected to baseball. After the United States officially entered World War I, a federal proclamation called for professional baseball to shorten its season and finish competition by Labor Day. Initially, officials wanted to cancel the World Series altogether because of the war, but they did not want to disappoint American soldiers in France, eager to hear the outcome of championship games. Thus, on the relatively early date of September 11, 1918, the Boston Red Sox triumphed over the Chicago Cubs for the championship title. Although many major league stars were "missing in action" from their teams because of military obligations, Carl Mays and Babe Ruth (in the days before he traded his red socks for pinstripes) made for exciting play, and while the atmosphere of war pervaded American headlines, the week of first-class baseball provided a respite from the news of bloodshed in Europe. The winning game of the 1918 World Series was a significant moment for Boston fans, because it marked the last time they would be champions for a still yet-to-be-determined period, but it also realized the debut of "The Star-Spangled Banner" on American playing fields. During its unannounced performance by the stadium band in the seventh inning stretch, fans and players alike took off their hats, stood, and sang.

At face value the anthem represents the ability of a nation to withstand the onslaught of warring fire and to emerge victorious. Although several other "patriotic" songs persevered throughout the nineteenth century, President Woodrow Wilson issued an executive order in 1916 for the ballad to be played as the national anthem at all military events. In 1931, a congressional decree confirmed Wilson's act.

World War II sealed the tradition of the anthem at sporting events. Yet it is not a tradition without controversy. On the whole, the national anthem is played at such events without much notice. Yet when its presence is jeopardized, fans and officials alike tend to vigorously champion its necessity and importance, directly connecting the responsibility and representation of national citizenship to the athletic action on the field. While the actions by Smith and Carlos in Mexico City and Collett and Matthews in Munich raised numerous eyebrows, in no way do they stand as isolated moments. In 1954, for example, the management of the Baltimore Orioles decided that the anthem would be played on special occasions rather than at every single game. The City Council overruled the decision and quickly passed a resolution for the anthem to be played at every home game. In 1966, the Chicago White Sox introduced "God Bless America" at a game in place of the anthem, producing a heated backlash. When polled, 74 percent of Chicago's fans voted in support of bringing back "The Star-Spangled Banner" to Comiskey Park. Of all such incidents, perhaps the strangest occurred at an Atlanta Falcons game in the mid-1970s, when the hold that "The Star-Spangled Banner" has on sports fans, and Americans as a whole, was made acutely obvious. At the conclusion of the game, the scoreboard flashed "PLEASE RISE AND JOIN IN SINGING OUR NATIONAL ANTHEM" instead of the usual banner that thanked fans for their attendance. Fans stood for some time before the announcer finally convinced them to leave. "Let's face it," concludes Sports Illustrated's Jack McCallum, "Americans are intimidated by the national anthem, fearful that some cosmic chandelier will come crashing on their heads if they put it out to pasture."[17]

Not only does the song intimidate fans into standing at attention; it also presents an array of problems for those brave enough to attempt singing it in public. In 1965, at the famed Ali-Liston fight in Lewiston, Maine, for example, Broadway star Robert Goulet forgot the words to the notoriously difficult song. In 1991, leaving no room for such mishap, diva Whitney Houston recorded her version ahead of time and proceeded to lip-synch through her performance at the Super Bowl in Tampa. Within a few days, 720,000 Americans, likely infused with the patriotic fever that surrounded the Persian Gulf War, purchased her recorded rendition. The previous year, Roseanne (then Barr) had not been quite as fortunate, nor was the San Diego audience of Padres and Reds fans who witnessed her "patriotic exhibition" on a baseball diamond. The comedic actress finished her dismal attempt by grabbing her crotch and spitting, ostensibly in imitation of the players, and prompted President George Bush (the elder) to declare her offering "disgraceful."[18]

On October 7, 1968, days before the Opening Ceremony in Mexico City, rising singing sensation José Feliciano created one of the most notable stirs in the history of "The Star-Spangled Banner." Performing in Detroit's Tiger Stadium during Game 5 of the World Series, Feliciano staged what one music critic has called a "soul-churned, bluesy rendition" of the anthem, provoking many of the 53,634 Tiger and Cardinal fans to boo and throw things onto the field. Still one year away from a Grammy Award for Best New Artist, the Puerto Rican musician was known at the time primarily for his cover of the Doors' "Light My Fire," but the song he produced that day on the baseball diamond would focus a new spotlight upon him. Days after the game, RCA released Feliciano's version of the national anthem as a single and watched it climb as high as number fifty on the Billboard charts amid the controversy.[19]

The degree of contention that surrounded Feliciano's performance, which was televised in the Olympic Village in Mexico City, should not be underestimated, particularly since the use of a popular performer to sing the anthem was not unprecedented. Aretha Franklin, for example, had sung it at the Democratic National Convention in Chicago just a few weeks earlier, and Marvin Gaye had rendered his own version from the pitcher's mound just a few days before Feliciano took the field. Both Franklin and Gaye did so without conflict, while Feliciano's unconventional interpretation produced a heated and immediate reaction. Telephone calls from angry television viewers, numbering at least four hundred in New York City alone, poured into the National Broadcasting Company (NBC), which had broadcast the game. The response propelled the network to state publicly that the Tigers had hired Feliciano, not the network, which had "just covered it, that's all." For his part, Feliciano confessed that he had been worried that people might think he was "making fun" of the anthem but was baffled about why anyone found his rendition to be, in the words of one spectator, nonpatriotic. "America is young now, and I thought maybe the anthem could be revived now," Feliciano said in his own defense. "This country has given me many opportunities. I owe everything I have to this country. I wanted to contribute something to this country, express my gratification for what it has done for me."[20]

The 1960s were an era in which the flag itself was continually being wrenched out of place and provocatively redefined—at times even burned. As a performer, Feliciano felt he had staged a tribute to nation, but much of his audience interpreted the performance as pejorative at best and as an act of sedition at worst, indicative of the turbulent recasting of identity politics going on in the period. This conflicted situation became further apparent in the definitive deconstruction of "The Star-Spangled Banner" that took place in the hands of Jimi Hendrix at Woodstock the year after Feliciano's performance. In his unorthodox rendition, Hendrix dismantled the central ideas and mythologies of the United States and put them back together in a new order, one that paid homage to the country and at the same time fully critiqued it in an attempt at redemption. His interpretation presented a counteranthem of realism in the era of Vietnam, one that quite literally evoked "bombs bursting in air" and symbolized a loss of faith in that which embodies America. In his elegy for what had been lost, he rendered both a celebratory acknowledgment of the promise and potential of the nation and a dirge about the death of innocence, recognizing that promises remained unfulfilled, because the United States subsisted as a corruption of all for which it allegedly stood.

As posited by British music critic Charles Shaar Murray, Hendrix intimately knew what he was "talking" about. Instead of standing on a stage in Bethel, New York, playing for the newly formed "Woodstock Nation," he was supposed to be in Vietnam with the 101st Airborne Division—the "Screaming Eagles"—but he had been honorably discharged because of a training injury. His army experience lent a personal voice to his perceptions of Vietnam, and he continually equated the warring in Southeast Asia with that which took place on the inner-city streets of America. "I'd like to dedicate this one to all the soldiers that are fightin' in Chicago, Milwaukee and New York," Hendrix announced before playing "Machine Gun" at a New Year's Eve performance in 1969 in New York. "Oh yes," he continued, "and all the soldiers fightin' in Vietnam." With such statements and the subsequent sounds of unrest he summoned from his instrument, he was "neither jiving his audience nor indulging in cheap irony," observes Murray. "Hendrix knew *exactly* who was paying the price of the politicians' games, and when he used the uncanny onomatopoeic power of his guitar to evoke the sounds of urban riots and jungle fire-fights ... he used every atom of that knowledge."[21]

Although he played "The Star-Spangled Banner" many times, it is Hendrix's Woodstock performance that is best known. Murray vividly described it, at length:

> The ironies were murderous: a black man with a white guitar; a massive, almost exclusively white audience wallowing in a paddy field of its own making; the clear, pure, trumpet-like notes of the familiar melody struggling to pierce through clouds of tear-gas, the explosions of cluster-bombs, the screams of the dying, the crackle of the flames, the heavy palls of smoke stinking with human grease, the hovering chatter of helicopters.... The "Star Spangled Banner" is probably the most complex and powerful work of American art to deal with the Vietnam war and its corrupting, distorting effect on successive generations of the American psyche. One man with one guitar said more in three and a half minutes about that peculiarly disgusting war and its reverberations than all the novels, memoirs and movies put together. It is an interpretation of history which permits no space for either the gung-ho revisionism of Sylvester Stallone and Chuck Norris or the solipsistic angst of Coppola and Oliver Stone; it depicts, as graphically as a piece of music can possibly do, both what the Americans did to the Vietnamese and what they did to themselves.[22]

Hendrix's Woodstock performance correlates to the black power action of Smith and Carlos, because they all, as organic figures, encompass what can be termed *performative nationalism*. The relationship that

exists between performer and audience within black culture, Lawrence
Levine notes in his discussion on secular music, is one of interaction
and participation: "What appears on the surface to be mere popular
entertainment in fact has a ritual significance; that such black performers as singers, *musicians*, comedians, disc jockeys, and even some *athletes*
share the expressive role occupied by the preacher."[23] Levine's point
becomes critical when examining the aspects of protest of such organic
figures, whether athletes or musicians. Alternative modes of protest, he
explains, were essential after emancipation in the nineteenth century,
because the more traditionally sanctioned channels of dissent were generally unavailable to African Americans.[24] Thus, it became necessary to
redraw the lines of protest and resistance to fit, perhaps on an Olympic
victory dais or at a rock concert, within the reality experienced by much
of the black population in the United States.

Such performances are not static but rather are infused with a
variety of intentions. Upon his return home from Mexico City, for
example, a reporter asked John Carlos if he would ever stand for the
national anthem again. "I'm not concerned about the National Anthem,"
he answered. "It was written for white people."[25] While Feliciano had
indicated that he created his version of the anthem to express his love
of country, Carlos, along with Smith, drew upon the anthem to demonstrate discontent, anger, and salvation, as Hendrix did. Yet while all of
these acts acknowledged the anthem in some way and attempted to
alter its meaning in a more inclusive interpretation of the nation, they
were largely perceived as unpatriotic, with little or no recognition of
how they existed as transformative moments of national expression
that simply questioned who was able to *speak* for America. Each of these
moments offered a representative national voice, but always one that
myriad people did not want to recognize or accept, because each served
as an illustration of the nation that embodied voices of the dispos-
sessed. Thus, all these performances served as attempts to respond to
the national anthem in a manner that included those not overtly embraced in the vision it was designed to symbolize, and all the performers assumed rebellious stances that were based on the very founding

ideologies imposed on them as national subjects. Each of these people exerted his right to freedom of expression, the ideology arguably held most dear in American politics, and yet was condemned as treasonous for exercising it.

The centrality and consequence of the national anthem in the sports arena, then, is undeniable, particularly in terms of how national identity is constructed within the broader transnational geopolitical context of the black athlete, as evidenced by the extraordinary legacy of Smith and Carlos. In 1996, such a case dramatically, albeit briefly, demonstrated the resilience of this process when the National Basketball Association (NBA) suspended Mahmoud Abdul-Rauf (Chris Jackson until his conversion to orthodox Islam in 1991) for failing to stand with his teammates at attention during the national anthem as dictated by his league contract. The dispute raised a discussion regarding race, nation, and sport when Abdul-Rauf invoked a religious argument to back his action. While this action was seemingly a small infraction of the rules, the NBA is, in actuality, rather explicit regarding the national anthem. In Section II (J:2) of its *Basic Principles*, it states, "Players, coaches and trainers are to stand and line up in a dignified posture along the sidelines or on the foul line during the playing of the national anthem." As a member—the leading scorer—of the Denver Nuggets, Abdul-Rauf's avoidance of "The Star-Spangled Banner" initially did not cause much hue and cry: he simply remained in the locker room until it was over each night and then took to the court to play his game. Eventually, however, management forced him to appear courtside with his teammates, where he remained seated on the bench for the duration of the song. His "outing" coincided with the announcement that the Oklahoma City bombing trial would take place in Denver, after which callers to local talk radio programs began to debate Abdul-Rauf's absence during the anthem, which at that point had continued for some sixty games. Callers questioned his allegiance to game and country, associating the action of the devout Muslim with that of a *foreign* entity, placing the practice of Islam within a distinctly foreign realm that the NBA and its audience could not accommodate or even tolerate. "If he doesn't like it here," one caller suggested, "why don't they deport his butt back to the country he came from?"[26] What such callers failed to realize, of course, was that Abdul-Rauf's so-called country of origin was Mississippi, and he had been an NBA draft pick out of Louisiana State University. Such condemnation directed at him by these callers likely fulfilled a void left by convicted Oklahoma bomber Timothy McVeigh, who did not comply with the standard image of a terrorist (read: Arab) to which the majority of the American "imagined community" subscribed.[27] Abdul-Rauf, then, satisfied the need, based on a particular national framework of pseudoknowledge, to place the blame of the state of the union on a foreigner—*any foreigner*—to avert the transformation of what was once described by the media as "terror *in* the heartland" into "terror *is* the heartland."

Once the NBA handed down the suspension, Abdul-Rauf's action, or more precisely *inaction*, gained national attention. The dispute raised a deep interrogation regarding the relationship among race, religion, citizenship, and sport. The American sports press as well as television programs ranging from ESPN's *Sportscenter* to CNN's *Crossfire* to *CBS This Morning* engaged in a critical, though short-lived, dialogue regarding the responsibility of citizenship in the sporting arena.[28] At the center of the discussion was Abdul-Rauf's assertion that his constitutional rights of freedom of speech and religion enabled him to refuse to stand for a flag that he felt, on the basis of his reading of the Koran, represented tyranny and oppression. "You can't be for God and for oppression," Abdul-Rauf responded. "It's clear in the Koran, Islam is the only way. I don't criticize those who stand, so don't criticize me for sitting."[29] Thus, despite his attempt to defend what he saw as a pious position, taken via the most oft-repeated tenets of the Bill of Rights, his stance encountered an overwhelming number of Americans who found his behavior, and him, treacherous and objected to his alleged breach of patriotism. Indeed, at the core of the debate was his employment of the U.S. Constitution to participate in an activity the majority of raised voices considered "un-American," an apparent attempt by a foreigner, as they saw it, to exercise inappropriately the most important of national principles. Further offensive, scores of people reiterated, was that his betrayal took place in an arena that paid him so well—$2.6 million per season, or $31,707 per game.

Ironically contending that the American flag stands for freedom and democracy, the *New York Daily News* roared "SHOW SOME RESPECT," echoing Abdul-Rauf's fellow NBA Muslim, Hakeem Olajuwon.[30] The press focused on the notably devout Olajuwon, who prominently juxtaposed his ardent posture to that of Abdul-Rauf. "It's tough for me to understand his position," Olajuwon said, "but in general the Muslim teaching is to obey and respect. To be a good Muslim is to be a good citizen." In line with Olajuwon, many Muslim leaders also questioned Abdul-Rauf's rationale behind his protest and argued that nothing in the Koran required such action. The athlete remained firm in his stance, nonetheless, stating that he was "a Muslim first and a Muslim last" and declaring, "My duty is to my creator, not to nationalist ideology." Maher Hathout, of the Islamic Center of Southern California, begged to differ and deemed such beliefs wrong. "Muslims give a pledge to respect their country and honor its symbols," Hathout said. "The American flag does not represent oppression. It represents the United States of America."[31]

Although supported by the players' union and the American Civil Liberties Union, Abdul-Rauf received little backing in the sports press. The press did, however, raise some of the significant implications of the debate. Famed sportswriter Frank Deford, for example, incisively questioned why the national anthem remained a part of *any* sporting event, a ritual during which "itchy patriots in the stands start screaming 'Dee-fense' along [with] ... 'whose broad stripes and bright stars.'" Deford judiciously pointed out how "The Star-Spangled Banner" remains a relatively invisible and generally antiquated portion of any game until, of course, "someone on the field decides to treat it badly." Deford also fretted about the state of Islam in the United States, finding Abdul-Rauf to be "another public-relations nightmare" that added to an injurious image advanced by "the ghastly celebrity of Louis Farrakhan and his ersatz Nation of Islam, and ... the Muslims' fundamentalist bombers,... too often taken as representative of the great peaceful majority." But despite Deford's appreciation for the nuances of Abdul-Rauf's stance, he, like many others, found that it came down to money in the end, creating a situation of "self-righteousness" more than anything else. "If the national anthem is such an obvious symbol of tyranny and oppression," Deford asked, "why isn't the national dollar bill likewise to be denied?"[32]

A notable exception to the backlash regarding Abdul-Rauf's paycheck was Harvey Araton of the *New York Times*, who found hypocrisy inherent in any situation in which the NBA tried to take a moral high road and transform its marketing campaign motto of "I Love This Game" to "Love It or Leave It." Araton found NBA deputy commissioner Russ Granik's declaration that "all our rules apply equally to all our players" to be absurd, noting that the NBA allowed Michael Jordan to change his jersey number midseason in breach of official rules and remained untroubled when "Jordan, Charles Barkley and other Republic of Nike pitchmen shamelessly used the flag to cover competing corporate logos on the Olympic medal stand in Barcelona, Spain, four years ago."[33] Like Araton, many *Sports Illustrated* writers also appreciated the series of ironies embedded in the Abdul-Rauf affair and posited, like Deford, that the time had come to put the national anthem to rest. Feted columnist Rick Reilly called the controversy "an ideological slam-dunk contest" that posed the players' union and the ACLU against seemingly the entire American public. Golfer Mike Sullivan personified the situation for Reilly. "I don't think they should suspend him," Sullivan told the press. "I think they should shoot him."[34]

After sitting out a home game against the Orlando Magic, Abdul-Rauf acquiesced to the NBA's demands and agreed to stand the following night in Chicago but stated that he would pray for its duration "for those who are suffering." However, according to Reilly, the Chicago crowd was not willing to forgive and forget, especially after the Denver Nuggets announced they would pay Abdul-Rauf $31,707 for the missed game. "This guy's making $3 million a year," protested Chuck Place, a Bulls fan seated next to his flag-adorned wife, "and he's oppressed?"

When the anthem played, all Nuggets and Bulls stood rigidly at attention, while the cheers and jeers of the Chicago fans completely drowned out the vocals of sixteen-year-old Suzanne Shields, a student at St. Ignatius College Prep. "I thought the point of the anthem was to face the flag," said Nuggets forward Reggie Williams. "It seemed to me everybody was facing Mahmoud."[35]

Working to Play: Rights, Commodity, and the "Big Shoe" Scandal

Of all those facing Abdul-Rauf, or at least paying attention to the matter in some way, it was Shaquille O'Neal, one of many players who supported him, who most succinctly acknowledged the history of such controversy. "Last time someone disrespected the national anthem they talked about them for about 20 years and that was those brothers in the 1968 Olympics, Mexico City," O'Neal said. "I wasn't even born yet, and I heard about it."[36] Perhaps more than anyone else, O'Neal astutely juxtaposed Abdul-Rauf to the action in Mexico City that had taken place some thirty years earlier, demonstrating once again how quickly the rules of national belonging change if an individual does not subscribe to the tenets of citizenship in the sanctioned way. As with members of the OPHR, many condemned Abdul-Rauf as ungrateful for the success granted to him by the American way of life allegedly embodied on the basketball court. The existence of the athlete as a commodity, whether via an exorbitant professional salary or commercial endorsements, works in conjunction with his or her responsibility to both team *and* nation. As Robin D. G. Kelley has made clear, the athlete is one who "plays" but is also a worker.[37] Yet few consider the relationship of the player *to* the worker, at least not with the same vigor as employed in Abdul-Rauf's censure. For example, as the furor regarding Michael Jordan's refusal to take Nike, the provider of his largest paycheck, to task for its "Third" world labor policies escalated during his final championship season in 1998, the player-worker relationship became increasingly relevant. Still, not many probed the postindustrial challenge of clarifying the affinity between the black athlete in the United States and the "Third" world worker who sews together his or her uniform, at least not with the force that eventually obligated Abdul-Rauf to stand at attention.

These circumstances indicate that a significant shift has taken place in the political rhetoric found in the national sports arena, particularly as matters of commodification and global visibility and responsibility were in a relatively embryonic state in 1968. While the black-gloved fists of Smith and Carlos demonstrated a mode of global civil rights struggle possible within the Olympic arena, sport can also be portrayed as a form of "neoslavery"—a realm where players are "bought" or "traded" and teams have "owners." In the late 1960s, the corporate underpinnings and profitability of sport grew swiftly, and yet those in power denied players free agency and access to unionization. Most famous, of course, was the case of Curt Flood, who challenged what he saw as a "master and slave relationship" in professional baseball by taking the so-called reserve clause, which bound a player and his contract to the mercy of the team, all the way to the Supreme Court. Flood lost not only his case but also the remainder of his financially lucrative career. Moreover, with the commercially lucrative relationship solidified between sport and network television in the postwar period, one forged before the emergence of players' associations, it became critically clear that athletes—all athletes—as workers had to become more attuned to dealing with their workplace as if it were a shop floor. By no accident, then, players' associations, described by Howard Cosell as "akin to labor unions," emerged in 1968, one of the concrete results of this incipient awareness. Of the new labor organizations in professional sports, Marvin Miller, the players' representative for major league baseball, said, "I think that the crux of the problem here is that the players are pieces of property; they are chattel, they are controlled by the owners, they are not free to talk to any club except the one that has signed them in the first place, whether they were eighteen years old or what have you...."[38]

Of course, one of the undeniable allures of joining the ranks of elite athletes remains the promise of financial stability and, for some, wealth. While Olympic athletes are officially branded as amateurs, the promise of fruitful commercial endorsements that accompany a gold medal remains. Given its outstanding results, the U.S. track and field squad in 1968 should have produced a wide array of successful and lucrative futures. As *Time* magazine was quick to point out in its summary of Mexico City, Americans hauled in 45 gold, 28 silver, and 34 bronze medals, for a total of 107, while the Soviet Union took home 29 gold, 32 silver, and 30 bronze medals, for a total of 91. On the track, *Time* found it to be an "utter debacle for the Russians," because they won only three events outright, while the United States inarguably dominated.[39] Yet despite this irrefutable success, American spikers did not get rich. "Black athletes won seven of the U.S. track team's twelve track and field gold medals in Mexico City and set six world records," Tommie Smith points out. "But none of us came home to be millionaires."[40]

But the lack of tangible riches had to be weighed against the ways in which the OPHR had attempted to redefine victory. After his suspension, Smith gave an interview to Brad Pye, sports reporter for radio station KGJF in Los Angeles, and indicated that he had no regrets, regardless of the consequences. When Pye specifically asked him if he was worried that he had jeopardized his career in professional football, particularly with his recent drafting by the Los Angeles Rams, Smith replied, "On the victory stands I was thinking about my black people. What will come after that will come."[41] Indeed, upon his return home, Smith lost his contract with the Rams, and the army, despite his good standing in the ROTC program at San Jose State, declared him unfit for Vietnam. Sprinter Mel Pender finds such lack of respect by the state a residual sore spot. "There has never been an Olympic team like ours and yet we are the only one that didn't go to the White House," he remembers. "That still sticks with me."[42] Like Pender, Jim Hines, too, remains bitter. After his definitive victory in the 100-meters, Hines expressed a desire to play professional football and told the press, "I hope to be in uniform with the Miami Dolphins within two weeks."[43] Yet after the black power protest, he lost his endorsement contract with Adidas, and the Dolphins greatly reduced the worth of his contract. Rather than blame the Olympic administration that ousted Smith and Carlos or the broader societal problems that motivated the OPHR in the first place, Hines concentrates his anger on what he sees as the negative upshot of political collectivity:

> I was an activist. We were all black and a unit, and we set out to speak against the racism of the country, but I believed in letting our winning speak. Our winning. The '68 team was the best in history, but it was discredited by what Tom and John did. The glove situation cost us all a lot.... They felt we were all in on the protest.... The gesture cost me a total of $2 million.[44]

Yet even the politics of association did not operate equally. While Tommie Smith, for example, eventually secured a job as athletic director at Oberlin College under the tutelage of progressive sports sociologist Jack Scott, John Carlos struggled. In 1971, when an attempt to get a job with his shoe sponsor failed, he tried a football career. Although he was a fifteenth-round draft pick for the Philadelphia Eagles, in training camp he found all he could do was run. Frustrated, he left the team and tried a variety of other occupations—inner-city outreach, other football leagues, professional track and field. He sent out resumes but found only dead ends. "My agent said one guy told him that after what I did in Mexico City," Carlos said, "no businessman in his right mind would hire me."[45]

However, during his stint in Mexico City, Carlos, as well as many of his teammates, could not shake escalating rumors regarding corporate sponsorship, illegal by Olympic standards. The same television lens that enabled Smith and Carlos to vividly create a protest gesture with political worth also benefited the unprecedented potential for commercial profit in the Olympic arena, a process fulfilled in contemporary society by the global recognition of Nike's indomitable swoosh. In the allegedly amateur realm of the Olympics, the promise of commercial revenue was not reserved solely for the network broadcasting the Games but also extended to the industries that manufactured the athletic equipment and clothing. While Olympic amateurism has always been, of course, a complicated notion, the entrance of network television further muddied the playing field. Communist nations had been under fire since their Olympic debut, with the "Free World" arguing that if nothing exists in the communist system outside the government then Eastern bloc athletes were state sponsored and subsidized, but new accusations of professionalism arose in Mexico City because of the pronounced role of corporations in getting athletes to the starting line. The majority of these accusations were aimed at several members of the OPHR with what became known in the sports press as the "big shoe scandal." Although always treated as a minor sidebar to the black power protest, the squall over shoes indicated just how closely money grimly loomed at the Games.

The controversy began days before the Opening Ceremony in Mexico City when Lee Evans, with support from John Carlos, raised an objection to a Mexican policy that prevented Olympic athletes from wearing the merchandise of all but one shoe manufacturer. While the IOC made some *styles* of shoes illegal, such as the "brush spikes" that both Carlos and Evans had worn during the Olympic Trials in Lake Tahoe, it did not forbid any specific shoemaker. This "exclusive contract" of the Mexicans, according to Evans, had left many athletes without their chosen brand and style. He emphasized how the practice created particular hardships for some athletes, such as American middle-distance runner Wade Bell, who suffered from a foot problem that required a special brand of shoe that was not allowed by Mexican officials. Some countries, including the United States and Great Britain, threatened to petition the IOC in protest, particularly after customs detained twenty-five hundred pairs of shoes that were made by a manufacturer used by approximately half of the Olympic runners but unacceptable to the Mexican government. In response, Derek Ibbotson, a former record holder in the mile who worked in Mexico City as an aid to the British track and field team, announced that a protest meeting would take place at the airport. "There is a question of principle involved," said Ibbotson. "These are the Olympics and if the Mexicans won't allow athletes to use the shoes which are best for them then they are going against the principles of the Olympics."[46]

Speculation began to find veracity with talk that a representative of one of the prohibited shoe manufacturers had been apprehended and jailed after trying to pass merchandise through Mexican customs. Louis Duino, of the *San Jose Mercury News*, countered such rumors with claims that it was actually a San Jose student who had tried to smuggle in the illegal shoes and that authorities had nabbed him, jailed him for five days, and fed him only bread and water.[47] The buzz then further escalated shortly before the Closing Ceremony with allegations that three members of the U.S. track team had accepted money from an unnamed sporting goods manufacturer. Conjecture followed that the United States would relinquish three gold medals if the claims were found true, which narrowed the list of suspects to Olympic champions. The prospect of losing medals undoubtedly threw the USOC into a tailspin. According to the U.S. State Department, the USOC reported to the American Embassy that it had "strong evidence" that two athletic shoe manufacturers, Adidas and Puma, had paid Smith and Carlos in "strict violation of Olympic and amateur rules and regulations" in the amount of thirty-five hundred dollars each. It also claimed that while another athlete had received similar payment, he or she "turned it over to the USOC." Further damning, according to the USOC, was verification that Smith and Carlos had held Puma and Adidas shoes during their medal ceremony, "theoretically for advertisement purposes." Subsequent payment, the USOC posited, could "have set Carlos' and Smith's minds more at ease concerning consequence of demonstration."[48]

For its part, the press, also working with little evidence and on rampant supposition, reported that a few American athletes had told the USOC that they received equipment with sums of cash—as much as seventy-five hundred dollars—hidden inside, a direct infraction of amateurism. Some accounts, such as the one delivered on the front page of the *San Jose Mercury News*, directly linked the accusations to the OPHR, contending that it was "certain black power militants on the

American track team" who had accepted the illegal sponsorship. Further incriminating were the remarks of Duino, who connected the question of the illegal shoes with the black power gesture specifically, noting that Smith and Carlos, standing in stocking feet, *carried* their white track shoes to the dais and dipped them "as if the gesture had some great significance." When later asked about it, Carlos told the press that the gesture had an importance only other black athletes would understand. However, the wives of Smith and Carlos gave a different explanation, contending that the gesture was aimed at the Mexicans for prohibiting their preferred shoes.[49]

Columnist Robert Lipsyte solidified the racial edge to the allegations when he determined that it was a *white* athlete who, in an obvious smear tactic aimed at militant athletes, had originally given a coach a shoe with a five hundred dollar bill in it and started the buzz that two African Americans had each accepted payment of seventy-five hundred dollars to wear a particular brand, and that another athlete had deposited an excessive number of pesos in an Olympic Village bank. However, Lipsyte alleged that this information was planted by the USOC and that the charges were fallacious, a stance he supported with the USOC's claim to be conducting an investigation, which, if true, would have made it "unlikely that undocumented charges would be released before direct action was taken."[50]

While few conclusions were reached, the "big shoe scandal" raised broader issues regarding the status of amateurism in the Olympics. USOC acting executive director Everett Barnes, while admitting that an investigation would continue, tried to lessen the seriousness of the situation by affirming that while "there have been rumors," the USOC had "nothing to substantiate" them. Daniel J. Ferris, secretary emeritus of the Amateur Athletic Union and an officer of the International Amateur Athletic Federation, found the controversy to be representative of a wider trend emerging in the amateur sports arena, averring that "virtually every country in the Olympics are [*sic*] guilty of violations in the equipment scandal." The big shoe scandal, in his opinion, reinforced his proposal to ban all equipment that exhibited a corporate trademark from all international amateur competitions, an idea that built upon Avery Brundage's move to rid the Winter Games in Grenoble of brand-name skis.[51]

An editorial in the *San Jose Mercury News* agreed that some kind of sweeping change had to take place but, in a familiar fashion, broadened the topic to directly question the state-sponsored teams of communist nations. The editorial admitted that while American athletes who had accepted money to wear a particular brand of shoe had, indeed, broken Olympic code, this was "far less sweeping a violation than that committed regularly by the Soviet Union and other Communist nations whose teams are, in fact, composed of state-paid professional athletes." The same newspaper that had condemned the attempt by Smith and Carlos days earlier to demonstrate for "human rights" within the Olympic arena now called for a policy allowing all athletes to "have access to the same equipment," permitting the Olympics to "be placed on a less hypocritical basis."[52] Arthur Daley of the *New York Times* concurred. The columnist argued that it might be time for the Olympics to surrender the spurious designations that "amateurism" entailed, because there were "few genuine amateurs in the world."[53] Legendary sportswriter Red Smith recognized that with the exception of U.S. collegiate athletics and "a few countries like Russia, a man can't make a living running 200 meters." If one is able to survive by "endorsing spiked shoes," Smith contended, "he injures nobody."[54] An article in the *Nation* vehemently agreed, declaring that the shoe scandal

and the as-yet-unsubstantiated rumors of money improperly distributed to allegedly amateur contestants, in themselves disagreeable, emphasize once again the hypocrisy of the Olympic rules. All athletes of Olympic caliber are subsidized in one way or another; the standards which must be met in modern world competition are so high that no one can train for them in after hours. The antiquated notion of amateurism should be scrapped, and a superb performer should be acknowledged worthy of his hire.[55]

The shoe controversy subsided without much further ado. In the present-day Olympics, corporate sponsorship and the ideals of amateurism are continually renegotiated, particularly with the recent inclusion of professional basketball and hockey players and the allowance of three World Cup soccer players per national Olympic team. Yet the economic imperatives of athleticism remain critical outside the specific Olympic venue, as exemplified by the contemporary commodification of black athletes, male and female, within media and entertainment industries. In the wake of the OPHR, the black athlete mediates this post–civil rights context, creating a bifurcated image that oscillates between black criminal youth and black upward mobility and compacts multiple racialized assumptions. In this vein, the contemporary black athlete, along with the masculine identity that accompanies it, creates anxiety within a white American imagination when traditional lines of racial coherence and cognizance are blurred. A random list of figures lumped under the heading of "black athlete" might include O. J. Simpson, Evander Holyfield, Mike Tyson, Tiger Woods, Dennis Rodman, Latrell Sprewell, and the Dallas Cowboy football squad, making central Hazel Carby's question, "How, exactly, can the white middle class distinguish between the good and bad black male?"[56]

Of course, the redrawing of such lines has been a feature of the transformations in civil rights struggles, as movements of Black Power, such as the OPHR, exemplify, and these modifications have continued into the post–civil rights period. When civil rights movements moved northward in the late postwar period, the struggle transformed as it combated a racism that was far more covert than voting restrictions, from the "state sponsored apartheid" of American suburbanization policies, in Nikhil Pal Singh's words, to the "spatial apartheid" that Mike Davis definitively demonstrates in "post-liberal" Los Angeles.[57] It is essential, then, that the strategies against such veiled oppression are duly skillful. In his treatment of the failure of the American working class to achieve successful and cohesive political representation, Davis continually reiterates how African Americans are *the* critical element to socialist ideology in the United States, arguing that the passing over of black political interests has crippled labor in the postwar period. Thus, when Davis contends that "the oppression of Blacks has remained a central contradiction at the heart of the American bourgeois democratic system," he makes it clear that African Americans have *the* unfinished democratic agenda.[58]

It is useful to go back to W. E. B. Du Bois, who created a framework of political ideology and national belonging that worked *within* the constraints of the nation. For example, in *The Souls of Black Folk*, Du Bois wrote:

> Freedom, too, the long-sought, we still seek,—the freedom of life and limb, the freedom to work and think, the freedom to love and aspire ... the ideal of fostering and developing the traits and talents of the Negro, not in opposition to or contempt for other races, but rather in large conformity to the greater ideals of the American Republic.... We the darker ones come even now not altogether empty-handed: there are to-day no truer exponents of the pure human spirit of the Declaration of Independence than the American Negroes; there is no true American music but the wild sweet melodies of the Negro slave; the American fairy tales and folklore are Indian and African; and, all in all, we black men seem the sole oasis of simple faith and reverence in a dusty desert of dollars and smartness. Will America be poorer if she replace her brutal dyspeptic blundering with light-hearted but determined Negro humility?[59]

In this fashion, the struggle for civil rights did not merely bring African Americans onto equal footing within the national sphere but rather tried to find a space to rehabilitate the broader definitions and implications of citizenship itself. In this context, the role of the black athlete as cultivated by the OPHR emerged as an overt attempt to make America fulfill its promises, understanding that while sport provides a vehicle to locate a black face in the most sweeping capacity, it also exists as a province that can be devastating in its outcome, alleviating America's racial culpability within the consequential framework of popular culture. In 1968, those, such as Harry Edwards, who understood the disparity that existed between the black athletic star and a broader African American community knew that the imbalance would only increase unless a cohesive and determined political movement went into combat with the same vigor and force. As Hazel Carby writes of the contemporary situation, "Despite the multimillion-dollar international trade in black male bodies, and encouragement to 'just do it,' there is no equivalent in international outrage, no marches or large-scale public protest, at the hundreds of thousands of black male bodies languishing out of sight of the media in the North American penal system."[60]

The movement that came to fruition around the figure of the black athlete in the late 1960s should not, however, be dismissed as having no structural result. As the Games began in Mexico, the *New York Amsterdam News* announced the possibility of a national corporation designed to aid black athletes with their financial and personal affairs.[61] One year after the close of the Mexico City Olympics, Kenneth Pitzer, the president of Stanford University, issued the "Right to Conscience" to allow black athletes to boycott any sporting event they objected to.[62] In 1971, Edwards concluded that "the onset of the revolt of the black athlete" had produced some substantial change, including "the hiring of unprecedented numbers of black coaches and administrative assistants at predominantly white educational institutions" and "the establishment of athletic boards and committees at many institutions to handle the grievances of black athletes." Perhaps most significant, Edwards noted "a highly visible increase in the number of black athletes doing paid television commercials."[63]

But does Edwards's summation undercut the purpose of staging such opposition in the first place? Does the scenario he describes defeat the purpose and significance of the protest? As exemplified by the case of Abdul-Rauf in 1996, the granting of profitable commercial endorsements to black athletes creates an atmosphere of resistance to any athlete who uses the athletic arena for political complaint, especially when the national anthem is part of one's contractual occupational obligation. The role sketched for O. J. Simpson in American society, as argued by Toni Morrison, epitomizes such a process. Simpson lived in an "all-white world" and was habitually accused of not doing anything for his racial community. In translation, Morrison argues, he was not a "vocal, high-profile activist."[64] Yet it was this same identity, what can be termed *apolitical blackness*, that allowed him to serve and profit as the corporate spokesman for companies like Hertz, Pepsi, Hanes, and Midas. Simpson, who had, for all intents and purposes, boycotted the NYAC in 1968, took on a social "whiteness." As Andrew Ross elaborates, "Despite his initial fame as a 'black athlete,' it was widely perceived that O. J. Simpson was less *socially* black than almost any other black man in America."[65] Because of this, Simpson was allowed access to the well-paying corporate domain denied to Smith and Carlos as well as Abdul-Rauf, who left the NBA in 1998 for a professional career in Turkey before returning to sign with the Vancouver Grizzlies.

"They Certainly Are Short": Tabloid Science and the Marketing of the Black Body

Although Simpson existed in a socially defined racial realm, the influence of science on understandings of race has persisted in the popular discourse on race in the contemporary United States. Movements such as the OPHR attempted to intervene in the scientific classifications that had become commonplace in the earlier part of the twentieth century, and in spite of the various rises and falls of Darwinian ideology, scientific arguments regarding the black athlete remained a critical part of contemporary popular discussions on race as the scientific discourse on the athlete continued to find its way into popular and public forums after World War II. Although many Americans had largely accepted the *language* of civil rights, it was clear that a discussion of racial biology could still comfortably take place on American playing fields.

Of course, in the wake of groups such as the OPHR as well as the Student Non-Violent Coordinating Committee and the Black Panthers, the late 1960s, perhaps more than any other period in the postwar era, represented the height of the shift in language influenced by the civil rights movements. Indeed, Harry Edwards and his cohort lent a great deal of political worth to the displacement of "Negro" by "black." Yet when members of the OPHR made their mark in both the athletic and the political arenas, their physical capabilities were questioned in a manner that resembled the scientific explorations of the Negro in the 1930s. A reporter, for example, asked John Carlos why black athletes were so fast. "Everything is hustle and bustle for a young black," Carlos answered. "Run to the bus, run with other kids, run from the cops. Maybe that's how we get so good at sprinting."[66] Carlos understood his speed to be environmentally driven rather than inherently derived. However, the persistence of an expert scientific language in mass-mediated conversations regarding the success of African Americans on the playing field indicated little consensus on the matter. A discussion of O. J. Simpson in 1968, for example, asked: "Is Simpson a born runner or have his coaches ... contributed to making him what he is?" John McKay, Simpson's college coach, emphasized how coaching was instrumental to Simpson's success. Yet in a vein reminiscent, again, of the laboratory assertions of the 1930s, another coach refuted, "NOBODY taught that boy how to run! We just left him alone."[67]

The latter response failed to acknowledge the contributions of hard work and dedication to Simpson's success, and while such a reply did not overtly cite scientific reasoning, its foundations resembled many laboratory conclusions. However, as the OPHR demonstrated, racialized questions of brain versus brawn have not been left solely to those in white coats. Early on, black intervention into the question of nature versus nurture emerged with the character of the trickster in slave tales. The trickster represented the slave's desire to be recognized as strong *and* intelligent, able to deal with an impossible situation against an insurmountable foe. Lawrence Levine draws parallels between the trickster and Muhammad Ali, finding that a large part of the fascination that surrounded the boxer was his ability to use words "to work on his adversaries long before he walked into the ring with them, predicting the round in which he would win, ridiculing his opponent, describing in advance the events to come...."[68]

Despite the legacy of characters such as the trickster and the political negotiations that Ali, for example, engaged in, the popularization of scientific racism continues with marked consequences. Connections between race and athletic ability endure in the lion's share of popular media, with pseudoscientific explanations augmenting various social beliefs and cultural constructions, whether counterfeit or not. Rather than having lost authority in the post–civil rights era, scientific claims of race persist in great number. Indeed, genetics has become such a part of the American vernacular that it is posed as an everyday, objective exegesis for a range of human behavior, including criminality, sexual orientation, and ethnic characteristics. This emphasis on a scientific basis for individual actions exonerates society of its responsibility for social problems.[69] Popular scientific understandings of the black athlete emerge in phrases such as "white men can't jump," the title of a popular film, and in related jests about "white man's disease." They are so prevalent and familiar that prominent sports figures such as Al Campanis, Jimmy "the Greek" Snyder, Marge Schott, and Sir Roger Bannister have comfortably stated, in public, racial and racist justifications for black athletic success in unparalleled mass forums.

In the early 1970s, the *Journal of Personality and Social Psychology* published two articles that dealt with racial differences in athletic ability. The first was designed because its authors, Morgan Worthy and Allan Markle, postulated that "recent comparative studies of differential performance are limited ... to ... intellectual tests ... in educational settings. Sports activities provide an additional area for meaningful comparisons."[70] The second study, written by James M. Jones and Adrian Ruth Hochner, was based on Worthy and Markle's conclusion: independent of socioeconomic class, black athletes performed better in reactive activities than self-paced ones. This latter study argued that juxtaposing "self-paced" and "reactive" was too simple, necessitating more intricate performance statistics to support any kind of theory that connected racial differences and physical ability.[71]

This advent of another round of popular treatments of the familiar subject was disturbing and demonstrated how academic disciplines such as sociology and psychology reacted to and were charged with interpreting the events of the 1960s. Within just a few years of the black power protest in Mexico City, a range of articles that dealt with the brain versus brawn question emerged in the popular press. Some four years after publishing its thought-provoking series "The Black Athlete," *Sports Illustrated* made a significant—infamous—contribution to the scientific debate regarding the physical abilities of African Americans. A piece by senior editor Martin Kane, "An Assessment of 'Black Is Best,'" used a variety of scientific studies, as well as theories regarding the "Middle Passage," to argue for both the dominance of African Americans and the budding success of "emerging nations" (read: black) in international sport. Passing over the "environmental factors" necessary for such achievement, Kane plunged into the "increasing body of scientific opinion which suggests that physical differences in the races might well have enhanced the athletic potential of the Negro in certain events." One such study among this body of opinion was J. M. Tanner's analysis of the Rome Olympics in 1960, which determined that "amongst competitors in both track and field events there were large significant racial differences in leg length, arm length and hip width."[72] While Kane explored the racialized consequences of this determination, Tanner's study, upon closer inspection, reveals that relatively little of his work was done in regard to race. Rather, his team sought to determine what kinds of anatomy enable elite athletic ability. Racial categorization played a role in Tanner's quest, but it was not a prominent feature of the work, nor was it the ultimate purpose for using the Olympics to this end.[73] Kane's use of Tanner's study as well as others, according to John Hoberman, is a common practice among "popularizing white journalists" who "accumulate suggestive but scientifically invalid or inconclusive evidence of black athletic superiority."[74]

Yet the importance of Kane's article can be seen in the flurry of impassioned reactions that followed it. In a response published later that same year, for example, Harry Edwards, this time in his role as a sociologist, took Kane directly to task for his specious assessment of the issues. While acknowledging the lengthy history of ideas on black physicality, Edwards argued that rarely had "the myth of racially-linked black athletic prowess been subject to so explicit a formulation and presentation" as Kane's piece.[75] But Edwards's review did not include even faint praise. In a detailed, methodical fashion, Edwards broke down each of Kane's major points to demonstrate their flaws, condemned the pseudoscientific evidence used to create his conclusions, and emphasized how Kane's antiquated definitions of race were based on a spurious idea of purity.

Edwards first delineated the various ways in which radical transformations had taken place in terms of the racial inequities firmly established in American sport, emphasizing the emergence of "a heightened consciousness among actual and aspiring black athletes as to their political responsibilities and potentials in the worldwide black liberation struggle."[76] Yet he also recognized that alongside the variety of political achievements and global extensions of the black athlete existed another so-called accomplishment: that "diverse and highly influential personas and publications ... have finally admitted what every objective observer of the sports scene already knew—to wit, that the performance of black athletes, on the average, is significantly superior to that of whites in all sports participated in by both groups in numbers." While Edwards did not question the conclusion of notable black athletic success, he did interrogate why it was so, asking for more "serious consideration to the broader implications of these arguments for either black athletes or the black population at large." He judiciously historicized, for example, what he called "the myth of the black male's racially determined, inherent physical and athletic superiority" in terms of mythical assumptions regarding sexual ability.[77] Last, as John Hoberman has pointed out, Edwards "rightly emphasized the persisting Darwinian context in which black athletic performances were still interpreted as evidence of retarded development."[78] Thus, Edwards responded to Kane by firmly illustrating how the success of the black athlete had to be considered as a socially and culturally derived product, no small part of which was the mental barrier inflicted upon "great white hopes"—Jim Ryun, Jerry Quarry, Pete Maravich—because of the belief in a scientific superiority.[79]

William Rhoden somewhat followed Edwards's intervention and extended the debate in a feature in *Ebony* in 1974. Rhoden built a scientific trajectory that called upon familiar sources, including Eleanor Metheny and W. Montague Cobb, to demonstrate where beliefs in black physical superiority came from and what kind of opposition they encountered. Perhaps most provocatively, Rhoden juxtaposed the work of Dr. Ernst Jokl, former director of the Exercise Research Laboratories at the University of Kentucky, to the work of Edwards. According to Jokl, "Negroes have enormously underdeveloped capacity (for athletics) due to their late coming into emancipation. With his emancipation, the Negro discovered ... where his abilities lay—and ... cultivated those abilities." Edwards, however, found that Jokl's reasoning "implies that blacks need only exercise their innate physical abilities to become successful athletes." With this theory, Edwards pointed out, "whites lose nothing," because intellectual capacity holds greater value in broader society.[80]

Some, including Hoberman, have accused Rhoden of not taking an overt side in his article. However, Rhoden, who was still a few years away from a prominent career as a *New York Times* sportswriter, used the work of prominent African American psychiatrist Alvin F. Poussaint to support Edwards's response.[81] Furthermore, he concluded the piece with what he called the "disheartening figures" that indicated the imbalance between the great number of elite black athletes and African Americans in "other fields of endeavors": one lawyer for every seven thousand African Americans, one doctor for every thirty-seven hundred. Last, Rhoden let Edwards have the impassioned final word, a warning that "until blacks come to understand athletics and what athletics means in their overall political, social and economic circumstances in this country, we're going to suffer."[82]

Yet no matter how fervent calls such as Edwards's were, the discussion persisted in tired and worn terms. A year later, for example, *Track and Field News* published "Is Black Fastest?" The writer, Jon Hendershott, offered little in the way of new material, focusing on a familiar cast of scientists, sociologists, and coaches. He summarized the debate of black athletic dominance as one between innate ability and socioeconomic determinism and concluded that the very discussion of the matter was self-perpetuating, a "monumental psych job done on whites."[83] While certainly not earth shattering in any way, the article demonstrated how the debate subsisted, regardless of how repetitive it continued to be, as long as African Americans maintained success in major athletic arenas.[84]

In 1988, however, the *Philadelphia Inquirer* offered an interesting variation on the subject with Michael Sokolove's "Are Blacks Better Athletes than Whites?" In what Hoberman has called "the first skeptical treatment of the subject," Sokolove's cautious discussion of race and physical ability included both extensive historical detail and a substantial examination of the increasing role genetics had started to play in the debate.[85] Sokolove summarized the various scientific and sociological theories that had dominated the landscape over the years and offered amateur explanations of the emerging work of geneticists, such as Gideon Ariel and Robert Malina, on the (ir)relevance of muscle twitch fibers. The body contains two types of these fibers, fast-twitch and slow-twitch, which work just as they sound: fast fibers are conducive to sprinting, whereas slow fibers are conducive to endurance. These geneticists, however, took the study to a new level and attempted to attach a preponderance of a particular kind of muscle twitch fiber to a racial group.

While on the surface the study of such fibers seemed to lend a new-found authority to the racialized brain versus brawn debate, Sokolove pointed out that "enough laymen" knew the meaning of muscle fibers that the Human Performance Lab, a prominent center conducting such research at Ball State University, continually received inquiries from parents who sought to have their children biopsied to determine the sport they were best suited for.[86] His air of caution regarding these genetic studies, however, was even more straightforward. While "most people with any knowledge of sports would agree" that numerous African Americans fill the ranks of elite athletes, he warned that it is a subject that is not "open for public discussion." According to Sokolove,

> On the face of it, it's fine to point out the remarkable achievements of black athletes: how blacks populate the rosters of professional baseball,

basketball and football teams far out of the proportion to their 11.4 percent of the U.S. population, how they account for more than half the players and the majority of the elite performers. The problem is that if you take it one step further and ask *why*—well, that's when it gets touchy and uncomfortable. Which doesn't mean people don't wonder. Even a casual viewer of sports, an hour here and there on television, might arrive at some seemingly obvious conclusions. Black competitors run faster than whites. They also jump higher. Their movements are quicker—whether it's flicking a left jab or scooting after a ground ball.... Thinking about why blacks excel in sports is OK. It doesn't make you a bad person, or a bigoted one. But to think out loud on the subject can be impolitic....[87]

Sokolove's primary example for the consequences of publicly engaging in the debate was an obvious one: Jimmy "the Greek" Snyder, who on January 15, 1988, in answer to a question about black football players posed by DCTV reporter Ed Hotaling, made a televised statement that caused CBS to fire him as a sports commentator.

The difference between blacks and whites goes all the way back to the Civil War when, during the slave period, the slave owner would breed his big black [man] with his big [black] woman so that he could have a big black kid—that's where it all started. The black is a better athlete to begin with because he's been bred to be that way because of his thigh size and big size. [They] jump higher and run faster. All the players are black; the only things that the whites control is the coaching job.[88]

Of course, Snyder's remarks were not the only such celebrated racial missteps. His theory had picked up where Los Angeles Dodgers' vice president Al Campanis had left off the previous year. Just as Snyder blundered on Martin Luther King's birthday, Campanis made his devastating statements on April 6, 1987, the fortieth anniversary of Jackie Robinson's major league debut, during an episode of ABC's *Niteline* designed to honor the event. As sports scholar Kenneth Shropshire suggests, it is worth quoting at length the exchange between Campanis and anchor Ted Koppel:

> KOPPEL: Why are there no black managers, general manager, or owners? ... Is there still prejudice in baseball today?
>
> CAMPANIS: No, I don't believe it's prejudice. I truly believe that they may not have some of the necessities to be, let's say, a field manager or perhaps a general manager.
>
> KOPPEL: Do you really believe that?
>
> CAMPANIS: Well, I don't say that all of them, but they certainly are short. How many quarterbacks do you have, how many pitchers do you have, that are black?
>
> KOPPEL: Yeah, but I got to tell you, that sounds like the same kind of garbage we were hearing forty years ago about players.
>
> CAMPANIS: No, it's not garbage, Mr. Koppel, because I played on a college team, and the center fielder was black, and in the backfield at NYU with a fullback who was black. Never knew the difference whether he was black or white. We were teammates. So it might just be, why are black men or black people not good swimmers? Because they don't have the buoyancy.[89]

The statements of both Snyder and Campanis fall into the category of what Shropshire has fittingly called the "lawn jockey mentality." Like Snyder, Campanis was fired for his comments, and many considered his remarks to Koppel far more egregious because he directly attacked African American intellectual capacity and did not attempt to provide the allegedly historical, albeit erroneous, argument regarding slavery that Snyder did. Indeed, one politically conservative response to Snyder commended him for bringing the issues into the forefront of public discussion and designated the incident "an epiphany." In defense of Snyder, the writer, a professor of law at George Mason University, saw the incident as a vehicle for delving into the subject more fully, declaring that "it is quite obvious that the races have different distributions of athletics skills, and those different distributions have a genetic root" and, to a further end, that "intelligence is the quintessential human characteristic, so surely we are most curious about how races differ in that dimension."[90]

The ramifications of the seemingly back-to-back statements by Campanis and Snyder were contradictory. According to Richard Lapchick, the public nature of the controversy prompted an increase in the number of African Americans hired in coaching and administrative positions in the sports industry, leading to what he considers "a dismantling of false perceptions regarding the ability of blacks to manage and coach at the highest levels."[91] Yet the controversy did not keep others with similar views at bay. While Cincinnati Reds owner Marge Schott's reference to two black players as "million-dollar niggers" took place behind closed doors, for example, she had to pay a twenty-five thousand dollar fine and was suspended for one year from daily club operations.[92] Yet her remarks, which also included references to "money-grubbing Jews," a declaration that "Hitler had the right idea ... but went too far," and the summation that players with earrings were "fruits," did not attain the same prominence as those of Snyder or Campanis, perhaps because few considered the female owner of a major league franchise to be a public authority. Besides, observed Harry Edwards, "Marge Schott is not the problem; she is a 64-year-old smoker and drinker with a weight problem. That's a problem that's going to take care of itself."[93]

While people were perhaps not surprised that a woman described in such terms would make such statements, the gaffe committed by Sir Roger Bannister, celebrated for breaking the four-minute barrier in the mile in 1954, shocked many. In 1995, in front of the British Association for the Advancement of Science, Bannister announced that he was "prepared to risk political incorrectness by drawing attention to the seemingly obvious but understressed fact that black sprinters, and black athletes in general, all seem to have certain natural anatomical advantages." A scientist, he cited as examples the "relative lack of subcutaneous fatty insulating tissue in the skin" and "the length of the Achilles tendon" in African Americans. While many reacted to Bannister's speech in horror, as they had with Schott and her coarse cohort, *Sports Illustrated* remarked that the knighted Bannister had "showed gumption" and "at least lent a thoughtful voice to what has been a taboo topic." Also, the magazine found that "the essence of what [he] said is not inherently racist" and as an example stated that "it would not ... be prejudicial to note that blacks tend to have different hair and lip structure than Asians, or that Asians, on average, are smaller than Caucasians."[94] In agreement with *Sports Illustrated*, another sports journalist found it unfair that figures like Bannister were not allowed to make such remarks. He noted that when watching "Dancin' Harry," a mascotlike figure in a sequined tuxedo who danced on the court during basketball games, basketball great Bill Russell once commented, "Well, that proves that not all of us have rhythm." According to the journalist, "Had Russell's wisecrack been delivered by a white broadcaster with one or two words changed, my, my.... But Russell could turn the stereotype into harmless and ironic humor because he, like Dancin' Harry, is African American."[95] The point, of course, was that the debate regarding racialized ideas of physical ability was unbalanced in terms of who was allowed to speak about it. Figures such as Campanis, Snyder, Schott, and Bannister made headlines, albeit unequally, while Russell's remark was considered merely a waggish observation.

Brooks Johnson, arguably the most prominent African American track and field coach in the United States, intervened in the debate when he boldly announced that his "mission" was to "find the white Carl Lewis." According to Johnson, who coached both Olympic and Stanford University teams, U.S. population statistics indicate that as many as nine top sprinters should be out there, but they are funneled in other directions because of the prevailing, and false, belief that, just as an African American athlete does not have the intellectual capacity to play quarterback, the white athlete does not have the physical capacity to succeed as a wide receiver. "Other countries produce white sprinters. We don't anymore. But we did back in the '50s. What happened? Did we have some kind of fantastic genetic metamorphosis over the course of 30 years? What Jimmy the Greek said, he got crucified for. The white community deserted him. But he was their most articulate spokesman. What he said, people generally believe."[96]

The essence of Johnson's argument was that training athletes according to race, which was endorsed by Dean Cromwell before World War II, created a self-fulfilling prophecy. The belief that black athletes excel at shorter distances and jump well not only directs them to such events but also excludes white athletes. Johnson bluntly made this assertion during one of the most popular and controversial public debates to take place regarding the black athlete: NBC's broadcast of "Black Athletes—Fact and Fiction" in 1989. Airing in the adult-oriented evening time slot of ten o'clock, it was to be, according to television listings, a conversation among NBC news anchor Tom Brokaw, athletes, and "experts."[97] Based on a series of greatly problematic scientific studies, the program attempted to find a link between racial difference and physical ability, or, as Brokaw clearly enunciated in the opening, "Are black athletes better than whites?"[98] The network presented its fundamental query in a literally explosive manner. Brokaw's voice was accompanied by the image of a white hand shooting a starter's pistol as two female runners, one black and one white, sprang out of the starting blocks. Yet despite the image of the two women, it was made clear from the beginning that the question of black dominance in sport, yet again, concerned men only. Brokaw further affirmed this when he explained that the program would focus on "how black males, especially, have made big time sports a mostly black world." It did not seem to be important, then, that *all* "big time sports"—presumably football, baseball, and basketball— tended to be arenas for men only.

Gender aside, the very premise, as well as tactic, of Brokaw's agenda was problematic. By focusing on domination, the program posed the black athlete as something in need of explanation. As Laurel R. Davis observes in her excellent analysis of the program, "The preoccupation itself is racist because it is founded on and naturalizes racial categories as fixed and unambiguous biological realities, obscuring the political processes of racial formation."[99] Thus, the ascendance of African Americans was posed as an abnormal occurrence, an aberration in need of scientific exploration and social understanding based on, promised Brokaw, a range of ideas and theories. To present these, he introduced members of a roundtable who would engage in discussion at the program's conclusion. The promise of this discussion reinforced the appearance that an open dialogue was to take place, juxtaposing prominent laboratory scientists to social scientists to create the ingredients for a classic nature versus nurture debate. Harry Edwards, Arthur Ashe, and Richard Lapchick, of the Center for the Study of Sport and Society at Northeastern University, joined Brokaw in the studio. Robert Malina, anthropologist of sports science at the University of Texas, and Claude Bouchard, of Laval University in Quebec, joined the conversation via the safety of a satellite uplink from Brussels. However, despite this varied cast of characters, the program twisted into a disturbing angle on race and sport that tried to justify the antiquated scientific mythologies. As John Hoberman points out, the program, "despite its scientific pretenses and apparently enlightened attitude toward the investigation of racial differences, ... was seriously flawed by the producers' ignorance of the historical context in which the myths and theories of racial physiology have developed."[100]

To be fair, the program did not completely avoid historical and social context. It offered, for example, a biographical profile of Phillip Crump, a talented young basketball player from Philadelphia, to demonstrate the environmental factors that contributed to the making of a great athlete. The segment opened with Crump dribbling down a sidewalk, passing a young black mother pushing a stroller, and, in doing so, using his ball to move past urban poverty. Brokaw's voice described the scene as the "most notorious ghetto in north Philadelphia," a place where some of the best basketball players started life. Over an image of Michael Jordan, Brokaw explained how Crump, the best high school guard in the city, dreams of a professional career not only to succeed but simply to survive. This life has made Crump, as described by Brokaw, "schoolyard smart." He lives with his mother, his sister, and her two children across the street from a crack house. The neighborhood is portrayed as a place to escape from, not live in, and basketball has been

Crump's best chance to do so. His neighbors, even those who have chosen an illicit approach to survival in the ghetto economy, support Crump's dreams. "I won't sell it to him," a darkened profile says into the camera. "He got a basketball career. He's smart, he not dumb, and he trying to make somethin'. Hey, I know he want to move out of the projects like I do."

Of course, Crump's chosen path, regardless of hard work, has proven difficult for all who have gone down it. As explained by Brokaw, historically Crump's "total dedication" has not been unique to young black men in the city; it began with the "white players" that ran the same concrete court fifty years before, namely Jewish immigrant youth. Citing various examples of the dominance exhibited by inner-city Jewish basketball teams from the first half of the twentieth century, such as the Spas (South Philadelphia Hebrew Association) and the Cleveland Rosenblums, Brokaw explained how basketball has not been a "black" game but rather what sportswriter Pete Axthelm termed "the city game."[101] Jewish players set out on a path similar to Crump's, because, as one former Spas star remembered, "We always thought, in Philadelphia, that every Jewish boy was born with a basketball in his hand." Yet the similarities found in this historical comparison end there. While African American and Jewish cagers had the inner-city environment in common, a far different language was used to explain why basketball prowess followed. When comparing the way the Rosenblums played against the New York Renaissance, for example, distinct words surfaced for the white versus black game. "Jews got by on strategy," translated Brokaw, "the blacks on quickness."

Thus, despite the casting of basketball as a vehicle for social mobility for urban residents, familiar ideas regarding innate traits and natural ability still prevailed with a racialized rhetoric that presented Jewish players as smart and black players as moving well. Brooks Johnson understood the importance of such beliefs in his quest to find his "white Carl Lewis." His mission, as an African American track coach, makes for an interesting parallel to the charge undertaken by white record mogul Sam Phillips decades earlier. Legend holds that when Phillips wanted to put his small Memphis studio, Sun Records, on the map, he said, "If I could find a white man who had the Negro sound and the Negro feel, I could make a million dollars." Phillips found his man, of course, in a young singer from Tupelo, Mississippi, named Elvis. The upshot, of course, was the commercial co-optation of rhythm and blues by the predominantly white music industry, paving the way for rock and roll.[102] If Johnson were to get his wish, as Phillips did, the ramifications could be equally dramatic and bring to fruition his intended point: racial stereotypes harm *all* people and, in this case, prevent *white* athletes from pursuing their goals.

However, rather than explore the racialized implications of inherent physical ability, Brokaw took Johnson's statement as proof of "reverse racism," lamented how the idea of black athletic superiority had made white athletes "the butt of jokes," and offered dramatic examples of the belabored white athlete. Brokaw introduced footage, for example, of runner Mike Cole, the lone white competitor at a track meet, false starting when he jumped out of the blocks early. "If I were Mike Cole I'd jump, too," laughed the announcer. "I would've jumped a long time ago, I'll tell ya!" agreed his sidekick. "I'd be running now in the second race to try to get ahead of these guys." In addition to this kind of comic relief was a clip of Howard Cosell, who once said of a stunning play made by football player Alvin Garrett, "That little monkey gets loose, doesn't he?"

While most excuse Cosell's famous misstep in light of his pioneering support of and relationship with Muhammad Ali, the use of such language, *monkey*, demonstrates a belief, as explained by Harry Edwards in the broadcast, that "blacks are closer to beasts and animals in terms of their genetic and physical and anatomical make than they are to the rest of humanity and that's where the indignity comes in." In terms of the roundtable of which Edwards was a part, however, Cosell's blunder paved the way for the scientists to make their point. Regardless of Brokaw's efforts to present basketball as a city game, the program's slant toward a scientific understanding of black athletic dominance became magnified in the discussion of "experts," building on language infused with ideas of evolution, such as *monkey*.

Of course, not everyone on the panel leaned in this direction. Edwards made impassioned calls for a sociological understanding of the situation, as Johnson did. But the few became greatly encumbered by their host. When Johnson, for example, exasperatedly posited that a racialized genetic difference *was not a factor* in sports success, Brokaw finished his thought with "But we *have* found that blacks do appear to have a genetic edge." Brokaw's stance, as Davis points out, helped present the scientists sitting on the panel as "more objective and knowledgeable" than the social scientists, such as Edwards and Lapchick, and therefore able to enunciate theories of racial superiority without political or social consequence.[103] "I know that the American system is sensitive to statements about blacks and whites," stated Bouchard, who had conducted muscle fiber tests on West Africans and created a theory that delineated differences between "white" and "black" muscle, "but you cannot defy science.... I mean, such things are *facts*." Edwards, for one, attempted to face such "facts" by substituting a more culturally, socially, and historically derived notion of race for the scientific one promulgated by Bouchard and company. In doing so, he directly, albeit futilely, reconfigured the debate in a way that a century of science had failed to do:

> Tom, we have a much more basic and fundamental problem here, and that has to do with the whole concept of race itself. We know, for example, that the African American population arose generally from an admixture of European American, native aboriginal or Indian stock, and African stock. Therefore, the issue emerges: How black does one have to be in order for this thing to make any sense that they're talking about? ... We approximate every color of the rainbow, and we didn't get that way by looking out the window too much or watching too much TV. So, what we have to begin to deal with is the basic concept of race: How black does one have to be in order to have these fast twitch muscles?

Edwards's point corresponds to Hoberman's judicious summary of the program: "The public was offered yet another examination of the black body rather than an examination of white fantasies about black bodies."[104] Unfortunately, that public was both large and won-over. The network reported an 11.1 national Nielsen rating for the prime-time broadcast of the show (with one point representing 904,000 homes) and a 20 percent audience share, finishing second in the time slot to ABC's *thirtysomething*. Also, the network fielded 71 phone calls that praised the segment, 209 calls that opposed it, and 41 requests for a cassette.[105] U.S. Olympic rowing medalist, IOC member, and black athlete Anita DeFrantz was one viewer who objected to the material presented. "If white American athletes think blacks are superior," she cautioned, "the rest of the world will laugh at us." Yet others, including Brokaw, were satisfied with the results. Claiming that the idea for the program was his own, Brokaw said that "most of his colleagues" were "impressed and relieved" with the outcome and that most of the opposition within NBC came "from rank and file, not from the highest level." Yet Brokaw did admit, "There are some in NBC, particularly some close friends who happen to be black, who also still have reservations about whether we needed to do it and that it did not advance the state of knowledge and will only leave stereotypes in the minds of people."[106] Perhaps making Brokaw's point for him was Jimmy "the Greek" Snyder. "I got fired for saying that and now they're doing specials on it," said Snyder, "You figure it out.... What I said was right. Maybe I didn't say it the right way, but it was true."[107]

Arguably the most egregious response to the program came from *Los Angeles Times* sports columnist Scott Ostler, who responded to Brooks Johnson's mission to find a "white Carl Lewis" with "Dear Brooks: Pack a lunch." Ostler continued, "And while you're out there searching, bring back a white Spud Webb, a white Dominique Wilkins, a white O. J. Simpson, a white Jerry Rice, a white Bo Jackson and a white Wilt Chamberlain." Modeling his column on the fact versus fiction theme of NBC's broadcast, Ostler attempted to reinforce theories of black superiority humorously from the perspective of a disgruntled white guy who did not have the athletic ability to play professional sports and therefore was resigned to writing about them. But in his roguish attempt to enter the debate, Ostler created yet another ahistorical analysis of race and physical ability. "Given the choice," he argued, apparently on behalf of all disgruntled white guys, "we'd rather slam, dunk you very much."[108] His point, of course, as one who had participated in team sports, was that he had never been aware of or participated in any kind of conscious racism. The racial situation in sport was simply what it was, with no one to blame, and there was no reason that anyone should be *complaining*, as Harry Edwards was, about the situation of African Americans. Indeed, from his perspective their situation was one to envy. But if his perspective is to be taken as any indication, Brokaw's belief that "The Black Athlete: Fact and Fiction" would accelerate the pursuit of an intelligent discussion of the subject seemed in vain. Rather, as Davis astutely concluded, "NBC Television, by legitimating the preoccupation itself, helped to produce consent for the racial status quo."[109]

In the post–civil rights moment, this "racial status quo" continues to enjoy a popular dominance. Just days before the Barcelona Olympic Games began in 1992, the August edition of *Runner's World* magazine featured a photo of a solemn Carl Lewis on its cover beneath the bold headline, "White Men Can't Run." Written by executive editor Amby Burfoot, the "special report" promised to demonstrate "why black runners win every race from the sprints to the marathon." The article dealt with subjects such as the oft-cited "fast-twitch muscle fibers" to determine why black men dominate the Olympic track, and it wondered why African Americans excel at sprinting while Kenyans top the ranks of the distance runners.[110] This line of questioning prominently continued with the December 1997 cover story in *Sports Illustrated*, "Whatever Happened to the White Athlete?" which included a sidebar feature entitled "Is It in the Genes?" In response, wise readers supplied their own answers to the cover's question, ranging from "he moved on to become a doctor, a lawyer or an engineer" to "he's coaching" to "he's playing hockey."[111] Rather than encode a racist perspective into the question, the magazine's readers seemed to understand that to locate "the white athlete," one must explore the implications of unequal access, providing a bit of hope that sports fans, perhaps, know more than sports writers about what is really going on.

Academics, too, continue to question the way in which the subject of race in sport is treated in the popular media. While Jon Entine, the producer of Brokaw's "Black Athletes" program, went on to publish an ineptly conceptualized book-length treatment of the subject, entitled *Taboo* (considered by many to be *The Bell Curve* of sports history), historian John Hoberman rightly opposes the work of "tabloid science" writers, because they "streamline their presentations and feign omniscience in order to excite their readers."[112] Yet even Hoberman makes the mistake of juxtaposing "tabloid science" with "real science," as if the work that occurs within laboratory walls does not deal with the same politicized problems of presentation and knowledge as those of the "gatekeepers" of the popular realms.

"It's about Time": Globalization and Commodification

One of the key complications that the nature versus nurture debate has recently undergone, as the *Runner's World* piece indicates, is the increasingly transnational concept of a black athlete. The dominance of African distance runners in the past several decades has forced many to rethink the blanket generalization that characterizes a black body as one that excels at short distances. One solution has been to regionalize the debate, with some scientists claiming that athletes of West African descent have different genetic makeups from those of East African descent. However, the face of the postmodern sports world is far more complex than a simple East versus West binary. The magnitude of sport's continuing multifaceted global expansion is exemplified by the increased presence of eastern European and African athletes in the NBA and the two hundred delegations associated with the Olympic movement. Some Olympic teams, whether Puerto Rican or Palestinian, are not members of a traditionally defined "nation" and therefore exist on a level that the IOC dances around, providing little clarity in regard to belonging. With this kind of expanded notion of identity accepted as nationality, there is a sustained proliferation of racial stereotypes projected onto the bodies of athletes. Such stereotypes are, of course, not limited to black bodies but rather constitute a conflation of racial, ethnic, and national identities in connection with physical attributes and abilities. When combined with the ever-growing commercialization and commodification of sport, an arena emerges in which companies such as Nike not only put their logo on the black athlete but also craft the actual athlete. Such was the case at the Winter Games in Nagano, Japan, where Nike sponsored Kenyans Philip Boit and Henry Bitok in the Nordic skiing competition.[113] The equation that produced the idea that a Kenyan athlete could be competitive in an event involving snow inarguably emanated, in the tradition of the laboratory studies of the 1930s, from a belief in "natural" ability and financial resource, making true Brooks Johnson's claim that the black athlete is a self-fulfilling prophecy.

The example of Boit and Bitok vividly illustrates how the tenets of science and culture can seamlessly blend together in the name of commerce. Indeed, it is important to realize that there are scientific and cultural aspects of "blackness" that are both sought after and magnified by the commodification of athletes. Gitanjali Maharaj has persuasively argued that the Nike-sponsored black basketball star, as a product of the postindustrial city and late capitalism, exists as a commodity and "an object of desire for mass consumption," a figure that represents both the "'nightmare' of the urban ghetto and the 'dream' of being a celebrity."[114] As an example, Maharaj deconstructs Nike's "NYC-Attack" advertising campaign, which featured celebrated street basketball star Peewee Kirkland. In 1980, Kirkland famously turned down an offer from the Chicago Bulls and chose to stay on the streets, where he eventually found himself homeless and with a drug addiction. One commercial in the Nike series ended with Kirkland telling the audience, ideally composed of a youthful demographic, that "the street takes lives." Maharaj concludes that Nike situated the black male body within this campaign "as a site of both play and pleasure" and simultaneously based the campaign on "the very same set of assumptions that stigmatize the urban black body as economically unproductive and biologically hyper-reproductive."[115] His conclusion judiciously takes Robin D. G. Kelley's observations of the postindustrial playground, that play *is* work, to the next level. Regarding black urban bodies, according to Kelley, the double-edged sword of capitalism creates profit out of their play but "is also responsible for a shrinking labor market, the militarization of urban space, and the circulation of the very representations of race that generate terror in all of us at the sight of young black men and yet compels most of America to want to wear their shoes."[116]

Nike portrays Kirkland's preference for life on the street instead of a professional contract as the wrong one to make, instructing its audience to *choose sport* if sport *chooses you*. The result, then, is not only to choose it over the street but to choose it over other options as well—medical school, law school, or, as established by Los Angeles Lakers phenom Kobe Bryant, even college itself. However, in August 1997, *Sports Illustrated* reinforced once again the glamorous possibilities of the street with its cover story "King of the Streets—New York Playground Phenom Booger Smith." With a gritty black-and-white cover of Smith in midair with the ball, the story was a revisitation of the playground game by writer Rick Telander, whose book *Heaven Is a Playground* (1995) had made the enigmatic asphalt stars—Kirkland, Joe "the Destroyer" Hammond, Earl "the Goat" Manigault, and Herman "the Helicopter" Knowings—history.[117]

The central question continually posed about these street players relates to their *value* compared with that of players in the NBA. While the so-called hoop dreams of some players have come to fruition, and others, such as Kirkland, have eschewed big league dreams for an alternative path, it is Nike and *Sports Illustrated* that have the surest campaigns for success, showcasing the ostensible essence and authenticity of street competition as part of the larger commodification of black athletes within broad realms of popular culture. The post–civil rights evolution of the black athlete demonstrates how the struggles for equality so crucial in the 1960s have receded into an expanding disjuncture between African American prosperity and poverty. It is a predicament exemplified by the contrast of basketball on concrete at the playground on West Fourth Street in Greenwich Village and basketball on a gleaming wood floor at the United Center in Chicago, played under the watchful gaze of Michael Jordan's retired number(s) to the tune of a national anthem whose last two words are, according to an old waggish maxim, "Play Ball!"

It is the realm of commercial endorsement working in concert with athletic excellence that speciously portrays sport as one of the most democratic vehicles of social mobility, if not *the* most, establishing firm boundaries between successful citizenship and condemned sedition. The suspension of the aforementioned Abdul-Rauf, perhaps most specifically, was applauded by an overwhelming number of Americans who objected to his alleged breach of patriotism, again, largely because it occurred in an arena that paid him so well. While brief and seemingly insignificant—"over in a couple of headline days,"[118] according to Frank Deford—the incident provided a moment in which multiple articulations regarding sport, race, nation, and commerce emerged. When a black athlete such as Jesse Owens, Jackie Robinson, Wilma Rudolph, Gail Devers, or Tiger Woods thrives, the story is read as the possibility of success offered by American society, a national and societal project of victory. However, such high points of achievement work in a constant dialogue with events such as the 1968 Olympic Games, Mike Tyson's rape conviction, O. J. Simpson's murder trial, and Abdul-Rauf's suspension, in which the "failure" of the individual involved is placed within a context of subversion antithetical to American national belonging. The individual, seen as an incapable citizen, is accused of misusing "natural" aptitude, transforming the ability to run fast into the ability to run *away* fast. With this blending of scientific and social implications and speculations of the black athlete, this process provides justification for broader perceptions regarding the role of the black community in American society. The black athlete—off the track, off the court, off the field—remains, in the words of Tommie Smith, "just another nigger."

This legacy has ensured that the promises of the black power action in Mexico City have had to do battle with competing forces in the increasingly profitable sport industry, clearly demonstrated at the conclusion of a "Where Are They Now?" segment aired during NBC's broadcast of the Barcelona Olympics in 1992. The segment featured Smith, exploring his life as the son of a sharecropper, a "model student" at San Jose State, a member of the ROTC, the owner of eleven of San Jose's eighteen world records in track and field, and what the decades after his turbulent moment on the victory stand in Mexico City held for him. Wrapping up the piece, commentator Jim Lampley stated, "Among many dramatic changes since 1968, one concrete one strikes us tonight: World record holders no longer go hungry, and it's entirely likely they never will again." His cohost, Hannah Storm, glibly added: "It's about time."[119] While Lampley was able to assure his audience that black athletes could now cash in their gold medals just like everyone else, he was unable to assure anyone about the state of racial oppression in America. As Nikhil Pal Singh dramatically asserts in his discussion of antiracism, "Yet today, as we sit on the threshold of the twenty-first century, the condition of poor communities of color, particularly black communities, is as dire as any time in recent history."[120] In 1968, the black power salute challenged the flag, contesting and claiming a denied national identity, and it cost those associated with it dearly. Instructively, the repercussions of the victory ceremony protest that took place in Barcelona with the "Dream Team" were far different, with what Robert Lipsyte has called the "perfect payback."[121] When Michael Jordan, under contract to Nike, refused to don his U.S. sweat suit because it was manufactured by Reebok, his solution was easier to come by than a black-gloved fist: he covered the Reebok logo by wrapping himself in an American flag.[122] His action indicated that a corporate emblem has replaced past global signifiers of black cultural politics and illustrated how both the flag *and* a logo can cover the "un-American" symbols of collective struggle.

It is difficult to imagine a world without an individual like Jordan reaping the gigantic financial benefits of athletic excellence. Perhaps even more significant, it grows harder to remember a time when society did not universally canonize Muhammad Ali as the quintessence of humanity. Indeed, the repatriation of Ali at the Olympic Games in Atlanta in 1996, during which he raised a shaky hand to light the flame in front of adoring millions, works to erase the battles he fought so long ago in the face of vitriolic discrimination, because society, in all of its white liberal tolerance, rests easy that it now "gets it." Moments such as Atlanta, alongside the extravagant paychecks of the lucky few who run the hardwood court, reinforce the exhausted belief that the sports world enjoys a racially harmonious neighborhood that the remainder of society does not. A figure like Jordan, then, completes the project of Reaganism. As the corporate protector and symbol of the politically reactionary 1980s and 1990s, he sits in dramatic contrast with and at times eclipses those who stood on a victory dais before him with clenched fists stretched overhead.

Yet the image of the black power protest remains because of its political malleability and potency. Members of the OPHR went to Mexico City with the intention of demonstrating their pursuit of racial equality and human rights individually when the collective strategy of a boycott proved too difficult to obtain. Arguably the greatest track and field squad ever assembled, the 1968 team did its country proud with remarkable achievements yet also established the degree to which some of them, as American citizens, were discontented with their prescribed circumstance. As Tommie Smith remembered on the thirtieth anniversary of the protest, "It's not something I can take off and lay on the shelf.... But it's a whisper—it's gone, and I continue.... it's been a lot of years ... and my heart and soul is still on that team, still [on] that stand, still in what we believed in the 60's for social change."[123] Thus, while the Nation of Jordan might overshadow the structural realities of racism in the United States, the memory and call of the black-gloved fist linger. It reminds us that the imperatives of a global citizenship require not merely civil rights but, as a group of terribly fast people in the late 1960s seemed to understand, *human* rights, and it reminds us that victory can be defined in multiple ways, including by the struggle itself.

Notes

Introduction

1. See Calvin Sinnette, *Forbidden Fairways: African Americans and the Game of Golf* (Chelsea, Mich.: Sleeping Bear Press, 1998); and John H. Kennedy, *A Course of Their Own: A History of African American Golfers* (Kansas City: Stark Books, 2000).

2. Sandra Harding, "Eurocentric Scientific Illiteracy—A Challenge for the World Community," in *The 'Racial' Economy of Science: Toward a Democratic Future* (Bloomington: Indiana University Press, 1993), 15.

3. Douglas Hartmann, "The Politics of Race and Sport: Resistance and Domination in the 1968 African American Olympic Protest Movement," *Ethnic and Racial Studies* 19, no. 3 (July 1996): 563n1. The perception that Edwards's role in the OPHR is inflated likely stems from his controversial comments in contemporary documentaries and his work with administrative institutions that he once disdained, such as major league baseball and professional football.

4. For more on identity and performativity, see Jane Blocker, *Where Is Ana Mendieta? Identity, Performativity, and Exile* (Durham: Duke University Press, 1999); Dana Nelson, *National Manhood: Capitalist Citizenship and the Imagined Fraternity of White Men* (Durham: Duke University Press, 1998); Robert Rydell, *All the World's a Fair: Visions of Empire at American International Expositions, 1876–1916* (Chicago: University of Chicago Press, 1984); and Richard Slotkin, "Buffalo Bill's 'Wild West' and the Mythologization of the American Empire," in *Cultures of United States Imperialism*, ed. Amy Kaplan and Donald E. Pease (Durham: Duke University Press, 1993), 219–36.

1. The Race between Politics and Sport

1. Robert Lipsyte, "Why Sports Don't Matter," *New York Times Sunday Magazine*, April 12, 1995, 51.

2. "Why Sports Matter," *New York Magazine*, April 17, 1995, 31.

3. Ken Burns, Letter to the Editor, *New York Times Sunday Magazine*, April 23, 1995, 10.

4. Quoted in David Gates, "The Story of Jazz," *Newsweek*, Jan. 8, 2001, 59.

5. Pierre Bourdieu, "Social Space and Symbolic Power," in *In Other Words: Essays Towards a Reflexive Sociology* (Stanford: Stanford University Press, 1990), 138.

6. Alexander Wolff, "The Bear in Winter," *Sports Illustrated*, Mar. 1, 1999, 56–66. On this tumultuous period in collegiate athletics, see David K. Wiggins, "'The Future of College Athletics Is at Stake': Black Athletes and Racial Turmoil on Three Predominantly White University Campuses, 1968–1972," *Journal of Sport History* 15, no. 3 (winter 1988): 304–33; Gary A. Sailes, "An Investigation of Campus Stereotypes: The Myth of Black Athletic Superiority and the Dumb Jock Stereotype," in *Sport in Society: Equal Opportunity or Business as Usual?* ed. Richard Lapchick (Thousand Oaks, Calif.: Sage Publications, 1996), 193–202; Ronald E. Marcello, "The Integration of Intercollegiate Athletics in Texas: North Texas State College as a Test Case, 1956," *Journal of Sport History* 14 (1987): 286–316; and Donald Spivey, "The Black Athlete in Big-Time Intercollegiate Sports, 1941–1968," *Phylon* 44, no. 2 (1983): 116–23.

7. I use *transnational* because, as recently defined, it allows for an investigation of how culture "passed *over* the nation, observing the nation as a whole; or how it passed *across* the nation ... or how it passed *through* the nation, transforming and being transformed." See David Thelen, "Transnational Perspectives on United States History," *Journal of American History* 86, no. 3 (Dec. 1999): 968.

8. George Katsiaficas, *The Imagination of the New Left: A Global Analysis of 1968* (Boston: South End Press, 1987), 17–20.

9. John Hoberman, *Sport and Political Ideology* (Austin: University of Texas Press, 1984), 1, 3.

10. Brenda Plummer, *A Rising Wind: Black Americans and U.S. Foreign Affairs, 1935–1960* (Chapel Hill: University of North Carolina Press, 1996), 4; Mary L. Dudziak, "Desegregation as a Cold War Imperative," in *Critical Race*

Theory, ed. Richard Delgado (Philadelphia: Temple University Press, 1995), 110–21.

11. Jules Tygiel, *Baseball's Great Experiment: Jackie Robinson and His Legacy* (New York: Oxford University Press, 1983), 334.

12. Quoted in Martin Bauml Duberman, *Paul Robeson: A Biography* (New York: Ballantine Books, 1989), 360, and in Tygiel, *Baseball's Great Experiment*, 334.

13. Quoted in Duberman, *Paul Robeson*, 360–61. Although Robinson stood by his HUAC statement, he eventually offered a more nuanced stance: "I have grown wiser and closer to the painful truth about America's destructiveness. And, I do have an increased respect for Paul Robeson, who ... sacrificed himself, his career, and the wealth ... he once enjoyed because ... he was sincerely trying to help his people." Quoted in Tygiel, *Baseball's Great Experiment*, 334.

14. Penny M. Von Eschen, *Race against Empire: Black Americans and Anticolonialism, 1937–1957* (Ithaca: Cornell University Press, 1997), 128. According to Von Eschen, that particular article was reprinted in Lagos, Nigeria, in 1952.

15. Quoted in Clayborne Carson, *In Struggle: SNCC and the Black Awakening of the 1960s* (Cambridge, Mass.: Harvard University Press, 1995), 135.

16. Quoted in Mary Jo Festle, *Playing Nice: Politics and Apologies in Women's Sports* (New York: Columbia University Press, 1996), 84–85.

17. Quoted in Donald J. Mrozek, "The Cult and Ritual of Toughness in Cold War America," in *Sport in America: From Wicked Amusement to National Obsession*, ed. David Wiggins (Champaign: Human Kinetics, 1995), 262, 267.

18. Quoted in Tygiel, *Baseball's Great Experiment*, 335.

19. "A Famous Athlete's Diplomatic Debut," *Life*, Oct. 31, 1955, 49.

20. Jack Olsen, *The Black Athlete: A Shameful Story* (New York: Time-Life Books, 1968), 20; quoted in Von Eschen, *Race against Empire*, 177. In his book, Olsen offers this description of the Globetrotters: "Running about the court emitting savage jungle yells, shouting in their Southern accents ('Yassuh, yas-suh!'), pulling sly larcenous tricks like walking with the ball when the (white) referee's back is turned, calling one another inane names like Sweetwater and Showboat, they come across as frivolous, mildly dishonest children, the white man's encapsulated view of the whole Negro race set to the bouncy rhythms of their theme song, *Sweet Georgia Brown*."

21. Quoted in Festle, *Playing Nice*, 85.

22. Rafer Johnson, "The Game of Good Will," *Newsweek*, July 20, 1998, 16.

23. Bourdieu defines *field* as "a network, or a configuration, of objective relations between position. These positions are objectively defined, in their existence and in the determinations they impose upon their occupants, agents or institutions, by their present and potential situation (*situs*) in the structure of the distribution of species of power (or capital) whose possession commands access to the specific profits that are at stake in the field, as well as by their objective relation to other positions (domination, subordination, homology, etc.)." Pierre Bourdieu and Loïc J. D. Wacquant, *An Invitation to Reflexive Sociology* (Chicago: University of Chicago Press, 1992), 97; Pierre Bourdieu, "Program for a Sociology of Sport," *Sociology of Sport Journal* 5 (1988): 153–61.

24. "A World Gone Mad," *Sports Illustrated*, June 22, 1998, 24–28.

25. Numbers cited in *Sports Letter* 8, no. 4 (Aug. 1996): 3. Despite the greater global merit of the Olympics, the AAFLA concludes that the final game of the World Cup is the most watched ninety minutes of sports programming in the world.

26. Numbers cited in *Sports Letter* 12, nos. 3-4 (Nov. 2000): 4–5. As the AAFLA explains, Nielsen Media research reveals that the average home now receives sixty cable channels, double the number received a decade ago. Yet NBC's prime-time percentages for Sydney were higher than both Barcelona (49 percent) and Seoul (35 percent) and not far behind those of Atlanta (125 percent).

27. David Wallechinsky, *The Complete Book of the Olympic Games* (New York: Penguin Books, 1988), xxiv.

28. See Richard Lapchick, "The Modern Olympic Games: A Political Cauldron," in *Sport in Society*, 253; Allen Guttmann, *The Olympics: A History of the Modern Games* (Urbana: University of Illinois Press, 1992); Allen Guttmann, *The Games Must Go On: Avery Brundage and the Olympic Movement* (New York: Columbia University Press, 1984); John Hoberman, *The Olympic Crisis: Sport, Politics, and the Moral Order* (New Rochelle: Aristide D. Caratzas, 1986); and Vyv Simson and Andrew Jennings, *The Lords of the Rings: Power, Money and Drugs in the Modern Olympics* (London: Simon and Schuster, 1992).

29. Gilbert M. Joseph, "Close Encounters: Toward a New Cultural History of U.S.–Latin American Relations," in *Close Encounters of Empire: Writing the Cultural History of U.S.–Latin American Relations*, ed. Gilbert M. Joseph (Durham: Duke University Press, 1998), 7.

30. Miguel de Moragas Spá et al., *Television in the Olympics* (London: John Libbey and Company, 1995), xvi.

31. Joseph, "Close Encounters," 8. Along these lines it is impossible to extricate the historical significance of the Olympics from what John Hoberman has termed their "redemptive and inspirational internationalism," which often blinds scholars from a fully developed grasp of the Games as a *movement*. See John Hoberman, "Toward a Theory of Olympic Internationalism," *Journal of Sport History* 22, no. 1 (spring 1995): 1–2.

32. Walter Benjamin, "The Work of Art in the Age of Mechanical Reproduction," in *Illuminations*, ed. Hannah Arendt (New York: Shocken Books, 1968), 217–51; Pierre Bourdieu, *On Television* (New York: Free Press, 1996), 79; emphasis and parenthetical aside in original.

33. Mary Louise Pratt, *Imperial Eyes: Travel Writing and Transculturation* (New York: Routledge, 1992), 4.

34. Robin D. G. Kelley, "'But a Local Phase of a World Problem': Black History's Global Vision, 1883–1950," *Journal of American History* 86, no. 3 (Dec. 1999): 1077.

35. C. L. R. James, *Beyond a Boundary* (Durham: Duke University Press, 1993), 65.

36. Allen Guttmann, "Who's on First? or, Books on the History of American Sports," *Journal of American History* 66, no. 2 (Sept. 1979): 351–52, 354. See also Melvin L. Adelman, "Academicians and American Athletes: A Decade of Progress," *Journal of Sport History* (spring 1983): 80–83.

37. Jeffrey T. Sammons, "'Race' and Sport: A Critical, Historical Examination," *Journal of Sport History* 21 (fall 1994): 204. See David Roediger, *The Wages of Whiteness: Race and the Making of the American Working Class* (New York: Verso, 1991); Barbara J. Fields, "Ideology and Race in American History," in *Region, Race, and Reconstruction: Essays in Honor of C. Vann Woodward*, ed. J. Morgan Kousser and James M. McPherson (New York: Oxford University Press, 1982); and Evelyn Brooks Higginbotham, "African-American Women's History and the Metalanguage of Race," *Signs* 17, no. 2 (winter 1992). Sammons problematically demarcates "race" from "class." He criticizes Fields's emphasis on the "reality" of class over race, finding that "perception and consciousness remain attached to identity even when at variance with actual condition," a response that seems to ignore the structural reality of class. He then (mis)uses Higginbotham to support his stance, asking, "What is 'the reality' of class when racism might prevent the enjoyment of its privileges . . . ?" and failing to develop fully the consequences of her argument that race is a "metalanguage" that can

conceal profound social differences, acting as its own source of reference. She sees race as a "double-voiced discourse," because it can adapt to multiple uses of power in society, functioning as a form of oppression *or* resistance and as a more general means of conceptualizing difference.

38. Sammons, "'Race' and Sport," 209–10, 215. While Sammons finds Edwards's multiple roles as activist, observer, and scholar, as well as his past relationships with professional baseball and football, problematic, he admits that his scholarship confronted "the orthodoxy of athletics as the embodiment of the American dream of meritocracy and success." For examples of Edwards's complicated status, see Harry Edwards, "Edwards vs. the University of California," *Black Scholar* 8, no. 7 (May 1977): 32–33; "The BCA-NCAA Rift: A Meaningful Resolution is Unlikely," *Sport*, December 1994, 70; "Black Youths' Commitment to Sports Achievement: A Virtue-Turned-Tragic-Turned-Virtue," *Sport*, July 1994, 86; "The Athlete as Role Model: Relic of America's Sports Past?" *Sport*, Nov. 1994, 32; "We Must Let O. J. Go: Separating Fact from Image," *Sport*, Feb. 1995, 80.

39. Grant Jarvie, *Sport, Racism, and Ethnicity* (London: Falmer Press, 1991), 2.

40. Sammons, "'Race' and Sport," 276–77.

41. Cornel West, "The New Cultural Politics of Difference," in *Out There: Marginalization and Contemporary Cultures*, ed. Russell Ferguson et al. (New York and Cambridge, Mass.: New Museum of Contemporary Art and MIT Press, 1990). West employs, of course, Foucault's definition of "genealogy," indicating a history with a presentist sense of the political. See also Stuart Hall, "What Is This 'Black' in Black Popular Culture?" in *Black Popular Culture*, ed. Gina Dent (Seattle: Bay Press, 1992), 21.

42. In addition to the founding texts of cultural studies like Richard Hoggart's *The Uses of Literacy* (1957) and Raymond Williams's *Culture and Society* (1958), see Richard Johnson, "What Is Cultural Studies Anyway?" *Social Text* (1986–87): 38–80; and Fredric Jameson's review of the *Cultural Studies* anthology in *Social Text* 34 (1993): 17–52.

43. Michael Denning, "The End of Mass Culture," *International Labor and Working-Class History* 37 (1990): 4. Denning finds that the terminology debate represents, in Great Britain, a choice between structuralism and culturalism, and in the United States, a choice between the Frankfurt School and populism. See Raymond Williams, *Keywords: A Vocabulary of Culture and Society*

(New York: Oxford University Press, 1983); Fredric Jameson, "Reification and Utopia in Mass Culture," *Social Text* 1 (1979): 130–48; and Stuart Hall, "Notes on Deconstructing 'the Popular,'" in *People's History and Socialist Theory*, ed. Raphael Samuel (London: Routledge, 1981). Denning agrees with Jameson and Hall that popular culture is never exclusively manipulative or authentic, but rather a Gramscian negotiation between dominant and subordinate sectors of society over popular thought and culture. See Antonio Gramsci, *Selections from the Prison Notebooks*, ed. Quintin Hoare and Geoffrey Nowell Smith (New York: International Publishers, 1971); Antonio Gramsci, "Hegemony, Relations of Force, Historical Bloc," in *An Antonio Gramsci Reader*, ed. David Forgacs (New York: Schocken Books, 1988), 189–221; and Jean Franco, "What's in a Name? Popular Culture Theories and Their Limitations," *Studies in Latin American Popular Culture* 1 (1982): 5–14.

44. Michael Denning, "'The Special American Conditions': Marxism and American Studies," *American Quarterly* (1986): 360.

45. Benedict Anderson, *Imagined Communities: Reflections on the Origin and Spread of Nationalism* (London: Verso, 1983).

46. Stuart Hall, "Culture, the Media and the 'Ideological Effect,'" in *Mass Communication and Society*, ed. James Curran, Michael Gurevitch, and Janet Woollacott (London: E. Arnold, 1977), 341; Stuart Hall, "Encoding/Decoding," in *Culture, Media, Language* (London: Hutchinson, 1980), 128–38; George Lipsitz, "The Meaning of Memory: Family, Class, and Ethnicity in Early Network Television," in *Time Passages: Collective Memory and American Popular Culture* (Minneapolis: University of Minnesota Press, 1990), 68.

47. Matthew Frye Jacobson, *Whiteness of a Different Color: European Immigrants and the Alchemy of Race* (Cambridge, Mass.: Harvard University Press, 1998), 6. See also Étienne Balibar, "Racism and Nationalism," in *Race, Nation, Class: Ambiguous Identities*, ed. Étienne Balibar and Immanuel Wallerstein (London: Verso, 1991), 37–67, a brilliant delineation of the inextricable relationship between race and nationalism that determines race to be the critical, yet fictive, element that defines who is to be kept within the nation and who is to be excluded, making racism a prominent feature of modern state-building and nationalism.

48. See Paul Gilroy, *"There Ain't No Black in the Union Jack": The Cultural Politics of Race and Nation* (Chicago: University of Chicago Press, 1991); and Hall, "What Is This 'Black' in Black Popular Culture?"

49. Nikhil Pal Singh, "The Black Panthers and the 'Undeveloped Country' of the Left," in *The Black Panther Party [Reconsidered]*, ed. Charles E. Jones (Baltimore: Black Classic Press, 1998), 61.

50. Nikhil Pal Singh, "Toward an Effective Antiracism," in *Beyond Pluralism: The Conception of Groups and Group Identity in America* (Urbana: University of Illinois Press), 230.

51. Daniel C. Hallin, "Network News: We Keep America on Top of the World," in *Watching Television*, ed. Todd Gitlin (New York: Pantheon Books, 1986), 11.

52. Hallin, "Network News," 23–25.

53. Katsiaficas, *The Imagination of the New Left*, 29–35.

54. Quoted in Marilyn Young, *The Vietnam Wars, 1945–1990* (New York: Harper Perennial, 1991), 226.

55. Quoted in Katsiaficas, *The Imagination of the New Left*, 33.

56. Carson, *In Struggle*, 288.

57. For more on U.S. student political activity, see Todd Gitlin, *The Whole World Is Watching: Mass Media in the Making and Unmaking of the New Left* (Berkeley: University of California Press, 1980); Todd Gitlin, *The Sixties: Years of Hope, Days of Rage* (New York: Bantam Books, 1987); Seymour Lipset, *Rebellion in the University* (New Brunswick: Rutgers University Press, 1993); David Farber, ed., *The Sixties: From Memory to History* (Chapel Hill: University of North Carolina Press, 1994); Robert Cohen, *When the Old Left Was Young: Student Radicals and America's First Mass Student Movement* (New York: Oxford University Press, 1993); and Sohnya Sayres, Anders Stephanson, Stanley Aronowitz, Fredric Jameson, eds., *The 60s without Apology* (Minneapolis: University of Minnesota Press, 1984).

58. Katsiaficas, *The Imagination of the New Left*, 3–4, 10.

59. "Czech TV Resumes," *New York Times*, Aug. 25, 1968, 41; "Czech and Soviet Athletes Separated at Olympic Meals," *New York Times*, Sept. 15, 1968, V: 11; Clyde H. Farnsworth, "Dubcek Fan Clubs Spring Up in Czechoslovakia," *New York Times*, Oct. 11, 1968, 12; "Plot to Kill the Olympics," *Newsweek*, Sept. 2, 1968, 59; Arthur Daley, "Awesome Pageantry," *San Jose Mercury News*, Oct. 13, 1968, 87; reprinted from the *New York Times*. Among Zátopek's accomplishments are eighteen world records and four Olympic gold medals. After an eminent stint in both the Czech army and the Communist Party, in 1968 he became an advocate of Czech independence and signed the "2000 Words Manifesto," which led to his eventual dismissal from the party.

60. It appears, for example, in Warren Beatty's film *Bulworth* (1998) as a poster in a Compton "crib"; as a political reference point in Mildred Pitts's inner-city coming-of-age story, *Lily of Watts Takes a Giant Step* (1971); in John Berendt's best-selling version of Savannah society, *Midnight in the Garden of Good and Evil* (1995); at a Whitney Museum exhibit, "Black Male" (1994); and again as a poster in the film *Remember the Titans* (2000).

61. Alice Echols, *Daring to Be Bad: Radical Feminism in America, 1967–1975* (Minneapolis: University of Minnesota Press, 1989).

62. The rise of American female athletes directly correlates with their increased presence in college. According to Susan Cahn, female college enrollment in institutions of higher education went from 85,000 in 1900 to 283,000 in 1920, creating a "ready-made constituency for athletic training." Vivian Bernice Lee Adkins contends that unlike European women, whose participation centered on track clubs, American women first hit the track at Vassar College in 1895. However, such activity was not widely encouraged, and numerous obstacles emerged. For example, the National Women's Track Athletic Association, founded in 1921, was not sanctioned by any professional physical education group, because such organizations were led by men, who generally discouraged female participation. See Susan Cahn, *Coming on Strong: Gender and Sexuality in Twentieth-Century Women's Sport* (New York: Free Press, 1994), 23; and Vivian Bernice Lee Adkins, "The Development of Negro Female Olympic Talent," unpublished doctoral dissertation, School of Health, Physical Education and Recreation, Indiana University, 1967, 25.

63. Quoted in Festle, *Playing Nice*, 92.

64. Festle, *Playing Nice*, 93.

65. Quoted in Festle, *Playing Nice*, 92.

66. Carroll Smith-Rosenberg and Charles Rosenberg, "The Female Animal: Medical and Biological Views of Women and Their Role in Nineteenth-Century America," in *From "Fair Sex" to Feminism: Sport and the Socialization of Women in the Industrial and Post-Industrial Eras*, ed. J. A. Mangan and Robert J. Park (London: Frank Cass, 1987), 19.

67. Cynthia Eagle Russett, *Sexual Science: The Victorian Construction of Womanhood* (Cambridge, Mass.: Harvard University Press, 1989), 116–17.

68. Grant Jarvie and Joseph Maguire, *Sport and Leisure in Social Thought* (London: Routledge, 1994), 166; Lynda Birke and Gail Vines, "A Sporting Chance: The Anatomy of Destiny?" *Women's Studies International Forum* 10, no. 4 (1987): 337–47.

69. Michel Foucault greatly influenced this feminist understanding of biology by enabling a discursive reading of the gendered body that dismisses any kind of rigid definition, making possible an understanding of the body from multiple locations, including sport, as well as the more traditional realms of science and medicine. See Michel Foucault, "The Body of the Condemned," in *The Foucault Reader*, ed. Paul Rabinow (New York: Pantheon Books, 1984); and M. Ann Hall, *Feminism and Sporting Bodies: Essays on Theory and Practice* (Champaign: Human Kinetics, 1996), 53.

70. M. Ann Hall, *Feminism and Sporting Bodies*, 16; Laura A. Wackwitz, "Sex Testing in International Women's Athletics: A History of Silence," *Women in Sport and Physical Activity Journal* 5, no. 1 (spring 1996): 51–60; Jennifer Hargreaves, *Sporting Females: Critical Issues in the History and Sociology of Women's Sports* (London: Routledge, 1994): 222–23. The International Amateur Athletic Federation abolished gender verification in 1992, but the IOC still requires it.

71. "Swimmers Snub Sex Test," *San Jose Mercury News*, Oct. 3, 1968, 42.

72. "540 Women Olympians Pass Exams," *Chicago Tribune*, Oct. 10, 1968, III: 5.

73. "Gals' Sex Test Dilemma: Grandma or Grandpa?" *San Jose Mercury News*, Oct. 12, 1968, 71.

74. "Gals' Sex Test Dilemma."

75. Jim Murray, "Chromosomes and Sex or Is a Girl Really a Girl?" *Los Angeles Times*, Oct. 16, 1968, III: 1.

76. Murray, "Chromosomes and Sex or Is a Girl Really a Girl?"

77. Murray, "Chromosomes and Sex or Is a Girl Really a Girl?"

78. "All Female Swimmers Take Sex Test, Ending Dispute," *New York Times*, Oct. 17, 1968, 62; "Dispute over Sex Settled at Olympics," *Chicago Tribune*, Oct. 17, 1968, III: 3.

79. Jim McKay, *Wide World of Sports*: "Highlights of the Sixties," ABC, aired Dec. 27, 1969, Museum of Radio and Television, New York; emphasis as spoken.

80. Quoted from "Fields of Fire: Sports in the 60's," HBO, 1995.

81. Quoted from "Fields of Fire."

82. Robin D. G. Kelley, "'We Are Not What We Seem': The Politics and Pleasures of Community," in *Race Rebels: Culture, Politics, and the Black Working Class* (New York: Free Press, 1994), 36.

83. Harry Edwards, *The Struggle That Must Be* (New York: Macmillan, 1980), 174–75.

84. Ali, as quoted in "Fields of Fire." See his autobiography, with Richard Durham, *The Greatest: My Own Story* (New York: Random House, 1975); David Remnick, *King of the World: Muhammad Ali and the Rise of an American Hero* (New York: Random House, 1998); Gerald Early, *The Muhammad Ali Reader* (New York: Ecco Press, 1998); Elliot J. Gorn, ed., *Muhammad Ali: The People's Champ* (Urbana: University of Illinois Press, 1995); and Mike Marqusee, "Sport and Stereotype: From Role Model to Muhammad Ali," *Race and Class* 36, no. 4 (Apr.–June 1995): 1–42.

85. Paul Gilroy, "It Ain't Where You're From, It's Where You're At: The Dialectics of Diaspora Identification," in *Small Acts: Thoughts on the Politics of Black Cultures* (London: Serpent's Tail, 1983), 120–21.

86. George J. Sanchez, "Reading Reginald Denny: The Politics of Whiteness in the Late Twentieth Century," *American Quarterly* 47, no. 3 (Sept. 1995): 388–94.

2. What Is This "Black" in Black Athlete?

1. Gail Bederman, *Manliness and Civilization: A Cultural History of Gender and Race, 1880–1917* (Chicago: University of Chicago Press, 1995), 3–4.

2. Quoted in Bederman, *Manliness and Civilization*, 2.

3. Bederman, *Manliness and Civilization*, 2.

4. Bederman, *Manliness and Civilization*, 4.

5. Joe Louis, *My Life Story* (London: Eldon Press, 1948), 99–104; Marqusee, "Sport and Stereotype," 5–7; Art Evans, "Joe Louis as a Key Functionary: White Reactions toward a Black Champion," *Journal of Black Studies* 16, no. 1 (Sept. 1985): 95–111; Chris Mead, *Champion: Joe Louis, Black Hero in White America* (New York: Charles Scribner's Sons, 1985). For an overview of sources on the Schmeling-Louis bout, see Lenwood G. Davis, *Joe Louis: A Bibliography of Articles, Books, Pamphlets, Records, and Archival Materials* (Westport, Conn.: Greenwood Press, 1983).

6. Brenda Gayle Plummer, *A Rising Wind: Black Americans and U.S. Foreign Affairs, 1935–1960* (Chapel Hill: University of North Carolina Press, 1996), 288.

7. Vaughan C. Mason, M.D., "Joe Louis—Model for the Physician," *Journal of the National Medical Association* 54, no. 1 (1962): 113–15.

8. For example, Randy Roberts and James S. Olson argue, "There was a time ... when sports knew its place in American culture. It was a pastime, diversion, leisure, recreation, play—fun. In sports people found relief from the

real things of the world and their own lives—wars, unemployment, social conflict, politics, religions, work, prices, and family. But after World War II, sports assumed an extraordinary significance in people's lives; games became not only a reflection of the changes occurring in the United States but a lens through which tens of millions Americans interpreted the significance of their country, their communities, their families, and themselves." Roberts and Olson, *Winning Is the Only Thing: Sports in America since 1945* (Baltimore: Johns Hopkins University Press, 1989), xi–xii.

9. Bederman, *Manliness and Civilization*, 8.

10. John Kasson, *Amusing the Millions: Coney Island at the Turn of the Century* (New York: Hill and Wang, 1978), 103.

11. Quoted in Kasson, *Amusing the Millions*, 104.

12. Walter LaFeber, *Michael Jordan and the New Global Capitalism* (New York: W. W. Norton, 1999), 33–34.

13. W. E. B. Du Bois, "On the Problem of Amusement," *Southern Workman* 27 (Sept. 1897): 182.

14. Du Bois, "On the Problem of Amusement," 182.

15. Du Bois, "On the Problem of Amusement," 184.

16. Dominick Cavallo, *Muscles and Morals: Organized Playgrounds and Urban Reform, 1880–1920* (Philadelphia: University of Pennsylvania Press, 1981), 15–18.

17. Quoted in Cavallo, *Muscles and Morals*, 29–30.

18. Cavallo, *Muscles and Morals*, 74.

19. Cavallo, *Muscles and Morals*, 49.

20. Du Bois, "On the Problem of Amusement," 184.

21. Patrick Miller, "To 'Bring the Race along Rapidly': Sport, Student Culture, and Educational Mission at Historically Black Colleges during the Interwar Years," *History of Education Quarterly* 35, no. 2 (summer 1995): 112. The belief in sport as a path of upward mobility still prevails, transforming the struggle for equality and national participation outlined within "muscular assimilationism" into a more economically grounded forum. "Midnight Basketball" perhaps best illustrates this process. The Midnight Basketball League (MBL) was created as a state-subsidized means by which "urban" youth could be channeled for success and simultaneously the "threat" of black criminality could be reduced—an idea with obvious roots in the play movement. Founded in 1986 by G. Van Standifer, with the motto "It's hoops for tonight and hope for tomorrow,"

the MBL wanted to keep youth occupied during the middle of the night, considered the prime period for drug use and trade, as well as require them to attend workshops on topics such as job interviews, financial management, health, and conflict resolution, preceding each game. Fifty cities adopted the program after reports of early success, and President George Bush declared it the 124th "Point of Light" in 1991.

22. David K. Wiggins, "Edwin Bancroft Henderson, African American Athletes, and the Writing of Sport History," in *Glory Bound: Black Athletes in a White America* (Syracuse: Syracuse University Press, 1997), 222–23. See also Leon N. Coursey, "Pioneer Black Physical Educators: Contributions of Anita J. Turner and Edwin B. Henderson," *Journal of Physical Education and Recreation* 51 (May 1980): 54–56; Edwin B. Henderson, "Physical Education and Athletics Among Negroes," *Proceedings of the Big Ten Symposium on the History of Physical Education and Sport at Ohio State University, Columbus, Ohio on March 1–3, 1971*, ed. Bruce L. Bennett (Chicago: Athletic Institute, 1972), 67–83; Edwin B. Henderson, *The Negro in Sports* (Washington, D.C.: Associated Publishers, 1949); Edwin B. Henderson, *The Black Athlete: Emergence and Arrival* (New York: Publishers Company, 1968).

23. William M. Bell, "The Sociological Contributions of Physical Education to the Needs of the Negro," *Research Quarterly* 10, no. 2 (May 1939): 137, 138, 140; parentheses in original.

24. As Harry Edwards, along with others, would later point out, "Given the functions of sport for the fans, the successful black athlete stimulates black people's individual hopes for eventually competing as equals in society. A major consequence, however, is that young blacks are encouraged toward attempts at 'making it' through athletic participation, rather than through pursuit of other occupations that hold greater potential for meeting the real political and material needs of both themselves and their people. Athletics, then, stifles the pursuits of rational alternatives by black people." See Harry Edwards, "The Black Athletes: 20th Century Gladiators for White America," *Psychology Today* (Nov. 1973): 44.

25. Guttmann, "Who's on First?" 353.

26. Jarvie, *Sport, Racism and Ethnicity*, 2.

27. Quoted in Miller, "To 'Bring the Race along Rapidly,'" 128.

28. Quoted in Miller, "To 'Bring the Race along Rapidly,'" 128.

29. Miller, "To 'Bring the Race along Rapidly,'" 130–31.

30. Kobena Mercer, "Reading Racial Fetishism: The Photographs of Robert Mapplethorpe," *Welcome to the Jungle: New Positions in Black Cultural Studies* (New York: Routledge, 1994), 178–79. A complex exception, of course, is Mike Tyson's rape conviction, in which the athletic hero leaves the sports page to take his place among other black figures. In many ways, American media are better equipped to deal with Tyson as a criminal, because the reference points are far more extensive.

31. Herman Gray, "Black Masculinity and Visual Culture," in *Black Male: Representations of Masculinity in Contemporary American Art*, ed. Henry Louis Gates Jr. (New York: Harry N. Abrams, 1994), 176–77.

32. In 1955, for example, French jazz critic André Hodeir wrote, "Astonishing to see that in important athletic tests of speed and jumping, that is to say in areas that require relaxation and flexibility, things that are so necessary in jazz, one always notes a certain superiority of black athletes. For example, in all the Olympic Games for twenty or thirty years the final of the 100 meters is invariably run with four or five blacks out of six runners. Transposed onto the plane of jazz, this supremacy is the same, I believe." See Hodeir, "Jazz noir; jazz blanc," *Jazz Hot* 102 (Sept. 1955): 9. I am grateful to Elizabeth Vihlen for this citation and the translation.

33. Stuart Hall, "Subjects in History: Making Diasporic Identities," in *The House That Race Built*, ed. Wahneema Lubiano (New York: Pantheon Books, 1997), 290; emphasis mine.

34. Sandra Harding, "Eurocentric Scientific Illiteracy—a Challenge for the World Community," in *The Racial Economy of Science: Toward a Democratic Future* (Bloomington: Indiana University Press, 1993), 9. Harding acknowledges Donna Haraway for expressing this point in this way.

35. Matthew Frye Jacobson, "Malevolent Assimilation: Immigrants and the Question of American Empire," in *Beyond Pluralism: The Conception of Groups and Group Identities in America*, ed. Wendy F. Katkin, Ned Landsman, and Andrea Tyree (Urbana: University of Illinois Press, 1998), 165.

36. Quoted in Lawrence W. Levine, *Black Culture and Black Consciousness: Afro-American Folk Thought from Slavery to Freedom* (Oxford: Oxford University Press, 1977), 5.

37. Paul Gilroy, "One Nation under a Groove," in *Small Acts*, 35; see also Eric Lott, *Love and Theft: Blackface Minstrelsy and the American Working Class* (New York: Oxford University Press, 1993), 145.

38. Foucault, "The Body of the Condemned."

39. Cynthia Eagle Russett, *Sexual Science: The Victorian Construction of Womanhood* (Cambridge, Mass.: Harvard University Press, 1989), 70–74.

40. Andrew Ross, "If the Genes Fit, How Do You Acquit? O. J. and Science," in *Birth of a Nation'hood: Gaze, Script, and Spectacle in the O. J. Simpson Case*, ed. Toni Morrison and Claudia Brodsky Lacour (New York: Pantheon Books, 1997), 244. Ross emphasizes how this trend is part of a conservative agenda that removes social problems from society.

41. Harding, "Eurocentric Scientific Illiteracy," 12. Similarly, Jacobson argues that "racializing sciences" contributed to "the political imperatives of the slavery question, questions of territorial expansion, and, later, the vexing immigration question, and at the same time creating in their wake new kinds of 'certainty' that 'explained' slavery, expansion, and the trouble with immigrants." Jacobson, *Whiteness of a Different Color*, 33.

42. See Stephen Jay Gould, *The Mismeasure of Man* (New York: W. W. Norton, 1981); Nancy Stepan, *The Idea of Race in Science: Great Britain, 1800–1960* (London: Macmillan, 1982); and Sander Gilman, "Appropriating the Idioms of Science: The Rejection of Scientific Racism," in *The Bounds of Race: Perspectives on Hegemony and Resistance*, ed. Dominick LaCapra (Ithaca: Cornell University Press, 1991), 72–103.

43. Quoted in John Burnham, *How Superstition Won and Science Lost: Popularizing Science and Health in the United States* (New Brunswick: Rutgers University Press, 1987), 34.

44. Burnham, *How Superstition Won and Science Lost*, 3.

45. Ross, "If the Genes Fit, How Do You Acquit?" 258.

46. Jacobson, *Whiteness of a Different Color*, 3.

47. G. D. Williams, G. E. Grim, J. J. Wimp, and T. F. Whayne, "Calf Muscles in American Whites and Negroes," *American Journal of Physical Anthropology* 14, no. 1 (Jan.-Mar. 1930): 45–58.

48. As Jacobson expertly determines, eugenics still heavily influenced discussions of immigration in the early part of the twentieth century; works such as Madison Grant's *Passing of the Great Race* (1916) was a notable exception to the emphasis on culture and environment by Boas and others. See Jacobson, *Whiteness of a Different Color*, 81–86.

49. While African Americans have overwhelmingly dominated international sprinting events in the last thirty years, that success has not been

uninterrupted throughout the twentieth century. See John George, "The Virtual Disappearance of the White Male Sprinter in the United States: A Speculative Essay," *Sociology of Sport Journal* 11 (1994): 70–78.

50. It should be noted that while the "broad" jump is now the "long" jump, and the "hop, step, and jump" is now the "triple" jump, I will use the historically proper terms to situate the discussion of the event.

51. As Wiggins points out, although the track athletes of this period were the first to succeed in great number, prominent black sporting accomplishments also occurred prior to the 1930s, such as Australian boxer Peter Jackson, who rose to prominence when John L. Sullivan refused to fight against him; cyclist Marshall "Major" Taylor, who was examined by a group of doctors at the Academy of Sciences in Bordeaux, France, in 1901; and University of Pennsylvania track star John B. Taylor, who dominated the quarter-mile in the early part of the century; as well as boxers such as Jack Johnson and Joe Louis. See Wiggins, "'Great Speed but Little Stamina': The Historical Debate over Black Athletic Superiority," in Glory Bound, 178–79. For more on Taylor, see Andrew Ritchie, *Marshall "Major" Taylor* (San Francisco: Bicycle Books, 1988).

52. Burnham, *How Superstition Won and Science Lost*, 175.

53. Glenda Gilmore, *Gender and Jim Crow: Women and the Politics of White Supremacy in North Carolina, 1896–1920* (Chapel Hill: University of North Carolina Press, 1996), 71.

54. The incident illustrated, as Bederman points out, a national preoccupation "with the connection between manhood and racial dominance." Bederman, *Manliness and Civilization*, 3–4.

55. Eleanor Metheny, "Some Differences in Bodily Proportions between American Negro and White Male College Students as Related to Athletic Performance," *Research Quarterly* 10, no. 4 (Dec. 1939): 41. The publication is the journal of the American Association for Health, Physical Education, and Recreation.

56. Metheny, "Some Differences in Bodily Proportions," 41, 51.

57. S. Robinson, D. B. Dill, P. M. Harmon, F. G. Hall, and J. W. Wilson, "Adaptations to Exercise of Negro and White Sharecroppers in Comparison with Northern Whites," *Human Biology* 13, no. 2 (May 1941): 140.

58. Frederick Lewis Allen, "Breaking World's Records," *Harper's Monthly*, Aug. 1936, 302–10. While Harper's is by no means a scientific journal, its reading audience was considered "highbrow."

59. Allen, "Breaking World's Records," 306.

60. Allen, "Breaking World's Records," 307–8. Of the "civilized countries," Allen notes the success of Finnish distance runners like Paavo Nurmi as well as the French and Italians. He also commends Sweden for producing the record in discus; Denmark, in the 3,000-meter run; and Japan, in the long jump.

61. Allen, "Breaking World's Records," 308.

62. Martha Lambeth and Lyle H. Lanier, "Race Differences in Speed of Reaction," *Journal of Genetic Psychology* 42, no. 2 (June 1933): 255–97. The journal was founded by G. Stanley Hall in 1891 at Clark University.

63. The study also provided an analysis of previous studies, beginning in 1895, regarding race and reaction time; see Lambeth and Lanier, "Race Differences in Speed of Reaction," 258–68.

64. Jacobson, *Whiteness of a Different Color*, 33.

65. Allen, "Breaking World's Records," 302–3. Note that he was referring to 100 yards, not the Olympic distance of 100 meters. In the latter, the world record mark of 10.2 was set by Texan Charley Paddock, who won the gold medal in the event at the 1920 Antwerp Games. Paddock's record was equaled by Metcalfe, Owens, Harold Davis, Lloyd LaBeach, and Barney Ewell, before being lowered to 10.1 by LaBeach.

66. Williams et al., "Calf Muscles in American Whites and Negroes," 45. In this study, Negro is continually written in the lower case and will be reflected as such hereafter as well.

67. Williams et al., "Calf Muscles in American Whites and Negroes," 57.

68. Lambeth and Lanier, "Race Differences in Speed of Reaction," 273.

69. Metheny, "Some Differences in Bodily Proportions," 45, 50–51.

70. Metheny, "Some Differences in Bodily Proportions," 51.

71. For example, the study determined that "working people, both Negroes and whites, were likely to accumulate a greater oxygen debt than people of higher financial rating, and were therefore likely to run for longer periods of time." Robinson et al., "Adaptations to Exercise of Negro and White Sharecroppers," 158.

72. Robinson et al., "Adaptations to Exercise of Negro and White Sharecroppers," 149; emphasis mine.

73. See Wiggins, "'Great Speed but Little Stamina'"; John Hoberman, *Darwin's Athletes: How Sport Has Damaged Black America and Preserved the Myth of Race* (Boston: Houghton Miflin, 1997); Jeffrey T. Sammons, "A Proportionate

and Measured Response to the Provocation That Is Darwin's Athletes" (Book Forum), *Journal of Sport History* 24, no. 3 (1997): 378–89; John Hoberman, "How Not to Misread Darwin's Athletes: A Response to Jeffrey T. Sammons" (Book Forum), *Journal of Sport History* 24, no. 3 (1997): 389–96; Gary A. Sailes, "The Myth of Black Sports Supremacy," *Journal of Black Studies* 21 (June 1990): 480–87; Roscoe Brown, "A Commentary on Racial Myths and the Black Athlete," in *Social Problems in Athletics*, ed. Daniel M. Landers (Urbana: University of Illinois Press, 1976), 168–73; Phillip M. Hoose, *Necessities: Racial Barriers in American Sports* (New York: Random House, 1989); Kenneth L. Shropshire, *In Black and White: Race and Sports in America* (New York: New York University Press, 1996); and Patrick Miller, "The Anatomy of Scientific Racism: Racialist Responses to Black Athletic Achievement," *Journal of Sport History* 25, no. 1 (1998): 119–25. Any bibliography regarding this subject matter is especially indebted to the work of Wiggins and Hoberman, who have assembled the most extensive body of primary and secondary work regarding the brain versus brawn debate in sport. Wiggins set the tone for historical debate by synthesizing the complex historical trajectory of the scientific discourse, clarifying how scientific interest in connections between race and physical ability worked in a direct relationship with ideas on intellectual capacity. He makes the especially critical point that the interest of science in the dialogue of race and athleticism and its influence on this dialogue have to be discerned in terms of power—as a matter of who controls science and its diffusion—in order to determine historically how the conclusions of someone like Eleanor Metheny came out of Jimmy "the Greek" Snyder's mouth decades later.

74. As Sammons rightly points out, despite Wiggins's initial premise that "the weight of the evidence indicates that the differences between participation patterns of black and white athletes are primarily a consequence of different historical experiences that individuals and their particular racial groups underwent," he abandons this understanding in his conclusion: "The spirit of science necessitates ... that academicians continue their research to determine whether the success of black athletes is somehow the consequence of racially distinctive chromosomes." See Wiggins, "'Great Speed but Little Stamina,'" 199; and Sammons, "'Race' and Sport: A Critical, Historical Examination," *Journal of Sport History* 21 (fall 1994): 270.

75. Among the most influential of such works is Hoberman's *Darwin's Athletes*. Hoberman argues that the assumed athletic dominance of African

Americans effects more harm than good for all parties involved. In terms of white America, which he never defines, the belief in black athletic superiority creates counterfeit notions of societal racial equality. In black America, which he only loosely defines, this belief creates an overwhelming emphasis on sport as a means of social mobility and economic stability, to the exclusion of other paths. In terms of the scientific mode in which this national discussion takes place, Hoberman rightly begins by arguing that "ideas about the 'natural' physical talents of dark-skinned peoples, and the media-generated images that sustain them, probably do more than anything else in our public life to encourage the idea that blacks and whites are biologically different in a meaningful way." Yet his conclusion, "The Fear of Racial Biology," is not executed as confidently as his premise, with a call for contemporary science to fully embrace race as a laboratory subject, ostensibly to dispel any lasting notions of racialized athletic ability and a condemnation of the "black elite," concluding that "today ... black eugenics comes at a very high price, for it is the black athlete, the product of another 'unnatural selection' and the most celebrated representative of black creativity, who carries the torch of eugenic advancement for his people. His tragedy is that he can neither advance nor lead his race in the modern world." See Hoberman, *Darwin's Athletes*, xiv, 242.

76. Williams et al., "Calf Muscles in American Whites and Negroes," 47.

77. See Jacobson, *Whiteness of a Different Color*; David R. Roediger, *The Wages of Whiteness: Race and the Making of the American Working Class* (London: Verso, 1991); Roediger, *Towards the Abolition of Whiteness: Essays on Race, Politics, and Working-Class History* (London: Verso, 1994); and Noel Ignatiev, *How the Irish Became White* (New York: Routledge, 1995).

78. Lambeth and Lanier, "Race Differences in Speed of Reaction," 255.

79. Lambeth and Lanier, "Race Differences in Speed of Reaction," 269, 274–76.

80. Lambeth and Lanier, "Race Differences in Speed of Reaction," 293–94; emphasis in the original.

81. Metheny, "Some Differences in Bodily Proportions," 42.

82. For a full listing of Cobb's affiliations and accomplishments, see Lesley M. Rankin-Hill and Michael L. Blakey, "W. Montague Cobb (1904–1990): Physical Anthropologist, Anatomist, and Activist," *American Anthropologist* 96, no. 1 (Mar. 1994): 74–96, an article based on a series of interviews with Cobb before his death in 1990.

83. Rankin-Hill and Blakey, "W. Montague Cobb," 79–80. For more on the development of the medical school at Howard, see Rayford W. Logan, *Howard University: The First Hundred Years, 1867–1967* (New York: New York University Press, 1969).

84. He explicitly outlined his beliefs in his address to the Association of Negro Life and History: "Anthropology can be hammered into an instrument for solving our most pressing problems of population, race or social status," he stated. "But if it is not hammered with the greatest care and skill it may turn out to be a dangerous weapon wounding alike him who wields it and the victims on whom it is applied." From T. Wingate Todd, "The Folly of Complacency," Oct. 28, 1930, quoted in Rankin-Hill and Blakey, "W. Montague Cobb," 80. Todd's work was well-known in the field. For example, Eleanor Metheny, in her 1939 study of athletes, used two of his studies as the basis of her own work: "Entrenched Negro Physical Features," *Human Biology* 1 (1928): 59; and, with Anna Lindala, "Dimensions of the Body: White and American Negroes of Both Sexes," *American Journal of Physical Anthropology* 12 (1928): 35–119. Cobb said, "It was a great joy to discover that Dr. Todd was already so advanced in his thinking and had amply demonstrated by his published work that prevalent American concepts in respect to race and human potential had no place in his laboratory," quoted in Rankin-Hill and Blakey, "W. Montague Cobb," 80.

85. Quoted in Rankin-Hill and Blakey, "W. Montague Cobb," 81.

86. For example, in 1921 he lectured that "there is no acceptable possibility ... that would make the white man wait upon the Japanese or Chinaman who is only a little bit behind, or the Negro who is a long way behind." Quoted in Rankin-Hill and Blakey, "W. Montague Cobb," 83, 77. Such words had a wide audience. Metheny, for example, cited Ales Hrdlicka's "The Full-Blood American Negro," *American Journal of Physical Anthropology* 12, no. 13 (1928): 15–33, in her 1939 study on athletes. On eugenics, see Daniel J. Kevles, *In the Name of Eugenics: Genetics and the Uses of Human Heredity* (Berkeley: University of California Press, 1985); Carl Degler, *In Search of Human Nature: The Decline and Revival of Darwinism in American Social Thought* (New York: Oxford University Press, 1991), chapters 2 and 6; and Richard Hofstadter, *Social Darwinism in American Thought* (Boston: Beacon Press, 1992), chapter 8.

87. Despite the racial bias evident in his academic conclusions, Hrdlicka not only worked closely with Cobb but also respected him, publishing parts of Cobb's dissertation in the American Journal of Physical Anthropology in 1933.

Cobb's recollection of an exchange with Hrdlicka is revealing: "Then one day I said, 'Dr. Hrdlicka, you accept me alright, why do you have these restrictive ideas about so called pure Negroes?' 'Well the Negro is alright when he's had the hardships the white man has had. You have the vigor of the hybrid,' he said. Well anytime you see anything you cannot explain, you invent an explanation." Quoted in Rankin-Hill and Blakey, "W. Montague Cobb," 83, 87.

88. W. Montague Cobb, "The Negro as a Biological Element in the American Population," *Journal of Negro Education* 8, no. 3 (July 1939) : 336–48. Cobb's construction of the "American Negro" as a modern entity works remarkably well within a discourse set by Richard Wright, who posed that black individuals—with connections among Africa, the United States, Great Britain, and the Caribbean—created a modernism that actually preceded modernity, because although slavery was a preindustrial labor force, it was also a global one. See Gilroy, *The Black Atlantic: Modernity and Double Consciousness* (Cambridge, Mass.: Harvard University Press, 1993), 159–86.

89. W. Montague Cobb, "Physical Anthropology of the Negro," *American Journal of Physical Anthropology* 24, no. 2 (June 1942): 113–93.

90. Cobb, "Physical Anthropology of the Negro," 121. Included in Cobb's survey was the work of his teacher, Hrdlicka, whose 1927 bibliography included 380 titles of anthropological work on the subject.

91. Cobb, "Physical Anthropology of the Negro," 130–31.

92. Cobb, "Physical Anthropology of the Negro," 133–34, 136–37. Cobb conveys a sense of urgency when he notes that there were but two other scientists besides himself who pursued such work, C. B. Day and K. B. M. Crooks. In addition, while a variety of anthropological organizations studied the American Negro, only one African American organization, the Daniel Smith Lamb Anthropological Society of Howard University, which he established in 1939, existed. Although the entire university was allowed membership, Cobb assessed the organization to include thirty members, all medical students.

93. For example, Cobb argued that living conditions and what he termed the "socially conditioned phenomenon" of race prejudice were two primary reasons the American Negro remained a separate group for study. Cobb, "Physical Anthropology of the Negro," 181–84.

94. Cobb, "Physical Anthropology of the Negro," 137–38, 141–42. Cobb argued that the amount of time necessary to become an anthropologist, along with a limited job market and a lack of financial resources for African American

students, kept many from pursuing the field, despite an "intrinsic interest of the subject," so he proposed the creation of a laboratory in an African American institution.

95. Cobb, "Physical Anthropology of the Negro," 143.

96. Cobb, "Physical Anthropology of the Negro," 144–45. To define "race," Cobb quoted a work of Harvard University's Earnest A. Hooton, *Up from the Ape* (New York: Macmillan, 1931). Hooton determined that members of a race, "though individually varying, are characterized as a group by a certain combination of morphological and metrical features, principally non-adaptive, which have been derived from their common descent." On Hooton, who focused primarily on the black criminal but also used examples of the black athlete, see Hoberman, *Darwin's Athletes*, 211–15.

97. Cobb, "Physical Anthropology of the Negro," 145.

98. Cobb, "Physical Anthropology of the Negro," 145–46. It is important that he does not dispute that race scientifically exists but refutes that "American Negro" is a race.

99. Cobb, "Physical Anthropology of the Negro," 168–69. Such a finding was not unprecedented. For example, according to Wiggins, Edwin Henderson concluded that University of Pennsylvania track standout John B. Taylor "was built more like a white runner, possessing larger gastrocnemius and soleus muscles than are found in the 'African Negro.'" See Wiggins, "Great Speed but Little Stamina," 178.

100. Cobb, "Physical Anthropology of the Negro," 169.

101. Cobb, "Physical Anthropology of the Negro," 171. Cobb was a three-time cross-country running champion and two-time boxing champion at Amherst College; see Harold Wade Jr., *Black Men of Amherst* (Amherst: Amherst College Press, 1976), 40–77.

102. Cobb, "The Negro as a Biological Element in the American Population," 342.

103. In 1942, he concluded, "Certainly those non-racial factors which make for general constitutional health and vigor must be possessed in abundance by the Negro, or his athletes, coming as they do from varied localities and backgrounds, could not manifest the high excellence they have regularly shown." Cobb, "The Negro as a Biological Element in the American Population," 342–43. In other work, he went further, indicating that the actual physique of the African American differs from whites, particularly in "proportions of limbs

and torso and cranial architectural pattern." See Cobb, "Physical Constitution of the American Negro," *Journal of Negro Education* 3 (1934): 387.

104. Cobb understood that his analysis was not broadly accepted, noting that other scientific conclusions focused on "a longer heel bone or strong tendon of Achilles than those of white competitors" to describe the success of stars like Owens, as well as Metcalfe and Tolan. C. Montague Cobb, "Race and Runners," *Journal of Health and Physical Education* 7, no. 1 (Jan. 1936): 3–7, 52–56.

105. Cobb, "Race and Runners," 3–5.

106. Cobb, "Race and Runners," 54; Cobb cites the work of Williams et al. in his discussion of the calf muscles.

107. Cobb, "Race and Runners," 56; emphasis mine.

108. Cobb, "Race and Runners," 56. The jumping performances of athletes representing Asian nations in the Olympics further illustrated Cobb's point. For example, the hop, step, and jump record that Nambu broke in 1932 was set by his countryman Mikio Oda, who won gold at the 1928 Amsterdam Games. Japanese jumper Naoto Tajima took the bronze in the broad jump and won gold in the hop, step, and jump at the 1936 Olympics in Berlin. His teammates Masao Harada and Kenkichi Oshima placed second and sixth, respectively, in the hop, step, and jump. In more recent broad/long jump history, athletes from China, Japan, and Korea placed in the top eight at the 1984 Los Angeles Games, and China's Huang Geng placed eighth in the 1992 Barcelona Olympics and seventh at the 1995 World Championships in Gothenburg, Sweden. In the hop, step, and jump, athletes from Japan and China have appeared in the top eight at the 1952 Helsinki Games, the 1956 Melbourne Games, and the 1984 Games in Los Angeles.

109. Cobb, "Race and Runners," 6.

110. Cobb, "Race and Runners," 7. Cobb noted that Owens considered his inspiration to be high school coach Charles Riley, as well as athletes De Hart Hubbard and Ned Gourdin. Additionally, it is critical to point out that athletic programs at historically black institutions of higher education were well under way by the 1930s, particularly with the founding of the Colored Intercollegiate Athletic Association in 1912.

111. The question of science's role is more clearly delineated in later writings; see Cobb, "Does Science Favor Negro Athletes?" *Negro Digest*, May 1947, 74–77, in which he pointedly asks, "Can science shed any light upon the Negro's evident 'racial superiority' in sports?" (74).

112. Cobb, "Race and Runners," 7.

113. Cobb, "Race and Runners," 7, 52.

114. Cobb, "Race and Runners," 52; emphasis mine.

115. Dean Cromwell, with Al Wesson, *Championship Techniques in Track and Field* (New York: Whittlesey House, 1941), 4.

116. Cromwell, *Championship Techniques in Track and Field*, 5.

117. Somewhat ambiguous is Cromwell's inclusion of American John Woodruff, who memorably won the 800-meters in Berlin. After running the fastest qualifying round (1:53) at the Games, the twenty-one-year-old from an impoverished black family in Pennsylvania was boxed in at the halfway point and slowed to a walk; once his competitors had all passed, he moved to the outside and sprinted into the lead. He won by two yards, the first Olympic 800-meters champion to run a faster second lap than the first, with an extraordinary display of a gifted distance runner thinking his way across the finish line. Yet Cromwell leaves out the details of his victory, simply stating that Woodruff's gold medal performance "adds to the laurels of the colored athletes." He makes Woodruff, as well as Canadian distance runner Phil Edwards, the exception to the rule, noting that "runs of any great length, however, are not ordinarily events in which the Negro excels" (*Championship Techniques in Track and Field*, 6).

118. Cromwell, *Championship Techniques in Track and Field*, 6.

119. Cromwell, *Championship Techniques in Track and Field*, 226. Hoberman notes that the "relaxation thesis" is widespread throughout "the racial folklore of sports" as a version of the Western notion of blacks as premodern and primitive. This belief also provides the basis for the false medical conclusion that blacks have lower blood pressure than whites, which Cobb explained as "indicative of greater inward serenity and less disturbance at outer circumstances, in contrast with worrying habits of the White engendered by the fitful pace of modern lives which causes the pressure to mount." See Cobb, "Physical Anthropology of the American Negro," 155; Hoberman, *Darwin's Athletes*, 199.

120. Cromwell, *Championship Techniques in Track and Field*, 233.

121. Cromwell, *Championship Techniques in Track and Field*, 9.

122. Cromwell, *Championship Techniques in Track and Field*, 9–10.

123. Cromwell, *Championship Techniques in Track and Field*, 11. Yet Cromwell felt the American generally performed better in athletic terms, because "he has become a bit more sports-minded than his brothers from across the sea and has made greater advances in training and technique."

124. Cromwell, *Championship Techniques in Track and Field*, 11. He notes in particular American success at the pole vault and hurdles, events that rely primarily on technique.

125. Marshall Smith, "Giving the Olympics an Anthropological Once-Over," *Life*, Oct. 23, 1964, 81–84; Hoberman, *Darwin's Athletes*, 192.

126. Smith, "Giving the Olympics an Anthropological Once-Over," 81.

3. An Olympic Challenge

1. Plummer, *A Rising Wind*, 218.

2. Edwards, *The Struggle That Must Be*, 27. Though invaluable resources, autobiographical works are problematic in that their bias often is slanted, perhaps more so than other works, to provide personal vindication for the author.

3. Edwards, *The Struggle That Must Be*, 89; emphasis in original.

4. Edwards, *The Struggle That Must Be*, 85–86; emphasis in original.

5. The categories symbolized the threatened OPHR and African boycotts, the Mexican student riots, the duels between runners Kip Keino and Jim Ryun, and the increasing turmoil surrounding Avery Brundage's leadership of the International Olympic Committee. John Underwood, "Games in Trouble," *Sports Illustrated*, Sept. 30, 1968, 46.

6. "Spell of the Olympics," *Newsweek*, Oct. 22, 1968, 64—65. The article made light of any remaining possibilities for a black protest, remarking that "the American blacks apparently will settle for some mild gesture like wearing Afro-style Dashikis over their U.S. sweatsuits on award stands."

7. Edwards, *The Struggle That Must Be*, 145; emphasis in original.

8. Sammons, "'Race' and Sport," 259.

9. *Black Journal*, 1969, Museum of Television and Radio, New York.

10. Donald Spivey, "'End Jim Crow in Sports': The Protest at New York University, 1940–1941," *Journal of Sport History* 15 (winter 1988): 285.

11. Spivey, "'End Jim Crow in Sports,'" 300–301. In 2001, NYU publicly admitted that the students should not have been suspended, but failed to issue an actual apology.

12. Spivey, "'End Jim Crow in Sports,'" 283–84.

13. Donald Spivey, "Black Consciousness and Olympic Protest Movement: 1964–1980," in *Sport in America: New Historical Perspectives* (Westport, Conn.: Greenwood Press, 1985), 239; Roberts and Olson, *Winning Is the Only Thing*, 16–18.

14. Quoted in Spivey, "Black Consciousness and Olympic Protest Movement," 240.

15. *Track and Field News* survey, Apr. 7, 1965, National Track and Field Hall of Fame Historical Research Library, Butler University, Indianapolis, Indiana. It is interesting to note that in his response, John Carlos wrote, "politics in track and field."

16. Harry Edwards, *The Revolt of the Black Athlete* (New York: Free Press, 1969), 41–44.

17. Edwards, *The Struggle That Must Be*, 161; Edwards, *The Revolt of the Black Athlete*, 46–47.

18. Edwards, *The Revolt of the Black Athlete*, 165.

19. Edwards, *The Revolt of the Black Athlete*, 50.

20. Dan Hruby, "Jordan Raps Olympic Fear," *San Jose Mercury News*, Nov. 13, 1967, 61.

21. Hruby, "Jordan Raps Olympic Fear," 61.

22. Hruby, "Jordan Raps Olympic Fear," 61.

23. "Negro Group in Boycott," *San Jose Mercury News*, Nov. 23, 1968, 117.

24. Scott Moore, "Negroes to Boycott Olympics," *San Jose Mercury News*, Nov. 24, 1967, 1.

25. Moore, "Negroes to Boycott Olympics," 2. I use "Lew Alcindor" instead of "Kareem Abdul-Jabbar" in order to situate his participation historically in the OPHR.

26. Scott Moore, "Olympics Boycott Final," *San Jose Mercury News*, Nov. 25, 1967, 1.

27. "Resolution Drafted at Black Youth Conference," in Edwards, *Revolt of the Black Athlete*, 55–56, and in Edwards, *The Struggle That Must Be*, 175.

28. Moore, "Negroes to Boycott Olympics," 2.

29. "'Bad Mistake'—Brundage," *San Jose Mercury News*, Nov. 25, 1967, 67; "'Concern Spreads,'" *San Jose Mercury News*, Nov. 25, 1967, 67. The initial news from Mexico came through Bud Winter, who said Olympic attaché Dave Curasco telephoned him from Mexico City to receive more information about the boycott declaration, indicating concern on the part of Mexican officials.

30. Arthur Daley, "Better Step: Participate," *San Jose Mercury News*, Nov. 28, 1967, 34; reprinted from the *New York Times*.

31. "'Bad Mistake'—Brundage."

32. David Wiggins, "The 1936 Olympic Games in Berlin: The Response of America's Black Press," in *Glory Bound*, ed. Wiggins, 63.

33. Wiggins, "The 1936 Olympic Games in Berlin," 75. See also Arnd Kruger, "Fair Play for American Athletes: A Study in Anti-Semitism," *Canadian Journal of History of Sport and Physical Education* 9, no. 1 (May 1978): 42–57; Bill Murray, "Berlin in 1936: Old and New Work on the Nazi Olympics," *International Journal of the History of Sport* 9 (1992): 29–49; Lapchick, "The Modern Olympic Games," in *Sport and Society*, ed. Lapchick, especially 255–59; W. J. Murray, "France, Coubertin and the Nazi Olympics: The Response," *Olympika: The International Journal of Olympic Studies* 1 (1992): 46–69; Stephen R. Wenn, "A Suitable Policy of Neutrality? FDR and the Question of American Participation in the 1936 Olympics," *International Journal of the History of Sport* 8 (1991): 319–35.

34. Daley, "Better Step: Participate," 34.

35. "Boycott Comment Divided," *San Jose Mercury News*, Nov. 25, 1967, 68.

36. "Boycott Wrong Says Negro Ump," *San Jose Mercury News*, Nov. 30, 1967, 106.

37. "Louis Frowns on Olympic Boycott," *New York Times*, Apr. 3, 1968, 54. Louis also commented that "Cassius Clay," while still the heavyweight champion, was wrong not to go into the army.

38. "Edwards Expands Boycott Plans," *San Jose Mercury News*, Dec. 14, 1967, 63.

39. "Boycott Comment Divided." The author of the article did not refer to Ali by his chosen name, but rather as Cassius Clay.

40. Robert Lipsyte, "Games Boycott an Obligation?" *San Jose Mercury News*, Nov. 25, 1967, 68; reprinted from the *New York Times*.

41. Louis Duino, "Olympic Team Will Survive Boycott by Negroes," *San Jose Mercury News*, Nov. 26, 1967, 73; emphasis mine.

42. Duino, "Olympic Team Will Survive Boycott by Negroes," 74.

43. For example, see "Aussie Sprinter Upsets Tommie," *San Jose Mercury News*, Dec. 14, 1967, 64, where report of Smith's defeat to Garey Eddy in a 220-yard race included the following: "Smith, who has said he will not represent the United States in the 1968 Olympic Games because of the racial situation, had defeated Eddy in a 130-yard race earlier in the day...."

44. Dan Hruby, "Smith: Rebel with a Cause," *San Jose Mercury News*, Nov. 27, 1967, 43.

45. Hruby, "Smith: Rebel with a Cause," 44.

46. Daley, "Better Step: Participate," 34.

47. Don Page, "ABC Eyes Olympic Action," *New York Times*, Oct. 15, 1968, IV: 20.

48. Miguel de Moragas Spá et al., *Television in the Olympics* (London: John Libbey, 1995), 20–21.

49. Sidney Wise, "Culture to Supplement Olympic Sports," *New York Times*, July 14, 1968, V: 10.

50. Eric Lott, *Love and Theft: Blackface Minstrelsy and the American Working Class* (New York: Oxford University Press, 1993).

51. Randy Roberts and James Olson, "The Roone Revolution," in *Sport in America*, ed. Wiggins, 270–71.

52. Roberts and Olson, "The Roone Revolution," 274, 277.

53. Joan Chandler, "American Televised Sport: Business as Usual," in *American Sport Culture: The Humanistic Dimensions*, ed. Wiley Umphett (Lewisburg: Bucknell University, 1985), 85. See also John J. MacAloon, "Sociation and Socioability in Political Celebrations," in *Celebration: Studies in Festivity and Ritual* (Washington, D.C.: Smithsonian Institution Press, 1982); John J. MacAloon, "Olympic Games and the Theory of Spectacle in Modern Societies," in *Rite, Drama, Festival, Spectacle: Rehearsals toward a Theory of Cultural Performance*, ed. John J. MacAloon (Philadelphia: Institute for the Study of Human Issues, 1984).

54. Bourdieu, *On Television*, 2.

55. "New U.S. Satellite to Relay TV Coverage of Olympics," *New York Times*, Aug. 21, 1968, 43; "'Dish' on Skyline Broadcasts Games," *San Jose Mercury News*, Oct. 16, 1968, 108.

56. Joseph M. Sheehan, "TV's Man in Sky Gets Clear View of Olympic Games," *New York Times*, Oct. 16, 1968, 52.

57. Susan M. Nattrass, "Television and the Olympics in Canada," in *The Olympic Movement and the Mass Media: Past, Present, and Future Issues* (Calgary: Hurford Enterprises: 1989), 5:9.

58. Jack Gould, "The Coverage Set Records, Too," *New York Times*, Nov. 3, 1968, II: 21.

59. John Hall, "Simple as ABC," *Los Angeles Times*, Oct. 14, 1968, III: 3.

60. Dr. G. Bodine, Letter to the Editor, *New York Times*, Nov. 3, 1968, II: 21.

61. Don Page, "ABC Eyes Olympic Action," *Los Angeles Times*, Oct. 15, 1968, IV: 20.

62. Spá et al., *Television in the Olympics*, 26.

63. "Numbers Tell Track Results, Cracking Language Barriers," *New York Times*, Oct. 15, 1968, 55; parenthetical aside in original.

64. Archived Olympic coverage, American Broadcasting Company, Oct. 17, 1968, tape 16, minutes 8:30–9:00.

65. Hall, "Simple as ABC."

66. Jack Gould, "TV: Olympic Games Brighten Screen," *New York Times*, Oct. 15, 1968, 95.

67. Gould, "The Coverage Set Records, Too."

68. Gould, "The Coverage Set Records, Too." He noted that computers also play a role, tabulating each nation's medal count almost instantly.

69. Tygiel, *Baseball's Great Experiment*, 269.

70. Chandler, "American Televised Sport," 87.

71. Gould, "The Coverage Set Records, Too"; Gould, "TV: Olympic Games Brighten Screen."

72. Chandler, "American Televised Sport," 94.

73. Hall, "Simple as ABC."

74. Arthur Daley, "Awesome Pageantry," *San Jose Mercury News*, Oct. 13, 1968, 87; reprinted from the *New York Times*; "Olympic Torchbearer Goes Out in Hurdles," *New York Times*, Oct. 15, 1968, 54. Basilio was eliminated from competition when she finished fifth in a heat for the women's 400-meter hurdles.

75. John Underwood, "Games in Trouble," *Sports Illustrated*, Sept. 30, 1968, 45.

76. Sam Lacy, "Mexican Mixers," *Baltimore Afro-American*, Oct. 19, 1968, 19.

77. Quoted in Lapchick, "The Modern Olympic Games," 262.

78. Arturo Escobar, *Encountering Development: The Making and Unmaking of the Third World* (Princeton: Princeton University Press, 1995), vii.

79. Eric Zolov, *Refried Elvis: The Rise of the Mexican Counterculture* (Berkeley: University of California Press, 1999).

80. Henry Giniger, "A Sports Capital-to-Be," *New York Times*, Jan. 13, 1968, 28.

81. "Mexico City's Olympic Feats," *Fortune*, Mar. 1968, 149.

82. "Mexico City's Olympic Feats," 149.

83. Carlo Rotella, *October Cities: The Redevelopment of Urban Literature* (Berkeley: University of California Press, 1998), 3.

84. "Mexico City's Olympic Feats," 149.

85. Underwood, "Games in Trouble," 46.

86. Arthur Daley, "A Brittle Brightness," *San Jose Mercury News*, Oct. 6, 1968, 106; reprinted from the *New York Times*.

87. Underwood, "Games in Trouble," 45; Bob Ottum, "Fresh, Fair and Golden," *Sports Illustrated*, Nov. 4, 1968, 25.

88. Steve Cady, "Amid Gun Salutes and Music, Mexico Bids a Colorful 'Adios' to Olympics," *New York Times*, Oct. 28, 1968, 59.

89. "Mexico City's Olympic Feats," 152. As early as January 1968, Mexico reportedly earned over thirty-two million dollars through such means.

90. Henry Giniger, "Mexicans Rushing Olympics' Complex," *New York Times*, July 21, 1968, V: 5; Henry Giniger, "Olympic Building Is Behind Schedule," *New York Times*, Sept. 8, 1968, V: 10.

91. "In 90 Days, Silent Stadiums Will Roar as Olympic Champions Are Crowned in Mexico," *New York Times*, July 14, 1968, V: 10; Arthur Daley, "A Triumph For Mexico," *San Jose Mercury News*, Oct. 8, 1968, 47; reprinted from the *New York Times*. Eventually the *Times* portrayed Mexico as an enjoyable Olympic destination and published a special section for Americans with an overview of the city's history, what to wear, a guide to Mexican food, an informative article about "Montezuma's revenge," medal predictions, the altitude factor, an ABC broadcast guide, the U.S. roster, a map of the Olympic venues, some Olympic history, and an article on language entitled "Basic Spanish, or Who Ordered Cactus Salad?" See *New York Times, Olympic Games Supplement*, Oct. 6, 1968, V.

92. Seth Fein, "Everyday Forms of Transnational Collaboration: U.S. Film Propaganda in Cold War Mexico," in *Close Encounters of Empire*, 405.

93. "Mexico Goes All Out for Video of 'Games,'" *San Jose Mercury News*, Dec. 25, 1967, 36.

94. *Olympic Charter*, Rule 44; the bylaw Rule 44 states that the cultural program has to be located both in the Olympic Village, in order to symbolize "the universality and the diversity of human culture," and throughout the host city, and must be open at least for the duration that the Olympic Village is open.

95. "Olympic Games Adding Culture," *New York Times*, Feb. 11, 1968, 94.

96. "Culture to Supplement Olympic Sports," *New York Times*, July 14, 1968, V: 10; Sanka Knox, "Olympics Press Culture Activity," *New York Times*, July 16, 1968, 33; Grace Glueck, "Not All Rowing or Discus Throwing," *New York Times*, July 21, 1968, II: 30.

97. "Dali Painting for Olympics," *New York Times*, Aug. 28, 1968.

98. The quoted portion of the section heading comes from the monument commemorating the twenty-fifth anniversary of the massacre at the La Plaza de las Tres Culturas: "The newspaper reported the weather as the chief news. And on television, on the radio, at the movies, there was no change in programming. There was no interruption for any announcement. Not a moment of silence at the banquet." See David Thelen, "Rethinking History and the Nation-State: Mexico and the United States," *Journal of American History* 86, no. 2 (Sept. 1999): 445.

99. Zolov, *Refried Elvis*, 119.

100. Zolov, *Refried Elvis*, 110.

101. Julio Scherer García and Carlos Monsiváis, *Parte de guerra, Tlatelolco, 1968: Documentos del general Marcelino Garcia Barragán: Los hechos y la historia* (Mexico: Aguilar Nuevo Siglo, 1999); "La conspiración del 68: El Estado mayor presidencial disparó contra los estudiantes y el ejército," *Proceso*, June 27, 1999, 6–11; Carlos Montemayor, "Tlatelolco 68: Las trampas, las mentiras, las contradicciones," *Proceso*, Oct. 2, 1999, 43–49.

102. Quoted in Thelen, "Rethinking History and the Nation-State," 442.

103. Barbara and John Ehrenreich, *Long March, Short Spring: The Student Uprising at Home and Abroad* (New York: Modern Reader Paperbacks, 1969), 8.

104. CIA Weekly Summary, July 19, 1968, the National Security Archive, George Washington University (http://www.gwu.edu/~nsarchiv/). Kate Doyle, the director of the Guatemala and Mexico Documentation Projects for the archive, has assembled the set of documents entitled "Tlatelolco Massacre: Declassified U.S. Documents on Mexico and the Events of 1968," which is indispensable for understanding La Nueva Noche Triste.

105. Evelyn P. Stevens, *Protest and Response in Mexico* (Cambridge, Mass.: MIT Press, 1974), 187.

106. John Womack Jr., "Unfreedom in Mexico: Government Crackdown on the Universities," *New Republic*, Oct. 12, 1968, 27.

107. Department of Defense Intelligence Information Report, Aug. 15, 1968, National Security Archive.

108. Stevens, *Protest and Response in Mexico*, 185–86, 200; William G. Bowdler, "Memorandum for the President," July 31, 1968, National Security Archive. A later Department of Defense Intelligence Information Report (Aug. 15, 1968) states that students claimed at least forty-eight were dead but had no "public confirmation of any fatalities."

109. Zolov, *Refried Elvis*, 121.

110. Department of Defense Intelligence Information Report, Aug. 15, 1968, National Security Archive.

111. Bowdler, "Memorandum for the President"; Department of State telegram, July 30, 1968; CIA Weekly Summary, Aug. 2, 1968; both in National Security Archive.

112. Quoted in Stevens, *Protest and Response in Mexico*, 203.

113. U.S. Department of Defense Intelligence Information Report, Aug. 15, 1968; Stevens, *Protest and Response in Mexico*, 203–4, 213; Zolov, *Refried Elvis*, 119–20.

114. Stevens, *Protest and Response in Mexico*, 212.

115. Quoted in Stevens, *Protest and Response in Mexico*, 213.

116. CIA Weekly Summary, Aug. 23, 1968, National Security Archive.

117. Womack, "Unfreedom in Mexico," 28; Stevens, *Protest and Response in Mexico*, 214–15.

118. White House memo with U.S. Embassy cable, Aug. 29, 1968, National Security Archive.

119. "Mexico City Collects Pistols for Safety at the Olympics," *New York Times*, June 8, 1968, 68.

120. "Plot to Kill the Olympics," *Newsweek*, Sept. 2, 1968, 59.

121. "Plot to Kill the Olympics," 59.

122. Henry Giniger, "Diaz Warns Dissident Mexican Students against Provocation," *New York Times*, Sept. 2, 1968, 10.

123. "Diaz Inaugurates Seven Olympic Sites," *New York Times*, Sept. 14, 1968, 6.

124. CIA Weekly Summary, Sept. 6, 1968; CIA cable, Sept. 9, 1968; both in National Security Archive.

125. Quoted in Stevens, *Protest and Response in Mexico*, 228.

126. White House memo, Sept. 19, 1968; Department of Defense Intelligence Information Report, Sept. 24, 1968; both in National Security Archive.

127. Department of Defense Intelligence Information Report, Sept. 24, 1968.

128. Henry Giniger, "3 Dead, Many Hurt in Mexico City Battle," *New York Times*, Sept. 25, 1968, 1, 21.

129. Department of Defense Intelligence Information Report, Sept. 24, 1968.

130. Henry Giniger, "Mexico City Death Toll Increases in Continuing Student Clashes," *New York Times*, Sept. 25, 1968, 21. Giniger states that the death toll reached at least seventeen with the second confrontation.

131. "Brundage Gets Assurances," *New York Times*, Sept. 24, 1968, 17.

132. Henry Giniger, "On an Embattled Campus, 8 Mexican Student Leaders Stress Moderate Aims," *New York Times*, Sept. 27, 1968, 16.

133. CIA Weekly Summary, Sept. 27, 1968, National Security Archive.

134. White House memo, Sept. 27, 1968; CIA Intelligence memo, Sept. 27, 1968, CIA memo, Sept. 26, 1968; all in National Security Archive.

135. Underwood, "Games in Trouble," 46.

136. Henry Giniger, "Easing of Tension in Mexico Sought," *New York Times*, Sept. 30, 1968, 13; "Students in Mexico to Continue Strike," *New York Times*, Oct. 2, 1968, 9.

137. Department of Defense Intelligence Information Report, Oct. 18, 1968, National Security Archive.

138. Zolov, *Refried Elvis*, 128–29; Paul L. Montgomery, "At Least 20 Dead as Mexico Strife Reaches a Peak," *New York Times*, Oct. 3, 1968, 1, 11; "Students Penned, Gunned," *San Jose Mercury News*, Oct. 3, 1968, 1, 2. The San Jose paper ran a banner headline over the masthead declaring "BLOODY MEXICO TRAP."

139. Carl J. Migdail, "On Olympic Eve—Biggest Flare-up Yet," *U.S. News and World Report*, Oct. 14, 1968, 8, 10.

140. Montgomery, "At Least 20 Dead as Mexico Strife Reaches a Peak."

141. Montgomery, "Deaths Put at 49 in Mexican Clash," *New York Times*, Oct. 4, 1968, 1, 3.

142. Montgomery, "Deaths Put at 49 in Mexican Clash," 1.

143. CIA Weekly Summary, Oct. 4, 1968, National Security Archive.

144. Steve Cady, "Brundage Declared Olympics Will Be Held Despite Riots," *New York Times*, Oct. 4, 1968, 60; "Soldiers Hunt Down Mexico City Snipers," *San Jose Mercury News*, Oct. 4, 1968, 1, 2; Louis Duino, "Valley Of Olympians," *San Jose Mercury News*, Oct. 6, 1968, 98. According to *Sports Illustrated*, Brundage was at the ballet when the massacre took place and claimed he

heard or knew nothing of it until the following day. See Bob Ottum, "Grim Countdown to the Games," *Sports Illustrated*, Oct. 1, 1968, 36–43.

145. FBI cable from director, Oct. 8, 1968, National Security Archive.

146. The athlete quotes are from Cady, "Brundage Declared Olympics Will be Held Despite Riots," 60. *Newsweek* reported that the Mexican government fired six of the press officers hired to facilitate information distribution to visiting journalists. Freelancer Jack Zanger, who quit in protest, stated, "We should have known what was coming at the first meeting when an official told us: 'There are no riots. If anyone asks you about riots, say it's not your department.'"

147. Quoted in Stevens, *Protest and Response in Mexico*, 238.

148. Ottum, "Grim Countdown to the Games," 43.

149. Henry Giniger, "Mexican Student Protest Appears to Be Crushed," *New York Times*, Oct. 5, 1968, 14; "Riot Rekindled in Mexico City," *San Jose Mercury News*, Oct. 5, 1968, 2; "Olympics Rioting Cools Off," *San Jose Mercury News*, Oct. 6, 1968, 106.

150. Henry Giniger, "Mexican President's Aides and Students Confer," *New York Times*, Oct. 10, 1968, 10. Student leaders claimed that over three hundred students had been missing since the October 2 clash.

151. Henry Giniger, "Leading Mexicans Linked to Protest," *New York Times*, Oct. 7, 1968, 13. Others named included Braulio Maldonado, former governor of Baja California, Victor Urquidi, director of the College of Mexico, and writer Elena Garro.

152. Department of State telegram, Oct. 12, 1968, National Security Archive.

153. CIA report, Oct. 10, 1968, National Security Archive.

154. White House memo, Oct. 5, 1968; CIA memo, Oct. 4, 1968; both in National Security Archive.

155. Womack, "Unfreedom in Mexico," 29.

156. FBI cable, Oct. 5, 1968, National Security Archive.

157. U.S. Department of State telegram, Oct. 12, 1968; Department of Defense Intelligence Information Report, Oct. 18, 1968; both in National Security Archive.

158. Giniger, "Mexican Student Protest Appears to Be Crushed," 13.

159. Steve Cady, "Olympic Tales Mix Facts, Fiction," *New York Times*, Oct. 7, 1968, 64.

160. "Mexican Disruptions—'Only a Few Hundred,'" *San Jose Mercury News*, Oct. 8, 1968, 48; Department of Defense Intelligence Report, Oct. 18, 1968.

161. *New York Times*, Oct. 9, 1968, 53.

162. "Ferment in Mexico," *New York Times*, Oct. 12, 1968, 36.

163. Ruben Salazar, "Wonder of Color Welcomes Olympics," *Los Angeles Times*, Oct. 13, 1968, 1, 8.

164. Ottum, "Grim Countdown to the Games," 36–43.

165. *Sports Illustrated*, Oct. 21, 1968.

166. "Olympics Site 'OK,'" *San Jose Mercury News*, Oct. 1, 1968, 49.

167. Underwood, "Games in Trouble," 46.

4. The Power of Protest and Boycott

1. Cady, "Olympic Tales Mix Facts, Fiction."

2. "Plot to Kill the Olympics," *Newsweek*, Sept. 2, 1968, 59; Edwards, *The Revolt of the Black Athlete*, 101.

3. FBI memo, Sept. 25, 1968, National Security Archive.

4. FBI memo, Sept. 26, 1968; letter from John Edgar Hoover, FBI director, Oct. 1, 1968; both in National Security Archive.

5. On France, see Jacques Capdevielle and Rene Mouriaux, *Mai 68: L'entre-deux de la modernite, histoire de trente ans* (Paris: Presses de la Fondation Nationale des Science Politiques, 1988); Keith Reader and Kursheed Wadia, *The May 1968 Events in France: Reproductions and Interpretations* (New York: St. Martin's Press, 1993); Herve Hamon and Patrick Rotman, *Generation* (Paris: Seuil, 1987); Alain Schnapp and Pierre Vidal-Naquet, *The French Student Uprising, November, 1967–June, 1968: An Analytic Record* (Boston: Beacon Press, 1971); Bernard Brown, *Protest in Paris: Anatomy of a Revolt* (Morristown: General Learning Press, 1974); Patrick Seale and Maureen McConville, *Red Flag/Black Flag: French Revolution 1968* (New York: Putnam, 1968).

6. Singh, "Toward an Effective Antiracism," 230.

7. Scott Moore, "12 Held in Dow Protest," *San Jose Mercury News*, Nov. 21, 1967, 1; "Expel Rioters, Reagan Urges," *San Jose Mercury News*, Nov. 21, 1967, 1. The stories regarding the riot were beneath a banner headline: "SJS ANTI-WAR RIOT ERUPTS."

8. Gil Bailey, "No Police Brutality Observed," *San Jose Mercury News*, Nov. 21, 1967, 1.

9. "Expel Rioters, Reagan Urges."

10. Lou Cannon, "Bradley Wants Clark's Scalp," *San Jose Mercury News*, Nov. 22, 1967, 1.

11. Scott Moore, "Protestors Try to Storm SJS," *San Jose Mercury News*, Nov. 22, 1967, 1, 2; Cannon, "Bradley Wants Clark's Scalp," 1, 2.

12. "Demonstrations: Too Far at SJS?" *San Jose Mercury News*, Nov. 28, 1967, 17; Edwards responded: "I think the cops have gone too far. I think the demonstrators have a right to demonstrate, they had a permit.... The police precipitated the violence. It's going to get to the point where the demonstrators are going to meet violence with violence."

13. Wes Mathis, "Smith Wins 300 Yard Dash," *San Jose Mercury News*, Jan. 6, 1968, 53.

14. "Edwards Expands Boycott Plans," *San Jose Mercury News*, Dec. 14, 1967, 63. The demand that specified the addition of two black coaches to the U.S. Olympic coaching staff stated that Stanley V. Wright did not count as a black coach because "he is a devout Negro and therefore is unacceptable." See Edwards, *The Revolt of the Black Athlete*, 58–59. Although the OPHR included Southern Rhodesia in its demands because of its own racist political system, South African apartheid remained the prominent center of the dialogue. Note that while Rhodesia accepted the IOC's invitation to send a team to Mexico, the team could not participate because of a UN Security Council resolution that denied admittance to anyone traveling under a Rhodesian passport. Brundage expressed public aggravation over the move, particularly with Great Britain's refusal to recognize Rhodesian independence, saying, "Here we have another case of throwing the Olympic movement in the middle of an international con-troversy when the cause is political and has nothing at all to do with sports." See "Rhodesia Accepts Bid to Olympics in Mexico," *New York Times*, June 3, 1968, 64; "U.N. Action on Rhodesia Bars Participation in Olympic Games," *New York Times*, June 8, 1968, 38.

15. "Brundage Ouster Demanded," *San Jose Mercury News*, Dec. 15, 1967, 73.

16. "Should Negroes Boycott the Olympics?" *Ebony*, vol. 23, no. 5, Mar. 1968, 112.

17. "Brundage Ouster Demanded."

18. Plummer, *A Rising Wind*, 1.

19. Kelley, "'But a Local Phase of a World Problem.'"

20. Quoted in John W. Dower, *War without Mercy: Race and Power in the Pacific War* (New York: Pantheon Books, 1986), 177–78.

21. Quoted in Singh, "Toward an Effective Antiracism," 228; emphasis mine.

22. George Lipsitz, "'Frantic to Join … the Japanese Army': Beyond the Black-White Binary," in *The Possessive Investment in Whiteness: How White People Profit from Identity Politics* (Philadelphia: Temple University Press, 1998), 94.

23. Quoted in Thomas R. Hietala, "Muhammad Ali and the Age of Bare Knuckle Politics," in *Muhammad Ali*, ed. Gorn, 138.

24. Robert Lipsyte, "Negroes' Boycott Strikes a Nerve," *San Jose Mercury News*, Dec. 16, 1967, 61; reprinted from *New York Times*.

25. Arthur Ashe, *A Hard Road to Glory: A History of the African-American Athlete since 1946* (New York: Amistad, 1988), 173. On "black internationalism," see Kelley, "'But a Local Phase of a World Problem,'" 1075–76.

26. "Another Olympics Boycott with 'Assist' of de Gaulle!" *San Jose Mercury News*, Jan. 11, 1968, 51.

27. Spivey, "Black Consciousness and Olympic Protest Movement," 240; Mihir Bose, *Sporting Colours: Sport and Politics in South Africa* (London: Robson Books, 1994), 69; William J. Baker, "Political Games: The Meaning of International Sport for Independent Africa," *Sport in Africa: Essays in Social History*, ed. William J. Baker and James A. Mangan (New York: Africana Publishing Company, 1987), 274; Richard Lapchick, *The Politics of Race and International Sport: The Case of South Africa* (Westport, Conn.: Greenwood Press, 1975), 80–81, 102; Peter Hain, *Don't Play with Apartheid: The Background to the Stop the Seventy Tour Campaign* (London: Ruskin House, 1971), 60. As Hain points out, critical to the SCSA's creation was the internal turmoil ongoing in South African sport. Mere months before its founding, the South African Non-Racial Olympic Committee (SAN-ROC), inaugurated in 1962, reenergized its international lobbying efforts after its president, Dennis Brutus, inarguably one of the most influential individuals in the fight for integration, fled the country for London. According to Lapchick, it was Brutus who provided the impetus for the inclusion of South Africa on the OPHR agenda; he asked a South African friend at UCLA, Dan Kunene, to ask Edwards to add a ban on South Africa to the other demands.

28. Quoted in Lapchick, *The Politics of Race and International Sport*, 80.

29. Edwards, *The Revolt of the Black Athlete*, 57.

30. Kenny Moore, "A Courageous Stand," *Sports Illustrated*, Aug. 5, 1991,

60. Edwards's class, which had averaged sixty students per semester, grew to six hundred students in 1967.

31. Edwards, *The Revolt of the Black Athlete*, 31–36. For an academic application of Edwards's political taxonomy, see Michael Govan, "The Emergence of the Black Athlete in America," *Black Scholar* 3, no. 3 (Nov. 1971): 16–28, but especially 26–27. In interesting juxtaposition to Edwards's racial hierarchy is a hierarchy that Jonathan Rieder found in his study of the fall of liberalism in the Jewish and Italian enclaves in Canarsie, New York; the words of one of his subjects indicated that the designation "Jew" had similar virtue and attainability: "We thought of Roosevelt in glowing terms. He saved the country, and we were all heartbroken when he died. My parents considered him Jewish. He was kindly and liberal and good. 'He should be a Jew,' they thought. 'He must be a Jew!'" Jonathan Rieder, *Canarsie: The Jews and Italians of Brooklyn against Liberalism* (Cambridge, Mass.: Harvard University Press, 1985), 50.

32. Edwards, *The Revolt of the Black Athlete*, 58. This kind of hierarchical classification is somewhat rooted in slave tales. As Lawrence Levine posits, slaves "possessed their own form of racial ethnocentrism and were capable of viewing the white race as a degenerate form of the black." See Lawrence Levine, *Black Culture and Consciousness: Afro-American Folk Thought from Slavery to Freedom* (Oxford: Oxford University Press, 1977), 85.

33. Lomax quoted in Edwards, *The Struggle That Must Be* (New York: Macmillan, 1980), 169.

34. Kobena Mercer, "'1968': Periodizing Politics and Identity," in *Welcome to the Jungle: New Positions in Black Cultural Studies* (New York: Routledge, 1994), 292, 300; emphasis in original.

35. Mercer, "'1968,'" 302. For an excellent summary of the creation of the Panthers and their ten-point program, see Manning Marable, *Race, Reform, and Rebellion: The Second Reconstruction in Black America, 1945–1990* (Jackson: University of Mississippi Press, 1991), 108–10.

36. Edwards, *The Struggle That Must Be*, 169.

37. Singh, "Toward an Effective Antiracism," 232.

38. Edwards, *The Struggle That Must Be*, 170.

39. William L. Van DeBurg, *New Day in Babylon: The Black Power Movement and American Culture, 1965–1975* (Chicago: University of Chicago Press, 1993), 306.

40. Ernesto Chávez, "'Birth of a New Symbol': The Brown Berets' Gendered Chicano National Imaginary," in *Generations of Youth: Youth Cultures and*

History in Twentieth-Century America, ed. Joe Austin and Michael Nevin Willard (New York: New York University Press, 1998), 209.

41. James A. Wechsler, "Strange Games," *New York Post*, Feb. 15, 1968, 49.

42. Bob Considine and Fred G. Jarvis, *A Portrait of the NYAC: The First Hundred Years* (London: Macmillan, 1969), 6–7. I would like to thank the NYAC for access to this volume.

43. Wechsler, "Strange Games."

44. Larry Merchant, "Right Time, Right Place," *New York Post*, Feb. 15, 1968, 88.

45. Homer Bigart, "Militants Lose 7th Ave. Scuffle," *New York Times*, Feb. 17, 1968, 19.

46. "Three New Groups Blast N.Y. Athletic Club Bias," *Pittsburgh Courier*, Feb. 17, 1968, 15.

47. David Wiggins, "'The Year of Awakening': Black Athletes, Racial Unrest and the Civil Rights Movement of 1968," *International Journal of the History of Sport* 9, no. 2 (Aug. 1992): 192.

48. Merchant, "Right Time, Right Place."

49. Wechsler, "Strange Games."

50. Merchant, "Right Time, Right Place."

51. C. Gerald Fraser, "Black Athletes Are Cautioned Not to Cross Lines," *New York Times*, Feb. 16, 1968, 41. In addition to Brown, other participants in the press conference included Callis Brown of CORE, C. Sumner (Chuck) Stone of the National Black Power conference, Lincoln Lynch of the United Black Front, and Omar Abu Ahmed of the Black Power Conference.

52. Robert Terrell and Paul Zimmerman, "Picket Plans Present High Hurdle to NYAC," *New York Post*, Feb. 15, 1968, 88. Brown's statement became prominent in various forms within the boycott coverage; Zimmerman later quoted Brown as saying, "Personally, if I didn't want people to run, I'd blow Madison Square Garden up." See "Will Boycott Stop Thomas?" *New York Post*, Feb. 16, 1968, 1.

53. Merchant, "Right Time, Right Place"; Frank Litsky, "Russians Out of N.Y.A.C. Track; Negro Pickets Ready," *New York Times*, Feb. 16, 1968, 41.

54. "Notre Dame Alumni Are Urged to Resign as N.Y.A.C. Members," *New York Times*, Feb. 16, 1968, 41.

55. Pete Axthelm, "Boycott Now—Boycott Later?" *Sports Illustrated*, Feb. 26, 1968, 25.

56. Merchant, "Right Time, Right Place."

57. Terrell and Zimmerman, "Picket Plans Present High Hurdle to NYAC"; "The Black Boycott," *Time*, Feb. 23, 1968, 61.

58. Paul Zimmerman, "Will Boycott Stop Thomas?" *New York Post*, Feb. 16, 1968, 88.

59. Quoted in David Wallechinsky, *The Complete Book of the Olympics* (New York: Penguin Books, 1988), 81–82.

60. Milton Gross, "TV's Eye in Storm Center," *New York Post*, Feb. 16, 1968, 84.

61. "Russians Withdraw from Boycott-Threatened Meet," *Los Angeles Times*, Feb. 16, 1968, III: 7; Zimmerman, "Will Boycott Stop Thomas?"

62. Zimmerman, "Will Boycott Stop Thomas?"

63. Axthelm, "Boycott Now—Boycott Later?"

64. "No Gate Sale," *New York Post*, Feb. 16, 1968, 88.

65. Zimmerman, "Will Boycott Stop Thomas?"

66. "Russians Withdraw from Boycott-Threatened Meet."

67. Milton Gross, "TV's Eye in Storm Center," *New York Post*, Feb. 16, 1968, 84.

68. Gross, "TV's Eye in Storm Center."

69. Frank Litsky, "9 Negroes Appear in Garden Action," *New York Times*, Feb. 17, 1968, 19. Of the nine African Americans who competed, five, including Beamon, were from UTEP: Kelly Myrick (hurdles), Chuck McPherson (60-yard dash), Leslie Miller (long jump and 1-mile relay), and Dave Morgan (1-mile relay). Rounding out the list, in addition to Lennox Miller and Franzetta Parham, were Al McPherson of Catholic University (1-mile relay) and James Rodman of Rutgers (freshmen 1-mile relay).

70. "Police, Demonstrators Battle—Track Meet Held," *Los Angeles Times*, Feb. 17, 1968, II: 2; Litsky, "9 Negroes Appear in Garden Action."

71. "Explained the Issues," *New York Post*, Feb. 17, 1968, 19.

72. Litsky, "9 Negroes Appear in Garden Action." Dennis was a teammate of Jim Hines in the Houston Striders Club and a military man, which cost him his easy entrance. "I made the mistake of wearing my air force uniform. I was easy to spot. A standing target. They knew who I was and they didn't let me through the picket line." See "Explained the Issues."

73. Dave Anderson, "Negro Athletes Apprehensive, but Compete in Meet Anyway," *New York Times*, Feb. 17, 1968, 19.

74. Anderson, "Negro Athletes Apprehensive, but Compete in Meet Anyway."

75. "Explained the Issues."

76. Homer Bigart, "Militants Lose 7th Ave. Scuffle," *New York Times*, Feb. 17, 1968, 19; Ralph Blumenfeld, "City Presses Ban on NYAC," *New York Post*, Feb. 17, 1968, 1.

77. "Explained the Issues."

78. "The Black Boycott."

79. Blumenfeld, "City Presses Ban on NYAC."

80. Paul Zimmerman, "Under the Gun," *New York Post*, Feb. 17, 1968, 19.

81. Zimmerman, "Under the Gun."

82. Frank Litsky, "An Olympian Problem," *New York Times*, Feb. 18, 1968, V: 2; "Explained the Issues."

83. Axthelm, "Boycott Now—Boycott Later?"

84. Milton Gross, "The Greeks Had a Word for It," *New York Post*, Feb. 19, 1968, 75.

85. Baker, "Political Games," 284; Robert Archer, "Politics and Sport in South Africa's Townships," *Sport in Africa*, ed. Baker and Mangan, 238. South African efforts to segregate domestic sports laid a substantial foundation for the IOC Baden-Baden decision long before the trials for Tokyo took place. As Archer notes, there existed some racial lines of fluidity among some of the "black" titled organizations, such as the Durban & District African Football Association. However, beginning in 1951 the Nationalist government began to work unequivocally against such mingling, particularly with visiting black athletes, and in 1956 issued its first public definition of the mode in which apartheid was to be utilized in sport. It was this transformation that provoked black associations to create the South African Sports Association (SAOC) in 1958 and subsequently SAN-ROC.

86. Quoted in Lapchick, *The Politics of Race and International Sport*, 52, 60–63. The IOC gave the South African Olympic Committee until December 31, 1963, to induce the South African government to alter its policies regarding sport. When the SAOC failed to meet the deadline, an extension to January 15, 1964, was granted; at this date, Otto Mayer, IOC chancellor, announced that the SAOC did not accept the IOC's demand concerning integration but still wanted to compete in Tokyo. The questions continued until August, when the IOC

officially invoked the suspension, with Mayer resigning his position, stating, "It is situations like this that make the job of Chancellor really unbearable" (Lapchick, *The Politics of Race and International Sport*, 52).

87. Walker won his gold medal in London in the 100-meters; he was the member of an all-white sports club. The next African medal would take another sixteen years. See Baker, "Political Games," 275.

88. Bose, *Sporting Colours*, 71–72; Lapchick, *The Politics of Race and International Sport*, 97–101. For a first-person account of the travels of the IOC committee, see Lord Michael Killanin, *My Olympic Years* (London: Secker and Warburg, 1983). As Jean-Claude Ganga was consistently quick to point out, Alexander, one of the three representatives of black Africa on the seventy-one-member IOC, was a white Englishman.

89. "So. Africa Gains in Olympics Bid," *New York Times*, Jan. 31, 1968, 34.

90. "Olympics Okay S. Africa," *New York Post*, Feb. 15, 1968, 96; "Integration Key to South Africa Reinstatement," *Los Angeles Times*, Feb. 16, 1968, 3; Lloyd Garrison, "Approval Is Given by Majority Vote," *New York Times*, Feb. 16, 1968, 41. The actual breakdown of the vote between the seventy-one member nations of the IOC was not released, so all numbers were speculation.

91. Bose, *Sporting Colours*, 39.

92. "South Africans Cheered by the News," *New York Times*, Feb. 16, 1968, 41.

93. Richard Thompson, *Race and Sport* (London: Oxford University Press, 1964), 15.

94. Baker, "Political Games," 284.

95. Quoted in Bose, *Sporting Colours*, 38.

96. Gross, "The Greeks Had a Word for It"; William Barry Furlong, "A Bad Week for Mr. B.," *Sports Illustrated*, Mar. 11, 1968, 19.

97. "Ethiopia Quits Summer Olympics Because of South Africa Issue," *Los Angeles Times*, Feb. 17, 1968, II: 2; "Ethiopia, Algeria Out of Olympics," *New York Times*, February 17, 1968, 19; Morris W. Rosenberg, "S. Africa in Olympics—Russia to Drop Out?" *New York Post*, Feb. 16, 1968, 81. The symbolic importance of Bikila cannot be underestimated. His 1960 win in Rome, involving a race whose route was guarded by Italian soldiers and whose finish line was reached through the Arch of Constantine, was constructed by him and his coach to demonstrate the irony of an Ethiopian runner dominating the

culminating event of Italy's Games. When previewing the route days before his start, Bikila and his coach noticed that almost a mile before the finish line was the obelisk of Axum, taken by Italian troops from Ethiopia; they decided the slight slope after the obelisk would be the suitable place for Bikila to make his move to take the lead. His victory, as well as his subsequent win in Tokyo a mere forty days after an appendectomy, elevated him to a status "not far below the Emperor Haile Selassie in the hearts of his countrymen." Indeed, rumors still abound that his 1973 death from injuries sustained in an automobile accident was arranged by Selassie, and that the leader formally prevented national radio from reporting on the funeral. See Wallechinsky, *The Complete Book of the Olympics*, 54–55; Baker, "Political Games," 281.

98. "S. Africa Readmission to Olympics Protested," *New York Post*, Feb. 16, 1968, 81; Robert Lipsyte, "Return of the Springbok," *New York Times*, Feb. 17, 1968, 19.

99. Frank Litsky, "65 Athletes Support Boycott of Olympics on S. Africa Issue," *New York Times*, Apr. 12, 1968, 28; Leonard Koppett, "Robinson Urges So. Africa Ban," *New York Times*, Feb. 9, 1968, 56; Robert Lipsyte, "Politics and Protest," *New York Times*, Feb. 11, 1968, 41. The American Committee on Africa had been on top of the South African issue several months before Edwards founded the OPHR, issuing a statement on May 8, 1967, with thirty prominent signatures—among them, those of Robinson, Ashe, Roy Campanella, Floyd McKissick, Bayard Rustin, Stokely Carmichael, Langston Hughes, Ruby Dee, Ed Sullivan, and Pete Seeger—urging the USOC to do all within its power to maintain the ban against South Africa. See Lapchick, *The Politics of Race and International Sport*, 96.

100. "5 More African Nations Join Boycott of Olympics," *New York Times*, Feb. 18, 1968, V: 1.

101. Quoted in Baruch A. Hazan, "Sport as an Instrument of Political Expansion: The Soviet Union in Africa," in *Sport in Africa*, ed. Baker and Mangan, 252.

102. Marable points out that "in the 1950s, the image of Africa as a cultural and political entity began to reassert its impact upon African-American intellectuals and artists," and he acknowledges that while there are several facets of a relationship between African Americans and Africans in the nineteenth and early twentieth centuries, such as missionary expeditions to Liberia and the elevation of a symbolic African home by Marcus Garvey, it is the

postwar period that provides the critical marking point. See Marable, *Race, Reform, and Rebellion*, 49.

103. Arthur Daley, "Dark Shadows," *New York Times*, Feb. 18, 1968, V: 2. Such rumination from Daley was not uncommon. For example, in a later column he deemed "ironic" the statement from a Soviet delegate to the IOC that the "Soviet Union never has used the Olympic Games for propaganda purposes." Daley submitted that the delegate "must have meant direct propaganda, because the entire Russian sports setup is indirect propaganda." See Arthur Daley, "The Incident," *New York Times*, Oct. 20, 1968, V: 2.

104. Hazan, "Sport as an Instrument of Political Expansion," 253–55, 259, 265; Von Eschen, *Race against Empire*, 125. Of course, as established earlier in the chapter, the Soviets were by no means the only ones to pursue a relationship with African athletes. For example, American gold medalist Mal Whitfield traveled to East Africa in 1953 to conduct aid programs and help coach national track teams, and Onni Niskanen, a Swedish citizen living in Ethiopia, was the original coach of Bikila. However, the Soviets had by far the most systematic program of establishing sporting ties with the continent. See Baker, "Political Games," 276.

105. Wechsler, "Strange Games."

106. Rob Nixon, *Homelands, Harlem and Hollywood: South African Culture and the World Beyond* (New York: Routledge, 1994), 2.

107. "Brundage Backs So. Africa Ruling," *New York Times*, Feb. 26, 1968, 50.

108. Robert Lipsyte, "After Thermopylae, What?" *New York Times*, Feb. 19, 1968, 53; Gilroy, "One Nation under a Groove," 46. For an excellent example of scholarship that directly takes up Gilroy's question, see Robin D. G. Kelley, "'This Ain't Ethiopia, but It'll Do': African Americans and the Spanish Civil War," in *Race Rebels*, 123–58. Of course, the decisive example of such work is that of C. L. R. James on Toussaint L'Ouverture. James writes without a *national* framework, creating a transnational perspective that conveys a historical moment that cannot be understood by looking in only one place; he presents many contexts in proximity to the Haitian Revolution. See C. L. R. James, *The Black Jacobins: Toussaint L'Ouverture and the San Domingo Revolution* (New York: Vintage Books, 1963). For a comparative look at American and South African systems of racism, see George M. Frederickson, *White Supremacy: A Comparative Study in American and South African History* (New York: Oxford University Press,

1981), particularly 239–82. For treatments of the relationship between the United States and South Africa, see Plummer, *A Rising Wind*; Thomas Borstelmann, *Apartheid's Reluctant Uncle: The United States and Southern Africa in the Early Cold War* (New York: Oxford University Press, 1993); Thomas J. Noer, *Black Liberation: The United States and White Rule in Africa, 1948–1968* (Columbia: University of Missouri Press, 1985); Martin Staniland, *American Intellectuals and African Nationalists, 1955–1970* (New Haven: Yale University Press, 1991); Christopher Coker, *The United States and South Africa, 1968–1985* (Durham: Duke University Press, 1986); Alfred O. Hero Jr. and John Barratt, eds., *The American People and South Africa: Publics, Elites, and Policymaking Processes* (Lexington: D.C. Heath, 1981); and Kenneth Mokena, *South Africa and the United States: The Declassified History* (New York: New Press, 1993).

109. "Syria 9th to Join Olympic Boycott," *New York Times*, Feb. 20, 1968, 57.

110. "Kenya, Sudan and Iraq Join Boycott of Summer Olympics," *New York Times*, Feb. 21, 1968, 39.

111. "Scandinavians Protest," *New York Times*, Feb. 21, 1968, 39.

112. "South Africa to the Olympics," *New York Times*, Feb. 21, 1968, 46.

113. Arthur Daley, "Some Second Thoughts," *New York Times*, Feb. 23, 1968, 21.

114. Quoted in Lapchick, *The Politics of Race and International Sport*, 112.

115. "Olympic Boycott Still Unofficial," *New York Times*, Feb. 22, 1968, 42.

116. "Brundage Backs So. Africa Ruling," *New York Times*, Feb. 26, 1968, 50.

117. "Africans Pressing Boycott of Olympics," *New York Times*, Feb. 25, 1968, V: 1, 2.

118. "Pressure Increases," *New York Times*, Feb. 25, 1968, 2; "Plea by Brundage," *New York Times*, Feb. 25, 1968. A critical agent in the movement against South Africa, Ganga became a full-fledged member of the IOC. However, he was expelled from the body in 1999 during the scandals that surrounded the Salt Lake City Winter Games for allegedly accepting $250,000 in gifts and services from the Salt Lake City organizing committee in exchange for his vote.

119. "Tunisia Decries Decision," *New York Times*, Feb. 25, 1968, 2; "Cuba Joins Criticism," *New York Times*, Feb. 25, 1968, 2; "Spur to U.S. Movement Seen," *New York Times*, Feb. 25, 1968, 2; Axthelm, "Boycott Now—Boycott

Later?" Edwards's understanding of the possibilities of international revolution was best enunciated in some of his later academic writings. See Harry Edwards, "Change and Crisis in Modern Sport," *Black Scholar* 8, no. 2 (Oct.-Nov. 1976): 60–65.

120. Katsiaficas, *The Imagination of the New Left*, 4.

121. "Boycott of Olympics Approved by 32-Nation African Council," *New York Times*, Feb. 27, 1968, 1, 48; "Boycott in Mexico?" *Newsweek*, Mar. 11, 1968, 84; "What Apartheid Policy Means," *Newsweek*, Mar. 11, 1968, 84; Frank Litsky, "Anatomy of a Boycott," *New York Times*, Feb. 27, 1968, 48, emphasis mine; Letter to the Editor, *New York Times*, Feb. 28, 1968, 46. The small article on apartheid defined it as a "separate racial development" and gave a short history of its evolution in government in South Africa, as well as defining what it meant in athletic terms in the outlawing of competition between whites and "non-whites" (categorized as African, "colored," and Asian). Such an article was critical, because, as Nixon points out, "the terms black, African, 'colored,' nonracial … have quite different valences and implications in the U.S.A. and South Africa"; Nixon, *Homelands, Harlem and Hollywood*, 3.

122. Nixon, *Homelands, Harlem and Hollywood*, 132.

123. Baker, "Political Games," 273.

124. Ian Robertson and Phillip Whitten, "The Olympics: Keep South Africa Out!" *New Republic*, Apr. 13, 1968, 12–14.

125. Litsky, "Anatomy of a Boycott."

126. "Soviet Stand Undecided," *New York Times*, Feb. 27, 1968, 48.

127. "France Deplores Olympics Boycott," *New York Times*, Feb. 29, 1968, 43.

128. "Africa Games Promised," *New York Times*, Mar. 2, 1968, 33.

129. "… and in the Olympics," *New York Times*, Mar. 2, 1968, 28.

130. "Special Meeting Called Unneeded"; "Amateur's Champion"; both in *New York Times*, Feb. 27, 1968, 48.

131. "The Olympics: Invitation Withdrawn," *Time*, May 3, 1968, 67–68.

132. Furlong, "A Bad Week for Mr. B.," 19.

133. Lloyd Garrison, "African Shock Waves," *New York Times*, Feb. 28, 1968, 57.

134. Garrison, "African Shock Waves." Garrison argued that the reluctance of the Soviets to withdraw was most closely connected to their "rivalry with the Chinese for the loyalty of the Left in the underdeveloped world," making

their absence in Mexico City "a major victory for Peking, which does not even participate in the Games."

135. "Move Is Growing for I.O.C. Session," *New York Times*, Feb. 28, 1968, 57.

136. Furlong, "A Bad Week for Mr. B.," 20; "Mexican Olympic Group Meets with Brundage about Boycott," *New York Times*, Mar. 1, 1968, 44.

137. "South Africa Forms Committee," *New York Times*, Mar. 1, 1968, 44.

138. "Brundage Calls Special Olympic Meeting after Talk with Mexican Officials," *New York Times*, Mar. 2, 1968, 33; "Boycotting South Africa," *Time*, Mar. 8, 1968, 74.

139. "Africa Games Promised," *New York Times*, Mar. 2, 1968, 33.

140. "South Africa Stands Firm"; "Cuba Joins Boycott"; both in *New York Times*, Mar. 2, 1968, 33.

141. "S. Africa Blacks Attack Boycott," *New York Times*, Mar. 3, 1968, V: 7.

142. "... and in the Olympics."

143. Quoted in Lapchick, *The Politics of Race and International Sport*, 117.

144. "Libya Joins Boycott," *New York Times*, Mar. 6, 1968, 54; "Sweden Bids I.O.C. Review So. Africa," *New York Times*, Mar. 7, 1968, 57.

145. "Soviet Asks I.O.C. to Bar South Africa," *New York Times*, Mar. 6, 1968, 54.

146. "Soviet Seeks Ban on South Africa," *New York Times*, Mar. 8, 1968, 30.

147. "Many Await Special Meeting," *New York Times*, Mar. 10, 1968, V: 1, 7.

148. "All Sports Will Be Represented," *New York Times*, Mar. 10, 1968, V: 1, 7.

149. "Mexico Asks for an Emergency Session of International Olympic Committee," *New York Times*, Mar. 7, 1968, 13.

150. "Brundage Takes Steps," *New York Times*, Mar. 7, 1968, 13; "Five Olympic Committee Nations Seek a Special Meeting," *New York Times*, Mar. 12, 1968, 53.

151. The histories on the reciprocal sporting relationship between New Zealand and South Africa are lamentably few. For a concise exposition on New Zealand's tours of South Africa with particular emphasis on cricket and rugby, see Richard Thompson, *Retreat from Apartheid: New Zealand's Sporting Contacts with South Africa* (London: Oxford University Press, 1975). For a solid overview

of the "Stop the Seventy Tour," which occurred during the 1969–1970 season, see Hain, *Don't Play with Apartheid*.

152. "Brundage Calls Executive Unit to April Session," *New York Times*, Mar. 13, 1968, 57; "Cambodia Not to Take Part in Olympics at Mexico City," *New York Times*, Mar. 20, 1968, 54; "So. Africa Gets Accreditation; U.S. Olympic Training Is Set," *New York Times*, Apr. 3, 1968, 57; "Negro Athlete to Carry Flag for So. Africa at Olympics," *New York Times*, Apr. 15, 1968, 53.

153. "Brundage Stands Firm on So. Africa," *New York Times*, Mar. 24, 1968, V: 14.

154. "Brundage, in So. Africa, Stirs Olympic Ban Talk," *New York Times*, Apr. 16, 1968, 59; "Brundage Leaves South Africa," *New York Times*, Apr. 20, 1968, 41.

155. Lloyd Garrison, "Olympic Committee Elders Weigh So. Africa Question," *New York Times*, Apr. 21, 1968, V: 1; "No Ruling on So. Africa by IOC Yet," *Chicago Tribune*, Apr. 21, 1968, II: 8.

156. Tex Maule, "Switcheroo from Yes to Nyet," *Sports Illustrated*, Apr. 29, 1968, 28.

157. "Wants S. Africa Out of the Olympics," *Chicago Tribune*, Apr. 22, 1968, III: 1, 5; Lloyd Garrison, "Olympic Unit, in Reversal, Votes to Bar South Africa," *New York Times*, Apr. 22, 1968, 1, 62.

158. Maule, "Switcheroo from Yes to Nyet," 28.

159. "S. African Says Olympic Officials Should Resign," *Chicago Tribune*, Apr. 23, 1968, III: 2.

160. "I.O.C. Won't Be Reliable: South Africa," *Chicago Tribune*, Apr. 22, 1968, III: 1.

161. "The Olympics: Invitation Withdrawn," *Time*, May 3, 1968, 67.

162. "Reversal in Lausanne," *New York Times*, Apr. 22, 1968, 46.

163. "Ban on Soviet Urged," *New York Times*, Apr. 24, 1968, 35.

164. "The Eclipse of the Olympic Ideal," *Chicago Tribune*, Apr. 23, 1968, 14.

165. "Favorable Vote Seen as Certain," *New York Times*, Apr. 23, 1968, 53; "S. Africa Out of Olympics," *Chicago Tribune*, Apr. 24, 1968, III: 1, 4; "Result Is Decided Early in Polling," *New York Times*, Apr. 24, 1968, 35; Thomas J. Hamilton, "Bid Is Withdrawn after 41–13 Vote," *New York Times*, Apr. 30, 1968, 59.

166. "'Will Accept It,'" *Chicago Tribune*, Apr. 24, 1968, 4.

167. Nixon, *Homelands, Harlem and Hollywood*, 61.

168. Arthur Daley, "A Question of Survival," *New York Times*, Apr. 23, 1968, 53.

169. "Two Negro Runners Change Attitude about Boycott," *New York Times*, Apr. 24, 1968, 35.

170. "Olympian Retreat," *Newsweek*, May 6, 1968, 90.

171. Gross, "The Greeks Had a Word for It."

172. Edwards, *Revolt of the Black Athlete*, 93.

173. "Foreign Trips Set for So. Africans," *New York Times*, Apr. 30, 1968, 59.

174. "African Olympic Groups Asked to Rescind Decisions," *New York Times*, May 3, 1968, 59. Note, in the article Ganga's name was spelled "Kanga."

175. "Olympian Retreat," *Newsweek*, May 6, 1968, 90.

176. "4 Countries Enter Olympics Making Total a Record 110," *New York Times*, July 24, 1968, 38.

177. Lipsyte, "Return of the Springbok"; Letter to the Editor, *New York Times*, Mar. 10, 1968, IV: 15.

178. Bose, *Sporting Colours*, 73.

179. Furlong, "A Bad Week for Mr. B.," 21.

180. Neil Amdur, "New Status for Olympic Athletes Urged," *New York Times*, Apr. 25, 1968, 58.

181. For a concise and coherent explanation of Vorster's policy, see Joan Brickhill, *Race against Race: South Africa's "Multinational" Sport Fraud* (London: International Defence and Aid Fund, 1976); Lapchick, *The Politics of Race and International Sport*, 208–9; Robert Archer, "An Exceptional Case: Politics and Sport in South Africa's Townships," in *Sport in Africa*, ed. Baker and Mangan, 229.

182. Nixon, *Homelands, Harlem and Hollywood*, 151; Spá et al., *Television in the Olympics*, 105.

5. Tribulations and the Trials

1. Dave Anderson, "Negro Athletes Apprehensive, but Compete in Meet Anyway," *New York Times*, Feb. 17, 1968, 19; emphasis mine.

2. "Mailbox: Sports and Civil Rights," *New York Times*, Feb. 25, 1968, V: 2.

3. C. Gerald Fraser, "Black Athletes Are Cautioned Not to Cross Lines," *New York Times*, Feb. 16, 1968, 41.

4. Lipsyte, "After Thermopylae, What?"

5. "Hayes, Unseld, White, Murphy Eye Olympics," *Pittsburgh Courier*, March 30, 1968, 15.

6. Sam Goldaper, "Alcindor Clarifies TV Remark, Criticizes Racial Bias in U.S.," *New York Times*, July 23, 1968, 31.

7. Clint Wilson Jr., "Should Alcindor Be Shut-Up?" *Los Angeles Sentinel*, Sept. 19, 1968, B2.

8. Letter to the Editor, *New York Times*, Apr. 28, 1968, IV: 19.

9. Hazel Carby, "The Multicultural Wars," in *Black Popular Culture* (Seattle: Bay Press, 1992), 195.

10. Hall, "What Is This 'Black' in Black Popular Culture?" 30.

11. Kelley, "'We Are Not What We Seem,'" 39.

12. Gilmore, *Gender and Jim Crow*, xviii.

13. Anne McClintock, *Imperial Leather: Race, Gender, and Sexuality in the Colonial Contest* (New York: Routledge, 1995), 352.

14. Hall, *Feminism and Sporting Bodies*, 101; Mariah Burton Nelson, *The Stronger Women Get, the More Men Love Football: Sexism and the American Culture of Sports* (New York: Harcourt Brace, 1994), 6.

15. Paul Gilroy, "It's a Family Affair: Black Culture and the Trope of Kinship," in *Small Acts*, 194.

16. Derrick Bell, *Faces at the Bottom of the Well* (New York: Basic Books, 1992), 109–26.

17. Bell, *Faces at the Bottom of the Well*, 98–99.

18. "The Olympic Jolt: 'Hell no, don't go!'" *Life*, vol. 64, Mar. 15, 1968, 11, 20.

19. "The Olympic Jolt," 22.

20. "The Olympic Jolt," 23.

21. Edwards, *The Struggle That Must Be*, 179.

22. "The Olympic Jolt," 23.

23. Kobena Mercer, "Black Hair/Style Politics," in *Welcome to the Jungle: New Positions in Black Cultural Studies* (New York: Routledge, 1994), 102. See also Robin D. G. Kelley, "Looking for the 'Real' Nigga: Social Scientists Construct the Ghetto," in *Yo' Mama's Disfunktional! Fighting the Culture Wars in Urban America* (Boston: Beacon Press, 1997), 29–30.

24. Mercer, "Black Hair/Style Politics," 98, 101; emphasis in original.

25. Mercer, "Black Hair/Style Politics," 98–99. Jeffrey Sammons makes an interesting point about the aesthetics of athletic style, noting that "a major

criticism of today's black athletes is their concern with style, articulated by Woody Harrelson's character in the feature film 'White Men Can't Jump,' that blacks value looking good over winning." Sammons, "'Race' and Sport," 256.

26. Andrew Ross, *No Respect: Intellectuals and Popular Culture* (New York: Routledge, 1989), 68.

27. Arnold Hano, "The Black Rebel Who 'Whitelists' the Olympics," *New York Times Magazine*, May 12, 1968, VI: 32. While Edwards's disdain for figures such as Owens fit with his ideologies on the designation "black," it also allowed him to pave a clearer path for himself as a pivotal political leader, exemplifying what Hazel Carby, in her discussion of Du Bois's renowned rejection of Booker T. Washington's ideologies, has termed "political displacement." See Hazel Carby, *Race Men* (Cambridge, Mass.: Harvard University Press, 1998), 41.

28. Hano, "The Black Rebel Who 'Whitelists' the Olympics," 32, 39; emphasis in original.

29. Hano, "The Black Rebel Who 'Whitelists' the Olympics," 41.

30. Hano, "The Black Rebel Who 'Whitelists' the Olympics," 41; emphasis in original.

31. Hano, "The Black Rebel Who 'Whitelists' the Olympics," 41.

32. Bill Nunn Jr., "Change of Pace," *Pittsburgh Courier*, Oct. 26, 1968, 14.

33. "Black Athletes, Brundage Talk, 'Kiss and Make Up,'" *Chicago Daily Defender*, Sept. 26, 1968, 42; "Brundage Makes Olympic Peace," *Baltimore Afro-American*, Sept. 28, 1968, 24.

34. Hano, "The Black Rebel Who 'Whitelists' the Olympics," 46.

35. Henry Louis Taylor, "The Hidden Face of Racism," *American Quarterly* 47, no. 3 (Sept. 1995): 396–97. "Occupational exclusion," according to Taylor, is the "process of keeping blacks from competing with whites in the labor market [and] is the foundation upon which American racism is built."

36. Hano, "The Black Rebel Who 'Whitelists' the Olympics," 50.

37. Charles Maher, "Sports: A World Where Blacks Are Just a Little More Equal," *Los Angeles Times*, Mar. 24, 1968, D1, 8.

38. Charles Maher, "Blacks Physically Superior? Some Say They're 'Hungrier,'" *Los Angeles Times*, Mar. 25, 1968, III: 1, 4.

39. Charles Maher, "Do Blacks Have a Physical Advantage? Scientists Differ," *Los Angeles Times*, Mar. 26, 1968, III: 1, 7, emphasis in original; Charles Maher, "Blacks' Arms OK —but They Run Better," *Los Angeles Times*, Mar. 28, 1968, III: 1, 11.

40. Charles Maher, "Off the Field, Players Do Not Mix So Well," *Los Angeles Times*, Mar. 29, 1968, III: 1, 6.

41. Maher, "Off the Field, Players Do Not Mix So Well," 6.

42. "Should Negroes Boycott the Olympics?" *Ebony* 23, no. 5, Mar. 1968, 110–11.

43. "Should Negroes Boycott the Olympics?" 112.

44. "Should Negroes Boycott the Olympics?" 112.

45. "Should Negroes Boycott the Olympics?" 114.

46. "Poll Reveals Range of Boycott Opinion," *Ebony* 23, no. 5, Mar. 1968, 113.

47. "Should Negroes Boycott the Olympics?" 114.

48. Edwards, *The Revolt of the Black Athlete*, appendix E, 184.

49. Edwards, *The Revolt of the Black Athlete*, appendix E, 190.

50. "Humphrey Urges Olympic Harmony," *New York Times*, Mar. 30, 1968, 42.

51. Edwards, *The Revolt of the Black Athlete*, appendix E, 190.

52. John Underwood, "The Non-Trial Trials," *Sports Illustrated*, July 8, 1968, 11.

53. Frank Litsky, "Resort Spends $250,000 to Stage Track Meet," *New York Times*, June 26, 1968, 56. Interestingly, in Mexico City, the first "official" controversy was whether Americans congregated too early in Tahoe. Adrian Metcalfe, an Olympic silver medalist in Mexico for British television, raised the issue when he asked USOC officials during a press conference if the high-altitude training in July violated the rule that a team is not allowed to congregate until twenty-eight days before the Opening Ceremony. Paul Zimmerman, "Olympus Rages," *New York Post*, Oct. 8, 1968, 105.

54. Ashe, *A Hard Road to Glory:... since 1946*, 174.

55. Kelley, "'We Are Not What We Seem,'" 51–52.

56. Underwood, "The Non-Trial Trials," 13.

57. "U.S. Olympic Boycott Leaders Remain Undecided on Course," *New York Times*, June 23, 1968, V: 1; Underwood, "The Non-Trial Trials," 13.

58. "U.S. Olympic Boycott Leaders Remain Undecided on Course," V: 1, 9.

59. Underwood, "The Non-Trial Trials," 13; emphasis in original.

60. Pete Axthelm, "The Angry Black Athlete," *Newsweek*, July 15, 1968, 56; emphasis in original.

61. Axthelm, "The Angry Black Athlete," 56; emphasis mine.

62. Axthelm, "The Angry Black Athlete," 57–59.

63. Michael MacCambridge, *The Franchise: A History of Sports Illustrated Magazine* (New York: Hyperion, 1997), 133–35.

64. Jack Olsen, "The Black Athlete—A Shameful Story: The Cruel Deception," *Sports Illustrated*, July 1, 1968, 12. The series ran weekly throughout July and eventually became a book, *The Black Athlete: A Shameful Story* (New York: Time-Life Books, 1968).

65. Linda D. Williams, "Sportswomen in Black and White: Sports History from an Afro-American Perspective," in *Women, Media and Sport: Challenging Gender Values*, ed. Pamela J. Creedon (Thousand Oaks, Calif.: Sage Publications, 1994), 50.

66. MacCambridge, *The Franchise*, 159.

67. Ric Roberts, "Racism in Sports," *Pittsburgh Courier*, Aug. 3, 1968, 15.

68. "'The Shameful Story' of the Black Athlete in U.S."; and Letter to the Editor, "Re: SI Story"; both in *New York Amsterdam News*, July 13, 1968, 31.

69. MacCambridge, *The Franchise*, 163.

70. Quoted in MacCambridge, *The Franchise*, 163.

71. MacCambridge, *The Franchise*, 163.

72. David Wiggins, "The Notion of Double-Consciousness and the Involvement of Black Athletes in American Sport," in *Glory Bound*, ed. Wiggins, 216–17.

73. See Nancie Caraway, *Segregated Sisterhood: Racism and the Politics of American Feminism* (Knoxville: University of Tennessee Press, 1991); and Patricia Hill Collins, *Black Feminist Thought: Knowledge, Consciousness, and the Politics of Empowerment* (New York: Routledge, 1990).

74. Christine Stansell, "White Feminists and Black Realities: The Politics of Authenticity," *Race-ing Justice, En-Gendering Power: Essays on Anita Hill, Clarence Thomas, and the Construction of Social Reality*, ed. Toni Morrison (New York: Pantheon Books, 1992), 251–53; Vron Ware, *Beyond the Pale: White Women, Racism and History* (London: Verso, 1992).

75. Clayborne Carson, *In Struggle: SNCC and the Black Awakening of the 1960s* (Cambridge, Mass.: Harvard University Press, 1995), 147–48.

76. Manning Marable, "Clarence Thomas and the Crisis of Black Political Culture," in *Race-ing Justice, En-Gendering Power*, ed. Morrison, 80.

77. Elaine Brown, *A Taste of Power: A Black Woman's Story* (New York: Anchor Books, 1992), 357.

78. For an excellent overview of Audrey Patterson-Tyler, see her obituary in *Jet*, Sept. 9, 1996, 53–54.

79. Quoted in Mary Jo Festle, *Playing Nice: Politics and Apologies in Women's Sports* (New York: Columbia University Press, 1996), 60.

80. Festle, *Playing Nice*, 60–61.

81. Marable, "Clarence Thomas and the Crisis of Black Political Culture," 74; emphasis in original. Marable illustrates his point with Bill Cosby, Douglas Wilder, Oprah Winfrey, and, of course, Michael Jordan.

82. Festle, *Playing Nice*, 62.

83. Cahn, *Coming on Strong*, 39. See also Cindy Himes Gissendanner, "African-American Women and Competitive Sport, 1920–1960," in *Women, Sport, and Culture*, ed. Susan Birrell and Cheryl L. Cole (Champaign: Human Kinetics, 1994), 83.

84. Edwin B. Henderson, "Negro Women in Sports," *Negro History Bulletin* 15 (Dec. 1951): 55. This entire issue of the *Bulletin* was devoted to sports.

85. Elaine Tyler May, *Homeward Bound: American Families in the Cold War Era* (New York: Basic Books, 1988), 16–18; Karal Ann Marling, *As Seen on TV: The Visual Culture of Everyday Life in the 1950s* (Cambridge, Mass.: Harvard University Press, 1994), 281.

86. Many women, for example, continued to work at the end of World War II despite the return of the "original" workforce, and those at home enjoyed a large enough degree of domestic economic power to incite many male-scribed articles in *Playboy* and *Look* magazines fearing a female economic takeover. See Barbara Ehrenreich, *The Hearts of Men: American Dreams and the Flight from Commitment* (New York: Anchor Books, 1983), 42, 37.

87. Quoted in Cahn, *Coming on Strong*, 114–15. The finish of the 800-meters in the 1928 Olympics, in which several competitors fell to the ground in exhaustion, proved to be an especially worrisome example, indicating to many that such competition was too taxing for women and pushing the IOC to eliminate such distance events—the 800-meters did not return until 1960. Didrikson's performance in 1932 at the Los Angeles Olympics somewhat averted these fears, because the young Texan handily won gold in javelin and hurdles and silver in the high jump and became a favorite of sportswriters for both her disarming sense of humor and her seemingly limitless athletic ability. See David

Wallechinsky, *The Complete Book of the Olympics* (New York: Penguin Books, 1988), 162–63.

88. Cahn, *Coming on Strong*, 111. One official, Norman Cox, suggested that the IOC create a hermaphrodite category. For an extended discussion comparing swimming with track and field, see Cahn, *Coming on Strong*, 129–30.

89. Tricia Rose, *Black Noise: Rap Music and Black Culture in Contemporary Culture* (Hanover, N.H.: Wesleyan University Press, 1994), 168. See also Sander L. Gilman, "Black Bodies, White Bodies: Toward an Iconography of Female Sexuality in Late Nineteenth-Century Art, Medicine and Literature," in *"Race," Writing, and Difference*, ed. Henry Louis Gates Jr. (Chicago: University of Chicago Press, 1986), 223–40; James Clifford, "Negrophilia," in *A History of New French Literature*, ed. Denis Hollier (Cambridge, Mass.: Harvard University Press, 1989), 901–7; and Marianna Torgovnick, *Gone Primitive: Savage Intellects, Modern Lives* (Chicago: University of Chicago Press, 1990).

90. Wini Breines, *Young, White, and Miserable: Growing Up Female in the Fifties* (Boston: Beacon Press, 1992), 96–97.

91. Patricia J. Murphy quoted in Williams, "Sportswomen in Black and White," 47.

92. Grant Jarvie and Joseph Maguire, *Sport and Leisure in Social Thought* (London: Routledge, 1994), 173. On the need for feminist scholarship to encompass a more finely tuned racial perception, see Evelyn Brooks Higginbotham, "African-American Women's History and the Metalanguage of Race," *Signs* (winter 1992): 251–74; and Hazel Carby, "'On the Threshold of Woman's Era': Lynching, Empire, and Sexuality in Black Feminist Theory," in *"Race," Writing, and Difference*, ed. Gates, 302.

93. Cahn, *Coming on Strong*, 37.

94. Collins, *Black Feminist Thought*, 78–82.

95. Cahn, *Coming on Strong*, 118–19; Ashe, *A Hard Road to Glory: A History of the African-American Athlete, 1919–1945* (New York: Armistad, 1978), 74–79; Gissendanner, "African-American Women and Competitive Sport," 85–86; Nolan Thaxton, "A Documentary Analysis of Competitive Track and Field for Women at Tuskegee Institute and Tennessee State University," unpublished doctoral dissertation, Springfield College, 1970; Michael Davis, *Black American Women in Olympic Track and Field: A Complete Illustrated Reference* (Jefferson, N.C.: McFarland and Company, 1992), 1. According to Davis, both Stokes and Pickett qualified for the U.S. squad in 1932 as members of the

400-meter relay team, but in a "controversial and unexplained decision," coaches replaced them with two white women they had previously beaten in time trials. In 1936, both qualified; Stokes again was replaced by a white competitor, while Pickett competed.

96. Mariah Burton Nelson, *Are We Winning Yet? How Women Are Changing Sports and Sports Are Changing Women* (New York: Random House, 1991), 158–59. Interestingly, Jessie Abbot, Cleveland Abbot's daughter, founded the Tennessee program. See Gissendanner, "African-American Women and Competitive Sport," 86.

97. Davis, *Black American Women in Olympic Track and Field*, 112. Temple designed his clinic, which ran for one month each summer, to impart track and field fundamentals to high school women. It cost each athlete only the transportation to get to the campus, and while the college was not later required to accept the participants as students, 90 percent did eventually attend the school. See Adkins, "The Development of Negro Female Olympic Talent," 33–34.

98. Davis, *Black American Women in Olympic Track and Field*, 114–15.

99. Barbara Heilman, "Like Nothing Else in Tennessee," *Sports Illustrated*, Nov. 14, 1960, 48. Note that while undeniably intended to be flattering, the comparisons of Rudolph to a gazelle work well within the inference that black athletic ability is as natural as that of the delicate African deer.

100. Heilman, "Like Nothing Else in Tennessee," 50.

101. Heilman, "Like Nothing Else in Tennessee," 52.

102. Davis, *Black American Women in Olympic Track and Field*, 125.

103. Quoted in Davis, *Black American Women in Olympic Track and Field*, 127.

104. Davis, *Black American Women in Olympic Track and Field*, 127–28.

105. Quoted in Davis, *Black American Women in Olympic Track and Field*, 146.

106. Wyomia Tyus, "Athletes in Gold, Silver, and Bronze," interview with Rick Ortiz, Long Beach, Calif., local access cable, 1993, Amateur Athletic Foundation, Los Angeles.

107. "Olympic Win Would Put Wyomia in Special Class," *Baltimore Afro-American*, Oct. 12, 1968, 24; emphasis mine.

108. Quoted in Wiggins, "The Notion of Double-Consciousness and the Involvement of Black Athletes in American Sport," 217.

109. Nellie Y. McKay, "Remembering Anita Hill and Clarence Thomas:

What Really Happened When One Black Woman Spoke Out," *Race-ing Justice, En-Gendering Power*, ed. Morrison, 282.

110. Paul Gilroy, *The Black Atlantic: Modernity and Double Consciousness* (Cambridge, Mass.: Harvard University Press, 1993), 85.

111. "Negro Vote Barring Games Boycott Told," *New York Times*, Aug. 1, 1968, 35.

112. "Edwards Hints of Plan," *New York Times*, Aug. 1, 1968, 35.

113. C. Gerald Fraser, "Negroes Call Off Boycott, Reshape Protest," *New York Times*, Sept. 1, 1968, V: 1, 4; "U.S. Olympic Boycott Leaders Remain Undecided on Course," *New York Times*, June 23, 1968, V: 1, 9.

114. Fraser, "Negroes Call Off Boycott, Reshape Protest"; "Athletes Ending Olympic Boycott," *Pittsburgh Courier*, Sept. 14, 1968, 1, 4. See Edwards, *The Revolt of the Black Athlete*, 98–100, and appendix D, for Edwards's written statement to the National Conference on Black Power in Philadelphia.

115. Howie Evans, "Sort of Sporty," *New York Amsterdam News*, Sept. 21, 1968, 33.

116. "Negroes Search for Gold," *Los Angeles Sentinel*, Sept. 26, 1968, B2.

117. "The Olympic 'Boycott,'" 6; "Stars Going to Olympics," 15; "End of the Season Good Deal," 6; all in *Pittsburgh Courier*, Sept. 21, 1968.

118. "Proposed Olympic Boycott Off; No Support: Edwards," 2; "The Proposed Boycott," 28; both in *Chicago Daily Defender*, Sept. 3, 1968.

119. A. S. "Doc" Young, "Good Morning Sports!" *Chicago Daily Defender*, Sept. 10, 1968, 24.

120. "Athletes Ending Olympic Boycott."

121. Fraser, "Negroes Call Off Boycott, Reshape Protest."

122. Robert Lipsyte, "The Spirit of the Olympics," *New York Times*, Aug. 1, 1968. Although the oarsmen indicated that they issued their statement in direct response to the boycott proposal, they waited until they had qualified for the Olympics before announcing it.

123. Lipsyte, "The Spirit of the Olympics."

124. "Athletes Take Breathing Lessons," *New York Times*, Sept. 15, 1968, V: 9.

125. Neil Amdur, "Evans Defeats James in Olympic Trial—Beamon Is Victor," *New York Times*, Sept. 15, 1968, V: 1, 9.

126. John Underwood, "Triumph and Tragedy at Tahoe," *Sports Illustrated*, Sept. 21, 1968, 19; emphasis mine. Much was made in the press about the

background of Carlos, in particular. For example, *Life* magazine, which noted that both Smith and Carlos were the sons of migrant laborers, emphasized that Carlos's father "ran a repair shop in Harlem, where John as a 10-year-old shined the shoes of white bill collectors. In his earliest contact with white men John Carlos bowed his head." See "Amid Gold Medals, Raised Black Fists," *Life*, vol. 65, no. 18, Nov. 1, 1968, 67.

127. "America's 'Finest' Track Team Ready for Mexico," *Baltimore Afro-American*, Sept. 21, 1968, 18.

6. "That's My Flag"

1. "U.S. Spikers Reach Mexico," *San Jose Mercury News*, Oct. 7, 1968, 61–62; George Strickler, "Olympic Site Ready," *San Jose Mercury News*, Oct. 8, 1968, III: 1.

2. U.S. Olympians United in Mexico," *San Jose Mercury News*, Oct. 8, 1968, 47.

3. Neil Amdur, "Soviet Reaffirms Stand on Barring South Africa from Olympics," *New York Times*, Oct. 11, 1968, 58.

4. "Brundage Is Opposed as Olympic Chief," *Chicago Tribune*, Oct. 10, 1968, III: 3; "Brundage Olympic Grip Challenged," *San Jose Mercury News*, Oct. 10, 1968, 71; "Brundage Reelected Chief; Big Trek to Olympics Begins," *Chicago Tribune*, Oct. 11, 1968, III: 1. For a superb overview of Brundage's presidency, see Guttmann, *The Games Must Go On*.

5. Sam Lacy, "Mexican Mixers," *Baltimore Afro-American*, Oct. 19, 1968, 19.

6. George Strickler, "Officials Work to Avert Confusion," *Chicago Tribune*, Oct. 11, 1968, III: 1.

7. "Refused to Kill Athlete; He's Thrown," *Chicago Tribune*, Oct. 17, 1968, III: 3; John Underwood, "A High Time for Sprinters—and Kenyans," *Sports Illustrated*, Oct. 28, 1968, 19.

8. "The Television Power of the 1996 Atlanta Centennial Olympic Games: A Research Report," Atlanta Committee for the Olympic Games, bid conclusion, 1992. The share figure represents the percentage of active sets that were tuned in to the broadcast; one rating point represents 1 percent of the television households in the United States.

9. Axthelm, "The Angry Black Athlete."

10. "Olympic Reaction," *Los Angeles Times*, Oct. 18, 1968, 2.

11. Edwards, *The Struggle That Must Be*, 189; emphasis in original.

12. Charles Maher, "Blacks Balk at Getting Medals from Brundage," *Los Angeles Times*, Oct. 16, 1968, III: 1; "No Medals by Avery," *San Jose Mercury News*, Oct. 16, 1968, 91; "America's Blacks Don't Share Winner's Circle with Brundage," *New York Times*, Oct. 16, 1968, 52.

13. "Amid Gold Medals, Raised Black Fists," *Life*, Nov. 1, 1968. According to the story, Evans raised his own gloved right fist from the stands during the Smith-Carlos action, although he did so in relative anonymity.

14. John J. MacAloon, "Double Visions: Olympic Games and American Culture," in *The Olympic Games in Transition*, ed. Jeffrey O. Segrave and Donald Chu (Champaign: Human Kinetics, 1988), 279–80. See also, John J. MacAloon, *This Great Symbol: Pierre de Coubertin and the Origins of the Modern Olympic Games* (Chicago: University of Chicago Press, 1981); MacAloon, "Sociation and Sociability in Political Celebrations"; MacAloon, "Olympic Games and the Theory of Spectacle in Modern Societies"; and Spá et al., *Television in the Olympics*, 83–91.

15. "The Olympics Extra Heat," *Newsweek*, Oct. 28, 1968, 74.

16. Maher, "Blacks Balk at Getting Medals from Brundage"; "No Medals by Avery"; "America's Blacks Don't Share Winner's Circle with Brundage."

17. Steve Cady, "Owens Recalls 1936 Sprinter's Ordeal," *New York Times*, Oct. 17, 1968, 59.

18. Louis Duino, "Smith, Carlos Qualify; Oerter Wins," *San Jose Mercury News*, Oct. 16, 1968, 91, 92.

19. Note that at the Olympic Trials in Lake Tahoe, John Carlos ran a 19.7 that was never officially recorded, because he raced with illegal "brush spikes."

20. Toni Morrison, "The Official Story: Dead Man Golfing," in *Birth of a Nation'hood*, ed. Morrison and Brodsky Lacour, xx.

21. Hall, "What Is This 'Black' in Black Popular Culture?" 27.

22. Olympic coverage, ABC archives, Oct. 17, 1968, tape 16, 8:39–8:44. Note that others, beginning with Harry Edwards, offer a grammatically sanitized version of this famous quotation.

23. Olympic coverage, ABC archives, Oct. 17, 1968, tape 16, 8:41–8:44.

24. Anderson, *Imagined Communities*, 135.

25. Hall, "What Is This 'Black' in Black Popular Culture?" 27.

26. Mike Marqusee, "Sport and Stereotype: From Role Model to Muhammad Ali," *Race and Class* 36, no. 4 (Apr.-June 1995): 21.

27. Olympic coverage, ABC archives, Oct. 17, 1968, tape 16, 8:41–8:44.

28. Olympic coverage, ABC archives, Oct. 17, 1968, tape 16, 8:44–9:00.

29. Paul Zimmerman, "Gambling Seagren Takes Pole Vault at 17½," *Los Angeles Times*, Oct. 17, 1968, III: 1, 4; Shirley Povich, "'Black Power' on Victory Stand," *Los Angeles Times*, Oct. 17, 1968, III: 1, 4.

30. Povich, "'Black Power' on Victory Stand," 4.

31. Joseph M. Sheehan, "Smith Takes Olympic 200 Meters and Seagren Captures Pole Vault for U.S.," *New York Times*, Oct. 17, 1968, 58.

32. "2 Accept Medals Wearing Black Gloves," *New York Times*, Oct. 17, 1968, 59.

33. George Strickler, "World Track Marks Fall in 3 Events at Olympics," *Chicago Tribune*, Oct. 17, 1968, III: 1, 3.

34. "Gold Medal for Smith," *San Jose Mercury News*, Oct. 17, 1968, 1; Louis Duino, "TOMMIE IN RECORD 200 WIN," *San Jose Mercury News*, Oct. 17, 1968, 73–74.

35. Paul Zimmerman, "Blacks Take Their Stand," *New York Post*, Oct. 17, 1968, 1 (back cover).

36. "IOC Calls Special Session," *New York Post*, Oct. 17, 1968, 1. Barnes temporarily replaced Arthur Lentz as USOC executive director during the Mexico City Olympics, because Lentz was detained in the United States with an undisclosed illness.

37. Quoted in "Olympic Reaction," *Los Angeles Times*, Oct. 18, 1968, 2.

38. "U.S. Apologizes for Protest by Blacks," *Chicago Tribune*, Oct. 18, 1968, III: 1; "U.S. Apologizes for Athletes, 'Discourtesy,'" *Los Angeles Times*, Oct. 18, 1968, III: 1.

39. "U.S. Apologizes for Athletes, 'Discourtesy,'" 1, 7.

40. "U.S. Apologizes for Protest by Blacks."

41. "U.S. Committee 'Sorry' about Discourtesy: Won't Stand for Repetition," *Chicago Tribune*, Oct. 18, 1968, 3; "Yanks Apologize for Race Protest," *San Jose Mercury News*, Oct. 18, 1968, 57.

42. "Yanks Apologize for Race Protest." As acting director, Barnes became the point person for the USOC in regard to Smith and Carlos. However, Arthur Lentz did issue a statement pertaining to the matter, indicating that the usual practice for such an action was to send the offending athletes home.

43. "U.S. Leaders Warn of Penalties for Further Black Power Acts," *New York Times*, Oct. 18, 1968, 55; Neil Amdur, "Davenport Gains Seventh Track Gold Medal for U.S.," *New York Times*, Oct. 18, 1968, 54.

44. "U.S. Committee 'Sorry' about Discourtesy."

45. "Amid Gold Medals, Raised Black Fists," 67.

46. "Reactions among Athletes," *New York Times*, Oct. 18, 1968, 55; "Black-Fist Display Gets Varied Reaction in Olympic Village," *Los Angeles Times*, Oct. 18, 1968, III: 1.

47. The *Baltimore Afro-American* ran a feature on Waddell, celebrating "the rare opportunity to root for a hometowner." Sam Lacy, "D.C.'s Dr. Waddell in Action Today at Olympics," *Baltimore Afro-American*, Oct. 19, 1968, 3.

48. Tom Waddell and Dick Schaap, *Gay Olympian: The Life and Death of Dr. Tom Waddell* (New York: Knopf, 1996), 104–9; emphasis mine.

49. Pete Axthelm et al., "The Olympics: Race Time at Mexico City," *Newsweek*, Oct. 28, 1968, 80; "Amid Gold Medals, Raised Black Fists," 68.

50. George Lipsitz, "'Frantic to Join ... the Japanese Army': Beyond the Black-White Binary," in *The Possessive Investment in Whiteness: How White People Profit from Identity Politics* (Philadelphia: Temple University Press, 1998), 184; "Reactions among Athletes," 55; "Black-Fist Display Gets Varied Reaction in Olympic Village"; "'Black Power' at the Olympics," *U.S. News and World Report*, Oct. 28, 1968, 10; "The Olympics Extra Heat," *Newsweek*, Oct. 28, 1968, 79; "Smith, Carlos Lead Press on Merry Chase in Airport," *Chicago Daily Defender*, Oct. 22, 1968, 26.

51. Jim Murray, "Excuse My Glove," *Los Angeles Times*, Oct. 18, 1968, III: 1.

52. John Hall, "It Takes All Kinds," *Los Angeles Times*, Oct. 18, 1968, III: 3.

53. Clint Wilson Jr., "Olympic Games' Events Most Disturbing," *Los Angeles Sentinel*, Oct. 24, 1968, 4B.

54. Louis Duino, "Americans Boo Smith, Carlos," *San Jose Mercury News*, Oct. 18, 1968, 58.

55. Olympic coverage, ABC archives, Oct. 17, 1968, tape 16, 8:41–8:44.

56. Department of State telegram, Oct. 18, 1968, National Archives and Records Administration, Record Group 59, Box 355.

57. Henry Louis Gates Jr., preface to *Black Male*, ed. Gates, 12. Gates attributes "already-read text" to Barbara Johnson.

58. Kobena Mercer and Isaac Julien, "True Confessions," in *Black Male*, ed. Gates, 197.

59. "Blacks All but Sweep Olympic Runs," *Pittsburgh Courier*, Oct. 26, 1968, 15.

60. "There's Gold in Mexico City," *Los Angeles Sentinel*, Oct. 10, 1968, B2.

61. Brad Pye Jr., "Olympiad Opens in Mexico on Note of Color," *Los Angeles Sentinel*, Oct. 17, 1968.

62. Brad Pye Jr., "Quiet and Loud Protests," *Los Angeles Sentinel*, Oct. 24, 1968, B1.

63. J. Paul Addleston, KHA, Oct. 18, 1968, Museum of Radio and Television, New York.

64. Danny Baxter, KHA, Oct. 18, 1968, Museum of Radio and Broadcast, New York.

65. Paul Zimmerman, "Dispute Dims U.S. Gold," *New York Post*, Oct. 19, 1968, 1 (sports.)

66. Joseph M. Sheehan, "2 Black Power Advocates Ousted from Olympics," *New York Times*, Oct. 19, 1968, 1, 45.

67. Department of State telegram, Oct. 18, 1968.

68. "Black Power Show Causes Banishment," *Chicago Tribune*, Oct. 19, 1968, 1.

69. Charles Maher, "U.S. Expels Smith, Carlos from Olympic Team," *Los Angeles Times*, Oct. 19, 1968, II: 1.

70. "The Natural Right of Being a Slob," *Chicago Tribune*, Oct. 19, 1968, 10.

71. John H. Sengstacke, "Olympic Black Power," *Chicago Daily Defender*, Oct. 21, 1968, 13.

72. "The Olympics: Black Complaint," *Time*, Oct. 25, 1968, 62–63; emphasis in original.

73. Dr. Ernst Jokl, physiologist and statistician, of the University of Kentucky, quoted in Kenny Moore, "Giants on the Earth," *Sports Illustrated*, June 29, 1987, 48.

74. Zimmerman, "Dispute Dims U.S. Gold"; Neil Amdur, "Beamon's 29-2½ Long Jump and Evans's 43.8-Second 400 Set World Marks," *New York Times*, Oct. 19, 1968, 44. After returning from Mexico City, Carlos himself supported such a notion at one point, indicating that the reason other athletes did not follow suit with black-gloved fists was that "they have minds of their own. This is an individual thing." See Scott Moore and Wes Mathis, "Banished Athletes Return," *San Jose Mercury News*, Oct. 22, 1968, 2.

75. "The Long Jump," *Sports Illustrated*, Oct. 28, 1968, 18; Underwood, "A High Time for Sprinters—and Kenyans," 22.

76. Sheehan, "2 Black Power Advocates Ousted from Olympics."

77. Scott Maher, "U.S. Duo Banned," *Los Angeles Times*, Oct. 19, 1968, II: 3; Paul Zimmerman, "Bob Beamon in Long, Long Jump, Sets Record at 29-2½," *Los Angeles Times*, Oct. 19, 1968, II: 1; Louis Duino, "Evans Sizzles; Beamon Soars," *San Jose Mercury News*, Oct. 19, 1968, 67; Louis Duino, "Evans Scores 'Double' via Record, Humility," *San Jose Mercury News*, Oct. 19, 1968, 65.

78. "Some Negro Athletes Threaten to 'Go Home' along with Smith and Carlos," *New York Times*, Oct. 19, 1968, 45.

79. Duino, "Evans Scores 'Double' Via Record, Humility."

80. "Black Power Show Causes Banishment," *Chicago Tribune*, Oct. 19, 1968, 1; Zimmerman, "Dispute Dims U.S. Gold."

81. "Suspend Two U.S. Negroes from Games," *Chicago Tribune*, Oct. 19, 1968, 2; Maher, "U.S. Duo Banned"; Zimmerman, "Dispute Dims U.S. Gold"; Red Smith, "The Black Berets," in *The Red Smith Reader* (New York: Random House, 1982), 38–39.

82. Duino, "Evans Sizzles, Beamon Soars."

83. Duino, "Evans Scores 'Double' Via Record, Humility."

84. "U.S. Suspends Smith and Carlos," *New York Post*, Oct. 18, 1968, 1 (sports); Zimmerman, "Dispute Dims U.S. Gold"; "Amid Gold Medals, Raised Black Fists," 67.

85. "Amid Gold Medals, Raised Black Fists," 67.

86. "U.S. Athletes Set 5 Records and Win 4 Finals at Olympics," *New York Times*, Oct. 20, 1968, 1; "'White Ones, Too,' Connolly States," *New York Times*, Oct. 19, 1968, 45; Charles Maher, "U.S. Expels Smith, Carlos from Olympic Team," *Los Angeles Times*, Oct. 19, 1968, 1, 3; "Confusion, Shock Grip U.S. Squad after Pair Ousted," *Los Angeles Times*, Oct. 19, 1968, II: 1; "Smith Explains the Gesture," *New York Post*, Oct. 18, 1968, 1 (sports); "Pride and Precocity," *Time*, Oct. 25, 1968, 63; "Amid Gold Medals, Raised Black Fists," 67. Many athletes in addition to Walker, including Connolly and Smith, brought up the United States' refusal to dip its flag in deference to the host nation in the Opening Ceremony. In fact, Connolly claims to have refused to carry the flag during the ceremony in Mexico City, because the USOC forbade him to depart from tradition. See "Amid Gold Medals, Raised Black Fists," 67.

87. "U.S. Athletes Set 5 Records and Win 4 Finals at Olympics"; "'White Ones, Too,' Connolly States"; Maher, "U.S. Expels Smith, Carlos from Olympic

Team"; "Confusion, Shock Grip U.S. Squad after Pair Ousted"; "Smith Explains the Gesture"; "Pride and Precocity"; Steve Cady, "U.S. Boxers Spurn Racial Fights," *New York Times*, Oct. 23, 1968. In his later writings, Edwards vilifies Foreman in the role of the "good Negro" perhaps more than anyone, arguing that Foreman "was applauded, celebrated, and praised by U.S. Olympic officials, the white media, and much of the American public, after parading around the ring waving an American flag moments after being declared the gold medallist in the Olympic heavyweight division. But that's sports politics for you." Edwards, *The Struggle That Must Be*, 204.

88. "U.S. Suspends Pair," *New York Post*, Oct. 18, 1968, 1 (sports).

89. "Amid Gold Medals, Raised Black Fists," 68.

90. Paul Zimmerman, "The Protest," *New York Post*, Oct. 19, 1968, 71.

91. "'White Ones, Too,' Connolly States."

92. "'White Ones, Too,' Connolly States."

93. "Suspend Two U.S. Negroes from Games," *Chicago Tribune*, Oct. 19, 1968, 2; Maher, "U.S. Duo Banned."

94. Booker Griffin, "Some Untold Tales of Mexico City," *Los Angeles Sentinel*, Oct. 24, 1968, B5.

95. "U.S. Suspends Pair," *New York Post*; note that the article referred to Carlos's wife as Denise, which was actually the name of Smith's wife.

96. Zimmerman, "Dispute Dims U.S. Gold."

97. Department of State telegram, Oct. 18, 1968.

98. Department of State telegram, Oct. 22, 1968, National Archives and Records Administration, Record Group 59, Box 325.

99. Arthur Daley, "The Incident," *New York Times*, Oct. 20, 1968, V: 2.

100. Scott Moore and Wes Mathis, "Newsmen Outrun Smith and Carlos," *San Jose Mercury News*, Oct. 22, 1968, 1. The front-page story on the return home included two photos of Smith and Carlos at the airport.

101. Maher, "U.S. Duo Banned," 3. As Maher notes in his story, Holm was not the only Olympian ever sent home from the Olympics by the United States. For example, wrestler Charles Trible was dropped from the U.S. squad for not maintaining the proper weight for his event, and in Mexico City, cyclist Dave Mulkey was sent back to the United States for training violations.

102. "Athletes 'Sheep,' Says Ex-Olympian," *San Jose Mercury News*, Oct. 19, 1968, 65.

103. "Shake-Up of I.O.C. Urged by Sayre," *New York Times*, Oct. 26, 1968, 45.

104. "Black Olympians Given No Hearing, Muskie Declares," *Chicago Daily Defender*, Oct. 22, 1968, 19.

105. "Robinson Supports SJS Pair," *San Jose Mercury News*, Oct. 22, 1968, 44.

106. Wes Mathis, "SJS Blacks Want Bronzan Booted," *San Jose Mercury News*, Oct. 22, 1968, 41; "Dr. Clark Defends Bronzan," *San Jose Mercury News*, Oct. 23, 1968; Scott Moore, "Dr. Clark Praises Smith and Carlos," *San Jose Mercury News*, Oct. 19, 1968, 1, 2.

107. Louis Duino, "Aftermath in Mexico," *San Jose Mercury News*, Oct. 20, 1968, 76; Scott Moore and Wes Mathis, "Banished Runners Return," *San Jose Mercury News*, Oct. 22, 1968.

108. "Letters: Black Power and the Olympic Games," *New York Times*, Oct. 27, 1968, 2.

109. Griffin, "Some Untold Tales of Mexico City."

110. Wilson, "Olympic Games' Events Most Disturbing."

111. Maggie Hathaway, "A Woman's View," *Los Angeles Sentinel*, Oct. 24, 1968, B5.

112. Jack Tenner, "Let's Take a Look ... at Quotes and Questions," *Los Angeles Sentinel*, Oct. 24, 1968, A6.

113. Brad Pye Jr., "Olympics No Platform for Problems," *Los Angeles Sentinel*, Oct. 24, 1968, 2B.

114. "Life on a Roller Coaster," *Los Angeles Sentinel*, Oct. 24, 1968, A6.

115. "Olympic Special," *Baltimore Afro-American*, Oct. 12, 1968, 1.

116. "World Mark Set by Tom Smith," *Baltimore Afro-American*, Oct. 19, 1968, 18–19.

117. Sam Lacy, "Lacy Hits 'Protest' at Olympics," *Baltimore Afro-American*, Oct. 19, 1968, 1, 17.

118. Ric Roberts, "U.S. Olympic Brass Lapses into Racism," *Pittsburgh Courier*, Oct. 26, 1968, 1.

119. *Pittsburgh Courier*, Oct. 26, 1968, 7.

120. *Pittsburgh Courier*, Nov. 2, 1968, 6.

121. "Olympic Committee Quits 'Making Ado' about Balled Fists," *Pittsburgh Courier*, Nov. 2, 1968, 15.

122. Olympic coverage, ABC archives, Oct. 17, 1968, tape 16, 8:41–8:44.

123. "Carlos Planning to Sue U.S. Group," *New York Times*, Oct. 20, 1968, V: 2.

124. Edwards, *The Struggle That Must Be*, 194–95.

125. Brad Pye Jr., "Jim Hines, Wyomia Tyus Set Records at Olympics," *Los Angeles Sentinel*, Oct. 17, 1968, 1. In an earlier article (Oct. 10, 1968), the newspaper sarcastically predicted that "the only U.S. contingent who will boycott the Games is Prof. Harry Edwards."

126. "Ousted Olympic Stars to File Suit," *San Jose Mercury News*, Oct. 20, 1968.

127. "Smith and Carlos Start Speaking Tour Today," *New York Times*, Oct. 24, 1968, 60; "U.S. Tour Slated for Smith, Carlos," *San Jose Mercury News*, Oct. 24, 1968, 65.

128. "'Malcolm X Medallion Real Medal'—Carlos," *San Jose Mercury News*, Oct. 23, 1968, 69; Adrienne Manns, "Olympics Stars Get Rousing Welcome," *Baltimore Afro-American*, Oct. 26, 1968, 31.

129. "Olympians Wave Farewell, U.S. Captures Team Title," *Pittsburgh Courier*, Nov. 2, 1968, 14.

130. Gertrude Wilson, "UFT Egos—and Black Athletes," *New York Amsterdam News*, Nov. 2, 1968, 19.

131. Lipsitz, "'Frantic to Join…the Japanese Army,'" 186.

132. "U.S. Women Dedicate Victory to Smith, Carlos," *New York Times*, Oct. 21, 1968, 60; Zimmerman, "There's a Certain Air to Olympic Records," *New York Post*, Oct. 21, 1968, 73.

133. Griffin, "Some Untold Tales of Mexico City," B5.

134. Underwood, "A High Time for Sprinters—and Kenyans," 22; "U.S. Women Dedicate Victory to Smith, Carlos," *New York Times*, Oct. 21, 1968, 60.

135. Quoted in "Ousted Olympic Stars to File Suit."

136. Daley, "The Incident."

137. Michael MacCambridge, *The Franchise: A History of Sports Illustrated Magazine* (New York: Hyperion, 1997), 165–66.

138. "U.S. Suspends Smith and Carlos." It is interesting to note the malleability with which Smith gave the symbolism of the gesture. For example, Smith also stated at different points that in addition to blackness the scarf signified dignity and/or lynching.

139. Harry Edwards, "The Olympic Project for Human Rights: An Assessment Ten Years Later," *Black Scholar* 10, nos. 6/7 (Mar.-Apr. 1979): 2–8; Kenny Moore, "A Courageous Stand," *Sports Illustrated*, Aug. 5, 1991, 60.

140. Jim McKay, *Wide World of Sports*, "Highlights of the Sixties," ABC, aired Dec. 27, 1969, Museum of Radio and Television.

141. *Black Journal*, premiere episode, 1968, Museum of Television and Radio.

142. "Spreading the U.S. Gospel Elsewhere," *New York Amsterdam News*, Oct. 26, 1968, 1.

143. Robert Lipsyte, "Closing the Rings," *New York Times*, Oct. 28, 1968, 59.

144. Gilroy, "It Ain't Where You're From, It's Where You're At," 125.

145. Amy Kaplan, "'Left Alone with America': The Absence of Empire in the Study of American Culture," in *Cultures of United States Imperialism*, ed. Kaplan and Pease, 16.

146. Bob Ottum, "Grim Countdown to the Games," *Sports Illustrated*, Oct. 14, 1968, 38.

147. Lapchick, "The Modern Olympic Games," 262.

148. Edwards, *The Struggle That Must Be*, 204.

149. "Fields of Fire: Sports in the 60's," HBO, 1995; emphasis spoken.

150. "The Olympics Extra Heat," *Newsweek*, Oct. 28, 1968, 74.

151. Paul Zimmerman, "The Protest," *New York Post*, Oct. 19, 1968, 71.

152. Zimmerman, "The Protest."

153. Daley, "The Incident."

154. Leroy S. Rouner, Letter to the Editor, *New York Times*, Oct. 27, 1968, 2.

7. Whose Broad Stripes and Bright Stars?

1. Letters to the Editor, *Ebony*, Dec. 1968, 20.

2. "Mills Proud of Carlos And Smith," *Los Angeles Sentinel*, Oct. 24, 1968, 1.

3. "Ousted Ex-Olympian Raps IOC," *San Jose Mercury News*, Oct. 19, 1968, 73.

4. Quoted in Ashe, *A Hard Road to Glory*, 179.

5. Quoted in Ashe, *A Hard Road to Glory*, 180.

6. Quoted in Wallechinsky, *The Complete Book of the Olympics*, 22.

7. *Entertainment Weekly*, Feb. 19–26, 1999, 65.

8. "Triumph and Tragedy: The Olympic Experience," ABC, aired Jan. 5, 1976, Museum of Radio and Television, New York. All subsequent references to the program and quotations from it pertain to this citation.

9. R. W. Apple, "Olympic Boxing Champion Is Used as Symbol by Both Major Candidates," *New York Times*, Nov. 3, 1968, 84.

10. Brenda Plummer, who erroneously states that Owens won "a" gold medal in "Munich," notes that on two occasions Owens "publicly praised Hitler as he campaigned for GOP vice-presidential candidate Alf Landon.... [His] remarks reflect a flippancy toward fascism originating in parochial interpretations of overseas crises." Plummer, *A Rising Wind*, 67.

11. Vijay Prashad, *The Karma of Brown Folk* (Minneapolis: University of Minnesota Press, 2000), 8.

12. Wallechinsky, *The Complete Book of the Olympics*, xxiv–xxv; emphasis in original.

13. "Fields of Fire: Sports in the 60's."

14. Lipsyte, "Closing the Rings"; "Amid Gold Medals, Raised Black Fists," *Life*, Nov. 1, 1968, 67.

15. Underwood, "The Non-Trial Trials."

16. "Triumph and Tragedy: The Olympic Experience."

17. Jack McCallum, "Oh, Say Should We Sing?" *Sports Illustrated*, Mar. 25, 1996, 50–54.

18. "Unforgettable Anthems," *Sports Illustrated*, Dec. 12, 1994, 16.

19. Cheo Tyehimba, "The Newfangled Banner," *Entertainment Weekly*, Oct. 11, 1996, 108.

20. "Soviets Dozed ... Turks Confused," *San Jose Mercury News*, Oct. 3, 1968, 41; "Fans Protest Soul Singer's Anthem Version," *New York Times*, Oct. 8, 1968, 54; "Our National Anthem ... from the Soul," *New York Post*, Oct. 8, 1968, 109; "Feliciano's Anthem Was 'My Thing,'" *Chicago Tribune*, Oct. 8, 1968, III: 1.

21. Charles Shaar Murray, *Crosstown Traffic: Jimi Hendrix and the Rock 'n' Roll Revolution* (New York: St. Martin's Press, 1989), 22–23; emphasis in original.

22. Murray, *Crosstown Traffic*, 24.

23. Levine, *Black Culture and Black Consciousness*, 234; emphasis mine.

24. Levine, *Black Culture and Black Consciousness*, 239. Of course, not *all* black secular song functions in the mode of protest, because not all of black culture exists as a *reaction* to white society and the injustices that stem from it. Yet it does remain a realm where such discussions take place. Ralph Ellison indicates this in his refutation of Gunnar Myrdal's *An American Dilemma*, "Can a people ... live and develop for over three hundred years simply by *reacting*? Are American Negroes simply the creation of white men, or have they at least helped to

create themselves out of what they found around them. Men have made a way of life in caves and upon cliffs, why cannot Negroes have made a life upon the horns of the white man's dilemma?" Quoted in Levine, *Black Culture and Black Consciousness*, 193; emphasis in original.

25. Moore and Mathis, "Banished Runners Return."

26. Rick Reilly, "Patriot Games," *Sports Illustrated*, Mar. 25, 1996, 51.

27. The term *imagined communities* comes from Anderson, *Imagined Communities*.

28. "The Reuter Television Daybook," Mar. 13–14, 1996.

29. Woody Paige, "Abdul-Rauf Has a Right Not to Stand," *Denver Post*, Mar. 13, 1996, D1; Roscoe Nance, "Abdul-Rauf Suspended over Anthem," *USA TODAY*, Mar. 13, 1996, C1; Lacy J. Banks, "NBA Suspends Nuggets Star over Anthem," *Chicago Sun-Times*, Mar. 13, 1996, 128; "NBA Update," *Dallas Morning News*, Mar. 13, 1996, B6; "Nuggets' Abdul-Rauf Suspended," *Chicago Tribune*, Mar. 13, 1996, 6; Jason Diamos, "Abdul-Rauf Vows Not to Back Down from N.B.A.," *New York Times*, Mar. 14, 1996, B13; "Sports Log," *Boston Globe*, Mar. 13, 1996, 38.

30. "Hakeem Tells Abdul-Rauf: SHOW SOME RESPECT," *New York Daily News*, Mar. 14, 1996.

31. "A Puzzled Olajuwon Speaks Out on Citizenship," *New York Times*, Mar. 14, 1996, B19; Larry B. Stammer, "NBA and Abdul-Rauf Are Standing Firm," *Los Angeles Times*, Mar. 14, 1996, C1; Jason Anders, "Muslims Say NBA Protest Is Out of Line," *Detroit News*, Mar. 14, 1996, 1.

32. Frank Deford, "Of Stars and Stripes," *Newsweek*, Mar. 25, 1996, 64.

33. Dave Krieger, "Abdul Rauf Vows to Fight Suspension," *Rocky Mountain News*, Mar. 13, 1996, A4; Jim Hodges, "NBA Sits Abdul-Rauf for Stance on Anthem," *Los Angeles Times*, Mar. 13, 1996, C1; L. C. Johnson, "Headliners," *Orlando Sentinel*, Mar. 13, 1996, C4; Mike Monroe, "Abdul-Rauf Suspended in Flap over Anthem," *Denver Post*, Mar. 13, 1996, D1; "Names in the Games," *Charleston Gazette*, Mar. 13, 1996, B1; Harvey Araton, "An Issue of Religion and Respect," *New York Times*, Mar. 14, 1996, B13.

34. Reilly, "Patriot Games."

35. McCallum, "Oh, Say Should We Sing?" 50–54; Reilly, "Patriot Games," 54.

36. Donna Carter, "Mutombo Goes to Bat for Suspended Guard," *Denver Post*, Mar. 13, 1996, D4.

37. Robin D. G. Kelley, "Playing for Keeps: Pleasure and Profit on the Postindustrial Playground," in *The House That Race Built: Black Americas, U.S. Terrains*, ed. Wahneema Lubiano (New York: Pantheon Books, 1997), 197.

38. *Wide World of Sports*: "Highlights of the Sixties," aired Dec. 27, 1969, Museum of Radio and Television, New York.

39. "The Olympics: Passionless Games," *Time*, Nov. 22, 1968, 50.

40. Robert Philip, "Gloved Fist Is Raised in Defiance," *Daily Telegraph*, Oct. 11, 1993.

41. Charles Maher, "U.S. Duo Banned," *Los Angeles Times*, Oct. 19, 1968, II: 3.

42. Robert Lipsyte, "Silent Salute, Ringing Impact," *New York Times*, Oct. 17, 1993, 8: 1.

43. "Pro Grid Next for Hines, *San Jose Mercury News*, Oct. 15, 1968, 47.

44. Kenny Moore, "A Courageous Stand," *Sports Illustrated*, Aug. 5, 1991, 60.

45. Ted Brock, "John Carlos' Fist Is Still Clenched," *Sport*, Mar. 1975, 83–86.

46. "Shoe Controversy Hits Evans, Olympic Athletes," *San Jose Mercury News*, Oct. 9, 1968, 28.

47. Duino, "Americans Boo Smith, Carlos."

48. Department of State telegram, Oct. 22, 1968, National Archives and Records Administration, Record Group 59, Box 325.

49. "3 U.S. Stars Accused of Using Equipment at Olympics for Pay," *New York Times*, Oct. 23, 1968, 50; Shirley Povich, "U.S. May Give Up Some Gold Medals," *San Jose Mercury News*, Oct. 23, 1968, 1, reprinted from the *Washington Post*; "Money in the Shoes?" *Time*, Nov. 1, 1968, 56; Duino, "Americans Boo Smith, Carlos."

50. Lipsyte, "Closing the Rings."

51. Joseph M. Sheehan, "Olympic Investigation of Illegal Payment to Athletes Expected to Widen," *New York Times*, Oct. 24, 1968, 60; "'Athletes from Almost All Countries Guilty,'" *San Jose Mercury News*, Oct. 24, 1968, 1.

52. "Overhaul the Olympics," *San Jose Mercury News*, Oct. 24, 1968, 2B.

53. Arthur Daley, "What Price Amateurism?" *New York Times*, Oct. 25, 1968, 54.

54. Red Smith, "Amateur Amity," in *The Red Smith Reader*, 41.

55. *Nation*, Nov. 11, 1968, 484.

56. Carby, *Race Men*, 176.

57. Nikhil Pal Singh, "'Race' and Nation in the American Century: A Genealogy of Color and Democracy," Ph.D. dissertation, Yale University, 1995 (Cambridge, Mass.: Harvard University Press, in press); Mike Davis, *City of Quartz: Excavating the Future in Los Angeles* (New York: Vintage Books, 1992), especially 223–63.

58. Mike Davis, *Prisoners of the American Dream: Politics and Economy in the History of the US Working Class* (London: Verso, 1986), 310–11. Davis is worth quoting at length on this matter: "... the failure of the postwar labor movement to form an organic bloc with Black liberation, to organize the South or to defeat the power of Southern reaction in the Democratic Party, have determined, more than any other factors, the ultimate decline of American trade unionism and the rightward reconstruction of the political economy during the 1970s. The frustration of any second Reconstruction was the pivotal event marking the end of the Rooseveltian epoch of reform and its underlying economic base: the integrative capacities of a Fordist mass consumption economy. The minimal democratic program of the civil rights movement, involving the claims to equal housing, equal employment and equal political representation, has proved to be an impossible set of reforms for contemporary American capitalism to enact.... The single most important organizational problem confronting the North American left today is the huge disjuncture between the progressive political consciousness of Black America and the weakness of any national Black socialist cadre (the same dilemma applies to Chicanos/Mexicanos in the Southwest). Faced with the catastrophic social deterioration that has resulted from the crumbling of inner-city employment structures, there is an understandable urgency in the ghettoes and barrios for a resumption of the liberation movements. But precisely because reformist options have become so restricted, it will be very hard for collective action to generate the immediate concessions and victories that could provide momentum for a wider popular militancy."

59. W. E. B. Du Bois, *The Souls of Black Folk* (New York: Signet, 1982), 52.

60. Carby, *Race Men*, 1.

61. Dick Edwards, "Form National Group to Protect Black Athletes," *New York Amsterdam News*, Oct. 12, 1968, 33.

62. Ashe, *Hard Road to Glory*, 178.

63. Harry Edwards, "The Sources of the Black Athlete's Superiority," *Black Scholar* 3, no. 3 (Nov. 1971): 32.

64. Morrison, "The Official Story," xx.

65. Ross, "If the Genes Fit, How Do You Acquit?" 262; emphasis mine.

66. Axthelm, "The Angry Black Athlete."

67. Dan Hruby, "O. J. 'Natural' or Man-Made?" *San Jose Mercury News*, Oct. 11, 1968, 71.

68. Levine, *Black Culture and Black Consciousness*, 349.

69. Ross, "If the Genes Fit, How Do You Acquit?" 243–44.

70. Morgan Worthy and Allan Markle, "Racial Differences in Reactive versus Self-Paced Sports Activities," *Journal of Personality and Social Psychology* 16, no. 3 (1970): 439.

71. James M. Jones and Adrian Ruth Hochner, "Racial Differences in Sports Activities: A Look at the Self-Paced versus Reactive Hypothesis," *Journal of Personality and Social Psychology* 27, no. 1 (1973): 86–96.

72. Martin Kane, "An Assessment of 'Black Is Best'," *Sports Illustrated*, Jan. 18, 1972, 74.

73. J. M. Tanner, *The Physique of the Olympic Athlete: A Study of 137 Track and Field Athletes at the XVIIth Olympic Games, Rome 1960; and a Comparison with Weight-Lifters and Wrestlers* (London: Ruskin House, 1964).

74. John Hoberman, *Darwin's Athletes: How Sport Has Damaged Black America and Preserved the Myth of Race* (Boston: Houghton Mifflin, 1997), 193. In particular, he notes that while the Tanner quotations Kane used indicate a scientifically determined racial difference among Olympic competitors, Tanner did not claim that these differences are the cause of athletic excellence but rather left the relationship open-ended.

75. Edwards, "The Sources of the Black Athlete's Superiority," 34. For subsequent detailed treatments by Edwards on Kane, see "The Black Athletes: 20th Century Gladiators for White America," *Psychology Today*, Nov. 1973, 47–52; and "Sport within the Veil: The Triumphs, Tragedies and Challenges of Afro-American Involvement," *Annals, American Academy of Political and Social Sciences* 445 (Sept. 1979): 121.

76. Edwards, "The Sources of the Black Athlete's Superiority," 32.

77. Edwards, "The Sources of the Black Athlete's Superiority," 32–34.

78. Hoberman, *Darwin's Athletes*, 195.

79. Edwards, "The Sources of the Black Athlete's Superiority," 40.

80. Bill Rhoden, "Are Black Athletes Naturally Superior?" *Ebony*, Dec. 1974, 141.

81. Hoberman, *Darwin's Athletes*, 196.

82. Rhoden, "Are Black Athletes Naturally Superior?" 146.

83. Jon Hendershott, "Is Black Fastest?" *Black Sports* 4 (May 1975): 18–35; reprinted from *Track and Field News* (Feb. 1975).

84. Examples of the many others contributing to the debate include but are not limited to James H. Jordan, "Physiological and Anthropometrical Comparisons of Negroes and Whites," *Journal of Health, Physical Education, and Recreation* 40 (Nov./Dec. 1969): 93–99; John C. Phillips, "Toward an Explanation of Racial Variations in Top-Level Sports Participation," *International Review of Sport Sociology* 3 (1976): 39–55; "Black Dominance," *Time*, May 9, 1977, 57–60; "The Right Kind of Excellence," *Black Enterprise* 10 (Nov. 1979): 9; Frank T. Bannister Jr., "Search for 'White Hopes' Threatens Black Athletes," *Ebony*, Feb. 1980, 130–34; Leonard H. Clegg II, "Why Black Athletes Run Faster," *Sepia* 29 (July 1980): 18–22; Larry E. Jordan, "Black Markets and Future Superstars: An Instrumental Approach to Opportunity in Sport Forms," *Journal of Black Studies* 11 (Mar. 1981): 289–306; and Mark Dyreson, "Melting-Pot Victories: Racial Ideas and the Olympic Games in American Culture during the Progressive Era," *International Journal of the History of Sport* 6 (1989): 49–61.

85. Michael Sokolove, "Are Blacks Better Athletes than Whites?" *Philadelphia Inquirer*, Apr. 24, 1966, 16–36; Hoberman, *Darwin's Athletes*, 204.

86. Sokolove, "Are Blacks Better Athletes than Whites?" 33.

87. Sokolove, "Are Blacks Better Athletes than Whites?" 16; emphasis in original.

88. Quoted in Shropshire, *In Black and White*, 23. For press reaction to Snyder's remarks, see Jonathan Rowe, "The Greek Chorus," *Washington Monthly*, Apr. 1988, 31–34; "Of Mandingo and Jimmy 'the Greek,'" *Time*, Feb. 1, 1988, 70; "Of Fingerprints and Other Clues," *Fortune*, Feb. 15, 1988, 123–24; "What We Say, What We Think," *U.S. News and World Report*, Feb. 1, 1988, 27–28; and "An Oddsmaker's Odd Views," *Sports Illustrated*, Jan. 25, 1988, 7.

89. Quoted in Shropshire, *In Black and White*, 21–22.

90. Lloyd R. Cohen, "The Puzzling Case of Jimmy 'the Greek,'" *Society* 31, no. 5 (July/Aug. 1994): 49–50.

91. Richard E. Lapchick, "The 1994 Racial Report Card," in *Sport in Society*, ed. Lapchick, 47.

92. Quoted in Shropshire, *In Black and White*, 23–24.

93. Quoted in Shropshire, *In Black and White*, 33.

94. "A Different Race for Sir Roger," *Sports Illustrated*, Sept. 25, 1995. This was not the first foray into the subject matter for Bannister, a physician, as evidenced by his article "The Meaning of Athletic Performance," in *Sport and Society*, ed. John T. Talamini and Charles H. Page (Boston: Little, Brown, 1973), 326–35.

95. Dave Kindred, "You Can't Be Color Blind," *Sporting News*, Oct. 2, 1995, 8; ellipsis in original.

96. Quoted in Sokolove, "Are Blacks Better Athletes than Whites?" 36.

97. See, for example, *Los Angeles Times TV Guide*, Apr. 25, 1989.

98. "Black Athletes: Fact and Fiction," NBC, aired Apr. 25, 1989, Jon Entine, producer, Museum of Television and Radio. All subsequent references to the program apply to this citation.

99. Laurel R. Davis, "The Articulation of Difference: White Preoccupation with the Question of Racially Linked Genetic Differences among Athletes," *Sociology of Sport* 7 (1990): 179; see also Gary A. Sailes, "An Investigation of Campus Stereotypes: The Myth of Black Sports Supremacy," in *Sport in Society*, ed. Lapchick, 482.

100. John Hoberman, "'Black Athletes—Fact and Fiction': A Racist Documentary?" unpublished paper presented at the 98th Annual Convention of the American Psychological Association, Boston, Aug. 14, 1990, 2. I am grateful to Professor Hoberman for sharing his work with me.

101. See Pete Axthelm, *The City Games: Basketball from the Garden to the Playgrounds* (Omaha: University of Nebraska, 1999); Harold U. Ribalow, *The Jew in American Sports* (New York: Bloch Publishing, 1948); Peter Levine, *Ellis Island to Ebbett's Field: Sport and the American Jewish Experience* (New York: Oxford University Press, 1992).

102. Greil Marcus, *Mystery Train: Images of America in Rock 'n' Roll Music* (New York: Plume, 1990), 11.

103. Davis, "The Articulation of Difference," 181.

104. Hoberman, "'Black Athletes—Fact and Fiction,'" 15.

105. John Carmody, "The TV Column," *Washington Post*, Apr. 27, 1989, B10.

106. George Vecsey, "Motivation Key Factor with Athletes," *New York Times*, Apr. 27, 1989, D27; Carmody, "The TV Column."

107. "After Telecast, Snyder Says He Was Right," *Los Angeles Times*, Apr. 27, 1989, III: 2.

108. Scott Ostler, "White Athletes—Fact and Fiction: Destroying Myths," *Los Angeles Times*, Apr. 27, 1989, III: 3.

109. Davis, "The Articulation of Difference," 179.

110. Amby Burfoot, "White Men Can't Run," *Runner's World*, Aug. 1992, 89–95.

111. S. L. Price, "Whatever Happened to the White Athlete?" *Sports Illustrated*, Dec. 8, 1997, 30–51; S. L. Price, "Is It in the Genes?" *Sports Illustrated*, 52–55; Letters, *Sports Illustrated*, Jan. 12, 1998, 19.

112. Hoberman, *Darwin's Athletes*, 206; Jon Entine, *Taboo: Why Black Athletes Dominate Sports and Why We're Afraid to Talk about It* (New York: Public Affairs, LLC, 1999); Richard J. Herrnstein and Charles Murray, *The Bell Curve: Intelligence and Class Structure in American Life* (New York: Simon and Schuster, 1995).

113. Kevin Sullivan, "Unofficially, Nike Is Payer at Winter Games," *Washington Post*, Feb. 13, 1998, C6; Mike Penner, "Winter Olympics 1998," *Los Angeles Times*, Feb. 12, 1998, N2; Philip Hersh, "Decision Made for Russia: Olympic Skating Champ Bows Out of Hunt," *Chicago Tribune*, Jan. 22, 1998, 10.

114. Gitanjali Maharaj, "Talking Trash: Late Capitalism, Black (Re)Productivity, and Professional Basketball," *Social Text* 50, no. 1 (spring 1997): 98.

115. Maharaj, "Talking Trash," 97, 106.

116. Kelley, "Playing for Keeps," 224.

117. Rick Telander, "Asphalt Legends," *Sports Illustrated*, Aug. 18, 1997, 60–72; Rick Telander, *Heaven Is a Playground* (Omaha: University of Nebraska Press, 1995). In a recent exploration of the playground game prompted by the return of Stephen Marbury to the New York metropolitan area (traded by the Minnesota Timberwolves to the New Jersey Nets), the *New York Times* ran through some of the highs and lows of famous street players, emphasizing the success of Marbury against that of Manigault, who died in 1998 of congestive heart failure after suffering a heroin addiction, and Hammond, who left an opportunity with the Lakers to become a drug dealer, addict, and eventually a prisoner; Charles LeDuff and Vincent M. Mallozzi, "A Hero's Homecoming," *New York Times*, Mar. 14, 1999, 37, 40. For more on concrete hoops, see also Ben Joravsky, *Hoop Dreams: A True Story* (New York: Harper Perennial, 1995); Darcey Fey, *The Last Shot: City Streets, Basketball Dreams* (New York: Touchstone Books,

1996); John Huet et al., *Soul of the Game: Images and Voices of Street Basketball* (New York: Workman Publishing, 1997); Lars Anderson et al., *Pickup Artists: Street Basketball in America* (London: Verso, 1998); Hal Lawson, "Physical Education and Sport in the Black Community," *Journal of Negro Education* 48 (spring 1979): 187–95; Jabari Mahiri, "Discourse in Sports: Language and Literacy Features of Preadolescent African American males in a Youth Basketball Program," *Journal of Negro Education* 60, no. 3 (1991): 305–13; John C. Gaston, "The Destruction of the Young Black Male: The Impact of Popular Culture and Organized Sports," *Journal of Black Studies* 16, no. 4 (June 1986): 369–84; and David Zang, "Calvin Hill Interview," *Journal of Sport History* 15, no. 3 (winter 1988): 334–55.

118. Deford, "Of Stars and Stripes," 64.

119. "Where Are They Now?" NBC, Barcelona Olympic coverage, 1992. For other recent revisitations around the time of the twenty-fifth anniversary of the black power protest, see the two-part *Sports Illustrated* series by Kenny Moore, "A Courageous Stand"; Kenny Moore, "The 1968 Olympians: The Eye of the Storm," *Sports Illustrated*, Aug. 12, 1991; Elaine Woo, "Olympics' Tommie Smith Still Delivering a Message," *Los Angeles Times*, July 3, 1991, B3; Charles Korr, "When Protest Made a Clean Sweep," *New York Times*, June 28, 1992, 8, 11; Bill Rhoden, "They Punched the Sky, and Ran into a Nation's Consciousness," *New York Times*, Oct. 17, 1993, 8:11; Lipsyte, "Silent Salute, Ringing Impact"; and Philip, "Gloved Fist Is Raised in Defiance." On the thirtieth anniversary, members of the U.S. track and field squad assembled in New Orleans and gave a series of interviews for CNBC's *The Olympic Show*, which aired July 25, 1998. I am grateful to Joe Gesue, Scott Boggins, and Lisa Lax at NBC for sharing both the footage and the interview transcripts of Tommie Smith, Dick Fosbury, Bob Beamon, and Wyomia Tyus.

120. Singh, "Toward an Effective Antiracism," 222.

121. Lipsyte, "Silent Salute, Ringing Impact."

122. "Don't Like the Sponsor? Just Zip It," *New York Times*, Aug. 5, 1992, B13; "Dream Team Will Dress in Reebok Suits," *San Diego Union-Tribune*, Aug. 5, 1992, D6; Scott Ostler, "Dropping the Other Shoe on the Olympics," *Los Angeles Times*, Aug. 10, 1992, B1; Jay Mariotti, "Even on Medal Stand, This Team Is a Dream," *Chicago Sun-Times*, Aug. 9, 1992, 2; Jay Mariotti, "Sweatsuit Solution Pleases Jordan," *Chicago Sun-Times*, Aug. 5, 1992, 96.

123. NBC transcript of interview by Scott Boggins with Tommie Smith, June 19, 1998, New Orleans.

Index

Abdul-Jabbar, Kareem. *See* Alcindor, Lew

Abdul-Rauf, Mahmoud, 310–15, 324–25, 346

Ademola, Ir Ade, 158

Alcindor, Lew, 31–33, 91, 94–95, 98–99, 186–87, 194, 206, 215, 254

Alexander, Reginald, 158, 390 n. 88

Ali, Muhammad: at the Atlanta Olympic Games, 347–48; on the black Olympic boycott, 96, 98; and Howard Cosell, 339; and the evolution of the black athlete, 32–35, 47, 194, 211–13, 281, 284; vs. Sonny Liston, 305; and the OPHR, 135, 138, 154, 186, 203; as a trickster, 326; and the Vietnam War, 138, 302, 375 n. 37

amateurism, 6, 316–22

American Broadcasting Company (ABC): and the black power protest, 25, 273; coverage of Mexico City Olympic Games, 83–84, 99–106; coverage of NYAC meet, 151–52; *Niteline*, 332–33; *Triumph and Tragedy*, 295–301; *Wide World of Sports*, 31–32, 101–2, 151, 280–81. *See also* Arledge, Roone

American Committee on Africa (ACOA), 161–62, 173

apartheid, 5, 84, 139, 157–61, 163–64, 166–67, 169, 177, 179–84, 188, 252, 322, 389 n. 85, 394 n. 121

Arledge, Roone, 99–103, 105, 106

Ashe, Arthur: "Black Athletes—Fact and Fiction" appearance, 337; *Black Journal* appearance, 86, 281–85; *A Hard Road to Glory*, 15; and the OPHR, 139, 208; and South Africa, 162; U.S. Open title, 32, 217

Ashford, Emmett, 95

Athens Olympic Games, 110

Atlanta Olympic Games, 12, 347–48

425

Axthelm, Pete, 142, 150, 210–12, 214, 338

Bailes, Margaret, 189, 279
Bannister, Sir Roger, 327, 334–35
Barcelona Olympic Games, 183, 184, 313, 342, 347, 371 n. 108
Barnes, Everett, 245, 246–48, 265, 320. *See also* United States Olympic Committee (USOC)
baseball, 2, 8–9, 16, 105–6, 304, 315
Basilio, Norma Enriqueta, 106–7, 130
Bates, Leonard, 86–87
Beamon, Bob: and NYAC meet, 149, 153–54, 157, 185; world record of, 32, 230, 262–64, 286, 298
Beaumont, Count Jean de, 170, 175–76, 234
Benjamin, Walter, 14
Berlin Olympic Games: compared to South Africa, 166, 171, 174; and Eleanor Holm, 270; Nazi salute at, 301; and Jesse Owens, 16, 47, 93–94, 96, 296–97. *See also* Riefenstahl, Leni
big shoe scandal, 317–22
Bikila, Abebe, 32, 161, 169, 225, 258, 270, 390–91 n. 97, 392 n. 104
blackface. *See* minstrelsy
Black Journal (PBS), 86, 281–85
Black Panthers: community programs, 5; image of, 144–45, 264–65; and the OPHR, 132–33; and SNCC, 20, 325; women in, 216
Black Power: historical significance of, 4–5; and masculinity, 189,

215–16; at the Mexico City Olympic Games, 244, 248, 257–59, 262, 263, 267, 274, 280, 294; and the OPHR, 138, 143–45; 156, 196, 205, 209, 211, 227, 322; and Smith and Carlos, 278–79
black power protest, Olympic: and boxing, 251, 267, 285, 295–96; construction of "blackness" in, 19, 257–58, 280, 285; in context of 1968, 24, 280, 315; foundations of, 35, 227; and 400-meters, 264–65; historical legacy of, 270, 277–89, 291–92, 294–95, 297–303, 314, 346–48, 357 n. 60; and long jump, 265; meaning and impact of, 24–25, 190–91, 235–36, 239–41, 320, 347; media representations of, 241–46, 272–77; and Munich Olympic Games, 300–301; post-Olympic ramifications of, 316–17; reaction to, 25, 246–56, 270, 305; suspension of Smith and Carlos for, 257–68, 286
Black September Movement. *See* Munich Olympic Games
Bond, Julian, 8, 34, 302
Boston, Ralph, 94, 97, 149, 153, 209, 243, 248, 264
Bourdieu, Pierre, 4, 10, 14, 102, 352 n. 23
boycott, Olympic. *See* Olympic Games; Olympic Project for Human Rights (OPHR)
Braun, Frank, 158, 159, 173, 176–80
Brokaw, Tom, 336–42, 343

Brown, Doris, 189

Brown, Elaine, 216

Brown, H. Rap, 146, 147–48, 156, 181, 196, 278

Brown, Jim, 202

Brown Berets, 145

Brundage, Avery: on the black Olympic boycott, 92, 197–98, 297; and the black power protest, 243, 246, 247, 260; and Eleanor Holm, 270; IOC presidency of, 234, 373 n. 5; and Mexican student movements, 120, 124, 129, 381–82 n. 144; on Mexico City, 107, 130; and Munich Olympic Games, 293; and Olympic corporate sponsorship, 321; and the OPHR, 136, 203, 236–37, 245; on South Africa, 164, 167, 168, 170–73, 175–78, 183, 384 n. 14; suspension of Smith and Carlos, 269

Brutus, Dennis, 385 n. 27

Burns, Ken, 2–3

Campanis, Al, 327, 332–35

Carlos, John, 211, 374 n. 15; and the big shoe scandal, 318–21; and the black power protest, 99, 190, 233–34, 235, 237–46, 308, 315, 410 n. 74; departure from Mexico City, 269–70; goatee, 195, 231, 243; historical legacy of the black power protest, 270, 277–89, 291–92; impact of the black power protest, 143, 235–36, 246–56, 271–77, 305; and the Munich Olympic Games, 294, 300–301; on the national anthem, 309; at the Olympic Trials, 209, 405–6 n. 126, 407 n. 19; post-Olympic career of, 317, 325; on South Africa, 162; suspension from Olympics, 257–68, 271, 286, 298; on winning, 84, 326

Carmichael, Stokely: and the black power protest, 277–78, 279; coinage of Black Power, 4, 205; and the OPHR, 196; on women, 216. See also Student Non-Violent Coordinating Committee (SNCC)

Cáslavská, Vera, 281. See also Prague Spring

ceremonial rituals, Olympic, 237, 239

Chicago Democratic Convention, 23, 306

civil rights movements: and the black power protest, 24, 294–95; and gender, 215–19; and Mexican student movements, 116; postindustrial moment of, 322–24, 325, 345–48, 419 n. 58; role of spectacle in, 20, 297, 302; and sports, 86–88, 138–39, 147, 185–86, 252; transnationalism of, 136–38, 163–64, 181, 216, 236, 315, 348

Clark, Robert. See San Jose State University

Clay, Cassius. *See* Ali, Muhammad

Cleveland Rosenblums, 338

Coachman, Alice, 217, 220

Cobb, W. Montague, 51, 78; on the American Negro, 65–68, 188, 189, 200–201, 330; on athletic coaches, 72–74; relationship with Ales Hrdlicka, 64–65, 66, 368–69 n. 87; relationship with T. Wingate Todd, 64, 66, 368 n. 84; study of Jesse Owens, 64, 67, 69–71

Cold War: House Un-American Activities Committee (HUAC), 7; "kitchen debate," 219; and the NYAC meet, 150; and the Olympics, 8–10, 90, 141, 162, 184, 278–79, 286; role of Africa in, 163–64, 179; role of black athlete in, 6–10, 92, 139, 140, 218, 224–25

Collett, Wayne, 292–93, 298, 299–300, 303, 305

Comité Anti-Olímpico de Subversion (CAOS), 118, 131–32. *See also* student movements, Mexican

commodification, 314–22, 324–25, 344–48

Congress of Racial Equality (CORE), 142, 146, 387 n. 51

Connolly, Hal, 249, 250, 266, 411 n. 86

corporeal capital, 46–47

Cosell, Howard: cohost of *Triumph and Tragedy*, 298–301; cohost of *Wide World of Sports*, 102; interview with Tommie Smith, 240–41, 256, 276; "monkey" comment, 339; on players' unions, 315

Coubertin, Baron Pierre de, 97

Cromwell, Dean B., 74–79, 336

Cuba: and the black power protest, 262, 279; and Joe Louis, 39; and Mexican student movements, 113, 114–15, 127, 235; and South Africa, 168, 173

cultural studies, 16–19, 354–55 n. 43

Daley, Arthur: on amateurism, 321; on black Olympic boycott, 99; on Cold War, 163; on Mexico City, 107, 109; on NYAC boycott, 185–86; on Jesse Owens, 94; on South Africa, 166–67, 180; on suspension of Smith and Carlos, 279–80, 288

Davenport, Willie, 243, 248

decolonization, 8–9, 16, 137–38, 140, 162–64, 169

DeFrantz, Anita, 341

development, discourse of, 107–9

Díaz Ordaz, Gustavo, 111–12, 117–19, 121, 126, 129. *See also* Partido Revolucionario Institucional (PRI)

Didrikson, Mildred "Babe," 220, 402 n. 87

doping, 13

dream team, 6, 313, 347

Du Bois, W. E. B.: on collegiate sport, 45–46; concept of double consciousness, 19; concept of national belonging, 323; play movement, 41–43

Edwards, Harry: autobiography of, 35, 82–83, 88–89; *Black Journal* appearance, 86, 281–85; and the black Olympic boycott, 91–92, 95, 135–36, 190–91, 198–99, 203, 206–7, 215, 226–29, 275; on the black power protest, 235–36, 407 n. 22; on Avery Brundage, 136; early years of, 82–83; on George Foreman, 411–12 n. 87; and the Harvard crew team, 229–30; on historical legacy of the black power protest, 277–78, 287; on language, 85, 89, 141–42, 146, 188, 325; and Louis Lomax, 143–44, 194, 277; and Mexican student movements, 131–32; and NYAC boycott, 147–49, 153, 154–55, 156, 157, 163; and Olympic Trials, 208–10, 226–27, 303; as OPHR leader, 4, 85–86, 138, 192, 193, 195–98, 202–3, 205, 254; at San Jose State University, 82, 85, 384 n. 12; on sports and civil rights, 33, 201, 202, 323–24; as sports scholar, 15, 280, 328–29, 330, 334, 337, 339–42, 354 n. 38; and South Africa, 168, 170, 172–73, 178, 180–81

Eisenhower, President Dwight, 8–9

Elder, Lee, xv, 252

Ellison, Ralph, 416–17 n. 24

Evans, Lee: and the big shoe scandal, 318; and the black Olympic boycott, 91, 92, 98, 205, 215, 226–27; and the black power protest, 249, 256, 257, 265–66, 299, 407 n. 13; and Avery Brundage, 237; on language, 141; and Munich Olympic Games, 292–93; and NYAC boycott, 150; at San Jose State University, 192–93, 201, 211; and South Africa, 162, 181; world record of, 262–64, 298

Feliciano, José, 302, 306–7, 309

femininity, 26–31, 219–21

feminism, 26, 215–16, 221

Ferrell, Barbara, 189, 279

Fetchit, Stepin, 56

Flemming, Peggy, 32, 139

Flood, Curt, 198, 302, 315

Flowers, Richmond, Jr., 155–56

Flowers, Vonetta, ix

Foreman, George, 267, 285, 295–96, 411–12 n. 87

Fosbury, Dick, 252

Foucault, Michel, 49–50, 354 n. 41, 358 n. 69

Freeman, Ron, 264, 266

Fuentes, Carlos, 114

Games of the New Emerging Forces (GANEFO), 140, 188

Ganga, Jean-Claude, 168, 182, 393 n. 118

Garrett, Mike, 198, 254

Garvey, Marcus, 53, 137, 391 n. 102

Gay Games. *See* Waddell, Tom

gender verification testing. *See*
    women in sports

Gibson, Althea, 217–18, 224

Gibson, Bob, 198, 254

Gourdin, Ned, 74, 371 n. 110

Great Migration, the, 54

Greene, Charlie, 95, 236

Gregory, Dick, 33, 87

Grenoble Winter Games, 100, 139,
    152, 171, 321

Griffith, D. W., 101

Gulick, Luther, 40–41

hair, political significance of, 144,
    194–95, 231, 243, 251, 299

Hamilton, Dr. Charles, 205–6

Harlem Globetrotters, 9, 351 n. 20

Harlem Renaissance, 53

Harvard University crew team,
    229–30, 250–51, 266–67

Hayes, Bob, 95

Henderson, Edwin Bancroft, 43–45,
    218–19

Hendrix, Jimi, 307–9

Herskovits, Melville, 63–64

Hines, Jim, 149, 153, 229, 236, 258,
    277, 316–17, 388 n. 72

Holm, Eleanor, 270

Hrdlicka, Ales. *See* Cobb,
    W. Montague

Hubbard, De Hart, 53, 75, 371 n. 110

Humphrey, Hubert, 207, 228, 295

International Olympic Committee
    (IOC): and Athens Olympic
Games, 110; and Berlin Olympic
Games, 94; and the big shoe
scandal, 318; and the black
power protest, 241, 245–48; and
the Harvard crew team, 251; and
Mexico City, 107, 109, 234; and
the Munich Olympic Games,
292–93, 294; and national
identity, 105; and Olympic
broadcasting, 100, 105; Salt Lake
City scandals, 13, 393 n. 118;
and South Africa, 139–40,
157–61, 170–84, 187, 191,
389–90 n. 86; and suspension of
Smith and Carlos, 257–68, 276,
280, 286, 288, 291; and women,
26, 106–7, 190. *See also*
Brundage, Avery

Jackson, Chris. *See* Abdul-Rauf,
    Mahmoud

James, C. L. R., 14–15, 392 n. 108

James, Larry, 264

Jim Crow, 62

Jimmy the Greek. *See* Snyder, Jimmy
    "the Greek"

Johnson, Brooks, 335–36, 338–39,
    340, 344

Johnson, Jack, 24, 37–38, 40, 54

Johnson, President Lyndon Baines,
    22, 196, 202, 228, 297

Johnson, Rafer, 10, 94

Jordan, Michael, 295, 313, 314, 337,
    346–48, 402 n. 81

Jordan, Payton, 90, 181, 227, 231,
    233–34, 243

Karenga, Ron, 203
Keino, Kipchoge "Kip," 166, 169, 298, 373 n. 5
Kennedy, Jackie, 259, 260, 261
Kennedy, President John F., 8, 20, 21, 297
Kennedy, Robert F., 8, 23
Killanin, Lord Michael, 158. *See also* International Olympic Committee (IOC)
Killy, Jean-Claude, 31–32, 139
King, Rev. Martin Luther, Jr., 302, 332; assassination of, 22–23, 178, 190; in Birmingham, 20; and the OPHR, 138, 142, 203, 206; and the Vietnam War, 22
Kiprugut, Wilson, 166, 169
Kirkland, Peewee, 344–45

Lambeth, Martha, 56, 58, 61–63
Lyle Lanier, 56, 58, 61–63
La Nueva Noche Triste, 124–25. *See also* Tlatelco massacre
Lee, Norvell, 95
Lentz, Arthur, 92–93, 139, 174, 203, 408 n. 36, 408 n. 42. *See also* United States Olympic Committee (USOC)
Lewis, Carl, 239, 335, 338, 341, 342
liberal integrationism, 218
Lipsyte, Robert: on the big shoe scandal, 320; on the black Olympic boycott, 96, 302; on the "emasculation of sports," 1–3; on the Harvard crew team, 229; on the NYAC boycott, 186; on

South Africa, 165, 166, 182; on suspension of Smith and Carlos, 286
Livers, Larry, 148, 157, 205
Lodge, Hilmer, 209, 227
Lomax, Louis, 143–44, 194, 277
Louis, Joe: on the black Olympic boycott, 95; on the black power protest, 254; and Althea Gibson, 218; vs. Max Schmeling, 16, 38–39, 40, 82–83

Malcolm X, 32, 85, 196, 212, 278
Manning, Madeline, 189
Mare, Matt, 159–60
masculinity, black: and the black power protest, 25, 257–58; and the body, 47–48, 189, 329, 344–45; and citizenship, 40, 322; and the OPHR, 189–90, 191, 204, 205, 215–26; representations in sports, 3, 336; in sports history, 16
Matthews, Vince, 249, 266, 292–93, 298–300, 303, 305
Mays, Willie, 198, 201–2, 253
McGuire, Edith, 204, 225
McKay, Jim: as cohost of *Triumph and Tragedy*, 297–98; and Mexico City, 106; and the Munich Olympic Games, 294–95; on sports in the sixties, 31–32, 280–81
McKissick, Floyd, 138, 142, 203, 391 n. 99
Metcalfe, Ralph, 53, 54, 55, 56, 71, 74, 75

Metheny, Eleanor, 54–55, 58–59, 63, 200, 330

Mexico City Olympic Games: altitude of, 208, 230; big shoe scandal at, 318–22; black power protest at, 237–68, 314, 346; building of, 110–12, Closing Ceremony, 270, 287, 319; corporate sponsorship of, 104–5; cultural Olympiad, 111–12; ethnic perceptions of, 106–10, 234–35, 378 n. 91; Opening Ceremony, 83–84, 99, 106–7, 115, 119, 122, 128, 129, 191, 306, 318; and South Africa, 158–84; 234; and student protest movements, 112–30; 234; television coverage of, 84, 99, 100–103, 106, 235–36. *See also* black power protest; Carlos, John; Edwards, Harry; Olympic Project for Human Rights (OPHR); Smith, Tommie

Mexico City Olympic Organizing Committee: on the black Olympic boycott, 93; on the black power protest, 260, 268–69, 272; building of Olympic venues, 108–12, 113; on South Africa, 168, 171, 172, 174, 175. *See also* Ramírez Vázquez, Pedro

Meyer, Debbie, 219–20

midnight basketball, 360–61 n. 21

Miller, Lennox, 153, 157

Mills, Billy, 32, 269, 270, 297

Minow, Newton, 21

minstrelsy, 49, 101

miscegenation, 54

model minority: concept of, 297

Montreal Olympic Games, 183–84, 292, 295

Munich Olympic Games: black protests at, 243, 292–93, 298, 299–300, 303; Black September Movement at, 293–95, 300–301

Murray, Jim, 29–31, 252–53

muscular assimilationism, 43–45

Muskie, Edmund, 271

Nagano Winter Games, 110, 344

Naismith, James, 41

Nambu, Chuhei, 71

national anthem. *See* "Star-Spangled Banner"

National Basketball Association (NBA), 310–14, 343, 345

National Broadcasting Company (NBC): and Roone Arledge, 101; "Black Athletes—Fact and Fiction," 336–42; Olympic broadcasts, 12, 347; World Series (1968) broadcast, 306

National Conference of Black Power, 88, 227, 229, 387 n. 51

national identity: and the black athlete, 6, 24–25, 34–35, 147, 189, 206–7, 239–41, 257–58, 285, 294–95, 310, 314, 346–48; and civil rights movements, 17, 322–24; concept of imagined community, 18, 241, 311; and

the Olympic Games, 105, 162, 237, 301, 343–44; and popular culture, 3, 17–19; and transnationalism, 285–89, 343–44. *See also* performative nationalism; transnationalism
nationalism. *See* national identity
Netter, Mildrette, 189, 279
Newcombe, Don, 95
New Left, 5, 19, 26, 133
New York Athletic Club (NYAC): boycott of, xix, 135–36, 145–57, 163, 170, 185–86, 191, 197, 204, 209, 325; and South Africa, 159, 162, 164, 165, 181
New York University (NYU), 86–87, 333
Nike, 313, 314, 317, 344–45
Nixon, Richard, 219
Noel, Ken, 85, 88, 154, 157
Norman, Peter, 238, 239, 240, 242, 245, 251, 267
Nurmi, Paavo, 69–70, 76, 365 n. 60

Oerter, Al, 238, 249
Oklahoma City bombing, 310–11
Olajuwon, Hakeem, 312
Olsen, Jack, 9, 210, 212–14, 280, 328
Olympic Charter, 111, 176, 288, 378 n. 94
Olympic Committee for Human Rights (OCHR), 89. *See also* Olympic Project for Human Rights (OPHR)
Olympic Games: African American medals in, 203–4, 217, 222, 224, 278–79, 316–17; boycotts of, 87, 139, 171, 183–84; corporate sponsorship of, 103–6, 317–18, 321–22; cultural Olympiad, 111–12; significance of, 12–14, 302, 343, 353 n. 31; women's participation in, 26–31, 217, 222–26. *See also* specific cities
Olympic Project for Human Rights (OPHR): and Muhammad Ali, 135; and the big shoe scandal, 318–20; and black Olympic boycott decision, 186–87, 191, 202–10, 226–29; and black Olympic boycott proposal, 84, 90–93, 135–36, 138–40, 280, 299, 314, 348; and the black power protest, 241, 247, 253, 256, 265, 277; collectivist ethos of, 188–91, 206–7; creation of, 3–4, 89–90, 213, 214; demands of, 135–36, 203, 206, 211, 384 n. 14; exclusion of women, 189–90, 204, 215–17, 226; and the Harvard crew team, 229–30, 250–51, 266–67; historical legacy of, 316–17, 324; ideology of, 5, 254, 257, 294–95, 316, 323–26; image of, 143–45, 186, 192–95, 210–14, 237, 258, 295; and Mexican student movements, 113, 116, 117, 121, 130, 131–33; and the Munich Olympic Games, 294; and NYAC boycott, 135–36, 145–57, 170; post-Olympic ramifications of, 316–17; reaction

to, 35, 92–99, 302; and South Africa, 135, 139–40, 145, 164–65, 168–70, 178, 180–81; strategy of, 5, 185, 203–4, 256; and transnationalism, 138–41, 197, 205, 229, 236, 267–68, 285–89; and the Vietnam War, 134–35. *See also* Carlos, John; Edwards, Harry; Evans, Lee; Smith, Tommie

Olympic Trials (1968): altitude of, 230–31; basketball players boycott of, 186–87, 194; demonstrations at, 207–10, 211; OPHR vote at, 226–27; use of brush spikes at, 318, 407 n. 19

O'Neal, Shaquille, 314

Onesti, Giulio, 170–71, 172, 176

Organization of African Unity (OAU), 162, 167–68

Owens, Jesse: and Berlin Olympic Games, 16, 47, 93–94, 96, 296–97, 298, 346; on the black Olympic boycott, 93–94, 98; and the black power protest, 248–49, 269, 270; and Avery Brundage, 136; and Dean Cromwell, 75, 76; and the OPHR, 196, 211, 238, 284; role in Cold War, 6, 9; in Schlitz commercial, 104–5; scientific analysis of, 50, 52–56, 64, 67, 69–71

Partido Revolucionario Institucional (PRI), 84, 108, 114, 116, 126. *See also* Díaz Ordaz, Gustavo

Patterson, Audrey "Mickey," 217, 220

Patterson, Floyd, 31, 33–34, 213, 254

Penn Relays, 69, 71, 72

performative nationalism, xx, 308–10. *See also* national identity

Phillips, Sam, 338–39

Pickett, Tidye, 222, 403–4 n. 95

play movement, the, 40–42

Prague Spring, 23–24, 84, 116, 234, 249, 281

Presley, Bob, 194–95, 211–12

Presley, Elvis, 195, 338–39

racial identity: and athletes, 47–48, 191–92, 199–202, 210–14, 284–85, 344, 398–99 n. 25; and the black power protest, 24–25, 239–41, 257–58, 294–95, 302–3; and class, 353–54 n. 37, 386 n. 31; and gender, 215–19; the OPHR and, 5, 192–95, 204–7, 210, 322, 325–26; and transnationalism, 286–87, 343

racism: and the black power protest, 239, 257, 273, 348; and national identity, 355 n. 47; science and, 3, 46–47, 50, 52, 326–27, 336–37; in sports, 35, 191–95, 198, 201–2, 204, 206–7, 211–14, 277, 281–85, 339–40, 342

Ramírez Vázquez, Pedro, 93, 111, 171, 172, 234

Randolph, A. Philip, 137

Reagan, Ronald, 134–35

resistance, cultural, 18–19, 34, 208–9, 239–40, 308–9

Riefenstahl, Leni, 99–102

Robeson, Paul, 7, 87

Robinson, Jackie: *Black Journal*

appearance, 86, 281–85; on the black Olympic boycott, 95–96, 98; and the black power protest, 254, 271; and the integration of baseball, 2, 24, 35, 47, 96, 147, 212, 217, 276, 332, 346; role in Cold War, 6–10, 351 n. 13; and South Africa, 162

Roby, Douglas, 110, 161–62, 170, 233, 261, 264, 265, 269, 288. *See also* United States Olympic Committee (USOC)

Rome Olympic Games, 100, 104, 149, 160, 222–24, 270, 328, 390–91 n. 97

Rudolph, Wilma, 31, 204, 222–25, 297, 346

Russell, Bill, 86, 150, 209, 281–85, 303, 335

Sample, Johnny, 281–85

San Jose Mercury News: on the big shoe scandal, 319–21; on the black Olympic boycott, 96–99, 135; on the black power protest, 244, 255–56, 264–65, 272; on gender verification testing, 29; on the Mexican student movements, 124, 381 n. 138

San Jose State University: antiwar movement at, 133–35; Robert Clark (president), 134–35, 271–72; and Harry Edwards, 82, 196; as OPHR base, 4, 192–93, 265; vs. UTEP, 88–89, 134, 135

Schenkel, Chris, 104, 106, 241, 242

Schmeling, Max. *See* Louis, Joe

Schott, Marge, 327, 334–35

science, laboratory: and the black athlete, 49–52, 200–201, 295, 325–43, 344, 346, 366 n. 74; brain vs. brawn debate, 56–57, 200–201, 326, 331, 365–66 n. 73; construction of race, 46–49; racial classification in, 59–64, 189, 199–200; studies of muscle twitch fibers, 331–32, 340, 342; study of calf muscles, 52, 57–58, 60–61; study of sharecroppers, 55, 59–60. *See also* Cobb, W. Montague; Lambeth, Martha; Metheny, Eleanor

science, popular: and black athletic superiority, 55–57, 59, 199–202, 327–43, 362 n. 32, 366–67 n. 75; definition of, 51; effect of Great Depression on, 53–54, and the Olympic Games, 78–79; and public discourse, 51–52; and racial discourse, 325–26

Scott, Jarvis, 189, 226

Seagren, Bob, 231, 242, 243, 244, 252

Sheridan, Martin, 298

Simpson, O. J., 148, 254, 322, 324–25, 326, 341, 346

sixties, the: and civil rights, 19–20, 169; role of spectacle in, 21–24, 302, 307; and television, 20–22; transformation in sports, 32–33, 141, 280–81, 283–84, 297, 315; and U.S. youth movements, 23, 133–35

Smith, Denise, 209, 237, 246, 412 n. 95

Smith, John, 292–93

Smith, Red, 204, 321

Smith, Tommie: and the big shoe scandal, 319–21; and the black Olympic boycott, 88, 90–92, 187, 215; and the black power protest, 235, 237–46, 308, 315; and Avery Brundage, 237; departure from Mexico City, 269; and the historical legacy of the black power protest, 270, 277–89, 291–92, 294–95, 297–99, 301–3, 310, 346, 348; and the impact of the black power protest, 143, 190, 235–36, 246–56, 271–77, 305; and the Munich Olympic Games, 300–301; at the Olympic Trials, 209, 211; as a political figure, 13, 35, 99, 192, 206, 375 n. 43; post-Olympic career of, 316–17, 323, 347; and the *San Jose Mercury News*, 96–98; at San Jose State University, 192–93, 198, 201, 211; and South Africa, 181; suspension from Olympics, 257–68, 271, 286, 298

Snyder, Jimmy "the Greek," 327, 332–34, 335, 341, 366 n. 73

soccer. *See* World Cup

South Africa: African boycott of, 140–41, 161–70, 172, 173, 174, 180, 182, 187–88, 252, 285; and the Davis Cup, 282; debate over Olympic participation of, 139–41, 145, 157–84, 185, 191, 192, 234, 280, 286, 288, 292; and international sporting federations, 175, 183; media representations of, 166–67; non-African boycott of, 165–66, 170–73, 174, 175, 176, 180; OPHR boycott of, xix, 135, 138, 187, 207; South African Olympic Games Association, 159; suspension from Mexico City Olympic Games, 177–84; television in, 180. *See also* Braun, Frank; Mare, Matt; Supreme Council for Sport in Africa (SCSA); Verwoerd, Hendrik; Vorster, John

Southern Christian Leadership Conference (SCLC), 4, 20, 138, 142

Soviet Union: and the black power protest, 249, 268, 274, 278; and Mexican student movements, 116; Mexico City Olympic medal count of, 316; and the NYAC boycott, 150–51, 152; and South Africa, 161, 162–64, 170, 171–72, 174, 179, 182, 234; sports programs, 8–10, 286, 321, 392 n. 103; women athletes, 26–27

Spas, the (South Philadelphia Hebrew Association), 338

sport: and citizenship, 40–42, 187, 278, 304–5, 311–14, 346; and civil rights, 33, 86–88, 139, 185–86, 199, 206, 252, 257, 282–83, 323–24; and gay rights, 250; globalization of, 343–44; golden age of, 39–40, 359–60 n. 8; history of, 15–19; and politics, 6–10, 141, 163–64, 169, 182–83, 184; and popular culture, 17; and upward mobility, 44–46, 83, 211, 218–19, 283–84, 315–16, 337–39, 345–46, 361 n. 24; women's participation in, 189, 215–26

Springboks, the. *See* South Africa

Squaw Valley Winter Games, 100

"Star-Spangled Banner," xx, 145, 210, 233, 240–44, 253, 262, 264, 281, 301–14, 324, 346

student movements, Mexican, 112–23, 234, 280, 285–87, 299, 301; U.S., 23, 133–35

Student Non-Violent Coordinating Committee (SNCC): African tour, 8; and the Black Panthers, 20, 325; and feminism, 216; and the NYAC boycott, 146, 148; and the SCLC, 4, 142; and the Vietnam War, 138

Supreme Council for Sport in Africa (SCSA), 140–41, 161, 167–70, 182, 188

Sydney Olympic Games, 12

tabloid science. *See* science, popular

television: and the black power protest, 25, 235–36; and Mexico City, 111, 128; and the Munich Olympic Games, 294–95; and national identity, 18; Olympic programming, 99–106, 317–18; and the OPHR, 143; and racial representation, 282–83; and the sixties, 20–22; in South Africa, 180

Temple, Ed, 204, 222–23, 404 n. 97

Tennessee State University. *See* Tennessee Tigerbelles

Tennessee Tigerbelles, 203–4, 217, 222–24. *See also* Rudolph, Wilma; Temple, Ed; Tyus, Wyomia

Tessema, Yidnekatchew, 161

Texas Western University. *See* University of Texas, El Paso (UTEP)

Thomas, John, 149–50, 153, 204–5

Tlatelco: massacre at, 112–14, 122–30, 235, 287, 379 n. 98. *See also* student movements, Mexican

Todd, T. Wingate. *See* Cobb, W. Montague

Tokyo Olympic Games, 87, 90, 92, 100, 104, 108–9, 149, 158, 159, 160, 162, 164, 168, 225

Tolan, Thomas "Eddie," 53, 54, 55, 56, 71, 75

Toomey, Bill, 250, 251–52, 298, 302

transnationalism: of civil rights movements, 136–39, 163–64, 181, 216; and the Olympic Games, 13–14, 269, 343–44; and the OPHR, 5, 136, 168, 236,

258–59, 285–89, 315; relationship to nationalism, 18, 350 n. 7; and student protest movements, 23, 133

Tuskegee Relays Carnival, 221–22

Tyson, Mike, 322, 346, 363 n. 30

Tyus, Wyomia, 189, 204, 223, 225–26, 238, 266, 279

United States Olympic Committee (USOC): and the big shoe scandal, 319–20; on the black Olympic boycott, 92–93, 139, 203–4; and the black power protest, 241, 245–49, 256, 272–73; and the Harvard crew team, 251; on Mexico City Olympic venues, 110; and the Munich Olympic Games, 293; and the Olympic Trials, 208–9, 230–31, 400 n. 53; and the OPHR, 135–36, 190, 227; and South Africa, 161–62, 174; suspension of Smith and Carlos, 257–69, 271, 276–80, 286, 288, 291, 408 n. 42

University of Texas, El Paso (UTEP), 4, 88–89, 148–49, 153–54, 213, 214, 388 n. 69

Verwoerd, Hendrik, 158

Vietnam War, 21–22, 34, 123, 138, 151, 197, 250, 259, 278, 297, 302, 307–8

Vorster, John, 158, 159, 183

Waddell, Tom, 249–50, 251

Walker, Art, 248, 266

Western Regional Black Youth Conference, 90–92, 97

White, Walter, 137

whiteness, social construction of, 61, 324–25

Whitfield, Mal, 87–88, 271, 392 n. 104

Winter, Bud, 85, 90, 92, 256, 264, 374 n. 29

women in sports, 357 n. 62; gender verification of, 26–31, 190, 403 n. 88; Olympic history of, 26; race and, 189–90, 204, 215–26; role in Cold War, 26–27, 218, 224–26

Woodruff, John, 372 n. 88

Woods, Tiger, xv–xvi, xxi, 322, 346

Woodstock, 302, 307–9

World Cup (soccer), 10–12

Wright, Richard, 137–38, 369 n. 88

Wright, Stan, 131, 197–98, 203–4, 209–10, 233, 236–38, 243, 384 n. 14

Zátopek, Emil, 23–24, 270, 356 n. 59

Amy Bass is assistant professor of history at Plattsburgh State University in New York. She has worked for NBC as a member of the research team during the Olympic Games in Atlanta in 1996, in Sydney in 2000, and in Salt Lake City in 2002.